# The Battle of Borodino

# Campaign Chronicles

# The Battle of Borodino
## Napoleon Against Kutuzov

## Alexander Mikaberidze

*Campaign Chronicles*
*Series Editor*
Christopher Summerville

Pen & Sword
**MILITARY**

First published in Great Britain in 2007 by
Pen & Sword Military
an imprint of
Pen & Sword Books Ltd
47 Church Street
Barnsley
South Yorkshire S70 2AS

Copyright © Alexander Mikaberidze 2007

ISBN 978-1-84415-603-0

A CIP catalogue record for this book is
available from the British Library

Typeset in Sabon 10.5/12pt by
Concept, Huddersfield

Printed and bound in England by
Biddles Ltd

Pen & Sword Books Ltd incorporates the Imprints of Pen & Sword Aviation,
Pen & Sword Maritime, Pen & Sword Military, Wharncliffe Local History,
Pen and Sword Select, Pen and Sword Military Classics and Leo Cooper.

For a complete list of Pen & Sword titles please contact
PEN & SWORD BOOKS LIMITED
47 Church Street, Barnsley, South Yorkshire, S70 2AS, England
E-mail: enquiries@pen-and-sword.co.uk
Website: www.pen-and-sword.co.uk

# Contents

# The Battle of Borodino

# Author's Note

I faced several challenges while working on this book. Dates in original Russian documents are given in the Julian calendar, which was effective in Russia at the time. Thus, for the Russians, Borodino was fought on 26 August 1812, while for the French (and Posterity) the battle occurred on 7 September. In my narrative, I have converted dates into the familiar Gregorian calendar, although some Julian-style dates remain in quoted extracts.

Similarly, French and Russian sources use different systems for weights and measures (e.g. *toises*, *lieue*, *versta*, *pud* etc.) and again I have endeavoured to render these intelligible to the modern reader (for those who are interested, explanations of these terms, among others, may be found in the glossary at the end of the book).

Meanwhile, readers should not be surprised to see Roman numerals attached to the surnames of Russian officers. This system was adopted by the Russian Army to differentiate between officers sharing the same surname. Thus we have Tuchkov IV, Ditterix III, Ilovaisky X, Grekov XVIII etc.

Another point to bear in mind is the use of Polish lancers by both the French and Russian Armies at Borodino. In order to distinguish these units I have opted to call those in French service 'Lancers' and those in Russian service 'Uhlans' (from the Polish 'Uan').

Russian regimental names are given in Russian transcription in the text, while the Order of Battle contains their generally accepted English translations in parentheses. Although named after specific locations, Russian regiments had no relation with these places, which is often (incorrectly) assumed when translating their names into English. Thus the Life Guard Lithuanian or Finland Regiments were *not* staffed with recruits from Lithuania or Finland, as might be assumed. Also, if one follows this principle, then Izmailovsk should be translated as Izmailovo, Akhtyrsk as Akhtyrka, Preobrazhensk as Preobrazhenskoye etc. Therefore, I made a decision to use transcribed regimental names: e.g. Akhtyrskii, Izmailovskii, Preobrazhenskii and so on.

Finally, the word 'tsar' is often used as the popular designation of the Russian ruler, although technically it is incorrect when applied to sovereigns of the eighteenth and nineteenth centuries. I have chosen to use the term 'Emperor' because this was the official title of Russian monarchs since 1721, when Peter the Great adopted it. The official title of a Russian emperor specifically stated that he was 'By the grace of God, the Emperor and Autocrat of all the Russias'.

# List of Maps, Diagrams and Illustrations

# List of Maps, Diagrams and Illustrations

# The Battle of Borodino

# Preface

———— ◄(●)► ————

'Every nation has critical moments when the strength and nobility of its spirit can be measured,' wrote prominent Russian writer Vissarion Belinsky. For Russia, one such moment was at Borodino on 7 September 1812. The battle – with over 280,000 men present on both sides and between 75,000 and 80,000 casualties – proved to be one of the largest battles of the 19th century and one of the bloodiest battles in military history. Its importance in military, political, social or cultural terms can hardly be overestimated.

Despite voluminous research on the Napoleonic Wars, the Battle of Borodino still requires additional study, especially with the fast approaching 200th anniversary of the battle. Most of the available material consists of memoirs and general studies of the 1812 campaign, which naturally prohibits detailed analysis of the battle itself. Among the English language books published in the last three decades, those by Holmes, Duffy and Smith deal specifically with the battle but utilize a limited number of non-French sources. There are also studies by Palmer, Curtis, Zamoyski, Riehn, Nicolson, Britten, James and Nafziger, but the general nature of their books limits discussion of the battle; still, Curtis, Zamoyski and Riehn were able to consult a variety of Russian sources to provide a Russian perspective of the conflict. In France, Hourtoulle produced the most recent, albeit brief, account of the battle, while Castelot, Thiry and Tranié studied the Russian campaign in general. However, their works share the common deficiency of describing the battle largely from the French perspective.

Russian historiography of Borodino is, unquestionably, the most extensive and counts in dozens of volumes. Yet, such overabundance of studies is not without its weakness. The battle was often discussed in overly patriotic tones and exploited for ideological purposes. Many Soviet studies are biased in their interpretation of events, and some even contain deliberate exaggeration or distortion of the facts. Pressure was often exerted on Soviet historians to conform to the official line. During and after the Second World War the Soviet government, under Joseph Stalin, tried to portray the struggle against the Nazi invader in the same terms as that against Napoleon's Grand Army, and historians followed this 'formula' for decades.

Prominent historians Zhilin, Beskrovny and Garnich set the tone and spent their careers fighting the 'evils of bourgeois historiography' that was critical of Russian actions in 1812. Kutuzov was gradually turned into a mythical figure dominating his epoch and contemporaries, while Borodino became a masterpiece of the Russian military art and Kutuzov its prime architect. Thus, in Beskrovny's version of the battle, 'Kutuzov prevented Napoleon from making any manoeuvres or achieving any success.'[1] Meanwhile, Garnich claimed that the Russians won Borodino so decisively that they pursued the routed French forces for over 7 miles after the battle![2]

Such views dominated Soviet historiography for almost four decades and prevented attempts to study the battle in a critical light. Scholars sought to best themselves in glorifying Russian actions and Kutuzov's role in them, often leading to comical incidents. At one scholarly meeting at the University of Leningrad, a scholar presenting his paper was interrupted by an angry fellow historian who told him, 'Comrade Stalin showed us that Kutuzov was *two heads* above Barclay de Tolly, while your paper shows he was only *one head* above him.'[3] In the same way, some scholars took Stalin's hypothesis at face value and sought to prove it by an outlandish formula: Kutuzov was *two heads* above Barclay de Tolly, who was *one head* above any French marshal and on a par with Napoleon: therefore Kutuzov was *two heads* above Napoleon! Such opinions and characterizations survived well into the 1980s and even the early 1990s, when historians continued to eulogize: Borodino remained the 'complete strategic and tactical victory' for the Russians, Kutuzov was 'a better military commander than Napoleon', and his military genius 'far superior to Napoleon's'.[4]

Among dissenters were Kochetkov, Shvedov, and Troitsky, who tried to bring much needed impartiality and objectivity into the Russian historiography but were largely ignored. Although passionate emotions about Borodino and Kutuzov were essentially abandoned in the 1990s, some Russian writers still follow this path, refusing to criticize Kutuzov or Russian actions because it is not patriotic.[5] Nowadays, Bezotosny, Popov, Vasiliev, Zemtsov, Tselorungo and others, have begun a new wave of Borodino research, their books contributing to the demolition of long held views and preconceptions on the battle. Their collective effort resulted in one of the most outstanding Napoleonic publication in any language: *Otechestvennaia voina 1812 goda: Entsiklopediia* (2004), a massive encyclopaedia of over 1,000 entries that will remain a standard work on this topic for many years to come. Unfortunately, such works remain largely unknown and underutilized outside Russia.

Thus the present book seeks to blend primary sources and material from various countries and produce a balanced account of the battle. This is a daunting task and I only hope to have succeeded in it. The battle will be covered from both sides, but the emphasis will be made on the Russian experiences. To meet the requirements of this series, I had to eliminate many details, but much information will be made available at the Napoleon Series website (www.napoleon-series.org).

The book opens with a general overview of the political situation in Europe and the causes of war. It then traces the opening moves of the main Russian and French forces in July and August 1812, describing events in

# Preface

closer detail as they move closer to the showdown at Borodino. The book covers actions involving only major combatant forces and excludes the northern and southern fronts, which are out of its scope. The battle narrative is divided into three phases and four sectors. Such division is tentative in nature and is simply utilized for better organization of the material. The final sections deal with the aftermath of the battle, casualties, and the subsequent history of the 1812 campaign.

The superfluity of primary sources – over 150 were consulted for this book – also reveals the limited value of personal testimonies about battles, especially as complex as Borodino. While major points of the battle are beyond dispute, careful comparison of statements and testimonies from participants reveal great differences and contradictions regarding details. This is especially true with respect to the timing of various attacks and manoeuvres, which differs widely in testimonies as a result of the confusion on the battlefield and/or memory lapses of participants writing years, if not decades, after the battle. This does not mean that memoirs should be ignored, but rather approached in a conscientious manner. They provide a unique insight into the human experiences of that war, and the horrendously savage nature of the Battle of Borodino, the like of which their authors had never experienced before.

# Acknowledgements

I was first introduced to the Battle of Borodino as a pupil in a Soviet elementary school, and I well remember the feeling of joy at discovering that Prince Peter Bagration was my compatriot from Georgia (then a Soviet republic). In later years I began researching Bagration's career for my doctoral study at Florida State University, which proved useful when I began writing this book.

I am grateful to Professor Donald D. Howard for his unwavering support and guidance during my stay at FSU. I was able to utilize the Napoleonic Special Collections of the Strozier Library (FSU), which remains one of the best collections in the United States. Special thanks to Interlibrary Loan Sections of Mitchell Library at Mississippi State University and to Marie Crusinberry of Santa Barbara Public Library, whose efficiency in locating materials proved to be indispensable. I am indebted to Jeff Graceffo, who sent me dozens of documents after my departure from FSU.

Living in the age of the Internet provides a unique opportunity to meet fellow scholars, and I was blessed to befriend many outstanding individuals at the Discussion Forum of the Napoleon Series website (www.napoleon-series.org), where I have been active for the past ten years. Steven H. Smith, Tony Broughton, Rory Muir and Robert Goetz generously shared their time and expertise and helped me procure obscure materials. Alain Chappet, Uwe Wild, and Fausto Berutti helped me with French, German and Italian materials, while Jerry McKenzie and Terry Doherty were helpful in clarifying some details of the French order of battle. Robert Mosher kindly sent me dozens of photographs of the battlefield. Michael Hopper volunteered to edit the manuscript and his amazing dedication and numerous insightful comments helped me to improve it.

I am grateful to Christopher Summerville who contacted me about writing this book and guided me through the rough waters of writing a manuscript within the publisher's requirements. Rupert Harding welcomed me to Pen & Sword and always acted with great professionalism.

On a personal level, this book could not have been written without the help and support of my family and friends. I extend my love and thanks to all of them, especially to my wife, Anna, for her unwavering support and love.

# Maps

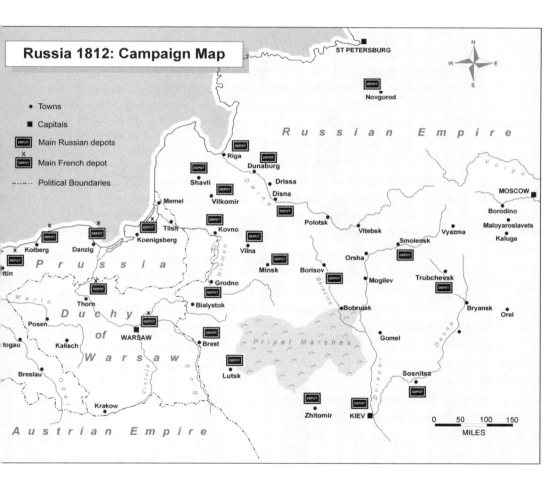

**Russia 1812: Campaign Map**

- • Towns
- ■ Capitals
- DEPOT Main Russian depots
- X / DEPOT Main French depot
- ----- Political Boundaries

ST PETERSBURG

R u s s i a n   E m p i r e

Novgorod

Riga

Dunaburg

Shavli

Drissa

Vilkomir

Disna

Memel

Polotsk

MOSCOW

Borodino

Kovno

Vitebsk

Vyazma

Maloyaroslavets

Tilsit

Vilna

Smolensk

Kaluga

Koenigsberg

Orsha

Kolberg

Danzig

Minsk

Borisov

Mogilev

Trubchevsk

ttin

P r u s s i a

Grodno

Bobruisk

Bryansk

Orel

Thorn

Bialystok

Posen

D u c h y

Pripet Marshes

Gomel

logau

Kalisch

of   WARSAW

Brest

Breslau

W a r s a w

Lutsk

Sosnitsa

Krakow

Zhitomir

KIEV

A u s t r i a n   E m p i r e

0   50   100   150

MILES

*Dwina*

*Niemen*

*Berezina*

*Dnieper*

*Desna*

*Volga*

*Warta*

*Oder*

*Vistula*

*Bug*

XV

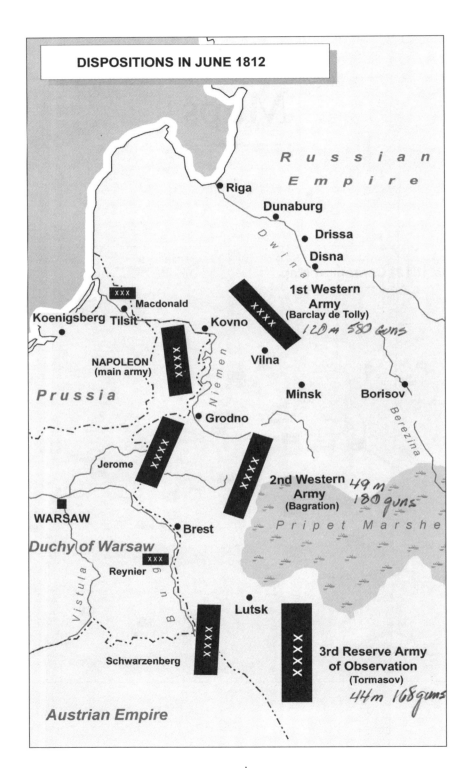

DISPOSITIONS IN JUNE 1812

*R u s s i a n*

*E m p i r e*

Riga

Dunaburg

Drissa

*D w i n a*

Disna

1st Western Army
(Barclay de Tolly)

*120 m 580 guns*

xxx

Macdonald

Koenigsberg  Tilsit

Kovno

*N i e m e n*

NAPOLEON
(main army)

Vilna

xxxx

*P r u s s i a*

Minsk

Borisov

*B e r e z i n a*

Grodno

Jerome

xxxx

xxxx

2nd Western Army
(Bagration)

*49 m*

*180 guns*

WARSAW

Brest

*P r i p e t   M a r s h e*

*Duchy of Warsaw*

xxx

Reynier

*B u g*

*V i s t u l a*

Lutsk

xxxx

Schwarzenberg

xxxx

3rd Reserve Army
of Observation
(Tormasov)

*44m 168 guns*

*Austrian Empire*

# SMOLENSK TO BORODINO

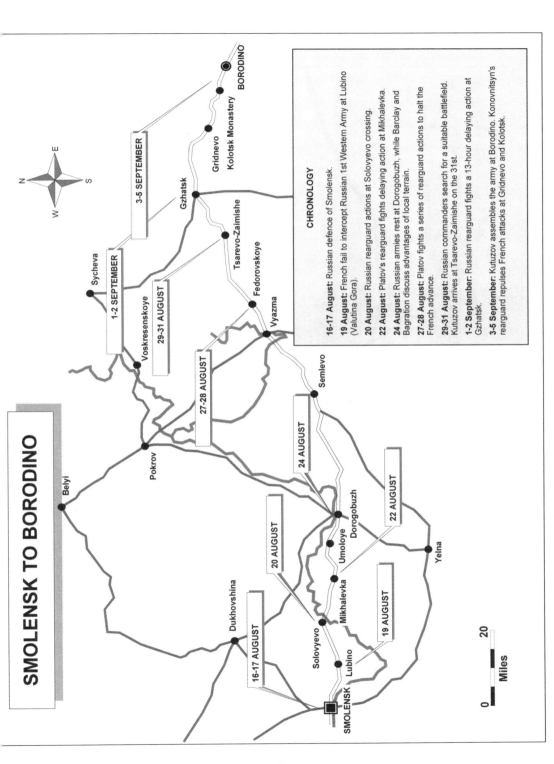

## CHRONOLOGY

**16-17 August:** Russian defence of Smolensk.

**19 August:** French fail to intercept Russian 1st Western Army at Lubino (Valutina Gora).

**20 August:** Russian rearguard actions at Solovyevo crossing.

**22 August:** Platov's rearguard fights delaying action at Mikhalevka.

**24 August:** Russian armies rest at Dorogobuzh, while Barclay and Bagration discuss advantages of local terrain.

**27-28 August:** Platov fights a series of rearguard actions to halt the French advance.

**29-31 August:** Russian commanders search for a suitable battlefield. Kutuzov arrives at Tsarevo-Zaimishe on the 31st.

**1-2 September:** Russian rearguard fights a 13-hour delaying action at Gzhatsk.

**3-5 September:** Kutuzov assembles the army at Borodino. Konovnitsyn's rearguard repulses French attacks at Gridnevo and Kolotsk.

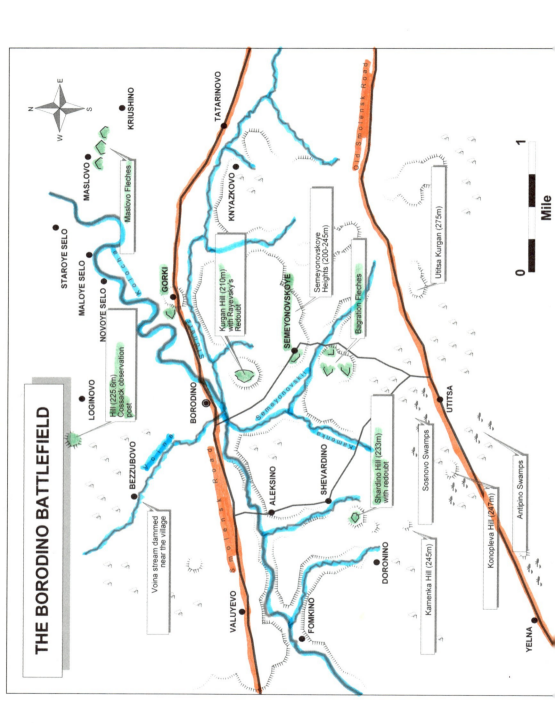

# THE BORODINO BATTLEFIELD

N E S W

Mile
0          1

TATARINOVO

Old Smolensk Road

KRIUSHINO

MASLOVO

Maslovo Fleches

STAROYE SELO

MALOYE SELO

NOVOYE SELO

GORKI

KNYAZKOVO

Kurgan Hill (210m) with Rayevsky's Redoubt

Semeyonovskoye Heights (200-245m)

Utitsa Kurgan (275m)

LOGINOVO

Hill (225.6m) Cossack observation post

SEMEYONOVSKOYE

Bagration Fleches

UTITSA

Kolocha

Stonets

Semeyonovskii

BORODINO

Sosnovo Swamps

BEZZUBOVO

Voina

Smolensk Road

Kamenka

Shardino Hill (233m) with redoubt

Antipino Swamps

Voina stream dammed near the village

ALEKSINO

SHEVARDINO

DORONINO

Konopleva Hill (247m)

VALUYEVO

FOMKINO

Kamenka Hill (245m)

YELNA

xviii

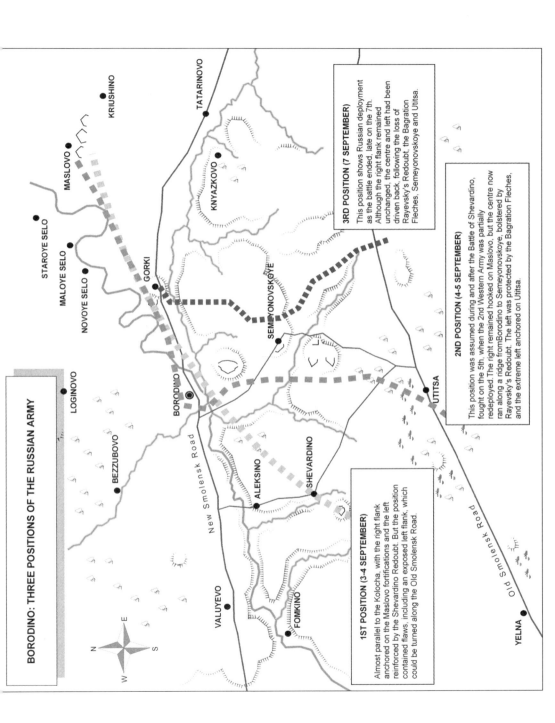

# BORODINO: THREE POSITIONS OF THE RUSSIAN ARMY

KRIUSHINO

TATARINOVO

MASLOVO

STAROYE SELO

KNYAZKOVO

MALOYE SELO

NOVOYE SELO

GORKI

SEMEYONOVSKOYE

LOGINOVO

BORODINO

BEZZUBOVO

New Smolensk Road

ALEKSINO

SHEVARDINO

UTITSA

Old Smolensk Road

VALUYEVO

FOMKINO

YELNA

**3RD POSITION (7 SEPTEMBER)**

This position shows Russian deployment as the battle ended, late on the 7th. Although the right flank remained unchanged, the centre and left had been driven back, following the loss of Rayevsky's Redoubt, the Bagration Fleches, Semeyonovskoye and Utitsa.

**2ND POSITION (4–5 SEPTEMBER)**

This position was assumed during and after the Battle of Shevardino, fought on the 5th, when the 2nd Western Army was partially redeployed. The right remained hooked on Maslovo, but the centre now ran along a ridge from Borodino to Semeyonovskoye, bolstered by Rayevsky's Redoubt. The left was protected by the Bagration Fleches, and the extreme left anchored on Utitsa.

**1ST POSITION (3–4 SEPTEMBER)**

Almost parallel to the Kolocha, with the right flank anchored on the Maslovo fortifications and the left reinforced by the Shevardino Redoubt. But the position contained flaws, including an exposed left flank, which could be turned along the Old Smolensk Road.

N E S W

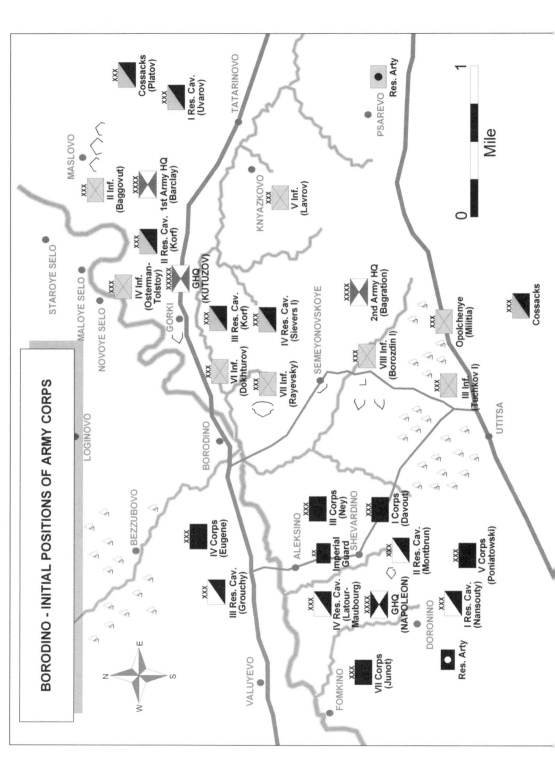

# BORODINO - INITIAL POSITIONS OF ARMY CORPS

Mile

0   1

xx

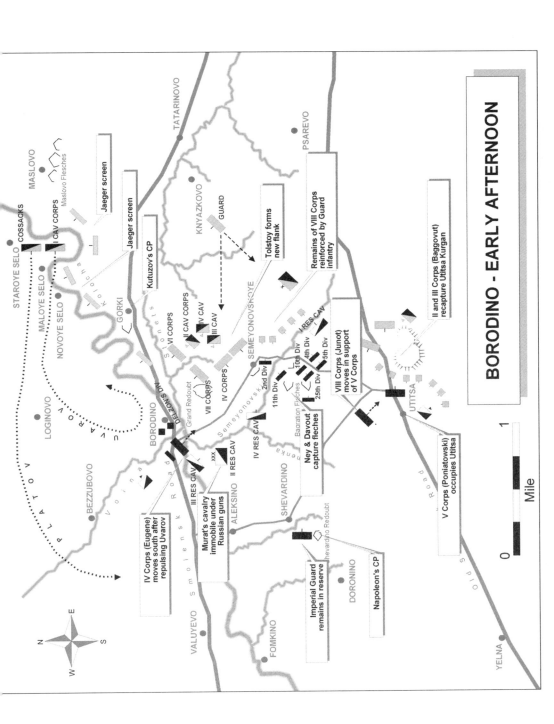

# BORODINO - EARLY AFTERNOON

MASLOVO

STAROYE SELO

COSSACKS

I CAV CORPS

Maslovo Fleches

Jaeger screen

Jaeger screen

Kutuzov's CP

MALOYE SELO

NOVOYE SELO

GORKI

VI CORPS

II CAV CORPS

IV CAV

III CAV

KNYAZKOVO

GUARD

Tolstoy forms new flank

TATARINOVO

PSAREVO

Remains of VIII Corps reinforced by Guard infantry

II and III Corps (Baggovut) recapture Utitsa Kurgan

SEMEYONOVSKOYE

I RES CAV

10th Div

4th Div

5th Div

BORODINO

Grand Redoubt

VII CORPS

IV CORPS

2nd Div

11th Div

25th Div

VIII Corps (Junot) moves in support of V Corps

UTITSA

BEZZUBOVO

LOGINOVO

IV Corps (Eugene) moves south after repulsing Uvarov

III RES CAV

Murat's cavalry immobile under Russian guns

II RES CAV

ALEKSINO

IV RES CAV

Bagration Fleches

Ney & Davout capture fleches

V Corps (Poniatowski) occupies Utitsa

VALUYEVO

SHEVARDINO

Shevardino Redoubt

Imperial Guard remains in reserve

Napoleon's CP

DORONINO

FOMKINO

YELNA

N
E
S
W

0    Mile    1

xxi

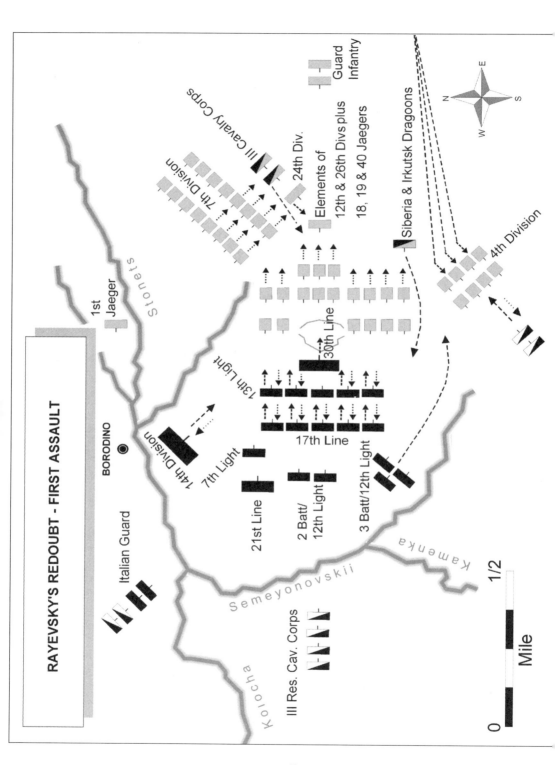

# RAYEVSKY'S REDOUBT - FIRST ASSAULT

Italian Guard

BORODINO

1st Jaeger

Stonets

III Cavalry Corps

7th Division

24th Div.

Elements of
12th & 26th Divs plus
18, 19 & 40 Jaegers

Guard Infantry

Siberia & Irkutsk Dragoons

4th Division

14th Division

7th Light

13th Light

30th Line

17th Line

21st Line

2 Batt/
12th Light

3 Batt/12th Light

Kamenka

Semeyonovskii

Kolocha

III Res. Cav. Corps

N
E
S
W

0   1/2   Mile

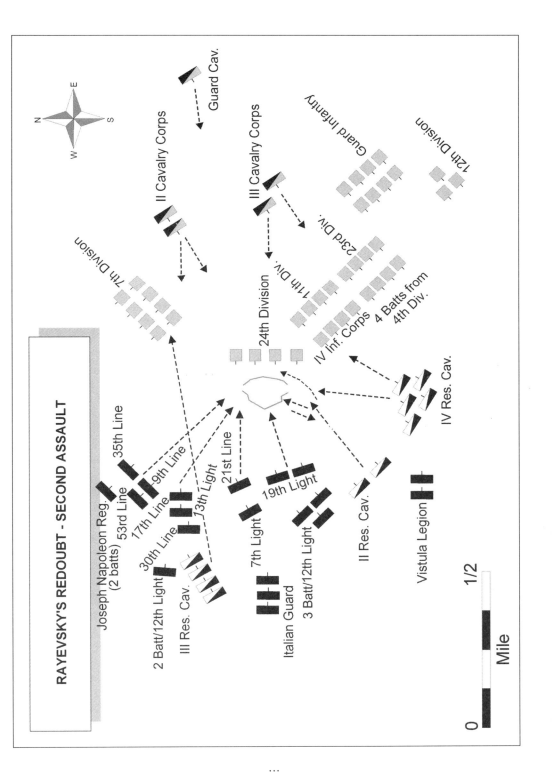

RAYEVSKY'S REDOUBT - SECOND ASSAULT

Guard Cav.

II Cavalry Corps

III Cavalry Corps

Guard Infantry

12th Division

7th Division

23rd Div.

11th Div.

24th Division

IV Inf. Corps     4 Batts from
                  4th Div.

IV Res. Cav.

35th Line

Joseph Napoleon Reg.
(2 batts)   53rd Line

9th Line

17th Line

13th Light

21st Line

30th Line

2 Batt/12th Light

III Res. Cav.

7th Light

19th Light

Italian Guard

3 Batt/12th Light

II Res. Cav.

Vistula Legion

N   E   W   S

0        1/2

Mile

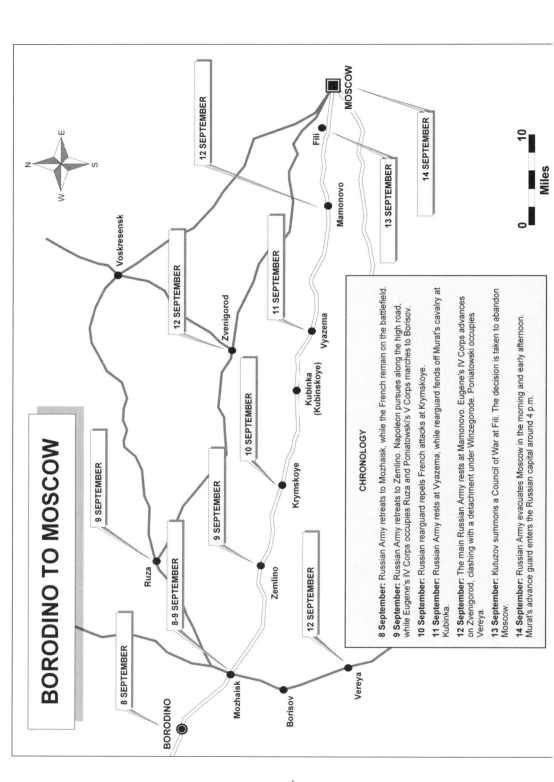

# BORODINO TO MOSCOW

**CHRONOLOGY**

**8 September:** Russian Army retreats to Mozhaisk, while the French remain on the battlefield.

**9 September:** Russian Army retreats to Zemlino. Napoleon pursues along the high road, while Eugene's IV Corps occupies Ruza and Poniatowski's V Corps marches to Borisov.

**10 September:** Russian rearguard repels French attacks at Krymskoye.

**11 September:** Russian Army rests at Vyazema, while rearguard fends off Murat's cavalry at Kubinka.

**12 September:** The main Russian Army rests at Mamonovo. Eugene's IV Corps advances on Zvenigorod, clashing with a detachment under Winzegorode. Poniatowski occupies Vereya.

**13 September:** Kutuzov summons a Council of War at Fili. The decision is taken to abandon Moscow.

**14 September:** Russian Army evacuates Moscow in the morning and early afternoon. Murat's advance guard enters the Russian capital around 4 p.m.

8 SEPTEMBER

9 SEPTEMBER

8-9 SEPTEMBER

9 SEPTEMBER

12 SEPTEMBER

10 SEPTEMBER

11 SEPTEMBER

12 SEPTEMBER

12 SEPTEMBER

13 SEPTEMBER

14 SEPTEMBER

BORODINO

Mozhaisk

Borisov

Vereya

Zemlino

Krymskoye

Kubinka (Kubinskoye)

Vyazema

Ruza

Zvenigorod

Voskresensk

Mamonovo

Fili

MOSCOW

N / E / S / W

0    10
Miles

# Background

As the sun rose on 24 June 1812, a small figure in an army uniform and bicorn hat stood high on a hill overlooking the Nieman river. Around him, as far as the eye could see, every valley, ravine and hill was covered by an enormous host that swarmed like an anthill. This colossal army was moving in three columns across the bridges constructed the night before. Many soldiers looked with awe at the distant figure of their leader, Emperor Napoleon, watching silently as the advance units almost came to blows, disputing the honour of being the first to step onto foreign soil. Later, near Kovno, a French officer witnessed a Polish squadron fording the river:

> They swam together to the middle of the stream but there the swift current swept them apart [...] Helplessly adrift, they were carried along by the violence of the current [...] [and] no longer tried to swim and lost headway completely [...] but as they were about to go down, they turned toward Napoleon and shouted 'Vive l'Empereur!'

These were the first casualties of a fateful war that would bring down the French Empire and change the course of European history.

## The Road to Borodino

The war between Russia and France did not come as a surprise to many contemporaries, since relations between them became increasingly tense after the Treaty of Tilsit of 1807. Emperor Alexander I of Russia did not forget the painful lessons of 1805–07, when his armies were repeatedly defeated by Napoleon, and was well aware of the widespread displeasure prevailing in Russia, particularly in the Army, over the 'ignominious' peace of Tilsit. The Russian nobility was irritated by what it perceived as the Russian submission to France, as Prince Sergei Volkonsky described:

> The defeats at Austerlitz and Friedland, the Peace of Tilsit, the haughtiness of French ambassadors in St Petersburg, the passive reaction of [Tsar] Alexander to the policies of Napoleon – all were deep wounds in the heart of every Russian. Vengeance, and vengeance alone, was the unshakable feeling with which we all were burning. Those who did not share this feeling – and there were only a few of them – were rejected and despised ...

Although Napoleon and Alexander seemed to have reconciled at Erfurt in 1808, the fissures became evident the following year, when the latter

1

was reluctant to support France against Austria. Russia was concerned by Napoleon's aggressive foreign policy, especially after the annexation of Holland, the Hanseatic cities and Germanic states, including the Duchy of Oldenburg, whose ruler was Tsar Alexander's brother-in-law.

Meanwhile, the Continental Blockade, which Napoleon initiated in response to the British blockade of 1806, had a profound effect on Europe, and on Russia in particular. It proved disadvantageous to the Russian merchants and nobility, leading to a sharp decrease in Russian foreign trade. Britain was the leading trade partner to Russia, exporting 17.7 million roubles' worth of goods in 1802, compared to just 500,000 roubles' worth from France that same year. Prior to 1807, a total of 17,000 great masts were sent from Riga and St Petersburg to the shipyards in England, but this number sharply declined to 4,500 in 1808, and to just over 300 in 1809–10. Besides timber, Russia also actively traded in grain, hemp and other products with Britain, and in 1800 the British Consul noted in the minutes of a Board of Trade meeting that: 'British merchants had such extensive dealings in all sorts of Russian articles as to export from two-thirds to three-quarters of the whole in commodities.' Indeed, in 1804, twelve English companies controlled a quarter of Russia's imports and half of its exports, while other English merchants issued long-term credit to the Russian merchants and nobility. Napoleon's protective tariff system, on the other hand, sought to safeguard French manufacturers and industry, limiting Russian imports while boosting French exports. Yet the French could provide neither the volume nor the quality of products required in Russia; neither could they replace British spending power when it came to buying raw materials.

The financial strains created by Napoleon's Continental System quickly developed into a serious problem, distressing merchants and nobles and crippling the Imperial treasury, which struggled to deal with a deficit that increased from 12.2 million roubles in 1801 to 157.5 million in 1809. Such economic tribulations forced the Russian government to gradually relax the enforcement of the blockade, especially with respect to neutral shipping. By 1810 American ships – and English ships with false papers – freely docked in Russian ports, and such 'neutral' trade was finally officially sanctioned by Emperor Alexander's decree of 31 December 1810, which limited the import of French products and allowed trade in non-French merchandise. As English goods found their way from the Russian ports into Eastern and Central Europe, Napoleon realized that the new Russian policy constituted a heavy blow to his Continental Blockade, and St Petersburg's cooperation in this system could only be enforced by war.[6]

France and Russia also disagreed on several political issues, the most important being the fate of Poland. Russo-Polish relations can be traced back for centuries and they were largely overshadowed by the rivalry between the two states. In the 1600s Polish invasions of Russia were commonplace and Moscow itself was captured in 1612. But just as Russia turned into a first-rate power, the Polish state declined and was partitioned

# Background

three times by neighbours Russia, Prussia and Austria in the second half of the 18th century. Russia was the prime beneficiary of these partitions, extending its territory deep into North East Europe. Any discussion of a Polish revival naturally threatened Russian strategic interests in the region. Yet the ink was hardly dry on the Tilsit agreement when Napoleon created the Duchy of Warsaw (albeit under the nominal control of the King of Saxony): an act that St Petersburg immediately considered hostile to its interests.

Napoleon's interest in consolidating his control over the Poles was further revealed when, after the defeat of Austria in 1809, he incorporated Western Galicia into the Duchy of Warsaw, which, in effect, further expanded the Polish principality. Polish demands for eventual restoration of their kingdom only increased Russia's concerns that she would be obliged to cede territory. Thus Alexander opposed French designs in Poland and tried to persuade Napoleon to give up his plans. Both emperors spent two years (1809–10) wrangling over this issue and by 1811, the discussions were in deadlock with neither side willing to concede.

Another aspect to Franco-Russian enmity lay in the Balkans, where Russia supported the local Slavic population against the Ottomans. In the 18th century alone, Russia and the Ottoman Empire were engaged in four wars and a fifth had been under way since 1806. At Tilsit Napoleon agreed to give Russia a free hand in the Balkans, but Alexander gradually became convinced that France was far from willing to allow Russian expansion into the Balkans.

Of a minor importance – but still relevant to personal relations between the two emperors – was the matter of Napoleon's marriage to the Austrian princess Marie-Louise. Back at Erfurt in 1808, Napoleon suggested the possibility of reinforcing a Franco-Russian alliance through his marriage to Alexander's sister. The Russian royal family was reluctant to allow the 'Corsican upstart' to enter its circle and found various excuses to rebuff Napoleon. His initial choice, Grand Duchess Catherine, was quickly married off to the Duke of Oldenburg, while the Empress Mother, Maria Feodorovna, bitterly opposed the marriage of her other daughter, Anna, for whom Napoleon also put in a formal offer. Napoleon considered these rejections as personal slights and a certain distrust began to pervade his relations with the Russian court. Interestingly, when Napoleon eventually married the Austrian princess, the St Petersburg court was somewhat piqued, since it signalled the rapprochement between France and Austria and a decline in Russian influence.

In the summer of 1811 Napoleon began preparing for the 'Second Polish Campaign', as he called it, attempting to ensure a rapid victory over Russia. The enormous Grand Army of more than 600,000 soldiers and over 1,300 field guns was gathered in German and Polish lands. Approximately half its manpower consisted of troops from Napoleon's allies, including Austria, Prussia, Saxony, Spain, Bavaria, Poland and Italy. Anticipating an unavoidable war, Russia and France cast around for allies, both seeking support

3

# The Battle of Borodino

from Austria and Prussia. But the French presence in the Germanic states and the recent defeat of Austria in 1809 left little choice for these countries but to submit to Napoleon.

Napoleon's overall strategy for the war considered the use of Sweden and the Ottoman Empire to form his extreme flanks, but he was unable to exercise influence on either power. Sweden, protected by the sea and the British Royal Navy, formed an alliance with Russia (April 1812) in return for the promise of Russian assistance in annexing Norway, then in Denmark's possession. As for the Ottomans, they appeared to be a natural ally for Napoleon but their war had been a failure, with their armies defeated by the Russians and their finances exhausted. By June 1812, Alexander I managed to achieve a significant diplomatic success by concluding the Treaty of Bucharest (26 May) with the Turks.

## Preparing for Battle

Napoleon's Army was deployed in three groups from Warsaw to Königsberg:

### Left Flank
- X Corps, under Marshal Jacques-Etienne Macdonald

### Central Army Group

**Main Army under Napoleon's direct command**
- Imperial Guard, under Marshals François Joseph Lefebvre (Old Guard), Edouard Mortier (Young Guard) and Marshal Jean-Baptiste Bessières (Guard Cavalry)
- I Corps, under Marshal Louis Nicolas Davout
- II Corps, under Marshal Nicolas Charles Oudinot
- III Corps, under Marshal Michel Ney
- I Reserve Cavalry Corps, under General Étienne Nansouty
- II Reserve Cavalry Corps, under General Louis Pierre Montbrun

**Army of Italy under the command of Prince Eugène de Beauharnais**
- IV Corps, under Prince Eugène de Beauharnais
- VI Corps, under Marshal Laurent Gouvion Saint-Cyr
- III Reserve Cavalry Corps, under General Emmanuel Grouchy

**Second Support Army under Jérôme Bonaparte, King of Westphalia**
- V Corps, under General Józef Poniatowski
- VII Corps, under General Jean Louis Reynier
- VIII Corps, under King Jérôme and General Dominique Vandamme
- IV Cavalry Corps, under General Marie-Victor Latour-Maubourg

### Right Flank
- Austrian Corps under General Prince Karl Philip Schwarzenberg

# Background

## Reserves in Second and Third Lines
- IX Corps under Marshal Claude Victor-Perrin
- XI Corps under Marshal Pierre François Charles Augereau

Napoleon's strategy was simple and resembled that of his earlier campaigns. Keeping the enemy ignorant of his army's exact aims, he intended to concentrate overwhelming superiority at a chosen point, attack and destroy the enemy's field forces, and then dictate peace on his own terms. Knowing the vast scope of the Russian Empire, he sought to engage the Russians as soon as possible. The Emperor had every confidence that he could achieve a desired victory within a few weeks by waging decisive battles in frontier regions. Still, he was well aware of the difficulties ahead. Together with a study of the history and geography of Russia, his previous campaigns in Poland had provided him with experience of fighting in underpopulated areas lacking good roads, and in extreme weather. In 1811 he made extensive logistical preparations and enormous quantities of supplies were amassed in depots in Poland and Germany, and a vast network of supply trains was organized to bring food, ammunition caissons, forges, and ambulances to the Army.

In 1812, Russia's military forces had over 650,000 men, but these were scattered throughout its vast regions. Some were situated in the Danubian Principalities, others in the Crimea, the Caucasus and Finland, leaving approximately 300,000 men with over 900 guns to face Napoleon's army during the initial stages of the invasion. The Russian forces facing the Grand Army were deployed in three army groups along the western frontiers of the Empire. The 1st Western Army of General Mikhail Barclay de Tolly (120,000 men and 580 guns) was deployed in the vicinity of Vilna, covering the route to St Petersburg. The 2nd Western Army of General Prince Peter Bagration (49,000 men and 180 guns) was assembled in the area of Volkovysk and Belostock, covering the route to Moscow. General Alexander Tormasov commanded the 3rd Reserve Army of Observation (44,000 men and 168 guns), deployed in the vicinity of Lutsk, to cover the route to Kiev. This force was later renamed the 3rd Western Army.

The three major armies were supported by several reserve corps that constituted a second line of defence. The Russian extreme flanks were covered by Lieutenant General Baron Faddey Steingell's corps in Finland and Admiral Paul Chichagov's Army of the Danube in the south.

The three main Russian armies on the eve of 1812:

## 1st Western Army under General of Infantry Mikhail Barclay de Tolly
- I Infantry Corps of Lieutenant General Peter Wittgenstein
- II Infantry Corps of Lieutenant General Karl Baggovut
- III Infantry Corps of Lieutenant General Nikolai Tuchkov I
- IV Infantry Corps of Lieutenant General Count Pavel Shuvalov
- V Reserve (Guard) Corps of Grand Duke Constantine Pavlovich

- VI Infantry Corps of General of Infantry Dimitry Dokhturov
- I Cavalry Corps of Adjutant General Fedor Uvarov
- II Cavalry Corps of Adjutant General Baron Fedor Korf
- III Cavalry Corps of Major General Peter Pahlen III
- Cossack Corps of General of Cavalry Matvei Platov.

### 2nd Western Army under General of Infantry Prince Peter Bagration
- VII Infantry Corps of Lieutenant General Nikolai Rayevsky
- VIII Infantry Corps of Lieutenant General Mikhail Borozdin
- IV Cavalry Corps of Major General Count Karl Sievers

### 3rd Reserve Army of Observation under General of Cavalry Alexander Tormasov
- General of Infantry Sergei Kamenski I's Infantry Corps
- Lieutenant General Yevgeny Markov's Infantry Corps
- Lieutenant General Baron Fabian Osten-Sacken's Infantry Corps
- Major General Count Karl Lambert's Cavalry Corps

Facing Napoleon's extensive preparations, the Russian government sought to strengthen its defence. But was there an actual plan to lure Napoleon deep into Russia, or was the Russian retreat inevitable considering the circumstances? Historians are divided on whether the Russians truly had a 'Scythian plan' or not. Some argue that Barclay de Tolly contemplated this strategy as early as 1807, when he discussed enticing French forces deep into Russia before destroying them. Other scholars reject such suggestions, claiming the Russian government had no tangible plan of retreat and the withdrawal was conducted of necessity when facing a superior enemy force.

The Russian military planning in 1810–11 represents a complicated, if not confusing, picture. Mistrustful of his generals, Alexander concealed military intelligence as well as military plans that were discussed within a close circle of his advisers. Preparations for the war started as early as 1810 and initially the strategy was offensive in nature. But these preparations were halted after Józef Poniatowski, whom Czartoriski tried to persuade to defect to Russia, informed Napoleon about Russian intentions. The strategic planning was still carried on and was conducted in such secrecy that General Bennigsen complained about his exclusion: 'The Emperor [Alexander] did not show me any parts of the operational plan and I do not know any person who had seen it.' Meanwhile, the Chief of Staff of the 1st Western Army, Major General Yermolov, still believed in the spring of 1812 that: 'at the present moment everything is arranged for an offensive ...'

In the two years leading up to the war, plenty of ink was wasted in drafting various plans and one Russian scholar, in fact, counted as many as thirty submitted by various officers.[7] Many of these officers studied the Duke of Wellington's operations in Spain, as well as Peter the Great's plans against

# Background

King Charles XII of Sweden in the 1700s, while Prussian officers, including Gerhard von Scharnhorst, advised the Russians to pursue 'a defensive war'.[8]

Among these plans several are worthy of discussion. Minister of War Mikhail Barclay de Tolly presented his plan of action as early as the spring of 1810, proposing to establish a main defensive line along the Western Dvina and the Dnieper rivers. He wanted to: 'face the enemy on the frontiers, fight the superior enemy forces in the Polish provinces as long as possible and then retreat to the defensive lines, leaving the enemy in a scorched countryside, without bread, cattle or any other means of supplying itself.' Then, when the enemy exhausted his forces, the Russian armies would launch a counter-offensive.[9] Alexander approved this plan later that year and preparations were carried out between August 1810 and December 1811. Cartographic and reconnaissance works were conducted in Western Russia, fortresses at Riga, Dvinsk, Bobruisk and Kiev were repaired, and large depots situated at Vilna and Grodno and other towns.

In early 1812, however, Prince Peter Bagration reflected the opinion of more hard-line officers when he called for an aggressive stance towards the French. He proposed establishing a demarcation line on the River Oder, and its violation, 'even by a single French Battalion', would be considered a *casus belli*. Bagration suggested using 'any means possible' to ensure Austria's support – or at least its neutrality – while an agreement with Britain would provide necessary funding. Depending on Napoleon's actions, Bagration called for an invasion of Poland and the Germanic lands to raise a national movement against the French and 'to remove the theatre of war from the boundaries of the Empire.'[10]

Ludwig Wolzogen, a Prussian officer who joined the Russian Army in 1807, contemplated a more defensive strategy and proposed deploying two armies along the western frontiers. If the French attacked, one of them would withdraw to a special line of well-supplied fortresses, organized along the Dvina, Dnieper and other rivers, where it would make a stand. The second army would operate against the enemy's lines of communication. Wolzogen's ideas can be compared to an insightful, albeit largely overlooked, memo by Lieutenant Colonel Peter Chuikevich of the Secret Chancellery of the Ministry of War. Addressed to Barclay de Tolly, Chuikevich's memo argued that Napoleon would seek a decisive battle to eliminate the enemy armies, therefore the Russians should avoid one as much as possible. Referring to the Spanish example, he contended that 'it is necessary to conduct a war that [Napoleon] is not accustomed to' and to start a guerrilla war utilizing flying detachments to harass French communications and supply lines. Chuikevich anticipated that the Russians would have to abandon vast territories to Napoleon but then, having gathered sufficient forces, they would be able to give battle to the exhausted, overextended and significantly reduced enemy forces: 'The loss of several provinces should not frighten us since the integrity of the Empire resides with the integrity of the Army.'[11]

# The Battle of Borodino

Chuikevich's memo, submitted in early April 1812, certainly indicates that the 'Scythian plan' was considered and discussed in its various aspects by the Russian high command on the eve of war. In the month preceding the start of the war, Barclay de Tolly and Bagration were already discussing evacuating large supply depots and laying waste to the countryside to create obstacles for the enemy to overcome. The Minister of War's instructions specified: 'We should prevent the enemy from using any of our supplies during the offensive, cut his lines of communication and always employ a "scorched earth" policy during our retreat.'[12] Such a 'Scythian plan', however, was limited in nature and contemplated retreating only as far as the western Dvina. Barclay de Tolly himself was ready to surrender the recently acquired Polish–Lithuanian provinces and retreat towards 'our ancient frontiers'. Lieutenant General Kankrin agreed that: 'at the start of the war, no one anticipated retreating beyond [the] Dvina, and certainly not as far as Smolensk; as a result very few supply magazines were established beyond that river.'

At first glance the proposed defensive and offensive plans seemingly contradicted each other, but as S. Shvedov argued:

> the intentions of the Russian command to invade the Grand Duchy of Warsaw and Prussia did not contradict the concurrent groundwork for a lengthy retreat [into Russia]. The purpose of the pre-emptive offensive was to move the 'scorched earth' zone, where the Russians wanted to engage Napoleon, as far west as possible. If achieved, the entire burden of the war would be removed from the shoulders of the Russian nation and placed on its neighbours.[13]

Among the mentioned plans, Wolzogen's ideas had particular effect, since they caught the attention of Lieutenant General Karl Ludwig August von Pfuel, a former Prussian officer who now advised the Russian Emperor. Recognizing that the western frontier of Russia was divided by the bogs of Polesye into two parts – northern and southern – Pfuel suggested that Napoleon could only approach from one of two directions: north of Polesye or south of it. He proposed to concentrate two armies and deploy one in the north and the other in the south. Should Napoleon approach from the north, the first army would retreat to the 'Drissa camp' on the western Dvina river and hold him there. The second army would then act on the enemy's flanks and rear. But if Napoleon approached from the south, the second army would retreat to Zhitomyr and Kiev and the first army would attack the his rear, as well as his lines of communication.

This plan was flawed for several reasons. For a start, it did not take into consideration the possibility of a French attack along both approaches. Meanwhile, the limited strength of Bagration's army made an attack on the flank and rear of the enemy unrealistic, since Napoleon only had to oppose it with an equivalent force to halt its advance. Furthermore, the Russian armies would be divided into several components, each isolated from the others by long distances and difficult terrain. And finally, the location of the camp at Drissa was poorly selected, and its construction was not completed before the war began. Carl von Clausewitz, who served in Barclay de Tolly's army, studied this fortification shortly before the 1st Western Army retreated, declaring that: 'if the Russians had not voluntarily abandoned this position, they would have been attacked [...] driven into the semi-circle of trenches and forced to capitulate.'[14]

Nevertheless, Alexander, trusting Pfuel, approved the plan. Accordingly, the 1st Western Army was deployed north of Polesye, in the area of Vilna, and the 2nd Western Army was posted south of it. Further complicating matters was the fact that Alexander was reluctant to renounce previous strategic arrangements, even though the situation in Europe had changed and offensive war became impossible. The lack of logistics complicated the problems of transporting supplies that were stored in new depots along the border. As a result, during the first days of the war in June–July, the retreating Russian armies were compelled either to abandon huge magazines to the French or destroy them.

During 23–25 June, Napoleon's army crossed the Russian border at the River Nieman, motivated by the grandiloquent rhetoric of a new imperial proclamation:

> Soldiers!
> The second Polish War has begun. The first war ended at Friedland and at Tilsit; at Tilsit, Russia swore an eternal alliance with France and war against England. Today she is violating her pledged word. She is unwilling to give any explanation for her strange conduct until the French Eagles have crossed back over the Rhine, leaving our allies there to her discretion. Russia is led on by fatality! Her destiny must be accomplished. Does she then believe us to be degenerates? Are we then no longer the soldiers of Austerlitz? She places us between dishonour and war. Our choice cannot be doubted, so let us march forward! Let us cross the Nieman! Let us carry the war into her territory. The second Polish war will be glorious for French arms, like the first; but the peace we shall conclude will carry with it its own guarantee, and will put an end to that proud influence Russia has exercised for fifty years over the affairs of Europe.

As the Russian armies retreated, discontent about the conduct of the war quickly increased among Russian officers and soldiers. Russia had not sustained a foreign invasion since that of Charles XII's Swedes in 1709, and even that was defeated at Poltava. A contemporary recalled: 'The victories of [Field Marshals] Peter Rumyantsev and Alexander Suvorov made the very word "retreat" reprehensible.'[15] Throughout the 18th century, Russia fought victorious wars against Sweden, the Ottoman Empire, Persia and Poland. The 1799 Campaign in Italy, conducted by Alexander Suvorov, was regarded as a true reflection of Russian military spirit, and the setbacks in the Alps were overshadowed by heroic Russian exploits. The defeat at Austerlitz in 1805 was largely blamed on the Austrians, while the memories of Friedland were soothed by victories in Finland and Wallachia. So, on the eve of the French invasion, an offensive psychology prevailed in the

# The Battle of Borodino

Russian military. Many officers were unwilling to accept defensive warfare within Russia and were inflamed by a belligerent ardour to fight Napoleon. According to one Russian nobleman:

> All letters from the Army are filled with aspiration of war and animation of the souls [...] It is said that soldiers are eager to fight the foe and avenge the past defeats. The common desire is to advance and engage Napoleon in Prussia, but it seems that the Sovereign's advisers are against this notion. They decided to wage a defensive war and let the enemy inside our borders; everyone aware of this *German* [italics added] strategy [...] is extremely upset, considering it as the greatest crime.

And a few days into the war Colonel Zakrevsky complained:

> We are retreating to that dreadful Drissa position that seems to doom us for destruction. [Our commanders] still cannot agree on what to do and, it seems, they make the worst decisions. The cursed Pfuel must be hanged, shot or tortured as the most ruinous man ...

A letter written by General Rayevsky expressed similar sentiments: 'I do not know what the Sovereign's intentions are [...] Pfuel's voice is stronger than anyone's [...] Lord save us from such traitors.' But Ivan Odental perhaps expressed the Army's frustration best, writing: 'it seems to me that Bonaparte gave our leaders large doses of opium. They are all dozing off while [worthless] men like Pfuel and Wolzogen are acting instead of them.'[16]

Despite increasing criticism of Pfuel's strategy, the Russian armies continued to withdraw towards the Drissa Camp. The 1st Western Army reached the camp on 8 July, when Alexander finally realized the flaws of Pfuel's plan and discarded it. Urged by his advisers, Alexander then left the Army without appointing a supreme commander. Barclay de Tolly took over the command of the 1st Western Army and also enjoyed authority over the 2nd Western Army based on his position as Minister of War.

On 14 July Barclay de Tolly abandoned the Drissa camp, detaching General Peter Wittgenstein with some 20,000 men to cover the route to St Petersburg. Barclay de Tolly then withdrew toward Smolensk, fighting rearguard actions at Vitebsk and Ostrovno. In the south, Bagration withdrew first on Minsk and then to Nesvizh and Bobruisk, eluding Napoleon's enveloping manoeuvres and gaining minor victories at Mir and Romanovo. When Marshal Davout's forces finally intercepted the 2nd Western Army at Moghilev, Bagration fought a diversion at Saltanovka on 23 July, while his troops crossed the Dnieper to the south and marched toward Smolensk through Mstislavl. On 2 August, the two Russian armies finally united at Smolensk, bringing their total strength to 120,000 as opposed to some 180,000 in Napoleon's main force.

Meanwhile, in the north, French forces Marshal Oudinot attacked Wittgenstein, protecting the road to St Petersburg, taking Polotsk on 26 July. But in combats near Klyastitsy on 30 July–1 August, the French suffered a defeat, forcing Napoleon to divert Saint-Cyr to support Oudinot's operations. And in the Baltic provinces, Macdonald's corps was fighting near

# Background

Riga, while the Russians redirected reinforcements from Finland. Finally, in the south, Tormasov defeated French forces at Kobrin and then pinned down Schwarzenberg and Reynier in the Volhynia region. On 31 July Chichagov's Army of the Danube moved from Moldavia to support Tormasov.

Thus, by August 1812, Napoleon's initial plan to destroy the Russian forces in a decisive battle had largely failed. The two main Russian armies eluded piecemeal destruction and united at Smolensk, while the Grand Army suffered high losses from strategic consumption and desertion.

# Campaign Chronicle

By the time they reached Smolensk, the Russian armies were already reeling from an ongoing crisis of command. The continuous retreat stirred up discontent among the troops, with many senior officers opposing Barclay de Tolly's defensive strategy. Relations between the two commanders-in-chief deteriorated after they began to exchange recriminating letters, each unaware of the difficulties the other faced. Yet this discord was far from a simple quarrel between two generals: it also represented political friction between foreign officers and members of the Russian aristocracy, most of whom preferred a straightforward stand-up fight and bitterly resented the surrender of every inch of Russian soil, blaming the outsiders for all their misfortunes. Needless to say, chances of a harmonious partnership between Barclay de Tolly (a Livonian of Scottish ancestry) and Bagration (a Georgian prince) were thus severely compromised.

Indeed, the two commanders gradually came to represent opposing fractions within the officer corps. Barclay de Tolly was surrounded by the so-called 'German Party', consisting of émigrés or the descendents of settlers. The latter were usually thoroughly Russified, but they still had foreign-sounding names, and many professed Protestantism or Catholicism, unlike the Orthodox Russians. The 'Russian' group naturally resented numerous foreign officers, who filled Alexander's army in the wake of Napoleon's European conquests. For many Russians, such an influx of foreign officers seemed to have undermined the very spirit of the Russian Army and many identified with Bagration's complaint that: 'our headquarters is so full of Germans that a Russian cannot breathe.' Besides, many newcomers were incompetent or inexperienced but took advantage of their social standing and connections to obtain promotions, as Bagration observed: 'wishing to become field marshals without reading any military journals or books [...] Today the rogues and impudent upstarts are in favour.'

## 2–7 August: Mutiny of the Generals

Leading the Army against the French, Barclay de Tolly acted under great stress and would later note that 'no other commander-in-chief operated in more unpleasant circumstances than I did.'[17] Although his Scottish family settled in Russia in the 17th century and loyally served its new motherland for decades, Barclay de Tolly was still perceived as a foreigner by the 'real'

12

## 2–7 August: Mutiny of the Generals

Russians. According to Jacob de Sanglen, head of the Military Police, on the eve of the war he warned Barclay de Tolly that: 'it is troublesome to command the Russian troops in their native language but with a foreign name.'[18] Barclay de Tolly could not boast ancient nobility or titles – and he never became a wealthy estate and serf owner as many around him did – but his successful career and high social status caused envy and hostility among fellow officers, and this was exacerbated by his foreign origins.

The Russian prejudice against foreign officers had deep roots, and by 1812 it was ingrained in both the Army and society. Russian senior officers gradually formed an anti-Barclay opposition party aimed at his dismissal. Barclay's own staff members, headed by Major General Yermolov – 'the sphinx of modern times' as he was described for his inscrutable, conspiratorial mind – intrigued against him. Unaware of the actual circumstances and exasperated by the retreat, officers taught the rank and file to call Barclay de Tolly by the nickname 'Boltai da i tolko' ('All talk and nothing else'). Soldiers complained about the continual retreat since: 'they were prejudiced against the word "retirada" [retreat], considering it alien to the dignity of the courageous soldiers, whom [Field Marshals] Rumyantsev and Suvorov trained to advance and gain victory.'

Thus, confidence in the Commander-in-Chief was undermined and every new stage of the retreat intensified the malicious rumours about him. It was hard for Barclay de Tolly to parry thrusts of criticism since his cautious, albeit sensible, policy contrasted with the popular ideas of Bagration and his fire-eating supporters. One of the Russian officers understood that Barclay's defensive strategy was 'prudent' but also noted 'the extremely negative impact' it had on the commander-in-chief: 'The common view about him was that of a treacherous German; naturally, this was followed by mistrust and even hatred and contempt that were openly expressed.'[19]

Bagration, with his impeccable reputation and eagerness to fight, certainly fared much better in the eyes of the common soldier. A contemporary remarked: 'The difference in the spirit of the two armies was that the 1st Army relied only on itself and the Russian God, while the 2nd Army also trusted Prince Bagration [. . .] His presence, eagle-like appearance, cheerful expression and keen humour inspired soldiers.' Similar sentiments are echoed by Yermolov, who noted a dramatic difference in the state of the armies as they reached Smolensk:

> The 1st Army was exhausted by the continuous withdrawal and soldiers began to mutiny; there were cases of insubordination and agitation [. . .] At the same time, the 2nd Western Army arrived [at Smolensk] in an entirely different state of mind. The music and joyful songs animated soldiers. These troops showed only pride for the danger they had overcome and the readiness to face and overcome a new danger. It seemed as if the 2nd Western Army did not retreat from the Nieman to the Dnieper, but covered this distance in triumph.[20]

Such were the passions on the eve of the junction at Smolensk, and the impending meeting of the two generals was naturally expected to be intense.

Yet, to everyone's surprise, when they encountered each other on 2 August both commanders displayed unusual tact, realizing the importance of restoring a workable partnership.

When Bagration arrived, accompanied by his generals and aides-de-camp, Barclay de Tolly met him wearing a parade uniform complete with medals, sash, and plumed bicorn in hand. The two commanders then had a private conversation and each apologized for any injustice he might have caused the other. Bagration praised Barclay's withdrawal from Vitebsk and Barclay de Tolly complimented Bagration on the skilful manner in which he had eluded Napoleon's trap.

Bagration was pleased with this meeting and though senior in rank, agreed to subordinate himself to Barclay de Tolly. Unity of command was thus achieved for the moment. Alas, such cordiality between the generals would survive a mere seven days.

## 7–14 August: Offensive at Last

With the Russian armies concentrated at Smolensk the question was what to do next? Should the armies continue retreating or take advantage of their combined strengths and launch an offensive? The majority of officers, and Russian society in general, demanded a more vigorous conduct of the war. Minor successes at Mir, Romanovo, Ostrovno, Saltanovka, and Klyastitsy were already portrayed as great victories, which only intensified calls for an offensive. In early August, Pavel Pushin, serving in the 3rd Battalion of the Semeyonovsk Life Guard Regiment, noted in his diary the general restlessness prevailing in the Army: 'We all are burning with impatience to fight, each of us is willing to shed blood to the very last drop, and, if commanded properly, we will inflict heavy losses on the enemy.' Three days later the Army learned about Count Wittgenstein's victory at Polotsk and the news only intensified the sentiments.

To many soldiers it seemed that the fruits of these victories were wasted by their high command (coincidentally full of 'German' officers) and Russian soil was being surrendered to the enemy without a fight. Bagration certainly echoed the opinion of many when he wrote to Barclay de Tolly:

> With our armies finally uniting, we accomplished the goal set by our Emperor [Alexander]. With so many experienced troops gathered together, we now enjoy a superiority, which [Napoleon] tried to exploit while we were separated. Now, our goal must be to attack the [French] centre and defeat it while [the French] forces are scattered [...] We would seize our destiny with one blow [...] The entire Army and all of Russia demand [attack].[21]

Conceding to public pressure, Barclay de Tolly called a council of war on 6 August. The council agreed to an attack and next day the Russian armies advanced westward in three columns on a 20-mile front. The weather was dry and the advance rapid. Yermolov recalled that the soldiers were in high spirits because: 'the order to attack was finally given and it [was] impossible to describe the joy of our troops! Smolensk watched in bewilderment at our forces' eagerness to fight; the Dnieper vociferously flowed, proud of the orderly movement of our troops!'

But the advance also revealed an ongoing disagreement between Bagration and Barclay de Tolly. One day after the offensive began Barclay de Tolly received news, later proved incorrect, that the French were advancing towards Porechye, north of Smolensk. Fearing Napoleon would turn his right flank, Barclay de Tolly ordered his troops to veer to the right to cover the Porechye–Smolensk route. Bagration opposed the change in direction of the 1st Western Army's advance, since he anticipated Napoleon's actual attack on the left flank.[22]

Barclay de Tolly ignored Bagration's pleas and remained on the Porechye route, awaiting new intelligence. His order to Platov (leader or *Ataman* of the Don Cossacks) to halt did not reach him in time, and acting under original instructions, Platov continued his march north-west, making a sudden attack on General Sébastiani's division near Inkovo (Molevo Boloto). Instead of trying to exploit this initial success by mounting a major attack in this direction (as envisaged by the council of war), Barclay de Tolly remained idle on the Porechye route, still believing that the main threat to Smolensk lay from the north. A Russian general complained:

> Instead of rapid movement that would have secured our success, the armies were given a useless rest and the enemy gained additional time to concentrate his forces! [...] Circumstances still favoured us and had our Commander-in-Chief showed more firmness in his intentions [we would have succeeded]. Of course, the defeat at [Inkovo] awakened the French, but they were about to suffer from further attacks and had no time to avoid them. Yet, the Commander-in-Chief not only evaded executing the adopted plan but completely changed it.[23]

This was a decisive blow to the Russian counter-offensive. The Russian armies remained inactive for days as Barclay de Tolly dithered, thus alerting Napoleon to Russian intentions and permitting him to prepare his troops accordingly. Finally, on 12 August, Barclay de Tolly learned that his intelligence regarding a French concentration at Porechye was incorrect and that Napoleon had assembled his army at Babinovichi, on the Dnieper, threatening the left flank of the Russian Army, as Bagration had anticipated days before. He responded by withdrawing his troops from the Porechye road to the Rudnya route on 13 August. The Russian troops reacted bitterly: the soldiers were grumbling and, after marching several times through the village of Shelomets, they called Barclay's manoeuvres 'oshelomelii' or 'dumbfounding'.[24]

The sudden cancellation of the planned attack, lack of information on Barclay de Tolly's plans, constant changes in orders and delayed manoeuvres aroused feelings of dismay in many Russian officers, and in Bagration above all. He clearly saw the threat to the Russian left flank but could not convince Barclay de Tolly to believe him. He complained:

> I still believe that there are no enemy forces [in the direction of Porechye] [...] I would be glad to coordinate my actions with [the 1st Western Army] but [Barclay de Tolly] is making twenty changes in a minute. For God's sake, please do not change the strategy every minute; [we] must have some kind of system to act upon.[25]

Russian senior officers who disliked Barclay de Tolly before now openly despised him. Conspiracy theories flourished in this fertile ground: especially after the Russians, searching Sébastiani's headquarters at Molevo Boloto, found a message from Marshal Murat describing the Russian offensive. Could it be that someone at Barclay de Tolly's headquarters had notified the enemy about the counter-offensive? On 12 August, Pavel Pushin of the Semeyonovskii Life Guard Regiment noted in his diary:

> A few days ago, General Sébastiani's personal papers were captured. Notes were found in his portfolio that contained numbers, places and day-by-day movement of our corps. Rumours have it that, as a result, all suspicious persons were removed from headquarters, including *Flügel Adjutants* and Counts ...

Not surprisingly, all of these persons were non-Russians, mostly Poles. It later transpired that the Polish Prince Lubomirski, one of the adjutants, accidentally overheard several generals discussing Russian offensive plans in the street and had sent a message to his mother, urging her to flee the coming bloodshed. Murat – who was billeted at Lubomirski's family home – had intercepted this letter. Another incident further increased Russian suspicions against the Poles in particular. As the troops marched back and forth between Prikaz Vydra and Shelomets, some soldiers noticed:

> a woman following our columns and, when asked, she always replied that she was with General Lavrov. Everyone was satisfied with her answer until one joker decided to flirt with her and, in a moment of passion, tore off her hat, which revealed a male head underneath. It appeared that he was a spy; he was [arrested] and sent to headquarters.[26]

## 14–19 August: Napoleon Strikes Back – The Battles of Krasnyi, Smolensk and Lubino

Russian hesitation gave Napoleon enough time to adjust his plans. His first reaction to news of the action at Inkovo had been to suspend preparations for the drive on Smolensk, followed by an order to concentrate the Grand Army around Lyosno, in order to meet the Russians. But by 10 August Barclay de Tolly's indecision convinced Napoleon that the Russian offensive presented no significant threat. Meanwhile, an opportunity to deal the enemy a decisive blow had presented itself.

Napoleon's manoeuvre on Smolensk was a masterpiece. He concentrated his corps on a narrow front between Orsha and Rosasna on the northern bank of the Dnieper; then, under cover of a heavy cavalry screen, the Grand Army crossed to the southern bank. Napoleon's plan was to advance eastwards along the left bank, taking Smolensk while the Russians were preoccupied with the northern approaches.

# 20–29 August: The Retreat Continues

By daylight on 14 August almost the entire Grand Army was across the Dnieper and advancing on Smolensk. However, Napoleon's plan was thwarted by a small Russian detachment led by General Neverovsky, which Bagration had deployed at Krasnyi to watch for any potential flanking manoeuvres. Neverovsky's troops made a successful fighting retreat to Smolensk, 'retreating like lions' as one French officer described it. Their exploits enthralled the Russian Army, and future guerrilla leader Denis Davidov reflected what many felt at the time: 'I remember how we looked at this division, as it approached us in midst of smoke and dust. Each bayonet shone with an immortal glory.'

Without Neverovky's staunch resistance at Krasnyi, the French might well have reached Smolensk by the evening of the 14 August and taken the city, cutting the Russian line of retreat. However, as a result of this action, Napoleon decided to halt his advance for a day in order to regroup his forces, missing his chance of taking Smolensk by surprise.

Hearing of Napoleon's flanking attack, both Russian armies rushed back to Smolensk. On 15–16 August the Russians repulsed French assaults on Smolensk but were nonetheless forced to abandon the city. Smolensk was almost completely destroyed and of 2,250 buildings only 350 remained intact. Meanwhile, of the city's 15,000 inhabitants only 1,000 remained in its smoking, smouldering wreck. The Russians lost about 10,000 men in the two-day battle. French losses reached a similar figure, though Russian sources often claim as many as 20,000 French casualties.

As the Russians withdrew to Moscow, Napoleon attempted to cut their line of retreat but at the Battle of Valutina Gora (Lubino) on 19 August Barclay de Tolly's army succeeded in clearing its way to Dorogobuzh. Once again the fighting proved bloody, this battle claiming over 7,000 French and around 6,000 Russian casualties.

## 20–29 August: The Retreat Continues

As the retreat continued, Barclay de Tolly concentrated his troops at Soloveyovo, crossing on four bridges to the left bank of the Dnieper. His army was now deployed at Umolye, while Bagration gathered his forces between Mikhailovsky and Novoselok. On the 21st, the 2nd Western Army proceeded to Dorogobuzh while Barclay de Tolly remained at Umolye until late evening, beginning his movement towards Usvyatye around 9pm by crossing the River Uzha. The French tried to cross the river in his wake but the Russians fought a successful rearguard action at Pnevo Boloto, destroying the bridges. This temporarily reduced the pressure on Barclay de Tolly, who realized a battle would have to be fought before moving much closer to Moscow. He instructed several officers, including Quartermaster-General Colonel Toll, to seek advantageous terrain for battle. As a result, two positions were found: one at Usvyatye, on the River Uzha, and the other at Tsarevo–Zaimische, near Vyazma.

On 21 August Barclay de Tolly and Bagration – accompanied by Grand Duke Constantine (Alexander's brother), Toll, and various aides-de-camp –

met at Usvyatye to inspect the site. Barclay de Tolly initially favoured the position but changed his mind when Bagration, among others, found it faulty on several counts: including an unprotected left flank, and the fact that it was overlooked by a range of heights where the enemy might site his batteries. Bagration then suggested another site near Dorogobuzh.[27] But Toll arrogantly defended the position he had selected, going so far as to insult Barclay de Tolly, who refrained from an angry reply. Bagration, however, resented Toll's insolence and defended Barclay de Tolly, censoring the young Quartermaster-General.[28]

On 24 August the 1st and 2nd Western Armies halted at Dorogobuzh, while their top brass spent the morning surveying positions that also proved to be unacceptable. Returning from a reconnaissance the Commanders discovered that the troops were so poorly deployed by Toll that: 'the 1st Army's front, facing the Dnieper, was perpendicular to the enemy's front and its reserves were arranged with their rear facing the enemy.' General Yermolov later remarked: 'This fact was immediately concealed! Bagration insisted on punishing [Toll], who deployed the Army with its rear facing the French [. . .] and he requested reducing him in rank for this unjustifiable blunder.' Barclay de Tolly quipped that: 'Toll must be either a traitor or madman for mishandling this task.' And yet, a favourite of Mikhail Kutuzov (hero of recent Russo-Turkish clashes along the Danube and future Commander-in-Chief), Toll would avoid punishment.

Next morning the Russians left Dorogobuzh and retreated to Vyazma, where they found a strong position at Tsarevo–Zaimische. Although Bagration still was not completely satisfied with the terrain, he agreed with Barclay de Tolly that no better position could be found at a safe distance from Moscow.[29]

Nevertheless, the failure of the Russian counter-offensive at Smolensk and the subsequent surrender of the city led to a rapid deterioration in relations between the two Russian commanders. Anti-Barclay sentiments also increased among senior officers, who intrigued behind the Commander-in-Chief's back. These generals not only demanded a change in strategy but also Barclay de Tolly's dismissal, threatening to disobey orders if they didn't get their way. This alarming development has been described by one Russian historian as 'the Mutiny of Generals'.[30] Thus, Dokhturov considered Barclay de Tolly a 'stupid and loathsome person', while Platov reportedly told Barclay de Tolly: 'As you see, I wear only a cloak. I will no longer put on a Emperor, requesting that Barclay de Tolly be replaced by Bagration.

Unaware of Yermolov's initiative, Bagration continued to obey Barclay de Tolly's orders, much to the Army's annoyance, as one contemporary recalled: 'the reconciliation of the commanders infuriated all our generals and officers, who unanimously detested Barclay.' These misguided officers tried to induce Bagration to oppose Barclay de Tolly publicly and Vistitsky even admitted that '[some] senior officers urged Bagration to replace Barclay by force.'[31] To his credit, Bagration rejected such treasonous suggestions and refused to publicly oppose Barclay de Tolly, though his passionate temper often burst forth in private correspondence. Yermolov urged Bagration to write directly to the Tsar and boldly suggest that he be named supreme commander of the Russian armies. But while this was undoubtedly Bagration's ambition, he hesitated to go that far: 'I will not write to the Tsar asking for the command, because this would be attributed to my ambition and vanity, not my merit and abilities.'[32]

After the loss of Smolensk, Barclay de Tolly's position in the Army became tenuous. The British Commissioner to the Russian Army, Sir Robert Wilson, recalled: 'The spirit of the Army was affected by a sense of mortification and all ranks loudly and boldly complained; discontent was general and discipline relaxing. The removal [of Barclay de Tolly] [...] had become a universal demand.'[33]

The withdrawal through Lithuania and Byelorussia, though far from popular, had been reluctantly accepted in view of the enemy's numerical superiority. But now the war was blighting ancient Russian soil and Smolensk, a holy city for many Russians, lay in ruins. As a senior Russian officer (Benckendorff) described: 'Drowned in sorrow, we were abandoning our provinces and their generous population to the enemy's devastation. How many curses the honest and noble General Barclay attracted ...' Fedor Glinka wrote in his memoirs: 'Soldiers were eager, demanding to fight!' And another officer complained: 'We are running away like hares. Panic has seized everyone [...] Our courage is crushed. Our march looks like a funeral procession.'[34] Meanwhile, Lieutenant Radozhitsky saw many junior officers and soldiers gathering in small groups and talking 'of the impending destruction of the fatherland'. They wondered, 'what fate awaited them [since] the arms which they had borne so bravely in defence of their fatherland now seemed useless and cumbersome.'[35] Yermolov reflected the opinion of his fellow senior officers when he wrote:

> The destruction of Smolensk introduced me to a completely new feeling which wars outside your native land cannot inspire. I had never witnessed the destruction of my native land or seen the burning cities of my motherland. For the first time in my life, my ears heard the moans of my compatriots and for the first time did my eyes see the horrors of their terrible conditions. I do consider magnanimity a gift from God, but I would never have allowed it into my heart before revenge was satisfied!

Most Russian officers had opposed the surrender of Smolensk, General Kutaisov actually pleading with Barclay de Tolly to continue the battle. The Commander-in-Chief listened attentively and then replied: 'Let everyone mind his own business and I shall mind mine.'[36] Later, Zakrevsky complained to Vorontsov that: 'no matter how much we appealed to our Minister not to surrender the city he did not listen to us [...] No, the Minister is not a military commander, he cannot lead the Russians ...' The following day Zakrevsky noted:

# The Battle of Borodino

I cannot ascribe our Minister's aloofness and indifference to anything but treason [...] I say this as a Russian, with all my heart and tears. When was there a time in our past when we abandoned our ancient cities? I cannot watch without tears the many residents who follow us with their children, bemoaning and losing their native land and property.[37]

In Dorogobuzh, some officers complained to Grand Duke Constantine of Barclay de Tolly's leadership, claiming the 'soldiers were disappointed, downcast [...] concerned with the future of the Army.'[38] To their dishonour, many officers publicly slandered Barclay de Tolly – especially Grand Duke Constantine, who publicly grumbled that 'there is not a single drop of Russian blood in our Commander's veins.' He even insulted him in the presence of aides-de-camp and Staff members: 'You are German, a traitor, vermin, and you are betraying Russia!'[39] And as Zhirkevich justly noted: 'When such words can be heard from the Emperor's brother himself, one can imagine what was spoken by the rank-and-file.'

Later, a Russian veteran neatly summed up why Barclay de Tolly was so detested in the Army: 'Because in 1812 he was called Barclay de Tolly [a foreign-sounding name] and not Kutuzov or Bagration.'[40]

Some generals felt such antipathy towards Barclay de Tolly and the 'German Party' that radical proposals were mooted. For example, one day Platov approached Yermolov to discuss 'untrustworthy and useless persons that overwhelmed the headquarters' and the name of Colonel Wolzogen, Barclay de Tolly's trusted adjutant, cropped up:

Being in a joyous mood, Ataman Platov told me in his peculiar, humorous manner, 'Here, brother, is what we need to do. You can suggest sending him on a reconnaissance of the French Army and direct him to me, and leave it to me to separate these Germans [i.e. Wolzogen and Barclay]. I will assign him special [Cossack] guides, who will show him the French in such a manner that he would never see the light of day again.'

## 29–31 August: Looking For a New Commander

Meantime, Emperor Alexander cautiously followed military events, as the reports from the Army were far from cheerful. Wittgenstein's success at Klyastitsy and Polotsk, and Tormasov's at Kobrin, were overshadowed by the loss of Smolensk and Napoleon's continued march on Moscow. The anxiety in society grew daily, while news from the Army was so disturbing that a new commander-in-chief had to be appointed immediately. In his letter to Alexander on 17 August, General Count Shuvalov, the Tsar's friend and advisor, painted a devastating picture of a grumbling, demoralized and ill-fed Army, blaming Barclay de Tolly for indecision and mismanagement: 'The Army has not the least confidence in the present Commander [...] A new commander is necessary, one with authority over both armies and Your Majesty should appoint him immediately; otherwise, Russia is lost.'[41]

The letter reflected the sentiments of a large number of senior Russian officers and motivated Alexander to make a decision. On 17 August he convened a committee to select a new commander. The committee considered

# 29–31 August: Looking For a New Commander

only full generals, while excluding two elderly field marshals (76-year-old Count Saltykov and 70-year-old Count Gudovich) on the grounds of age.

The committee members initially discussed the candidacies of Bagration, Bennigsen, Tormasov, Dokhturov and Pahlen but none of them were supported unanimously.[42] Kutuzov's candidacy was discussed last, since it was a delicate question. Though the nobility and most of the Army had long been talking of Kutuzov's appointment, the members of the committee were well aware that, after the disaster at Austerlitz in 1805, the Tsar disliked Kutuzov, who felt likewise about the Sovereign. For several hours the committee hesitated to make its proposal but finally gathered the courage to recommend Kutuzov. Alexander vacillated for three days before finally signing the decree on 20 August. Lord Cathcart noted that:

> in appointing Koutousof [*sic*], it was considered that his long-standing in the Army, his recent able conduct of the Turkish campaign, and his former military reputation, would place him above rivalry, and that in consequence he might be a kind of head to unite all parties.[43]

Imperial orders were sent to Barclay de Tolly and Bagration, informing them that 'various dire complications occurring after the two armies united, have impelled me to appoint one commander above all others. I have chosen for this post General of Infantry Prince Kutuzov.' Russian society – and especially St Petersburg – celebrated Kutuzov's appointment, an eyewitness describing how: 'the people surrounded him [Kutuzov], touched his clothes and appealed, "Save us and defeat this cruel enemy." Kutuzov's departure to join the Army turned into a majestic and touching procession.'[44]

Despite the popular Western perception of him, Kutuzov was far from being a sluggish, simple-minded man. Although his career was largely based on victories against the decadent Ottoman Empire, Kutuzov's military talents are hard to deny. He was a shrewd diplomat and adroit courtier, who rarely spoke his mind openly and could skilfully manipulate people around him, causing Suvorov to observe: 'Shrewd, he is very shrewd, no one can trick him.' His was a subtle personality, which Sir Robert Wilson found 'polished, courteous, shrewd as a Greek, naturally intelligent as an Asiatic and well-instructed as a European.' Yet Kutuzov was also a sybarite, who valued power and honours, and the effects of this indulgent life were evident by 1812. The 65-year-old Kutuzov had grown stouter since Austerlitz, walked heavily, often out of breath, and had difficulty riding a horse, preferring his carriage. Although his rival Bennigsen claimed that Kutuzov had lost the habit of mental work, below that drowsy and absent-minded appearance was keen judgement, cunning and patience.

While he was hailed by society, Kutuzov was not as universally welcomed in the Army. Alexander himself was not overly thrilled about his appointment and later confided to his aide-de-camp: 'The public wanted Kutuzov to be appointed and I appointed him; as for me, I wash my hands of it.' Many generals were also disenchanted by Kutuzov's appointment. Bagration described him as a 'swindler', Rayevsky considered him a 'mediocrity',

# The Battle of Borodino

Miloradovich called him 'a petite courtier', while Dokhturov regarded him a 'coward'. Still, the appointment of Kutuzov – an ethnic Russian of ancient noble family and considerable military reputation – silenced disgruntled officers.

On the French side, Brandt recalled learning of the appointment of 'old Kutuzov, nicknamed "the runaway of Austerlitz" by the French troops [. . .] This change seemed to augur well for us . . .'

Barclay de Tolly received his copy of the imperial decree regarding Kutuzov's appointment on 27 August, as his army marched through Vyazma. He was certainly disappointed by the news, especially since the Tsar's order was not accompanied by any personal note or message. Such casual treatment – even more than the decision itself – was particularly depressing for him. The timing was also unfortunate: for Kutuzov's appointment came just as Barclay's strategy was showing results and Napoleon's superiority in numbers was significantly reduced. Nevertheless, he assured Alexander of his desire to prove his:

> eagerness to serve the country at any post or assignment [. . .] Had I been motivated by blind and reckless ambition, Your Majesty would probably have received a number of reports of battles fought, and nevertheless the enemy would still be at the gates of Moscow without Russia retaining sufficient forces to resist him.

Like many others, Colonel Benckendorff, one of the imperial Flügel Adjutants, would later praise Barclay de Tolly for his actions, noting that: 'his great self-sacrifice [in 1812] was a hundred times more deserving of praise than all the victories that later crowned him with laurels and brought him the title of prince and the rank of field marshal.'

The Russian armies reached Tsarevo–Zaimische on 29 August 1812. The village may not have been a perfect defensive position, but it had several features to recommend it. Located at the edge of a plain with a virtually unobstructed view for miles around, it was dominated by gently rising ground, which provided the Russians with vantage points for observing enemy movements and for deploying their artillery batteries. Beyond the ridge the Smolensk–Moscow route stretched eastward across marshland and offered an unimpeded avenue of withdrawal in case of retreat. Barclay and Bagration agreed that this was one of the best defensive positions to be found between Smolensk and Moscow: so they immediately put the soldiers to work, building redoubts and other fortifications. The same day Kutuzov arrived at Gzhatsk, followed by an impressive suite of generals and aides-de-camp.

Kutuzov's actions on that day reveal his cunning. He, without a doubt, shared Barclay de Tolly's belief in the necessity of retreat, but unlike him, he appreciated that popular opinion demanded the Army make a stand, ending the policy of incessant withdrawal. Kutuzov's initial orders to attack were aimed at calming the rank-and-file, addressing the common soldiers in their own simple language. The fact that he was Russian to the marrow of his bones, while Barclay de Tolly was of foreign extraction, made Kutuzov more acceptable to the troops in the moment of national crisis, when most foreigners were suspected of treason. In the words of Clausewitz: 'Kutuzov [...] knew Russians and how to handle them [...] He could flatter the self-esteem of both populace and army, and sought by proclamation and religious observances to work on the public mind.'[45]

Kutuzov did just the right things and said exactly what was needed to foster the impression that he was going to stand and fight. After climbing out of his carriage at Tsarevo–Zaimische he nodded approvingly at the sight of the honour guard drawn up to greet him and then muttered audibly: 'How can one go on retreating with young lads like these?'[46] The comment, repeated from mouth to mouth, was on everyone's lips within hours. Meanwhile, knowing well what everyone expected of him, Kutuzov, shortly after his arrival, instructed a Cossack detachment to scout the woods some distance from the main road. Later, accompanied by a magnificent suite of generals and Staff officers, he set off down the road on a grand reconnaissance. When the party approached the woods Kutuzov pointed to the horsemen in the distance, asking: 'Who can that be?' No one was able to distinguish their uniforms and some suggested it was a French patrol. 'No, they are Cossacks,' Kutuzov assured them and calmly ordered some of his adjutants to investigate the identity of the horsemen. As they returned, confirming Kutuzov's opinion, everyone was stunned by the old man's sharp eyesight and confidence.

Kutuzov made several changes at headquarters that had important consequences. He effectively ignored the regulations established within the official 'Yellow Book' adopted under Barclay de Tolly's command. Kutuzov was well known for his preference for issuing oral instruction and avoiding official channels of correspondence, advising Yermolov: 'My dear boy, you know that not everything can be written in reports so keep me informed via separate messages.' Several persons soon emerged as the centres of power at headquarters and covetously guarded access to Kutuzov. Yermolov, a perceptive witness to this development, remarked:

> Age, serious wounds and [the] years of abuse [Kutuzov] endured significantly reduced his powers. His previous mannerisms, proven in numerous trials, were now replaced by timid caution. It was easy to gain his confidence with open flattery and it was as easy to lose his trust because of outside influence. His associates, having studied his character, could even direct his will. Because of this, many undertakings, either just starting or already in progress, were cancelled by new orders. Among his close associates were some with limited abilities who, through shrewdness and intrigues, managed to become indispensable and get appointments. There was constant intriguing [at headquarters]; intriguers rose quickly and their fall was hardly discernible.

Colonel Toll was Kutuzov's old-time favourite, having studied under Kutuzov's direction as an adolescent: he now became the Commander-in-Chief's right-hand man. Alexander Sherbinin, serving in the quartermaster service, noted that after Kutuzov's appointment General Vistitsky, the Quartermaster of the 2nd Western Army, became the Quartermaster General of the united armies. However:

> the moral influence Colonel Toll wielded over officers was so strong that we all continued to gather around him while Vistitsky, a tall and lean old man, rode alone like the Commendatore in *Don Juan*. He finally ordered me angrily to remain with him and I initially followed his command but when he joined the suite surrounding Kutuzov, I immediately left him and joined my comrades.[47]

Two other persons around Kutuzov were Nikolai Kudashev (Kutuzov's son-in-law) and Paisii Kaisarov, both known for their tendency towards intrigues. Yermolov lamented the chaotic situation that quickly emerged at the headquarters:

> Following Kutuzov's arrival I became aware of the tension he was creating with Barclay de Tolly, who was exasperated by the disorder in the Army, something which was now becoming incredibly widespread. Initially, the Prince's orders were sent to the Chiefs of Staff, that is to me and Count Saint Priest, via Colonel Kaisarov, who served as duty officer to Kutuzov as well as through many other officers; frequently, they contradicted each other, which caused misunderstanding, confusion and unpleasant recriminations. Sometimes, the orders were delivered directly to the corps and local commanders, who carried them out and reported to the Army commanders only when their troops left camp or returned. [Toll and Kudashev] were also authorized to publicize orders personally on behalf of the commander-in-chief.

Upon reaching the Army, Kutuzov inspected the position at Tsarevo–Zaimische and initially approved it, telling Barclay de Tolly and Bagration that it is 'very advantageous and strong'. However, later that night, Kaisarov, Kudashev and Toll went to work on Kutuzov, appealing to his vanity by saying that he could not fight on ground selected by another general, especially when that general was Barclay de Tolly. Swayed by their arguments, Kutuzov rescinded his initial decision and ordered a withdrawal beyond Gzhatsk. 'That unbearable drum woke us up at 3 o'clock in the night and we immediately marched on the road to Moscow,' recalled Captain Pushin.

## 1–4 September: Arrival at Borodino

As the Russian Army left Tsarevo–Zaimische, the Russian generals examined several positions at which to fight a decisive battle. None of them proved acceptable, since, as Clausewitz noted:

> Russia is very poor in positions. Where the great morasses prevail, the country is so wooded that one has trouble to find room for a considerable number of troops. Where the forests are thinner, as between Smolensk and Moscow, the ground is level without any decided mountain ridges and without any deep hollows; the fields are without enclosures, therefore everywhere easy to be passed; the villages of woods and so ill adapted for defence [...] There is therefore little choice of positions.

# 1–4 September: Arrival at Borodino

Bagration reflected the frustration of many officers when he wrote to Rostopchin: 'As usual we have yet to make a decision where and when to give a battle – we are still selecting places and are finding each new one to be worse than the previous.'[48]

Kutuzov's initial choice was the terrain near the Kolotsk Monastery, and on 2 September he wrote to the Governor of Moscow: 'Even half an hour ago I could not tell anything specific about the position for the anticipated decisive battle. Yet, after examining all locations before Mozhaisk, it seems that the position we currently occupy [near the Kolotsk Monastery] seems to be the best.' Still, Kutuzov's next message to Rostopchin reveals that his earlier letter was too optimistic: 'the position, which was selected today, is very good but also too vast for our army and could expose one of the flanks.'[49]

Discussing this initial Russian choice of battlefield, Yermolov noted that:

Kutuzov intended to give battle near the Kolotsk Monastery. Fortifications were constructed there but the position was soon abandoned as it had some advantages but just as many flaws. The right flank was placed on some vital heights, which dominated the surroundings along our entire line, but a failure to hold them would have complicated our retreat since a narrow valley lay behind them. Our rearguard was left there and another position was selected some 12 verstas [12.8km] further back near the village of Borodino located near the Moscow river.

The Russian Army marched eastward in three columns: the right column consisting of Bagration's army; the middle column of the III, V and VI Corps, under the command of Dokhturov; and the left column, of the II and the IV Corps, led by Miloradovich. Cavalry was left behind to support the rearguard while the artillery proceeded along the main road.[50] On 3 September the official *Journal of Military Operations* recorded that: 'the Army set up its camp near the village of Borodino.'

The position at Borodino, 105 verstas (112km) from Moscow and 279 verstas (297km) from Smolensk, was selected by Toll, and later reviewed by Kutuzov on 3 September. His contemporaries, as well as subsequent generations, have debated its flaws and advantages ever since. Yermolov, Bennigsen, Barclay de Tolly and other senior officers criticized Kutuzov for blindly trusting Toll and being reluctant, due to obesity and lethargy, to examine it more closely. Bennigsen, who had strained relations with Toll, blamed him for selecting this inferior position, since he 'has gained complete control over the mind of Prince Kutuzov.' Bennigsen lamented:

I never described Borodino as a favourable position but Colonel Toll, appointed [by Kutuzov] to the position of Quartermaster General, selected it himself [. . .] He was satisfied by the mere fact that its front was protected by shallow rivulets that could be forded everywhere, and ignored the fact that both flanks were exposed and not reinforced.

In his *Izobrazhenie voyennikh deistvii*, Barclay de Tolly remarked that the position at Borodino was 'favourable in the centre and on the right flank, but the left flank was completely exposed'. He then placed the responsibility on Bennigsen's shoulders, who 'denounced everything that he did not come up with or that was not suggested by him.'

Bagration, reconnoitring the area around Semeyonovskoye, immediately voiced his criticism of the position and highlighted the exposed position of the 2nd Western Army, which, he felt, was threatened the most.

Vistitsky remembered that Kutuzov initially disapproved of the position but then weighed its flaws and advantages, and under Toll's influence, finally decided to accept it. Clausewitz agrees: 'It was thus that Colonel Toll could find no better position than that of Borodino, which is, however, a deceptive one, for it promises at first sight more than it performs.'

Kutuzov himself displayed a mixture of optimism and caution in a letter to Alexander, dated 4 September:

> The position at the village of Borodino in which I have stopped [...] is one of the best to be found in the vicinity [of Moscow]. The weak point of this position is on the left flank, which I will try to rectify.[51]

The terrain was rolling, intersected by several streams and sharp valleys, and littered with woods and hamlets. The battlefield stretched from the confluence of the Moscow and Kolocha rivers in the north to the hamlets of Utitsa on the Old Smolensk Road in the south. The Kolocha and several other brooks flowed along the north of the plain, eventually joining the Moscow river. The streams were deeply scored in the ground and marked with steep banks that would have proved serious obstacles for the French attacks, had the hot summer not rendered some of them shallow. There were about two dozen small settlements and four major villages, the most important being the village of Borodino, which gave its name to the battle. The village was noteworthy for its white two-storey Church of the Nativity, the bell tower of which would serve as an advantageous observation point for Russian scouts.

The lower stretch of the Kolocha, between Borodino and the Moscow river, had a steep right bank overlooking the opposite bank, which made it easier for the Russians to defend their positions. Beyond the river was a vast field, convenient for cavalry action. Still, the terrain here was hilly with the gullies of the Voina, Stonets and Ognik brooks cutting across it. In the centre the Russians held heights that dominated the surrounding area in all directions. In the south the Russian positions were covered only by the shallow gullies of the Semeyonovskii and Kamenka streams. The village of Semeyonovskoye occupied a key position on a hill on the east bank of the Semeyonovskii brook, but its wooden houses were useless for defence so they were dismantled. Further south, the extensive Utitsa forest separated Semeyonovskoye from the Old Smolensk Road. As Clausewitz elaborated:

> The ground taken up by the left wing presented no particular advantages. Some hillocks with a gentle slope, and perhaps twenty feet high, together with strips of shrubby wood, formed so confused a whole, that it was difficult to

pronounce which party would have the advantage of the ground. Thus, the best side of the position, the right wing, could be of no avail to redeem the defects of the left. The whole position too strongly indicated the left flank to the French as the object of operation, to admit of their forces being attracted to the right.[52]

The Russian troops reached Borodino on 3 September and Avraam Norov recalled that by the time he reached the battlefield: 'all nearby heights were glittering with the steel of our bayonets and the copper of our guns. The air was filled with the voices of hordes of men and the neighs of horses.'[53] The stories of the enemy pillaging nearby villages and the local populace courageously defending itself spread through the Army. Pushin noted in his diary on 3 September that during a French raid on a nearby village:

> the peasants repulsed the attack, killing 45 enemy soldiers and capturing 50. Remarkably, women were also fighting with consternation. Among the dead was one 18-year-old girl, who fought with particular gallantry. Despite receiving a mortal blow, she was so strong in spirit that, with her last breath, she still managed to thrust her knife into the Frenchman who shot her ...

Fedor Glinka recounted the peasant exploits and described 'two young peasant girls who were wounded to their hands as one of them rushed to protect her grandfather while the other killed a Frenchman who injured her mother ...' Stories like these, describing women – even innocent girls – fighting the enemy while the Army was still retreating, only further increased the soldiers' eagerness to fight.

The Russian Army was initially deployed in a line parallel to the Kolocha river, with its right flank near Maslovo and the left flank at Shevardino. This arrangement is sometimes referred to as the 'first Russian position'. Clausewitz, the perceptive Prussian officer serving at Kutuzov's head-quarters, was critical of this position:

> The road from Smolensk to Moscow runs unfortunately not at right angles to the Kolocha, but parallel to it for some distance, and, after it has passed the river, diverges from it at an obtuse angle [...] The consequence is, if the position be taken up parallel to the stream, the Army stands obliquely to its line of retreat and exposes its left flank to the enemy [...] half a mile from the great road, a second road to Moscow issues from the village of Yelnya, and leads straight behind the rear of such a position.

On 3 September Bagration called upon all generals of his 2nd Western Army to make a detailed reconnaissance of the position. He was dissatisfied with the position for several reasons, including the fact that: 'the position was selected by the same eyes that selected all previous positions for Barclay, that is the eyes of Colonel Toll.' As we have already seen, Bagration distrusted Toll and even threatened to have him demoted for incompetence.

It was quickly realized that the left wing, anchored on Shevardino, was greatly exposed, since the French could take advantage of the Old Smolensk Road to outflank the Russian position. This oversight – whether made by

# The Battle of Borodino

Toll or Bennigsen – was later covered up in official reports and battle histories, but many participants voiced their criticisms in their memoirs. As we know, Clausewitz argued that the road from Yelnya led 'straight behind the rear of such a position' and he was supported by Yermolov's comment that: 'the old postal [Old Smolensk] road to Mozhaisk wound through the forest for one mile from the left wing, gradually skirting around our positions,' as well as Norov's remark that: 'the position could be flanked through the woods adjacent to the Shevardino Redoubt, where the Old Smolensk Road was located.'

The decisions made that day had important consequences for the Russian deployment, but their course remains disputed. One of the issues at stake is who made the decision to reinforce the left flank with the series of fortifications? Many Russian, and later Soviet, historians sought to give sole credit to Kutuzov, who, they claimed, devised and supervised everything on the battlefield. But Bogdanov's study suggests that it was Bagration who closely examined the terrain of his position and finding it deficient, suggested constructing a redoubt at Shevardino and then *flèches* at Semeyonovskoye. Kutuzov consented to this. Saint Priest made it clear in his diary that:

> the village of Semeyonovskoye was selected as the key to our positions. [However,] the enemy could easily get around [the Russian left wing] position by moving along the Old Smolensk Road from Yelnya to Utitsa, and then approach Semeyonvskoe [...] through the woods. To prevent this, [Bagration] arranged to reinforce the village and construct several flèches. The heights, near the village of Shevardino, in front of the village [of Semeyonovskoye] were also reinforced.[54]

According to Barclay de Tolly, Bagration told Kutuzov that his position 'was currently under the greatest risk' and that:

> the Old Smolensk Road, located at some distance from the village of Semeyonovskoye on the left flank, could be used by the enemy to turn his left flank but Prince Kutuzov and Bennigsen claimed that this road could be easily defended by irregular ['nestroevymi'] forces.[55]

Bagration then suggested moving his troops to the eastern bank of the Semeyonovskii ravine, which would give them a positional advantage over the advancing French. Barclay de Tolly noted that, after hearing Bagration, Kutuzov decided that: 'in case of an enemy attack, this flank would retreat and take position between the mentioned [Kurgan] Heights and the Semeyonovskoye village. Orders were issued to construct batteries and redoubts here.'

While pleased with Kutuzov's decision, Barclay de Tolly 'still could not understand why such movement was to be done only after the enemy attacked and not beforehand.' Yermolov, on other hand, gives credit to Kutuzov, who:

> after reconnoitring the deployment of the troops, ordered the left wing to move back so that deep [a] ravine lay in front of it; he also ordered the flank to be strengthened with several flèches. Following this change, the redoubt

# 5 September: Prelude to Borodino – The Battle of Shevardino

[at Shevardino] was out of our artillery range and so was rendered completely useless to us [...] The straight line formed by the Army position was now bent at its very centre.

This deployment is sometimes dubbed the 'second Russian position'.

## 5 September: Prelude to Borodino – The Battle of Shevardino

By early September the French Army advanced by forced marches, closely pressing Konovnitsyn's rearguard. Brandt, an officer in the Vistula Legion, remembered the exhausting pursuit from Smolensk to Gzhatsk, when:

the temperature would swing dramatically from burning heat to freezing cold. The heat was terrible and the wind swept up huge billowing clouds of dust that were so thick it was often impossible to see the great trees on either side of the road [...] The dust was a real torment. In order to at least protect their eyes, the soldiers improvised goggles out of glass from windows; others marched with their shakos tucked under their arms and with their heads swathed in handkerchiefs, with openings left open just enough to see and to breathe; still others made garlands out of leaves. The Army presented a comical appearance, but all signs of this masquerade would vanish at the slightest shower of rain.[56]

Captain Girod de l'Ain, veteran of the Spanish campaign, also lamented:

The heat was excessive: I had never experienced worse in Spain [...] The main road [...] is sandy, and the Army, marching in several serried columns abreast, raised such clouds of dust that we could not see one another two yards away and our eyes, ears and nostrils were full of it, and our faced encrusted. This heat and dust made us extremely thirsty [...] [but] water was scarce. Will you believe me when I say that I saw men lying on their bellies to drink horses' urine in the gutter![57]

Meanwhile continual retreat, agitation over the perceived treason of Barclay de Tolly and his adjutants, lack of supplies, and the emotional strain of war was affecting the Russian soldiers. In late August Kutuzov was informed of increasing disturbances among the troops and had to acknowledge in one of his orders that: 'up to 2,000 itinerant soldiers had been captured.' On 30 August he complained that:

such enormous number of soldiers abandoning their units reveals remarkable loosening of discipline on the part of the regimental commanders. A tendency towards marauding, facilitated by the weakness of their superiors, had an effect on the soldier's morale and now almost evolved into this habit that must be eradicated through the strictest measures.

Forthwith, the Russian Commander-in-Chief ordered the execution of any soldier caught pillaging. But even draconian measures like this barely influenced the rank and file, forcing Kutuzov to repeat his order on 2 September.[58]

On 1 September, in unbearable heat, the Russians fought a delaying action lasting almost thirteen hours around Gzhatsk, and three days later the rearguard repulsed French attacks at Gridnevo. Meanwhile, Kutuzov's main forces concentrated at Borodino.

# The Battle of Borodino

Early in the morning of 5 September the sound of gunfire was heard from the direction of Kolotsk and by 1pm Konovnitsyn's troops came into view, pursued by the French advance guard. As the French advance guard proceeded from Gridnevo to Kolotsk, Konovnitsyn called for reinforcements, especially in cavalry, to hold the French cavalry at bay, consequently General Fedor Uvarov arrived to support him. Although senior in rank, Uvarov gallantly subordinated himself to Konovnitsyn, telling him: 'This is not the time to discuss seniority. You are leading the rearguard and I am sent to assist you – so command me.' Uvarov's cavalry made frequent charges and the Russian artillery acted with relative success while, as Konovnitsyn reported, 'the infantry largely did not participate in the fighting due to the [broken] terrain.'

A Württemberger serving in the Grand Army remembered how:

[The Russians] chose very advantageous positions. On the left flank, their artillery was covered by a wide building of the monastery that was firmly occupied by the *Jägers*. Numerous cavalry covered the right flank. We unlimbered our guns and the fighting soon turned into a hell. The Russians persisted for a quarter of an hour before they hastily retreated.[59]

## Air Blitz at Borodino?

Some months before the French invasion, the Russian Minister to Stuttgart, D. Alopeus, met a young German inventor Franz Leppich, who had earlier approached King Frederick of Württemberg with the grand idea of constructing a new kind of flying machines.

After Joseph and Étienne Montgolfier first flew them in 1783, hot air balloons had been used by the French military for reconnaissance. Leppich suggested improving their performance and turning them into fighting machines. The trouble with balloons, he explained, was their inability to fly against the wind, but by attaching wings they could be made to move in any direction. Although the idea seemed enticing, the King of Württemberg initially passed on it, especially after Napoleon rejected Leppich's similar offer. But King Frederick later changed his mind and provided modest funding for Leppich's experiments. The inventor was busy building his machine when, in early 1812, the Russian Minister approached him with a tempting offer to work in Russia. In his letter to Emperor Alexander, Alopeus described in detail a machine 'shaped somewhat like a whale', capable of lifting '40 men with 12,000 wounds of explosives' to bombard enemy positions and sailing from Stuttgart to London in an incredible thirteen hours.

Leppich's project appealed to Alexander, especially as war with Napoleon was looming, and any ideas that promised to give Russia an edge sounded attractive. On 26 April Alexander approved the project and Leppich's workshop was set up at a village near Moscow, where

Governor Rostopchin provided Leppich – now working under the alias 'Schmidt' – with all necessary resources. Officially, 'Schmidt' was supervising the production of artillery ammunition.

Maintaining secrecy over the project was of paramount importance, but difficult to maintain. Suspicions were immediately aroused when guards were deployed around the estate. And they were further heightened when Rostopchin placed large orders for fabric, sulphurid acid, file dust and other assets, totalling a staggering 120,000 roubles. By July, some hundred labourers were working 17-hour shifts at the workshop. Leppich assured Rostopchin that the money was well spent and the flying machine would be completed by 15 August: by autumn entire squadrons would soar into the skies above Moscow!

On 15 July, Alexander personally visited the workshop and was shown various elements of the flying machine, including wings and a large gondola 15m long and 8m wide. The Emperor soon informed Kutuzov of the secret weapon and instructed him and Leppich to closely coordinate their actions in the future 'air blitz' against the French.

However, the deadline of 15 August passed without any results.

By now the invasion was under way and Napoleon was already at Smolensk. Rostopchin, beginning to suspect Leppich, demanded results. The scientist promised to deliver the machine by 27 August, but when nothing was forthcoming, Rostopchin wrote a letter to Alexander denouncing Leppich as a 'crazy charlatan'. The machine was not completed by the time Borodino was fought, and the subsequent French advance threatened Leppich's secret workshop: so it was loaded onto 130 wagons and moved to Nizhni Novgorod, while Leppich himself was recalled to St Petersburg.

Back in Moscow, Napoleon, already aware of rumours about a flying machine, ordered an investigation. Reports came back that some work had been done 'by an Englishman who called himself Schmidt and claimed to be a German'. The purpose of this secret weapon, it was alleged, was to destroy Moscow before the French could seize it.

Meantime, Leppich continued his experiments at the famous Oranienbaum observatory. In November 1812 his first prototype balloon collapsed as it was wheeled out of the hanger. By September 1813 he finally built a flying machine that could ascend 12–13m above the ground – a far cry from his earlier promises of soaring squadrons in the skies above Russia.

In October 1813 General Alexei Arakcheyev launched an investigation into Leppich's experiments and branded him 'a complete charlatan, who knows nothing whatever of even the elementary rules of mechanics or the principles of levers'. Deprived of funding and in disgrace, Leppich left Russia in February 1814. By that time the Russian government had spent a staggering 250,000 roubles on Leppich's project.

# The Battle of Borodino

Konovnitsyn had no choice but retreat, since he was facing numerically superior forces that were trying to turn his right flank. As Eugène's troops pressed forward, a French officer described advancing in Konovnitsyn's wake: 'Coming out of the woods, which were full of Cossacks who were routed by the Italian cavalry, we passed through several villages devastated by the Russians. The devastation, which these barbarians left in their wake, showed us the way.'[60]

To cover Konovnitsyn's rearguard, the Russian command dispatched the Leib-Guard Jäger Regiment to secure crossings across the Voina and Koloch streams. Colonel Karl Bistrom sent Colonel P. Makarov with the 3rd Battalion to deploy in a line along the right bank of the river. To accelerate Konovnitsyn's retreat, Makarov instructed his subordinates to locate fords, since there was only one bridge that could have delayed the Russian retreat.

Quickly retreating from the Kolotsk direction, the Leib-Guard Cossack Regiment and part of Konovnitsyn's cavalry forded the stream on the left side of Borodino, while the Izumsk Hussars led the remaining cavalry across another ford on the right side of the village. This allowed the artillery and other transports to move across the bridge without delay and the rearguard wasted no time in taking up positions on the right bank.[61] The bridge itself was defended by Makarov's troops.

Around 2pm Prince Eugène, accompanied by his staff and escort, arrived at the advance guard to reconnoitre the Russian positions. Eugène had hardly begun his observations when the Emperor himself galloped in front of the Allied cavalry and approached his stepson. Labaume, who witnessed this moment, later recalled that Napoleon carefully studied the terrain, and after a brief conversation with Prince Eugène, galloped back towards the troops of Marshal Davout. Then Eugène dispatched aides-de-camp with orders to begin an attack towards Borodino.[62]

Leaving the Italian guard in reserve, Eugène directed the 13th and 14th Divisions to occupy the nearby heights west of the Voina stream, in order to threaten the Russian right flank. In the meantime, the troops of General Gérard (from Davout's Corps) supported Eugène from the south, and in fact, had already engaged the Russian skirmishers.

The 13th and 14th Divisions reached the Voina stream but failed to take up positions there. As Barclay de Tolly reported: 'the enemy's repeated attempts to seize the village of Borodino were repelled by the Guard Jägers, the Elisavetgrad Hussar Regiment and an [artillery] battery set up on the right bank of the river.' Major General Vsevolodsky particularly distinguished himself as he led his hussars in several charges against the French. Supported by artillery and reinforced with three Cossack regiments from Bagration's 2nd Army, Vsevolodsky was able to defend his position until late into the night.[63]

While Prince Eugène's troops were engaged in the north, the rest of the Grand Army was slowly approaching the site of the future battle. Near Valuyevo, the French advance guard encountered the Russian skirmishers, firing from bushes and ravines along the Kolocha river. Compans dispatched four *voltigeur* companies (under the command of Adjutant Major Duchesne of the 25th Line) to the right and, supported by the two companies of the 1st and 2nd Battalions, they seized the village of Okinshino, which was abandoned by the Russians.[64] General Montbrun, commander of the II Cavalry Corps, soon reported to Murat that a major fortification had been observed between the villages of Doronino and Shevardino. According to Dumonceau, the French could see:

> a broad, tall hillock, like a truncated cone, which we took for a redoubt. Some individuals were visible on its summit, probably put there to observe. At its base and behind its flanks we could make out two black masses, which could only be the heads of columns intended to support it.

Shaped like a pentagon, the redoubt at Shevardino was initially designed to anchor the left wing of the Russian positions at Borodino, but eventually became a forward fortification, protecting the approaches to Kutuzov's left flank. Who decided to construct this fortification, and why, is still disputed. As we have seen above, Bagration considered building it by 3 September and had made some arrangements for this purpose before discussing the flaws of his position with Kutuzov. At the same time, Clausewitz argued that this fortifications was constructed after Colonel Toll suggested an observation post to 'discover the direction from which the French forces were advancing and possibly to discover Napoleon's intentions.' Vistitsky also noted: '[The Redoubt] was constructed at a distance [from Borodino] to halt the enemy advance and keep [the current] positions intact.' Kutuzov himself considered the redoubt as: 'a separate fortification whose loss would not have had any effect on the defence of Russian positions and was mainly designed to delay the enemy from approaching [positions] for some time.'[65]

Among historians, Buturlin based his narrative on Kutuzov's report and naturally repeated the Russian commander's opinion that 'the redoubt was built only to determine the direction of the advance of the French column.' Mikhailovsky-Danilevsky thought that one of the purposes of the redoubt was 'to facilitate attacks into the flank of the enemy columns advancing along the main road towards Borodino.'[66] The latter opinion influenced later histories of Borodino and N. Neyelov used it to suggest that the redoubt was built for two main reasons: to prevent the French 'from seizing this location, which would have allowed them to observe the entire disposition of the Russian troops'; and 'to delay the enemy advance along the main road by acting against his flank.'[67] Among later Russian historians a small group of scholars (E. Bogdanovich, I. Bozheryanov etc.) continued to sustain this idea but many – including M. Dragomirov, A. Witmer, G. Ratch, M. Bogdanovich, N. Polikarpov, A. Skugarevsky, A. Gerua, B. Kolyubyakin, V. Kharkevich – rejected the notion that the Shevardino Redoubt could threaten the flank of the French Army advancing along the main road, since the fortification was located beyond its effective artillery range (the road was about 1,700m away to the north). Soviet historians, breaking with the imperial historiography, sought to tread their own path, leading to frequent overstatements and factual errors. Thus Garnich claimed that the Shevardino Redoubt placed the French flank in grave danger from Russian cannon-fire, later producing nonsensical data on artillery ranges that had Russian guns capable of firing at 2,500m with a target range of over 1,200m. This idea was slightly revised in later works, which downplayed the role of artillery, asserting that Napoleon was more concerned about flank attacks from Russian troops deployed around Shevardino.[68]

Kutuzov's report, cited above, is a little misleading. One can wonder what was the purpose of sacrificing men in defending this place if, as he claimed, its loss 'would not have had any effect' on his overall position? This is especially interesting in view of the considerable effort the Russian command committed to protect the Shevardino Redoubt. More plausible suggestions are voiced in contemporary memoirs. As we noted above, the initial Russian left flank was anchored near the village of Shevardino but Bagration and other generals complained about this exposed position and Kutuzov agreed to their suggestions, ordering the left wing to be withdrawn to Semeyonovskoye. As Bagration began gradually withdrawing his troops to new positions near Semeyonovskoye, he left the so-called 'Corps de Bataille' under General Andrei Gorchakov to cover his movement and support the Russian rearguard if necessary. With the withdrawal of the 2nd Western Army, the Redoubt at Shevardino had lost its early task of reinforcing the Russian left flank and now became a forward fortification that could hinder Napoleon's deployment. Some participants suggested that the battle at Shevardino began because the French:

> noticed our movement [as Bagration withdrew to Semeyonovskoye] and wanted to take advantage of it. This battle quickly escalated and no one on our side expected such rapid onslaught by the French Army. Yet we had to defend the redoubt while the new disposition of our left wing at Semeyonovskoye was completed.

This opinion is repeated in the memoirs of Yermolov, who, as the Chief of Staff of the 1st Western Army, was certainly better informed. Yermolov explained that Prince Kutuzov had earlier ordered the left wing to move back but during the rearguard action near the Kolotsk Monastery:

> a part of the rearguard, comprising some troops from the 2nd Army, withdrew so hastily, and without warning the Army, that the pursuing enemy appeared on the heights before the position had been changed by the orders of Prince Kutuzov. Thus, our change of position was conducted in front of the enemy, and, notwithstanding the speed in which it was made, the enemy was presented with a chance to attack. An otherwise useless redoubt now had to be defended out of necessity, in order to give the troops time to occupy their [new] positions, since the enemy could try to impede and even to throw our entire army into confusion.[69]

The construction of the Redoubt was begun by some thirty pioneers led by Lieutenants Bogdanov and Oldengren in the evening of 4 September. However, hard ground and lack of manpower greatly delayed the process.

# 5 September: Prelude to Borodino – The Battle of Shevardino

According to Bogdanov, after seven hours of work, his pioneers barely managed to dig a foot-deep trench to defend the fortification, and constructed a 1.5m-high walls of the redoubt, which, however, were not reinforced. Because the redoubt had been hastily constructed, some of its guns had been positioned in improper embrasures that compromised their effectiveness, while the rest had to fire over the crude earthwork.[70] The redoubt's key weakness lay in the fact that it was exposed to the fire from a hill located some 200m away south-west. This spot was not protected and would allow the French to deploy a battery that would inflict heavy casualties on the redoubt's defenders.

On 5 September, as the French Army approached Shevardino, Marshal Murat informed the Emperor about the Russian fortification and Napoleon soon arrived to make a personal reconnaissance. Across the battlefield, Paskevich could see 'a cavalry group standing on the heights in front of us. Two generals left the group, one of them in a grey coat and three-cornered hat. He reconnoitred positions for about fifteen minutes and waved his hand to the right.'[71] Despite thick smoke from burning villages and a drizzling rain, both of which obscured his view – as Lejeune and Constant inform us – Napoleon spent some time reconnoitring the enemy positions.

Napoleon assumed that Gorchakov's troops constituted the left wing of the Russian Army and believed the redoubt at Shevardino would impede the deployment of the French troops. Gourgaud recalled that: 'Napoleon considered it highly important to gain possessions before night of this position, which covered the left centre of the Russian line.' However, Pelet suggested that the entire Battle of Shevardino was fought in vain, since Napoleon was misled by his maps that misrepresented the flow of the Kolocha river, and had Napoleon known the terrain better, he would not have attempted this attack but simply forced the Russian to retreat through a flanking manoeuvre.[72]

As the French engineers put up bridges across the Kolocha, Napoleon, 'without waiting for the other Divisions of the first Corps to arrive', ordered General Compans' 5th Division of Davout's corps to attack the redoubt from north-west, while the 16th and 18th Divisions of Poniatowski's V Corps, which was approaching Yelna, would make a flanking attack through the wooded terrain from the south-west. Followed by the two cavalry corps of Nansouty and Montbrun, Compans' troops crossed the Kolocha at Fomkino around 3pm. The total number of French forces committed, including Murat's cavalry, was approximately 34,000–36,000 men with about 194 guns.[73]

On the Russian side, Prince Andrei Gorchakov, the nephew of the renowned Field Marshal Alexander Suvorov, commanded about 8,000 infantry, 4,000 cavalry and thirty-six guns.[74] The 27th Division was deployed in battalion columns behind the redoubt, with the Odesskii and Simbirskii Regiments in the first line and the Vilenskii and Tarnopolskii Regiments in the second. The 2nd Cuirassier Division was arranged further behind, between the fortification and the Utitsa woods. The 49th, 41st and

# The Battle of Borodino

the 6th Jägers, under Colonel Glebov I, were in skirmishing chain around Doronino, while the 42nd, 5th and 50th Jäger, under Colonel Gogel I, were south of Doronino, extending to the Old Smolensk Road. To the north-west of the redoubt were the Kharkovskii and Chernigovskii Dragoon regiments of the IV Reserve Cavalry Corps. In the south-west, the Novorosiiskii and Kievskii Dragoons stood behind Doronino while two squadrons of the Akhtyrskii Hussar Regiment, protected the eight gun battery of the 9th Horse Artillery Company.

Most scholars acknowledge that the twelve pieces of the 12th Battery Company were placed inside the Redoubt, and twenty-four other guns (the 23rd (Lieutenant Colonel Sablin) and 47th (Capt. Zhurakovski) Companies) placed in support around it. However, the redoubt itself was relatively small (smaller than the southern flèche at Semeyonovskoye) and could not have accommodated a twelve gun battery. Lieutenant Bogdanov, who supervised construction of the redoubt and saw the deployment of the guns, specifically mentions only three guns inside the redoubt, while the remaining nine were unlimbered on a hill on the northern side of the fortification; the fact that not all guns of the 12th Battery Company were inside the redoubt is also confirmed by the memoirs of Sub Lieutenant Raspopov, who served in this company and was deployed outside the redoubt. This evidence may explain why Russian battle reports refer to the loss of three guns at the redoubt.

The Russian reserves included the 2nd Grenadier Division, deployed behind the 27th Division. The 2nd Combined Grenadier Division was initially deployed near the village of Semeyonovskoye but its four battalions were later committed to the fighting at Shevardino. Major General Karpov II's detachment of seven Cossack regiments was further south on the Old Smolensk Road.

The initial attack on Shevardino came from the south-west, where Polish cavalry encountered the Cossacks near Yelna. After a brief skirmish, the Cossacks retreated towards Utitsa and Poniatowski turned his forces northward to attack the left wing of the Russian positions at Shevardino. Preceded by several voltigeur companies, the 16th Division (Krasinski) moved over

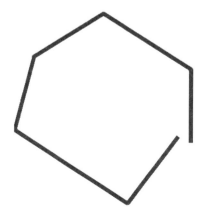

the ravine and through brushes, while the 18th Division and the cavalry secured the road and protected the flank against any Cossack attack. Krasinski's troops suffered from the Russian guns at Shevardino and the Russian Jäger skirmishers. The Poles deployed twenty-four guns to bombard the enemy positions but they were exposed on a disadvantageous position and suffered from Russian counter-fire. Seeing the 5th Jägers under attack, Colonel Emmanuel

*The Shevardino Redoubt (based on a study by Nefedovich and Kolubyakian)*

charged with the Kievskii Dragoon Regiment and was supported by two squadrons of the Akhtyrskii Hussar Regiment. The charge briefly halted the Polish advance but could not stop it. Among the Polish casualties was Major Sowinski, Chief of Artillery of the 16th Division, who was seriously injured in the leg but continued commanding lying on the ground.[75]

Meantime, Compans was preparing to attack from the north-east. Colonel Griois was fascinated by the scene that:

> was enhanced by the splendid sky and the setting sun that was reflected from the muskets and sabres. From its positions the rest of the Army cheered [Compans'] troops as they marched on, proud to have been chosen to open the battle.[76]

But his comrade-in-arms, Labaume seemed less optimistic as he noticed the Russians 'sending considerable forces to defend the Redoubt's approaches.'

Compans took full advantage of the rolling terrain, where, as a participant noted: 'the hillocks provided platforms from which [Compans'] cannon could batter the redoubt, and sheltered the infantry as they formed into columns for attack'.[77] The French enjoyed superiority in artillery, and a Russian officer reported that 'strong French batteries deployed on both sides' of the redoubt soon bombarded the Russian troops, provoking an artillery duel lasting about two hours.[78]

Between 2pm and 2.30pm the 1st Battalion of the 57th Line was ordered to seize the village of Doronino and woods adjacent to it, and was soon engaged in a heated action with the Russian Jägers defending the village.[79] As Kutuzov reported, 'our Jägers, lodged in the ravines and amidst the bushes on the right bank of the Kolocha and inside the villages [...] made it very difficult for the enemy to advance along the main road'.[80]

The French battalion was soon reinforced by a company of the 2nd Battalion and the entire 3rd Battalion of the 57th Line, which drove the Russians back and secured initial positions near Doronino. Simultaneously, two other columns (1st and 2nd Voltigeur Companies of the 57th, led by Captain Simon), covered by a thick chain of *tirailleurs* from Duchesne's 1st Combined Voltigeur Battalion, drove the Russian skirmishers near the village but suffered from the Russian artillery. Furthermore, they were soon charged by the Novorossiiskii Dragoon Regiment, led by Major Terenin, who had been sent by Count Sievers to support the Jägers. The Russian dragoons tried to cut off the French tirailleurs by moving in-between Doronino and the woods, where the French sought cover. Three Russian squadrons, led by Captain Sievers, Lieutenant Stanikovich and Major Borgraf, charged the French, while the fourth squadron (under Major Milfeld) tried to cut them off.[81] The voltigeur companies were caught on an open plain but organized an unexpectedly stiff resistance to the dragoons, deploying into squares to repel the attacks.[82]

Retreating towards the woods, the French were supported by the newly arriving cavalry, which charged the Russian cavalry and forced it to retreat, inflicting heavy casualties, Sievers acknowledging 'considerable loss in staff junior officers and the rank-and-file'.[83] The French – four companies of tirailleurs under Duchesne and two companies under Simon[84] – then resumed their assault on Doronino, which was defended by the few remaining Russian Jägers, and seized it after a brief but tenacious fight.[85] The Novorosiiskii Dragoons, meantime, rallied for the second charge after which they covered the retreating Jägers and helped the Kievskii Dragoon Regiment in removing the guns of the 9th Horse Artillery Company from the nearby heights.

As the fighting intensified, Murat's cavalry moved across the river to fill the gap between the I and V Corps. The Divisions of Friant and Morand also crossed the river in the vicinity of Aleksino. Both divisions were instructed to flank the Russian right wing while Poniatowski threatened the Russian left.[86] Behind them moved Gérard's 3rd Division and Girardin's light cavalry division. With such reinforcements, Compans was able to rally his division for a direct assault on the Shevardino Redoubt.

Around 5pm the French voltigeurs advanced in open order towards the redoubt, followed by the 57th Line and 61st Line. Gourgaud witnessed as Compans:

> hastened to throw five or six companies of voltigeurs [. . .] [and] these scattered over [the knoll], and covering themselves as much as possible, were ordered to keep up a constant fire on the artillery men at the guns on the redoubt [. . .] A Battalion [probably the 1st Battalion of the 61st] was placed in rear of the knoll to support the tirailleurs.[87]

Compans, at the head of the 61st and four battalions of the 57th Line with voltigeurs preceding them, directed his march toward the right side of the redoubt, while Duppelin (with the 25th and the 111th Line) moved towards the left wing. The 25th Line was to attack the village while the 111th was placed still farther to the left, in order to turn the Russian flank and get into the rear.[88] Simultaneously, Morand's division marched from the north-west towards Shevardino, threatening the Russian right flank.

The artillery fire had a devastating effect on both sides, but especially on the French, exposed on the rolling terrain. Karl Löwenstern, who was sent by Bennigsen and Bagration 'to examine the redoubt and determine if it was capable of repulsing the dynamic enemy attacks', reported that 'despite numerous killed and wounded due to our dreadful canister fire, the French boldly advanced towards our fortifications'. Compans exploited the terrain and 'a wattle fencing' that enabled him to continue his movement despite the Russian cavalry charge, 'and even to repulse it with considerable loss'. On his orders, a company of the 2nd Combined Voltigeurs Battalion seized the Doronino hill (or *Kurgan*) about 250m west of the Russian redoubt. Moments later, Compans deployed his artillery (eight or twelve guns depending on the source) there and bombarded the Russian troops in and around the fortification. To preserve his men, Gorchakov had most of his cavalry arranged in battle formation on the left flank behind the redoubt.[89]

South of the redoubt, the Poles continued their attack, which the Russian Jägers contained. Poniatowski sent the 2nd Polish Regiment through the

# 5 September: Prelude to Borodino – The Battle of Shevardino

woods south of the redoubt to flank the Russian defenders, while the 12th Regiment was sent to the left to protect the battery that operated against the Russians.[90] The Tarnopolskii Infantry Regiment was sent to assist the Jägers, and Nikolai Andreyev, an officer of the 50th Jägers, recalled seeing:

> [for] the first, and the last, time as the Tarnopolskii Regiment attacked in a column formation with music playing and soldiers singing. Right in front of my eyes, the regiment made a bayonet charge. The combat was brief and their regimental commander [Lieutenant Colonel Alekseyev] was wounded by a musket ball in the back of his head. He was carried out and the Regiment wavered.[91]

Simultaneously, Gorchakov sent the Fanagoriiskii Grenadier Regiment to relieve the 5th Jägers.

The combined French and Polish artillery and musket fire outgunned the Russian defenders of Shevardino and the 12th Battery Company, at its own discretion, began to withdraw from the redoubt. The 27th Division, deployed behind the redoubt, was also exposed to the enemy fire and began to waver. However, Löwenstern, who earlier left the battlefield to bring Bagration up to date, now returned in time to halt the Russian troops. Yet, it was one moment too late. A brief cessation of fire allowed the French to close in and charge the redoubt. The 27th Division was already falling back when Löwenstern turned it back against the French.[92] As Vossen, an officer of the 111th Line, recalled:

> we almost caught up with the retreating enemy, when it suddenly halted, turned back and opened fire at us. Our courageous *Chef de Bataillon* rushed in front of the 1st Battalion and ordered, 'Grenadiers en avant, croisez les bayonets!'

Meanwhile, Gourgaud saw:

> a most murderous fusillade [that] started between Compans' two regiments and the Russian infantry supporting the redoubt's left flank. Only separated by a couple of dozen yards, the troops on either side of the wattle fences were protected from each other up to chest level. Thus, this sanguinary fusillade lasted three-quarters of an hour; its vivacity and noise made it impossible to hear the generals' order to advance with the bayonet, a manoeuvre which would have cost us a lot of men.

Gourgaud's account is supported by Lieutenant Damploux, who recalled 'such confusion that no voices could be overheard [and] it was even impossible to give orders with signs,' and by Louis Gardier of the 3rd Battalion of the 111th Line, who also remembered that: 'division commanders could not hear orders and senior adjutants were forced to lead one [unit] after another into the battle'.

Realizing the gravity of the situation, Löwenstern led some units of the 27th Division in a bayonet counter-attack that briefly halted the French. Sievers watched as Löwenstern 'halted the [French] advance for some time until they received reinforcements and seized the redoubt'. Indeed, Compans brought in two reserve battalions and personally led a new attack on the redoubt. As Gourgaud described, he then:

# The Battle of Borodino

took a Battalion [probably the 2nd] of the 57th Line and, having opened up the fences on his right, made it advance in close column of divisions, covering four guns charged with grape that moved behind it. He led this battalion against the extreme right of the Russians flanking the redoubt. When, at 50 toises [~100m] from them, he unmasked his battery, which caused a dreadful destruction of the enemy [with its grapeshot]. Compans profiting by the disorder which he observed in their ranks, charged with his battalion at the point of the bayonet.

Despite the Russian counter-fire, a battalion of the 57th Line fought its way into the redoubt (Gourgaud says the battalion lost its major and 200 killed and wounded in the process), supported by Colonel Charles Bouge with the 1st Battalion of the 61st Line and two voltigeur companies of the 57th Line. The report of the 61st Line reveals that Captain Duhon, commander of the 1st Battalion, and Captain Destor were the first officers to break into the redoubt and showed 'remarkable courage' in the process.[93] The hand-to-hand combat proved vicious, leading to mounting casualties on both sides; the 2nd Battalion of 57th Line lost sixteen killed, including Major La Boulayer, and 178 wounded in this charge.[94]

Around 7pm the French seized the redoubt, capturing several guns the Russians could not evacuate. The Russian gunners rendered a stiff resistance and some tried to escape with the guns but were killed on the spot. Six French soldiers, led by Sergeant Rodant, turned one of the captured guns and tried in vain to fire at the retreating Russians.[95]

The precise number of Russian guns captured inside the redoubt remains in doubt. The Polish officer, Soltyk, claimed as many as twelve, Denniée referred to six, Chambray to five, while other French participants (Lejeune, Berthezene, François, Vaudoncourt etc.) acknowledged seven guns. On the Russian side, Sievers and Löwenstern failed to mention any losses, while Barclay de Tolly and Saint Priest referred to three pieces lost. As mentioned above, Lieutenant Bogdanov, who supervized the construction of the redoubt, saw only three guns deployed inside, which seem to have been captured in Compans' charge, while nine other cannon, deployed outside the redoubt, were safely removed by the defenders. Raspopov, who served with the 12th Battery Company, claimed that only two cannon were lost.

As evening approached, many participants hoped for the end of the carnage and Gorchakov later admitted that he 'wanted nothing better than for the darkest night to fall and bring an end to the battle'. The flames of burning villages lit some parts of the battlefield, which was now obscured by fast approaching darkness and thick smoke.

Compans rallied his battalions in and around the redoubt and brought up reinforcements, anticipating an attack. The initial Russian counter attack was made by the Sibirskii and Malorossiiskii Grenadier Regiments, which were motivated by priests who blessed the soldiers as they attacked. However, the French held their ground. Bagration soon ordered the 2nd Grenadier Division and four battalions of the 2nd Combined Grenadier Division to support Gorchakov.[96] As these forces – it is unclear who led the Grenadier attack, since Russian participants and scholars name both Gorchakov and

# 5 September: Prelude to Borodino – The Battle of Shevardino

Bagration – reached the battlefield after 7pm, a fierce hand-to-hand resumed. Murat reported that the Russians 'returned at a charge with two columns of infantry to retake the redoubt but it was vigorously received by Compans' division'.[97]

Some French participants disputed that the redoubt was ever recaptured by the Russians, and responding to Ségur's memoirs, Gourgaud defended his comrades: 'It is false that this redoubt, once in our power, ever was retaken by the enemy [and] it was, therefore, impossible there should be found any of our dead in it.' Napoleon's faithful companion was mistaken, since the redoubt did change hands at least three times and a battalion of the 61st Line, though fighting valiantly, was almost completely destroyed inside the redoubt.

As the Russian Grenadiers fought around the redoubt, the Russian 2nd Cuirassier Division was deployed in squadron columns some 300 paces behind the redoubt, ready to charge the enemy.[98] The Russians soon saw the French troops, which under cover of darkness, sought to march between the redoubt and Shevardino. Sievers reported that he:

> perceived the enemy's daring intention of attacking our infantry in flank and rear with two strong columns [probably the 25th and 111th Line] that were quickly moving between the redoubt and the village [of Shevardino]. I rushed to the right flank of the cavalry line that was under my command [and found] two newly arrived cuirassier regiments [Glukhovskii and Malorossiiskii Cuirassiers] deploying in front of the line [of dragoon regiments]. Their commander, gallant Colonel Tolbuzin met me and I directed him towards the enemy column that was the closest ...

Approaching the French, Tolbuzin charged with the Malorossiisk and Glukhov Cuirassiers, while two squadrons of the Kharkovskii Dragoons, led by Major Zhbakovsky, and two squadrons of the Chernigovskii Dragoons, under Major Musin-Pushkin, soon followed. Panchulidzev described his Chernigovskii Dragoons supporting the cuirassiers and 'impetuously charging the enemy column'. Sievers' report implies that Dragoons protected 'the right flank of the cuirassiers that was threatened by two enemy infantry columns that appeared on the other side of the village'. Colonel Yuzefovich's report reveals that:

> [when the] two enemy columns appeared near the burning village and began to harm our cavalry with their fire, I charged with my regiment; one of the columns was destroyed while the second was forced to flee and one enemy cannon, still loaded with canister, was captured before it could fire upon us.[99]

The Russian charge had a particularly devastating effect on the 111th Line, which was moving in the dark, north of Shevardino, when it was suddenly charged. Although it tried to organize a square, the impetus of the Russian charge pierced it and the regiment suffered heavy casualties. Louis Gardier, serving in the 3rd Battalion of this regiment, provides interesting details of this charge:

# The Battle of Borodino

It was already dark when a *division* of Russian cuirassiers, who claimed to be our allies and indeed looked like the Saxon cuirassiers, appeared [in front of us]. Assuming that they arrived to charge the enemy, we allowed them to pass nearby. But they rallied behind us and charged, killing anyone who came under their blows. We rushed as fast as we could to the orchard that was behind us and in front of the burning village.

Gardier's testimony is enhanced by Lieutenant Vossen, who noted that 'the cuirassiers overwhelmed the first battalion and broke through the square, which was so hastily arranged, and killed everyone they could find. Other battalions became disordered ...'

The Russian cavalry, Ségur recalled, 'fell upon [the French] and scattered them, capturing three guns and taking or killing three hundred men. The survivors immediately gathered themselves up in a compact mass, bristling with steel and firearms.'[100] Panchulidzev reported that 'over 300 men fell', and Vossen also referred to 'up to 300 killed, including [the] Chef de Bataillon and twelve non-commissioned officers'. As it retreated, the unfortunate 111th Line was subjected to friendly fire when, as Vossen recalled, 'a French infantry regiment, not far away, mistakenly took us for the Russians and opened fire until the courageous Adjutant Riston galloped there to explain that the troops standing near the village were the Frenchmen'.[101]

Meanwhile, Friant, whose 2nd Division was deployed north of Shevardino, ordered Colonel de Tschudy to lead the Spaniards of the 2nd and 3rd Battalions of the Joseph Napoleon Regiment, closer to Shevardino to protect the division's right flank. As it marched southward, the Joseph Napoleon Regiment approached Shevardino at the very moment when the Russian cavalry routed the 111th Line, and so it formed a square, in anticipation of a charge. According to E. Lopes, a non commissioned officer in the regiment, Colonel de Tschudy deployed a company of voltigeurs that lured the unsuspecting Russian dragoons of the Kharkovskii and Chernigovskii Regiments directly onto the Spanish square, which opened a surprise fire in the dark. 'The [enemy] cavalry retreated in disorder,' Tschudy later reported, 'having lost a dozen killed, including its commanding officer and large number of wounded men and horses; the battalion lost not a single man and the enemy made no further movement for the rest of the night.'[102] Indeed, the Chernigovskii Dragoon Regiment lost five officers killed, while the Kharkovskii Dragoons lost Captain Nesteley, commanding its Chef Squadron, and Captain von Nagel, leading the second squadron. The Russian cavalry soon retreated since, according to Panchulidzev, 'a strong enemy cavalry detachment appeared to support [the French infantry units] ...'[103]

The number and affiliation of guns seized in this cavalry charge remains unclear. Sievers reported that his men captured '[an] entire French artillery battery' in front of Doronino but removed only three guns. Saint Priest referred to six guns, while Kutuzov, Kaisarov, Toll, Harting and others, claimed as many as eight, with five of them removed and three damaged and left behind.[104] Cornet von Dreyling of the Malorossiiskii Cuirassier Regiment, who did not participate in the charge but certainly heard the stories from his comrades, wrote in his memoirs that his regiment seized an eight-gun battery, destroying four guns and removing the remaining four. An official Army report claimed eight guns captured by the cuirassiers. Modern Russian historians, however, believe that the Russian cuirassiers seized only three guns in this fighting. Russian regimental nominations for rewards provide interesting details in this respect. Privates Gregory Baranov, Ivan Velichko, Roman Pelikh and Arkhip Sergeiev, of the Kharkov Regiment, were commended for quickly dismounting and harnessing their own horses to remove the cannon.[105] Among other officers, Major Babarsov was first among the Kharkovskii Dragoons 'to attack the infantry column and seize an enemy gun', but three of his comrades, Lieutenants Spanovsky, Pereyaslavtsev and Pluzhansky, were killed in action as they tried to rally their troops after the death of Nesteley and von Nagel. An NCO named Fisenko and Dragoons Pavlenko, Gubskoy, Tereshenko and Gontarenko, seized a gun and helped to remove it under enemy fire.[106]

In his report to Bagration two weeks after the battle, Gorchakov sought to correct Kutuzov's praise of the Cuirassier Division for capturing 'five enemy guns'. He explained that, before the cuirassiers arrived:

> I sent a Battalion of the Simbirskii Infantry Regiment, under [the] command of Colonel Loshkarev, against the strong French column, which he attacked with bayonets and managed to capture two guns before the arrival of the Cuirassier Division, which completed the destruction of this enemy column and seized three more cannon.[107]

Panchulidzev reported that his troops captured two guns but because of haste and no horses to pull one of them, he was forced to abandon it, while the other gun was removed with the aid of three horses.[108] French sources are often silent on this issue, but some do acknowledge the loss of three guns belonging to the 111th. Most importantly, General Lonchan's report explained why the 111th lost its regimental artillery, noting that: 'an artillery officer, who had no orders to follow the regiment, moved to the left and, by accident, fell into a ravine, where he lost all guns without the regiment's knowledge'.[109]

The battle was raging south of Shevardino as well, where, as Gourgaud noted, 'notwithstanding all the efforts of [Poniatowski], the many obstacles he encountered in the wood retarded his march and only one of his batteries assisted in the battle'. The Polish advance was halted by combined efforts of the Russian Jägers, Tarnopol Infantry and Fanagoriiskii Grenadier Regiments, which held positions on the edge of the woods. Gorchakov later directed the Ekaterinoslavl and Military Order Cuirassiers to support them. The cavalry initially directed its efforts towards the Polish battery near Doronino but it failed to capture it due to counter-charges of Bruyère's 1st Light Cavalry Division and the Polish Lancers. A Grenadier Company of the 16th Polish Regiment, led by Captain Jan Skrzynecki (future general and leader of the 1831 uprising), distinguished itself as it fought off the Russian cavalry. As one participant described, the night was '[not] so dark we could not make

# The Battle of Borodino

out movement [but] dark enough to prevent us from seeing which arm [the Russian cavalry] was composed of'. This was significant, for the French could not see that the Russians wore cuirasses, causing General Nansouty to send the Red Lancers of Hamburg[110] against them. As Thirion de Metz described:

> This regiment flew to the attack, delivered its charge and fell on the enemy with felled lances aimed at the body. The Russian cavalry received the shock without budging and, in the same moment as the French lance-heads touched the enemy's chest, the regiment about-faced and came back towards us as if it in turn had been charged.

Indeed, Nansouty's lancers proved no match for the heavily armed Russian cuirassiers and sought cover behind their own cuirassiers, who opened intervals to let them through the line and then closed ranks to repel the Russians.

In the meantime, the Polish infantry (fourteen companies of voltigeurs and the 15th Polish Line), led by General Rybinski and supported by cavalry, occupied the hill south of the Shevardino Redoubt and threatened the left wing of the Russian forces Andreyev recalled that almost his entire regiment (50th Jägers) acted in skirmisher order and suffered heavy losses.

The confused nocturnal fight finally died down around 10.30pm when Kutuzov was informed of French reinforcements reaching the battlefield and the Poles flanking the Russian position from the left. It was already too late in the evening and there was no point in defending the destroyed redoubt any longer. So Kutuzov recalled the troops and abandoned the redoubt to the French. Virtually all Russian sources consulted asserted that the redoubt was in the Russian hands by then and it was abandoned to the French. Naturally, the French memoirs reveal claims to the contrary.

Bagration received the order around 11pm and immediately instructed Gorchakov to withdraw his exhausted troops under cover of darkness. The Russian cavalry regiments took position in two lines behind the redoubt and a line of skirmishers was deployed between the Utitsa woods and the left flank, while the Jägers moved to the north-western edge of the wood. The remaining troops retreated towards the Semeyonovskoye brook, which now became the new Russian left flank. The redoubt was occupied by the French, who also controlled the villages of Aleksinka, Fomkino, Doronino and Shevardino.

The Russian withdrawal from Shevardino is noteworthy for an interesting, albeit often overlooked, incident. As Gorchakov's men were falling back, the French cavalry moved around the redoubt in order to charge their right flank in an attempt to cut off some units. As Gorchakov noted, he heard

> the loud tramping of enemy horses. The night was already dark enough that it was impossible to make out the numbers, though from the sound alone it was clear that the enemy was cavalry and that they were coming on in fairly powerful columns.

# 5 September: Prelude to Borodino – The Battle of Shevardino

Gorchakov quickly issued orders for the Cuirassier Division to attack, but 'with all the haste, it would have still taken some time for it to engage the enemy'. Therefore, to gain time and confuse the enemy, Gorchakov exploited the darkness that concealed the strength of his troops near Shevardino, and ordered a mere battalion of the Odessa Infantry Regiment to thunder on its drums and shout 'Hurrah!' as loud as possible, in order to simulate the arrival of reinforcements (the battalion was strictly prohibited from firing, so as not to reveal its location and strength). The ruse apparently worked since, as Gorchakov described, 'the enemy movement was halted' and the Cuirassier Division arrived in time to charge and route the French. Gorchakov even claimed that the Cuirassier Division seized four guns, but 'the capture of these pieces was not mentioned anywhere and they were later counted instead of the pieces we lost during the battle of [the following day]'.[111]

The Battle of Shevardino was now finally over. Bagration submitted a glowing report of his troops: 'although the enemy forces gradually increased and [constantly] reinforcing its columns, endeavoured to overwhelm our troops, they were vanquished everywhere by the courage of the Russian troops ...' Kutuzov acknowledged in a letter to his wife that 'yesterday we had an infernal battle on the left flank'.[112]

The Shevardino Redoubt was almost completely destroyed and the area around it was strewn with the corpses of men and horses. Gourgaud says the French found 'every living thing [...] destroyed' inside the redoubt, while Brandt saw it 'covered in corpses'. The villages of Doronino and Shevardino were largely destroyed. As night descended over the battlefield, occasional gunfire disrupted the gloomy silence, since the advance elements of both armies were only 'at a distance of a pistol shot'.[113] Dutheillet de Lamothe, of the 6th Battalion, 57th Regiment, spent a grisly night inside the redoubt, which was full of dead and dying men, whose moans kept him awake all night. However, exhaustion – both physical and psychological – soon took over and, according to Labaume, the soldiers 'lay down amidst bushes and slept profoundly, despite the vehement wind and an excessively cold rain'.

The French wounded were more fortunate than their Russian counter-parts, since Larrey's flying ambulances spent the night removing them to the nearby infirmaries (although, according to Griois, the French medics picked up some Russian wounded as well). Larrey's subordinates worked tirelessly, and in the morning the results of their labours could be seen in 'a grass covered ravine near the road that was full of [amputated] hands and limbs as well as corpses'.[114]

Marauders were also busy that night, searching the dead for food, alcohol and valuables – in that order. The French did find some low-quality alcohol and barely edible biscuits on the Russian corpses. Hubert Charles Biot, aide-de-camp to General Pajol, accompanied his general to the redoubt late on the night of the 6th and found it 'cluttered with dead and wounded'. Meanwhile, French infantrymen

# The Battle of Borodino

were busy 'stripping' the Russian corpses of the bad brandy which they had in their water bottles; short of everything, they did not despise this frightful drink. I too wanted to taste it, but the pepper and vitriol burnt one's mouth.

That night, as usual, Russian officers gathered in small groups to spend the night. Most were sitting around the campfires but some fortunates lodged in a few remaining huts. Sergei Mayevsky, Bagration's adjutant, recalled that: 'since my title of duty officer worked magic in war and peace', he was able to secure one of the two remaining houses at Semeyonovskoye, where 'everyone, except for first-class generals, gathered and the leftovers of my tea tasted as a heavenly nectar to them'.[115]

Both Army commanders observed the Battle of Shevardino from afar. Kutuzov stayed at his headquarters, north-east of Shevardino, and briefly travelled along the Russian lines. Second Lieutenant Nikolai Mitarevsky, of the 12th Light Company, recalled seeing the aged field marshal approaching with his escort and setting up an observation post between the 7th and 24th Divisions, from where he was able to observe the New Smolensk Road and the action at Shevardino:

I had never seen Kutuzov before and now we all had a chance to observe him to the full, although we could not dare to approach him too close. With his head bowed, he sat in his frock-coat without epaulettes, with a forage cap on his head and a Cossack whip [nagaika] across his shoulder. Generals and staff officers of his suite stood around him, while messengers and Cossacks were behind him. Some of his young adjutants and messengers soon sat in a circle, took out cards and began to play a Schtoss [a popular card game among Russian officers].[116]

Kutuzov was often briefed by arriving officers and remained 'serious but calm' throughout the action. As the battle at Shevardino progressed, Bennigsen travelled south to meet Bagration, who shared his opinion that Napoleon would attack the left flank:

He foresaw what would happen if our Army remained in [its] current position and that the left flank would be driven back with casualties. I promised him to convey his concerns about the dangers facing this part of the Army to the Commander-in-Chief. Returning, I delivered a detailed report to Kutuzov and suggested, as I did the day before, to shorten our left flank. Yet, [Kutuzov made no decision] and everything was left intact.[117]

On the French side, Napoleon spent most of the day in his tent near Valuyevo, surrounded by his Imperial Guard. One participant saw him 'walking to and fro on the edge of the ravine, his hands behind his back, now and then observing what was going on through his spyglass'. His health was already weakened by the campaign and his personal physician, Baron Yvan, noted that the Emperor 'was eminently nervous'.[118] Furthermore, due to winds, rain, and continual horse riding, Napoleon suffered from a severe cold and high temperature, which only worsened his condition, causing nervous coughing and difficulty in urinating. Summoning another physician, Dr Mestivier, Napoleon complained, 'I am growing old, my legs swell, I urinate with difficulty, doubtless it is the humidity of these bivouacs.' After a quick check up, the doctor noted that the Emperor had 'a continual dry cough, breathing difficult and spasmodic, urine only coming out drop by drop and with pain [containing] sediment. The lower part of the legs and feet extremely oedematose, the pulse feverish ...' Both doctors were greatly concerned about Napoleon's health and had the Emperor's pharmacist prepare a special medicine for him, while General Lauriston helped to apply cataplasms on his stomach.

The Battle of Shevardino proved to be costly for both sides. Most Russian studies acknowledge that the Russians lost approximately 6,000 casualties and several guns. Neverovsky's memoirs revealed the scale of losses suffered by some Russian units, when he noted that:

> in this battle I lost almost all my brigade *chefs*, staff and junior officers [...]
> I received 4,000 recruits to reinforce my Division before the battle, and had
> some 6,000 in the front during the battle; I left the battle with only three
> [thousand].

Vorontsov, who brought four battalions of his Grenadier Division, also acknowledged that the battle claimed 'rather many lives'. There were virtually no Russian prisoners taken, and when General Caulaincourt reported this to the Emperor, Napoleon 'was astonished [and] questioned him over and over. "Didn't my cavalry charge in time? [...] Are those Russians determined to win or die?"'[119]

French losses are usually estimated at between 4,000–5,000 men and some French regiments were particularly hard-hit. The 57th Line lost approximately 500 men, though Dutheillet de Lamothe estimated its loss at 600. According to later studies of officer casualties by Martinien, the 57th lost three officers dead, three mortally wounded and six wounded, while in the 25th Line, one officer died of wounds and one was wounded. One more officer was killed in the 2nd Company of the 6th Horse Artillery, which was attached to Compans' division. Based on regimental reports, the 111th lost eighty-six killed (including four officers), 555 wounded (fifteen officers), thirty-three captured and another 138 missing. The combined voltigeur companies had twenty-five killed and 220 wounded (including six officers), the 30th Line (of Morand's Division) lost twenty-four killed and forty-two wounded. Meanwhile, the Polish troops suffered about 550 casualties. Among the French casualties was also Colonel Méda of the 1st Chasseurs, who shot Maximilian Robespierre during the Thermidorean coup in July 1794.[120]

The 61st Line, which distinguished itself in the assault on the Shevardino Redoubt, lost thirty killed, 238 wounded and seventeen captured. When, on the following day, Napoleon was surprised to see the much-reduced regiment and asked a colonel of the whereabouts of his battalion, the colonel supposedly replied: 'Sire, it is [lying dead] in the redoubt.' Among the men of the 61st who distinguished themselves that day was the 27-year-old Augustin Sommeillier, General Guyardet's aide-de-camp, who 'demonstrated sangfroid and calmness as he delivered various orders to the troops engaged in the action.' Among other troops, Fusilier Bovard was singled out for killing two Russian gunners, while Voltigeur Kaiser slew two others as they tried to remove an artillery piece. In the midst of the fighting, Adjutant-Major Fourgeau 'rallied a *peloton* of tirailleurs to repel a cavalry charge', and was helped by Captain Labroux, replacing the Major, who 'led a company to halt a cavalry charge and always demonstrated his courage'. Ricot, commander of the regimental artillery of the 61st, was commended for his skilful command of the battery.[121]

Meanwhile, Robert Guillemard recalled meeting a sergeant of the 57th Line, who told him: 'The Emperor came to our bivouac this morning at daybreak, and was able to convince himself, by the appearance of the ground round the redoubt, strewed with green-coated corpses that the enemy's loss was infinitely greater than ours.'

Some Russian officers criticized Kutuzov's decision to defend Shevardino, and Yermolov remarked that the construction of the Bagration Flèches had made the Shevardino Redoubt superfluous, 'because it stood out of our artillery range; consequently, there was no point in defending and maintaining it'. This opinion was shared by Norov, who lamented that the 'redoubt was defended longer than it was needed'. The opinion of many rank-and-file seems to have been expressed by a soldier of the 27th Division, who remarked many years after the war:

> There was no order at Shevardino [...] Before the cuirassiers arrived, we were badly mauled and our battalion head, in a fit of anger, grumbled, 'What a sham! First they [Russian command] cannot properly make any arrangements and then give us this nonsense![122]

Barclay de Tolly was enraged by the whole affair, since he had previously requested the redoubt to be abandoned. He blamed Bennigsen for this failure, since '[he] had chosen the position and did not want to lose his face. Consequently, Bennigsen sacrificed six or seven thousand valiant soldiers and three cannon on 5 September'.

Barclay de Tolly probably was overly critical in his assessment. The defence of Shevardino allowed the Russian troops (of the 2nd Western Army) to move to new positions around Semeyonovskoye. This redeployment certainly should have been done earlier, but it was not, and in given circumstances, Bagration and Gorchakov had little choice but to fight. Kutuzov later acknowledged that the battle gave the Russians time to continue the construction of fortifications at Borodino and determine the direction of Napoleon's main attack. Indeed, the loss of Shevardino should have convinced Kutuzov that Bagration and Barclay de Tolly were right in asserting that the left flank could not be adequately defended and should have induced him to make appropriate changes. As we will see, this was not the case and Kutuzov's reluctance to make changes in his battle formation would have important consequences ...

## Armies and Leaders

The strength of both armies varies depending on the source. The Russians tallied approximately 120,000 men at Smolensk and suffered up to 20,000 casualties over the following two weeks. The heaviest losses (about 16,000 men killed and wounded) were sustained at the battles of Smolensk and Lubino, the rest were lost during the fighting retreat to Borodino. Tsar Alexander's letter of 5 September indicates that Kutuzov reported 95,734 men in cavalry and infantry in late August. Alexander calculated that with the arrival of some 2,000 stragglers and Miloradovich's reinforcements of 15,589 men, the Russian Army would amount to 113,323 men; and in view of additional detached units rejoining the Army, he estimated over 120,000 men.[123] Army roll-calls, gathered in early September, provide further details. On 4 September, the 1st Western Army numbered 53,587 soldiers and 6,338 officers, while its artillery consisted of 132 position, 212 light and 52 horse guns. On 6 September, after receiving reinforcements, it showed 67,391 men and 7,982 officers with 420 guns.[124] In late August, Prince Bagration's army comprised 1,210 officers, 2,182 non-commissioned officers, 31,533 soldiers, with 53 heavy, 72 light and 48 Horse Artillery guns.[125]

Despite these reports, both participants and historians produced contrasting assessment of the Russian strength. Toll referred to 103,800 regular troops, Buturlin and Wolzogen estimated 115,000 regular troops and 17,000 Cossacks and *Opolchenye*. Duke Eugène of Württemberg was more specific, naming 96,000 men in infantry, 18,300 in regular cavalry, 5,000 Cossacks and 15,000 Opolchenye. Russian historians Mikhailovsky-Danilevsky and Bogdanovich calculated 128,000 men. The Soviet estimates of Kutuzov's army at Borodino varied from 120,000 (Zhilin) to 126,000 (Beskrovny) and sought to highlight the French numerical superiority, which was usually stated as 133,000 men. However, in 1987, S. Shvedov's research demonstrated that these estimates were flawed and Kutuzov, in fact, had some 157,000 soldiers, including 10,000 Cossacks and 33,000 Opolchenye. This study was largely ignored by Soviet scholars but was utilized by a new generation of Russian historians. Thus, in the mid-1990s, Aleksey Vasiliev and Andrei Eliseyev produced slightly lower estimate of 155,200 men. Accepting these numbers, it is clear that Kutuzov enjoyed the overall numerical superiority over the French but had about 20,000 less regular troops than Napoleon.

The Russian Opolchenye included 21,694 troops of the Moscow Opolchenye and 12,500 from the Smolensk Opolchenye. Of the latter, a couple of thousand militiamen were assigned to Major General Levitsky, the commandant of Mozhaisk, to maintain garrison duty: so the effective strength of the Smolensk Opolchenye was close to 10,000. These forces differed in their organization and combat readiness. The Moscow Opolchenye was organized into three divisions, which included three Jäger units armed with muskets and five dismounted Cossack regiments armed with lances. The Smolensk Opolchenye, however, consisted of eleven *uezd* (district) Opolchenyes, each divided into 500 (*pyatisotnya*), 100 (*sotnya*) and 50 (*polusotnya*) units. The weaponry was distributed unevenly and the

## Troop Estimates for the Battle of Borodino

| Author | Year | French | Russian | Total |
|---|---|---|---|---|
| Buturlin | 1824 | 190,000 | 132,000 | 322,000 |
| Ségur | 1824 | 130,000 | 120,000 | 250,000 |
| Chambray | 1825 | 133,819 | 130,000 | 263,819 |
| Fain | 1827 | 120,000 | 133,500 | 253,500 |
| Clausewitz | 1830s | 130,000 | 120,000 | 250,000 |
| Mikhailovsky-Danilevsky | 1839 | 160,000 | 128,000 | 288,000 |
| Bogdanovich | 1859 | 130,000 | 120,800 | 250,800 |
| Marbot | 1860 | 140,000 | 160,000 | 300,000 |
| Burton | 1914 | 130,000 | 120,800 | 250,800 |
| Garnich | 1956 | 130,665 | 119,300 | 249,665 |
| Tarle | 1962 | 130,000 | 127,800 | 257,800 |
| Grunward | 1963 | 130,000 | 120,000 | 250,000 |
| Beskrovny | 1968 | 135,000 | 126,000 | 261,000 |
| Chandler | 1966 | 156,000 | 120,800 | 276,800 |
| Thiry | 1969 | 120,000 | 133,000 | 253,000 |
| Holmes | 1971 | 130,000 | 120,800 | 250,800 |
| Duffy | 1972 | 133,000 | 125,000 | 258,000 |
| Tranie | 1981 | 127,000 | 120,000 | 247,000 |
| Nicolson | 1985 | 128,000 | 106,000 | 234,000 |
| Troitsky | 1988 | 134,000 | 154,800 | 288,800 |
| Vasiliev | 1997 | 130,000 | 155,200 | 285,200 |
| Smith | 1998 | 133,000 | 120,800 | 253,800 |
| Zemtsov | 1999 | 127,000 | 154,000 | 281,000 |
| Hourtoulle | 2000 | 115,000 | 140,000 | 255,000 |
| Bezotosny | 2004 | 135,000 | 150,000 | 285,000 |

militiamen from the Belsk, Gzhatsk and Krasnyi uezds had no firearms at all. The best-armed Opolchenye was that of the Sychov district, since its 1,336 men had 1,284 muskets, 6 carbines, 400 pistols and 1,309 pikes.[126] The battle value of the Opolchenye and other reinforcements had been long debated. In his letter to Tsar Alexander, Kutuzov himself complained that: 'although the newly arriving troops were dressed and equipped, they were composed largely of recruits and lacked staff, junior and non-commissioned officers.'[127] Neverovsky, whose division was reinforced by some of the newly arrived troops, reported that:

> the rank-and-file of the 5th Regiment from [Miloradovich's] corps are well trained, properly dressed and given all necessary primary guidance. However, the troops of the 1st Jäger [Opolchenye] Regiment fail these requirements and had not received necessary drill during their training.[128]

# Armies and Leaders

Still, the Opolchenye forces should not be dismissed completely, since they performed many auxiliary functions that freed up regular troops for combat, and some militiamen helped defend the Russian extreme left flank. Yet some Russian officers left less than flattering accounts of the Opolchenye. Nikolai Andreyev of the 50th Jägers noted that some militiamen, tasked with removing the wounded, robbed their charges.

As for artillery, most memoirs and studies cite 640 guns present at Borodino. In reality, the Russian Army had 624 guns on the battlefield and 12 guns in Mozhaisk, bringing the total to 636.[129] The 1st Western Army had 438 guns and the 2nd Army had 186 pieces (for a detailed discussion, readers should visit the book's companion website at www.napoleon-series.org).

*The Russian Army at Borodino*
(Based on the 1997 study by Vasiliev and Eliseyev)

| | Strength on 5 September 1812 |
|---|---|
| **1st Western Army** | |
| II Corps | 11,450 |
| III Corps | 10,800 |
| IV Corps | 12,000 |
| V Corps | 17,255 |
| VI Corps | 12,500 |
| I Reserve Cavalry Corps | 3,470 |
| II and III Reserve Cavalry Corps | 6,700 |
| Cossacks | 5,600 |
| Total | 79,775 men (excluding HQ escort and auxiliary) 82,400 (all forces) |
| **2nd Western Army** | |
| VII Corps | 12,500 |
| VIII Corps | 17,000 |
| 2nd Cuirassier Division | 2,800 |
| IV Reserve Cavalry Corps | 4,300 |
| Cossacks | 3,016 |
| Total | 39,616 (excluding HQ escort & auxiliary) 41,100 (all forces) |
| Moscow Opolchenye | 21,700 |
| Smolensk Opolchenye | 10,000 |
| Grand Total | 155,200 |

At the time, Russian headquarters estimated the French strength at 165,000 men with up to 1,000 guns, though Tsar Alexander and Kutuzov found this estimate 'somewhat exaggerated' and Bagration argued Napoleon could not have had more than 150,000 men.[130] Discussing the French Army, most scholars utilize estimates provided by Chambray, Fain and Pelet, based on roll-calls of 2 September. Fain showed 120,000 men in the French Army,

# The Battle of Borodino

including 40,000 on the left flank, 70,000 in the centre and 10,000 on the right flank. Pelet estimated 84,000 infantry, 27,000 cavalry, 15,000 artillery-men, for a total of 126,000 men and 563 guns. George Chambray is the most detailed of them and he showed the following numbers:[131]

*The French Army at Borodino*
(Based on figures quoted by George Chambray)

| Corps | Present Infantry | Present Cavalry | Detached (returned within 5 days) Infantry | Detached (returned within 5 days) Cavalry | Artillery (guns) |
|---|---|---|---|---|---|
| Imperial Guard | 13,932 | 4,930 | – | – | 109 |
| I Corps | 36,402 | – | 2,784 | – | 147 |
| III Corps | 10,314 | – | 964 | – | 69 |
| IV Corps | 20,063 | 3,465 | 1,466 | 27 | 88 |
| V Corps | 8,430 | 1,638 | 260 | – | 50 |
| VIII Corps | 7,932 | 936 | 529 | 259 | 30 |
| I Reserve Cavalry Corps | – | 4,999 | – | 160 | 25 |
| II Reserve Cavalry Corps | – | 3,943 | – | – | 29 |
| III Reserve Cavalry Corps | – | 2,907 | – | 676 | 10 |
| IV Reserve Cavalry Corps | – | 3,600 | – | – | 24 |
| Cavalry of I and III Corps | – | 3,007 | – | 196 | 6 |
| Total | 97,073 | 29,425 | 6,003 | 1,318 | 587 |

Thus, Chambray's table shows the total strength of the French Army as 133,819 men, of which 103,076 were infantry and 30,743 cavalry; artillery-men are certainly included in these numbers.

This is in stark contrast to the powerful Grand Army of some 450,000 men that crossed the Nieman in June, or to the estimated 182,000 men Napoleon had at Smolensk, a mere twenty days prior to the roll-call of 2 September. Still, these numbers, which are usually cited in most studies of the 1812 campaign, are somewhat misleading, since they do not seem to take into account the arrival of some French units and fail to mention additional troops assigned to the *État Major* (i.e. General Staff). Furthermore, they do not reflect losses that the French Army suffered during the five days subsequent to the roll-call on 2 September. At Shevardino alone, the French lost over 4,000 men, while a couple thousand stragglers are estimated during the French advance from Gzhatsk. Taking these factors into account, one might argue that at Borodino Napoleon's effective force probably amounted to between 126,000 and 128,000 men supported by 587 guns.

In fact, many French regiments were depleted, sick and weary from the constant marches, malnutrition and fighting. More importantly, the French cavalry was in poor condition after losing thousands of horses due to excessive heat, lack of forage and bloody encounters in the first months of the campaign. And as events will show, the Imperial Guard – some 19,000 élite French troops – remained idle during the entire battle, so the number of Allied troops that actually fought at Borodino was closer to 110,000.

## The French Army

Despite fatigue and losses, the French Army standing at the walls of Moscow represented by far the best fighting machine of its age. Inspired by Revolutionary ideology and led by one of the greatest military captains in history, French troops had dominated the Continent since 1805.

While the French Revolution saw the famous *levée en masse* in 1793, the recruitment system was later modified by a series of conscription laws. These laws required that all men between the ages of eighteen and forty register with the authorities, and those between eighteen and twenty-five (later thirty) years of age were called upon for service. Depending on strategic circumstances, an annual 'class' (the year in which men reached the age of eighteen) could be called up early.

The Revolution opened the officer ranks to non-nobles, making all citizens of the new French Republic admissible to every rank and appointment. This was a far cry from the military establishment of the *Ancien Régime*, which was dominated by the nobility. Naturally, many old officers – almost two-thirds in the Army and even more in the Navy – were dissatisfied with the loss of privileged status and left France to join the *émigré* forces in Austria and Russia. Despite its tremendous effect on the French Army in 1791–92, the mass departure of officers also had a positive consequence, allowing talented commoners to rise through the ranks.

Innovations resulting in the development of permanent divisions, and later corps, were already in place during the Revolution and Napoleon took full advantage of this to develop his concept of mobile warfare. In 1804 he refined a system that combined infantry and cavalry divisions, supported by artillery, into permanent army corps. These units became self-sufficient mini-armies – key elements of the French military machine. Divisions, however, remained as the major tactical unit that could be entrusted with a specific mission. Each division usually consisted of two or three infantry brigades (each with two to five battalions in one or more regiments) and an artillery brigade (with one or more batteries of four to six field guns and two howitzers).

The infantry was the main branch of the French Army and included both 'line' and 'light' units. After 1808, regiments had one depot battalion of four companies (training replacements and reinforcements) and four active battalions (*bataillons de guerre*), each consisting of six companies: four of fusiliers, one of grenadiers and one of voltigeurs. Regiments usually consisted of about 100 officers and some 3,800 rank-and-file.

French cavalry was categorized as heavy (employed in the charge) or light (used for reconnaissance and skirmishing). The cavalry included a number of

# The Battle of Borodino

different types, including: cuirassiers equipped with breastplates (cuirasses); *carabiniers*, who were armed with a carbine; dragoons, carrying the sabre and a musket with a bayonet; hussars, elaborately dressed light cavalry generally used for scouting and pursuit; *chasseurs à cheval*, light cavalrymen who operated as mounted Jägers; and *chevaux-léger*, light cavalrymen armed with lances. In addition, Napoleon's cavalry included various foreign units, including the famous Polish Lancers, the Croatian Hussars, Württemberg chevau-léger, etc.

The Imperial Guard was the élite organization within the Grand Army. In the decade since it was established, the Guard participated in all Napoleon's campaigns and earned a fearsome reputation. Its membership was by strict selection, since it entailed many privileges, including higher pay and better provisions. As a result, the Guard was both envied and resented by the line units. By 1812, it was an army within an army, with its own infantry, cavalry, artillery, engineers and marines. This imperial corps was organized into the Old Guard (the élite within the élite), the Middle Guard (created in 1806), and the newly established Young Guard. Attached to them were the Polish Vistula Legion and the Hessian Guards.

Having graduated as an artillery officer from L'École Militaire, Napoleon knew well the potential of this arm. The French artillery, after a lacklustre performance during the Seven Years War (1756–63), quickly developed and improved under the guidance of a series of capable officers. Jean Baptiste de Gribeuval was instrumental in modernizing the French artillery by simplifying and standardizing French guns. Gun barrels were shortened and lightened and accuracy was improved by means of elevating mechanisms and scale sights. Napoleon incorporated this Gribeuval system into his military concepts and employed artillery on an unprecedented scale. He often deployed a grand battery to soften the enemy position and provide massive artillery support for his main attack effort. By 1812, the ratio of guns to men rose from two guns per thousand to five guns per thousand. The artillery of the Grand Army was organized into regimental (i.e. attached to each regiment), divisional (i.e. assigned to infantry and cavalry divisions), army corps (i.e. an artillery reserve attached to a corps) and army reserve (i.e. organized into the army's main artillery park). A foot artillery regiment was comprised of several artillery companies (batteries), each with six guns and two howitzers; a horse artillery company included four guns and two howitzers.

The Grand Army, resting on the fields of Borodino, was an amalgamation of troops from almost every nation of Europe. The ethnic French made up only a part of this enormous army, while the rest included Prussians, Bavarians, Westphalians, Saxons, Dutch, Swiss, Italians, Austrians and others. The largest non-French contingent was provided by the Poles, who fielded an entire corps led by Józef Poniatowski. Time and again they would prove themselves excellent warriors, who would remain loyal to Napoleon to the very last. The Italians provided the second largest body of non-French troops, led by Prince Eugène, Napoleon's stepson and Viceroy of Italy. After so many centuries of division, Italians of different stock and regions were now united into a single force and some of the Italian officers even began to dream of the Roman legions and the sense of national pride they once instilled.[132] The Germanic troops came from a plethora of minor states that Napoleon placed under his sway over the previous decade. Among them were Bavarians (Napoleon's most reliable German allies), Saxons (whose ruler would eventually pay a dear price for his pro-French policy), Westphalians (whose King Jérôme Bonaparte was sent back home earlier in the campaign), and the reluctant Prussians (who were represented by a few regiments at Borodino, but whose entire corps was fighting in north-western Russia).

With such diverse group of nationalities, each with their own worldview and goals, it was naturally difficult to maintain cohesion and *esprit de corps*. Lieutenant Wedel of the 9th Polish Lancers confirms this in his memoirs: 'Three-quarters of the nations that were about to take part in the struggle had interests diametrically opposed to those, which had decided the opening of hostilities. There were many who in their hearts wished the Russians success.' However, the existing sense of union and purpose was cantered on Napoleon, whose legendary sway over his troops has been discussed in numerous books. This is why, according to Wedel:

> Whatever their personal feelings towards the Emperor may have been, there was nobody who did not see in him the greatest and the ablest of all generals, and who did not experience a feeling of confidence in his talents and the value of his judgement [...] thus, at the moment of danger, all fought as though they had been defending their own homes.

His view is echoed in the testimony of Lieutenant Calosso of the 24th Chasseurs à Cheval, who had a rare opportunity to meet Napoleon in person, an incident that seemingly changed his life:

> Before that I admired Napoleon as the whole army admired him. But from that day on I devoted my life to him with a fanaticism which time has not weakened. I only had one regret, which was that I only had one life to offer in his service.

Even his enemies had to acknowledge the effect Napoleon had on the battlefield. Arthur Wellesley, Duke of Wellington, famously proclaimed that the presence of Napoleon on a battlefield was itself worth 40,000 men, while a Russian officer, and future distinguished historian, remarked: 'Anyone

*Average Length of Service (in years) of French Officers (by ranks)*

| Rank | Infantry | Cavalry |
| --- | --- | --- |
| Sous-lieutenant | 11.4 | 10.7 |
| Lieutenant | 13 | 13.2 |
| Captain | 18 | 18.5 |
| Chef de Bataillon/Chef d'Escadron | 19.7 | 19.7 |
| Colonel | 21.9 | 20.9 |

who was not alive at the time of Napoleon simply cannot imagine the extent of the moral ascendancy he exerted over the minds of his contemporaries.'[133]

The French officers were products of the Revolution, which introduced principles of merit, talent and elections in the military. With the privileges of nobility abolished and many noble officers emigrating, the officer ranks were open to citizen-soldiers, who advanced according to their merits and talents. The mass departure of nobles and the influx of commoners produced a new amalgamation of strata. According to Oleg Sokolov's research, about half of the French officers serving in 1812 came from the bourgeoisie (30 per cent) and landowners (20 per cent), while nobles constituted only 5 per cent. Studying company grade officers serving in 1814, Jean Paul Bertaud found that 40.3 per cent were the sons of landowners, followed by those of farmers (34.8 per cent), merchants and tradesmen (20.3 per cent), artisans (18.1 per cent), rentiers (17.6 per cent), military men (14.4 per cent), lawyers (9.8 per cent), professors, teachers and engineers (8.3 per cent), commercial businessmen (8.3 per cent) and manufacturers (7.8 per cent). The government employees supplied 8.2 per cent of officers and nobles comprised almost 5 per cent.[134] Among 149 generals sampled for the present study, fifty-seven began service under the *Ancien Régime*, while the rest joined during the Revolution, with forty-five volunteering in the first three years of the Revolution (1789–91) and twenty-seven responding to the call, 'la patrie en danger', in 1792.

Napoleon inherited the military developed during the Revolutionary Wars and perfected it. He placed the Army at the centre of imperial society and lavished it with attention and honours. One-quarter of 300 prefects of the Empire were from a military background, and officers were in charge of major cities throughout the country. Between 1808 and 1814, 59 per cent of the 3,263 men who received noble titles were military men, and besides the marshals – who all had noble titles – the majority of generals were counts or barons, while colonels received a barony and company-grade officers were rewarded with the title of 'chevalier'. In addition to titles, Napoleon also provided substantial material privileges to his officer corps. Besides increased pay, the imperial government also provided free education or grants for officers' children, exempted garrison officers from certain taxes and granted retired officers priority in recruitment for certain government posts.

With troops from almost every corner of Europe, one might have expected a similarly diverse officer corps. Yet, while company grade officers were mostly of ethnic origin, general officers were largely French. Thus, out of 166 generals considered, 130 were French (plus one Corsican). Among the rest were seventeen Poles, four Westphalians, four Württembergers, two Italians, two Hessians, two Dutch, one Bavarian, one Portuguese, one Swiss and one Saxon. The average length of service of these officers (based on 149 cases) was 24.4 years, with General Ornano and Berthemy's thirteen years of service and Alexander Berthier's forty-six years setting the records for the shortest and longest careers, respectively.

# Armies and Leaders

Of the twenty-six marshals Napoleon created during the Empire, thirteen current and future marshals participated in the Russian campaign, nine of them (seven current and two future marshals) being present at Borodino. Two of Napoleon's ablest marshals – André Masséna and Jean Lannes – did not participate in the campaign since the former was in semi-retirement in France, while the latter had died in 1809. Pierre François Augereau was in Prussia, while Jean Baptiste Bernadotte, already in alliance with Russia, was in Sweden, after being elected Crown Prince in 1810. Four other marshals – Jean Baptiste Jourdan, the hero of Flerus; Nicholas Jean Soult of Austerlitz fame; Louis Gabriel Suchet, the conqueror of Catalonia; and Auguste Frederic Marmont, Napoleon's close friend and a future turncoat – were all tied down in Spain. Claude-Victor Perrin, Laurent Gouvion Saint-Cyr, Etienne-Jacques-Joseph-Alexandre Macdonald and Nicolas-Charles Oudinot were in Russia but commanded corps on other fronts.

## The Russian Army

The Russian Army of 1812 was, in many respects, quite different from the one Napoleon faced in 1805 and 1807. The lessons of Austerlitz, Eylau and Friedland led the Russian government to realize the need for change and to pursue a modernization through military reforms. It was a lengthy process, since Russia was at war for virtually the entire period between 1789 and 1812, fighting three campaigns against France, two wars against the Ottomans, two wars with Sweden, one war against Persia and participating in the partitions of Poland and annexations of the Caucasian principalities.

Able to draw on a population of almost 40 million by the late 18th century, Russian sovereigns drafted conscripts from the servile population that included serfs, state and Church peasants and townspeople. During the Napoleonic Wars, Russia raised levies every year except in 1814, raising some 1,100,000 men. In times of emergency, Russian sovereigns often ordered heavier levies or resorted to militia mobilizations. The heaviest levies were held in 1812, when three emergency levies were initiated within a six-month timeframe, calling for over 400,000 men.

The Russian officer corps primarily consisted of nobles. Over 86 per cent of the 2,000 officers present at Borodino belonged to the nobility, as did 96 per cent (728 out of 758) of senior officers. Nobles received preferential treatment on enlisting and also in subsequent promotions, while non-nobles were required to serve as non-commissioned officers for extended periods before further advancement. On paper, nobles were required to serve in the lower ranks, but naturally sought to circumvent regulations. The most prominent and powerful families often exploited a loophole in the system by enlisting their children in infancy: consequently, by the time these infants grew up, they already had extensive 'records of service', making them eligible for officer status without any real experience or training.

Of course, patronage and nepotism was of paramount importance in this practice, as well as subsequent career development. Obviously, non-nobles had a lesser chance of obtaining quick career advancement and usually had

# The Battle of Borodino

to wait between five and seven years to become officers. NCOs from the soldier ranks were in the worst position because they, on average, served up to a decade before reaching the officer ranks, but there were exceptions. At Borodino, sixty-four NCOs had already served between ten and twenty-five years, while three others had remained NCOs for an incredible twenty-four to twenty-seven years.

Directly linked to the length of service is the battle experience of the Russian officers at Borodino. Studying their records of service, it becomes clear that about 55 per cent of officers had some battle experience prior to 1812, while 45 per cent (or 925 officers) went through their baptism by fire in 1812. Among the officers with prior combat experience, some 1,305 served in the campaigns against the French and thus had some knowledge of their enemy; the largest number (357 and 640) had served in the 1805 campaign in Bohemia and the Polish campaign of 1806–07 respectively. About 247 officers had served in the Baltic campaigns against the Swedes in 1788–90 and 1808–09, while the careers of 395 officers included wars against the Ottoman Empire in 1770–90 and 1806–12.

Even more interesting is the data on the number of battles these officers participated in: some 580 (almost one-third or 28 per cent) had fought between three and five battles; 692 officers (33.4 per cent) between six and ten battles; 350 (over 16 per cent) between eleven and fifteen battles; 163 (7.9 per cent) between sixteen and twenty battles; and 59 (2.8 per cent) between twenty-one and twenty-five battles and combats. Remarkably, there were six officers who had previously fought thirty-six to forty battles, and two with experience of up to forty-five battles! Among these officers were A. Berger of the 6th Jägers and L. Rubachev of the Lithuanian Uhlan Regiment, who had served in thirty-eight and forty-four battles respectively.[135]

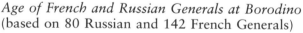

*Age of French and Russian Generals at Borodino*
(based on 80 Russian and 142 French Generals)

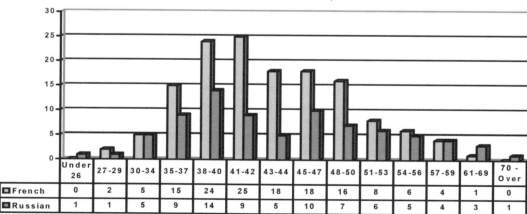

| | Under 26 | 27-29 | 30-34 | 35-37 | 38-40 | 41-42 | 43-44 | 45-47 | 48-50 | 51-53 | 54-56 | 57-59 | 61-69 | 70-Over |
|---|---|---|---|---|---|---|---|---|---|---|---|---|---|---|
| ☐ French | 0 | 2 | 5 | 15 | 24 | 25 | 18 | 18 | 16 | 8 | 6 | 4 | 1 | 0 |
| ☐ Russian | 1 | 1 | 5 | 9 | 14 | 9 | 5 | 10 | 7 | 6 | 5 | 4 | 3 | 1 |

# Armies and Leaders

*Russian and French Corps Commanders at Borodino*

| Russian | | | French | | |
|---|---|---|---|---|---|
| Name | Age | Years of Service | Name | Age | Years of Service |
| Baggovut | 51 | 33 | Bessieres | 44 | 23 |
| Bagration | 47 | 30 | Davout | 42 | 24 |
| Barclay de Tolly | 55 | 34 | Girardin d'Ermenonville | 36 | 25 |
| Borosdin | 45 | 32 | Grouchy | 46 | 31 |
| Dokhturov | 53 | 31 | Junot | 41 | 21 |
| Golitsyn | 41 | 27 | Latour-Mauborg | 44 | 30 |
| Karpov | 45 | 34 | Lefevbre | 57 | 39 |
| Korf | 39 | 25 | Montbrun | 42 | 23 |
| Lavrov | 51 | 35 | Mortier | 44 | 23 |
| Osterman-Tolstoy | 41 | 24 | Mourier | 46 | 20 |
| Platov | 59 | 46 | Murat | 45 | 25 |
| Rayevsky | 41 | 26 | Nansouty | 44 | 30 |
| Sievers | 40 | 23 | Ney | 43 | 25 |
| Tuchkov | 47 | 34 | Poniatowski | 49 | 32 |
| Uvarov | 39 | 36 | Eugene de Beauharnais | 31 | 16 |
| | Average 46.2 | Average 31.4 | | Average 43.6 | Average 25.8 |

The Russian system of military education was quite diverse and eight major institutions produced a steady stream of cadets. However, emphasis was usually placed on general subjects that broadened students' intellectual horizons and made them fit for both civil and military service. Many officers entered service untrained and semi-illiterate. A number of relatively competent foreign officers often transferred to the Russian service but, as we have seen, generated mistrust among the ethnic Russian officers and troops.

The records of service of the officers present at Borodino reveal that the majority (1,061 out of 2,074 men) could only read and write. Many officers were fluent in several languages, with 630 (30.4 per cent) speaking French and 522 (25.2 per cent) German, followed by 17 speaking English and 10 Italian. The ill-advised emphasis on general education is revealed by the fact that only 61 officers (2.9 per cent) studied military sciences and even fewer (7 or 0.3 per cent) had been taught military tactics. The artillery branch, naturally, fared better in this respect and many artillery officers were competent in arithmetic (23.2 per cent), geometry (10.6 per cent), algebra (6.5 per cent) and trigonometry (3.5 per cent). Over 67 per cent of the Russian artillery officers present at Borodino were graduates of institutions offering a higher military education, compared to 10.5 per cent in the Guard cavalry and 10 per cent in the regular cavalry. On a higher note, 21.6 per cent of the regular infantry officers studied in cadet corps and 21.2 per cent of Guard infantry officers studied at some of the highest military institutions. Non-commissioned officers, many of whom were promoted from the rank-and-file, still had a relatively high level of literacy at 38 per cent.

# The Battle of Borodino

*Average Length of Service of Russian Officers*

| Rank | Guard | | Army | | | | Artillery | Imperial Suite |
|------|-------|------|------|-------|------|------|-----------|----------------|
| | Inf. | Cav. | Inf. | Gren. | Jag. | Cav. | | |
| Ensign | 1.8 | – | 3.7 | 6.9 | 6.1 | – | 2 | 1.6 |
| Cornet | – | 3 | – | – | – | 7 | – | – |
| Sub-Lieutenant | 3.5 | – | 7.4 | 10.9 | 7.9 | – | 5 | 3.6 |
| Lieutenant | 6.2 | – | 6.9 | 9.7 | 8.9 | 9 | 6 | 6 |
| Staff-Captain | 9.7 | 8 | 9.3 | 11.3 | 12.3 | – | 9 | 9.1 |
| Staff-Rotmistr | – | 11 | – | – | – | 14 | – | – |
| Captain | 12.6 | 14 | 13 | 13.5 | 14.8 | – | 12 | 9.8 |
| Rotmistr | – | – | 17.7 | – | – | 18 | – | – |
| Major | – | – | 20.3 | 19.4 | 17.6 | 22 | – | – |
| Lieutenant Colonel | – | – | 20.3 | – | 28.2 | 24 | 18 | 13.7 |
| Colonel | 20.6 | 21 | 26.3 | 24.8 | 29.8 | – | 20 | 18.9 |

*Campaign Experience of Russian Officers at Borodino (by ranks)*

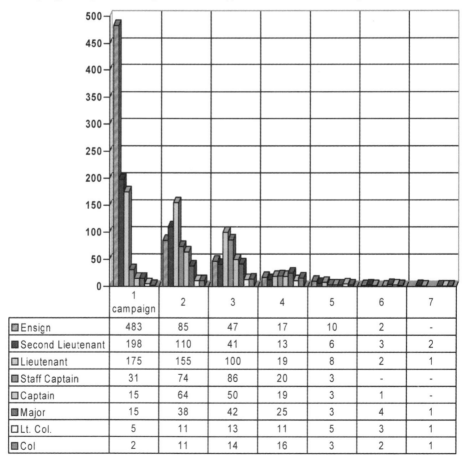

| | 1 campaign | 2 | 3 | 4 | 5 | 6 | 7 |
|------|-----------|-----|-----|-----|-----|-----|-----|
| Ensign | 483 | 85 | 47 | 17 | 10 | 2 | - |
| Second Lieutenant | 198 | 110 | 41 | 13 | 6 | 3 | 2 |
| Lieutenant | 175 | 155 | 100 | 19 | 8 | 2 | 1 |
| Staff Captain | 31 | 74 | 86 | 20 | 3 | - | - |
| Captain | 15 | 64 | 50 | 19 | 3 | 1 | - |
| Major | 15 | 38 | 42 | 25 | 3 | 4 | 1 |
| Lt. Col. | 5 | 11 | 13 | 11 | 5 | 3 | 1 |
| Col | 2 | 11 | 14 | 16 | 3 | 2 | 1 |

# Armies and Leaders

*ttle Experiences of Russian officers at Borodino (by branches)*

| | Guard | | | Army | | | | Cavalry | | | | | Artillery | Total |
|---|---|---|---|---|---|---|---|---|---|---|---|---|---|---|
| les | Infantry | Cavalry | Total | Grenadiers | Line | Jägers | Total | Cuirassiers | Dragoons | Hussars | Ulans | Total | Artillery | Total |
| | 68 | – | 68 | 10 | 37 | 34 | 81 | 18 | – | 3 | – | 21 | 18 | 188 |
| | 121 | 15 | 136 | 52 | 211 | 55 | 318 | 33 | 11 | 21 | 3 | 68 | 58 | 580 |
| ) | 45 | 45 | 90 | 79 | 232 | 131 | 442 | 53 | 16 | 45 | 6 | 120 | 40 | 692 |
| 15 | 8 | 4 | 12 | 50 | 129 | 61 | 240 | 17 | 14 | 45 | 6 | 82 | 16 | 350 |
| 20 | 1 | 10 | 11 | 24 | 48 | 27 | 99 | – | 14 | 20 | 11 | 45 | 8 | 163 |
| 25 | 2 | 2 | 4 | 12 | 5 | 13 | 30 | – | 4 | 6 | 13 | 23 | 2 | 59 |
| 30 | – | – | – | 3 | 2 | 5 | 10 | – | 10 | 2 | 3 | 15 | – | 25 |
| 40 | – | – | – | 6 | – | 5 | 11 | – | 2 | 1 | 1 | 4 | – | 15 |
| 45 | – | – | – | – | – | 1 | 1 | – | – | – | 1 | 1 | – | 2 |

*Battle Experience of Russian NCOs at Borodino*
(based on 1,518 NCOs sampled in Tselorungo)

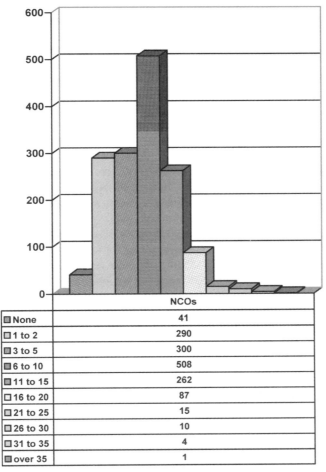

| | NCOs |
|---|---|
| None | 41 |
| 1 to 2 | 290 |
| 3 to 5 | 300 |
| 6 to 10 | 508 |
| 11 to 15 | 262 |
| 16 to 20 | 87 |
| 21 to 25 | 15 |
| 26 to 30 | 10 |
| 31 to 35 | 4 |
| over 35 | 1 |

# The Battle of Borodino

In the upper levels of the officer corps, out of some 500 generals participating in the 1812–13 Campaigns, 45 graduated from the Artillery and Engineer Corps (II Cadet Corps), 35 from the Infantry Cadet Corps (I Cadet Corps), 22 from the Page Corps, 7 from the Corps of Fellow Believers, 4 from the Schklov Cadet Corps and 11 from the Naval Cadet Corps. Some prominent commanders, such as Bagration and Platov, received no military education at all and contemporaries often highlighted this. On the other hand, Miloradovich studied at the Universities of Hottingen, Königsberg, Strasbourg and Metz, while Saint Priest graduated from the University of Heidelberg, and d'Auvray completed the Engineer Academy at Dresden.

Ever since Peter the Great employed large numbers of foreigners in his newly created regular Army, the foreign-born officers were a continual presence and many played an important role in its development. The ratio between Russian and foreign officers varied greatly throughout the 18th century, increasing during the reign of Empress Anna Ioanovna and decreasing in later decades. Tsar Paul's purges in the 1790s expelled many foreigners and shifted the percentages in favour of Russian officers. In 1812, out of 1,434 officers examined, some 1,228 (over 85 per cent) were from the Russian heartlands, 51 (3.6 per cent) were born in the Lithuanian provinces, many of them ethnic Poles, while 7.1 per cent were from the Baltic provinces, the majority of these being of German stock. Germans composed the largest non-Russian ethnic group, followed by Poles, French and Swedes. Relations between the Russian and foreign-born officers was tense at times but it became especially hostile during the 1812 campaign, as discussed earlier. Osterman-Tolstoy certainly reflected the attitudes of many when he told Italian Marquis Paulucci: 'For you, Russia is a uniform that you put on or off at will, but for me Russia is my skin!'[136] Foreigners were mostly concentrated in His Majesty's Suite on Quartermaster Service, the predecessor of the Russian General Staff, where foreign-born officers accounted for almost one-third of staff officers. They composed only 2.4 per cent in infantry and 3.1 per cent in cavalry and the Guard.[137]

Although the popular stereotype portrays Russian officers as wealthy serf owners and spoiled aristocrats, in reality most Russian officers lived in poverty, without any property or serfs. Young officers from the gentry often had nothing but a simple bundle of clothes when they joined a regiment. Records of service show that 77 per cent of the Russian officers at Borodino did not own any property or serfs and another 20 per cent had shared ownership of serfs and property with their respective families. Furthermore, 95.6 per cent of foreign officers in the Russian Army held no assets in Russia and depended on their salaries; the same condition applied to 88.6 per cent of Polish officers and 83.1 per cent of officers from the Baltic provinces. The data on the various Army branches also clearly shows the discrepancies in financial and property ownership status. Naturally, the Guard units had the most affluent officers, with 38 per cent of them owning serfs and property. The cavalry officers were less well off at 22 per cent, followed by infantry

# Armies and Leaders

officers at 20 per cent and artillery officers at 15 per cent. It is also surprising to discover that that among 295 generals, the majority (160 or 54.2 per cent) had no serfs or property, 13 owned less than 20 serfs, 34 possessed between up to 100 serfs and 79 owned over 100 serfs.

Following the purges and reforms of Tsar Paul I in the late 1790s, the first years of Alexander's reign saw a gradual transformation of the Russian military forces. After the 1802 reforms, an infantry regiment was organized into three battalions of four companies each, and the average strength of units varied between 1,500 and 1,700 men. Although the Russian Army had ad hoc divisions on campaign, the conversion to a divisional system was not initiated until 1806, when the first eighteen divisions were formed. The normal strength of a division was 18,000–20,000 men. Between 1809–12, the Russian Army was reorganized to accommodate a corps system along French lines. Thus, in 1812, the 1st Western Army consisted of six infantry, three cavalry and one Cossack corps, and the 2nd Western Army included two infantry and one cavalry corps.

An infantry corps was organized with two divisions, while cavalry corps included three brigades. The basic infantry division included three infantry brigades, where the 3rd often was composed of Jägers; in a grenadier division, all three brigades were composed of grenadier battalions. Each division had field artillery consisting of one heavy and two light companies (batteries). Divisions were designated with numbers and, by mid-1812, the Army had 1 Guard infantry division, 2 grenadier divisions and 24 infantry divisions. Later, additional divisions were established, including the 28th and 29th Divisions from the Orenburg and Siberia garrisons forces. The 30th through 37th Divisions were raised from the 2nd Battalions of the first twenty-seven divisions and the 38th through 48th Divisions were raised from the 4th Battalions.

The backbone of the Russian Army consisted of regular and light infantry regiments. Regimental chefs commanded the regiments and the 1st Battalion was designated the 'Chef's Battalion' and carried his name. In the Chef's absence, the regimental commander or commanding officer led the unit. After October 1810, a regular infantry regiment consisted of two active battalions (1st and 3rd) and one replacement (2nd *zapasnoi*) battalion. After November 1811 the 4th reserve (*rezervnii*) battalion was assigned to the recruitment depot. The grenadier companies of the 2nd Battalions were often united to establish 'combined grenadier battalions'. The Russian light infantry increased throughout the Napoleonic Wars and by 1812 consisted of two guard and fifty Jäger regiments, plus the Guard *Ekipazh*. In addition, special Jäger regiments and battalions were organized within the provincial Opolchenyes. The Jäger regiments had a similar organization to the line infantry units, and the regular infantry division had one Jäger brigade, usually the third. The light infantry regiments did not carry flags, while line infantry units usually had six flags (two for each battalion, except for the 4th Battalion, which had none). One of the flags was considered 'regimental' and often referred to as 'white', while other flags were known as 'colour' flags.

# The Battle of Borodino

After the 1801 reorganization, Russian heavy cavalry regiments comprised five squadrons each, of which four were active and one held in reserve. By 1812 the Russian cavalry arm included six guard, eight cuirassier, thirty-six dragoon, eleven hussar and five Uhlan (lancer) regiments. Two or three cavalry regiments were often organized into a brigade and three brigades (two heavy and one light) were united into a cavalry division. In 1812 divisions were further organized into cavalry corps. Cuirassier brigades had a separate designation from the general cavalry brigades. In 1812 there was one guard cavalry division plus two cuirassier divisions and eight cavalry divisions. In March of that year, eight new cavalry divisions were formed, with the 9th through 12th Divisions organized from the replacement squadrons, while the 13th through 16th Divisions were raised from the cavalry recruitment depots.

Alexander continued his father's reforms of the artillery. In 1805 the Inspector of All Artillery, Alexei Arakcheyev, launched a series of reforms to modernize the arm. Known as 'the 1805 System' these measures introduced standardized equipment, ammunition and guns. However, following the Russian defeat at Austerlitz, further changes were introduced. In 1806 artillery regiments were reorganized into brigades of two battery or heavy, one horse, and two light companies. These brigades were attached to infantry divisions. New artillery regulations prescribed specific instructions on artillery deployment and firing. Battery companies were armed with eight 12-pounders and four ½-pud (1 pud/pood = 16.4kg) *licornes*, while the light companies had eight 6-pounders and four ¼-pud licornes. Horse artillery companies had six 6-pounders and six ¼-pud licornes. Two guns were organized into squads (*vzvod*) commanded by a non-commissioned officer. Two squads formed a division and three divisions made up one company led by a staff officer.

## 6 September: Eve of the Bloodbath

The night of 5/6 September proved cool, as rain blanketed the battlefield, blown in by a piercing wind. By morning, a mist covered the ground, presenting a peaceful and eerie scene. After the battle at Shevardino, the French troops bivouacked on both banks of the Kolocha and some patrols reconnoitred the area beyond the Voina, reaching the Moscow river, where they watered their horses. The approaching battle was thus named *La Bataille de la Moskowa* by the French, and on the morning of the battle Napoleon would inspire his men by telling them that they were fighting 'sous les murs de Moscou' ('under the walls of Moscow'), while in reality the city was still about 112km away.

Early on the morning of the 6th,[138] after taking some rest and attending to political and administrative affairs, Napoleon decided to reconnoitre the area where he hoped the Russians would finally stand and give him the battle he had sought so long. Ségur noted that:

# 6 September: Eve of the Bloodbath

the generals as well as the Emperor were worried lest the Russians, discouraged by the day's losses, might slip away under cover of the night. Murat had warned us of that possibility; and several times it seemed to us that their campfires were growing fainter, and we imagined we could hear the noise of their departure.

As Lejeune tells us, the Emperor:

rode all along the front lines, drawn up on high ground at right angles with the Moscow road and separated from us only by the winding stream of the Kaluga [Kolocha], with its muddy banks, which flows into the Moskowa at Borodino. Everywhere our *vedettes* were barely a pistol-shot distance from those of the enemy, but neither fired on the other, both sides being probably too exhausted by the struggle of the evening before to feel any further irritation against each other.

However, at one point, Napoleon and his companions suddenly came upon a patrol of twenty Cossacks, a mere four paces away. Lejeune continues:

Thinking themselves surprised, they were already turning their horses to escape, when seeing our small numbers galloping away from them they pursued us for some hundred yards. Fortunately the fleetness of our horses and the protection of some fences saved us from the embarrassing predicament.

According to Pelet, Napoleon

studied in great detail the vicinity of Borodino and the valleys of Kolocha and Voina. He ordered construction of several fortifications (one central *lunette*, supported by three *redans* and two batteries) opposite them to divert enemy attention and establish a pivot for the rest of the Army and ensure communications between the Corps

Napoleon then travelled southwards to Shevardino, where he took advantage of a light haze to approach and examine the Russian positions near the Kurgan Hill and the Semeyonovskoye. He could see that the Russians had thrown up several earthworks in this region but the mist prevented him from noticing details. Moving south, he reached Poniatowski's V Corps, where, Pelet tells us, he ascended a hill and observed terrain through a spyglass placed on Murat's shoulder. Seeing the Old Smolensk Road winding through thick woods, he told Poniatowski: 'tomorrow you will advance forward and sweep away anything you may encounter on your way'. The Poles were then to turn left to flank the Russians and support the rest of the army.[139]

On his way back, Napoleon instructed some officers to conduct a detailed examination of specific sectors of the battlefield. Consequently, Labaume was awakened by General Armand Charles Guilleminot, who instructed him 'to traverse the entire line and try to approach the enemy as closely as possible to disclose the accidents of the ground he was encamped on, and above all, make sure there were not any masked batteries or ravines'. And Lejeune was told to 'ride carefully along the enemy's lines once more, to make a sketch of them, and to bring a few views of the ground occupied.' Later that morning, Jean Rapp, one of the Emperor's aides-de-camp, was also sent with orders to get as close as he could to the Russian positions: 'I removed my white plumes,' Rapp recalled, 'and put on a soldier's shako, and examined everything with the greatest precision.'[140] Simultaneously, Davout, probably accompanied by Poniatowski, reconnoitred terrain on the French right flank.

Returning to his tent, Napoleon found two newly arrived messengers. Baron Louis-François-Joseph de Bausset, Prefect of the Imperial Palace, reached the camp around 9 o'clock that morning, delivering a letter from Empress Marie Louise and a large portrait of Napoleon's son, painted by François Gérard. The portrait was packed in a case that filled the whole top of the carriage and de Bausset thought that, in view of the impending battle, Napoleon would 'put off opening the case for a few days'. But he was mistaken and Napoleon, 'eager to experience the joy of a sight so dear to his heart', abandoned his business to gaze upon his son's features, which served as great contrast to the weary, war-hardened men surrounding him. He was overjoyed at seeing his son's image – lying in a cradle, toying with a miniature sceptre and orb – and only regretted not being able 'to press him against his heart'. Napoleon then placed the picture before his tent and summoned his staff officers and generals to share his paternal joy. 'Gentlemen,' he told them, 'you may be sure that if my son were fifteen years old, he would be here, among so many brave men, and not in a picture.' After a brief pause, he added, 'It is an admirable portrait.' It remained before the imperial tent for the rest of the day, gazed at by the officers and soldiers of the Old Guard. According to Brandt, 'The soldiers, especially the veterans, seemed greatly touched by the picture; but the officers were now seriously worried about the outcome of the campaign and seemed as anxious as ever.'[141]

Napoleon's mood, however, was marred by Captain Charles Fabvier,[142] aide-de-camp of Marshal Auguste Marmont, who brought gloomy news from Spain. On 22 July, Anglo-Portuguese troops under Arthur Wellesley, Duke of Wellington, gained an important victory at Salamanca, which, as one modern historian described it: 'was the greatest French defeat for over a decade'.[143] The battle claimed about 12,500 casualties on the French side and broke Napoleon's grip on North and Central Spain. Equally important was its propaganda value, which could stir up anti-French sentiments in the rest of Europe. According to Thiers, Napoleon:

> heard, with a singular mixture of raillery and humour, the account of the Battle of Salamanca given by Fabvier, who had just arrived. When Fabvier had concluded his account, Napoleon dismissed him, saying that he would repair on the banks of the Moskowa [river] the faults committed at Arapilles.

Ségur tells us that Napoleon 'received graciously the aide-de-camp of the vanquished general [because] on the eve of a battle, the fate of which was so uncertain, he felt disposed to be indulgent to a defeat'. In his response to Ségur, Gourgaud rejected this account as 'wholly incorrect' and claimed that the Emperor:

# 6 September: Eve of the Bloodbath

testified the most violent disappointment, when he learnt that Marshal Marmont had compromised the French Army to satisfy a personal ambition, in giving a battle without waiting and in the face of the orders he had received for the arrival of Soult, which would have insured him the victory.

Hearing the Emperor's criticism, Fabvier, who was wounded at Salamanca and was 'imbued with the most noble and elevated feelings', considered it as a slight to his honour and during the battle the next day, 'fought on foot, as a volunteer, in the most perilous situations, as if to prove, that the soldiers of the Army of Spain did not yield in courage to those of the Army of Russia'.[144]

News of the French defeat in Spain was suppressed to avoid demoralization in the army on the eve of the battle and, as Brandt noted, 'many officers, even of high rank, would know nothing of it until they got back from the campaign'.

In the afternoon, Napoleon decided to make his second reconnaissance of the day. The morning mist was long gone by now and the Emperor could better examine the enemy positions across the field.[145] Accompanied by his staff, Napoleon first travelled along the Voina stream to reconnoitre the Russian right flank, before proceeding southwards. In the process, he was noticed and fired upon by some Russian batteries and Muravyev could hear 'occasional artillery fire here and there and, according to some, these were directed against Napoleon, who was reviewing his troops and reconnoitring our positions'.[146] Despite this 'nuisance' Napoleon still could notice 'numerous redoubts that covered the Russian positions'.[147] According to Lejeune: 'The enemy's line was protected by well-chosen and formidable positions, supplemented by redoubts and redans, the firing from which would cross each other.' As Saxon Dragoon officer von Leissnig described:

> As far as my inquisitive eye could see the whole ground to the left and right and straight ahead was covered with a growth of hazel bushes, junipers and other brushwood which rose to at least a man's height. To the left centre [...] stood a village [Borodino] and a nice Byzantine church which rose from a gentle tree covered slope and had a pretty tower plated in green copper [...] To the right, a ridge was covered along almost all its length with masses of Russian infantry and artillery. As I could clearly see through my telescope, the Russians had thrown up earthworks on some of the highest points of the ridge. These fortifications were cut into notches, which seemed to be embrasures for the artillery. Obliquely to the right of our regiment and beyond the ridge there rose the towers of the churches of Mozhaisk and the nearby monastery. They were an hour's march away, but they succeeded in lending a touch of beauty to the brooding gloom of the wild and barren neighbourhood.[148]

Travelling south, Napoleon observed Russians constructing a large and imposing redoubt (Rayevsky's Battery) on a hill north of Semeyonovskoye, which could sweep the entire plain in front of it. Slightly south-west of it, he observed two fortifications resembling shallow redans. As Rapp indicates, seeing these fortifications convinced Napoleon that the enemy would not retreat and he immediately returned to headquarters.

# The Battle of Borodino

As a result of his reconnaissances, Napoleon realized that the Russian right flank was difficult to assail, as it was located on the steep banks of the Kolocha river and was further reinforced by newly built batteries and earthworks. On the other hand, the left flank was much more exposed and provided an opportunity to launch a massive assault, and, if necessary, a flanking manoeuvre. However, Napoleon's observations were not complete, since Russian Jägers plus thick forest and brushwood barred him from gaining a full understanding of Kutuzov's position. He thus confused the Kamenka stream with the headwaters of the Semeyonovskii stream, believing that the Bagration Flèches and Rayevsky's Redoubt were located on the same ridge and could be assaulted at the same time. A similar error was made by Labaume and other French officers who prepared maps for the Emperor. Furthermore, Napoleon and his staff officers failed to notice that there was a third flèche behind the two forward ones, and this slip-up would play an important role in the subsequent fighting.

Based on his observations, Napoleon made arrangements for the battle. By late afternoon, Poniatowski's V Corps was lined up between Shevardino and the old road to Utitsa on the French right flank. To the right-centre, east of Shevardino, stood Davout's I Corps, with the cavalry corps of Nansouty, Montbrun and Latour-Maubourg behind it. Ney's III Corps was on Davout's immediate left, with Junot's VIII Corps and the Imperial Guard behind it. Eugène's IV Corps, reinforced by two divisions from I Corps, formed the left wing of the Grand Army, across the Kolocha river near Borodino, while General Ornano's cavalry covered the extreme left. Many troops remained in their bivouacs during daylight on 6 September, assuming their attack positions under cover of night, in order to prevent the Russians from determining the direction of the coming assault. Still, some corps made minor adjustments in their positions during the day and the cavalry was moved closer to the corps of Ney and Davout. Most importantly, Napoleon moved his headquarters from Valuyevo to the Shevardino Redoubt, and was followed by some units of the Imperial Guard, while the rest of the Guard crossed the Kolocha during the night.[149]

Napoleon's plan of attack was hardly inspiring, and Kutuzov himself was somewhat startled by this, writing to his wife: 'It is difficult to recognize [Napoleon] because he is unusually cautious, everywhere entrenching up to his ears ["zakapyvaetsia po ushi"].'[150] The plan called for a heavy bombardment of enemy positions followed by a frontal attack with minor diversions on the flanks. Eugène was to seize Borodino and then swing right across the Kolocha, while Poniatowski was to advance along the Old Smolensk Road and threaten the Russian left flank. Eugène's attack on Borodino had the twofold purpose of attracting Kutuzov's attention to his right wing and centre, thus preventing him from diverting forces to other sectors. Napoleon's main assault was directed against the Russian left flank, where Davout would launch the initial assault. According to Gourgaud, while planning Davout's attack, the Emperor sent for Compans 'to inform him that he destined him to attack [Bagration's southward flèche]'. Ney was present at this meeting and when Compans proposed to lead his division through the wood to avoid the enemy's fire, Ney argued it would delay the attack. However, Compans, who had reconnoitred the spot, declared that it was 'a passable copse and the Emperor approved of his plan'. Compans then noted that he was more concerned that his right flank would be exposed to the Russians attacking the gap between him and Poniatowski.[151] Once Davout's attack was under way, Ney was to advance to Semeyonovskoye, with Junot's VIII Corps and Murat's Reserve Cavalry providing support. As usual, the Imperial Guard was kept in the reserve.[152]

Much has been said about Napoleon's plan. Some argued that it lacked the ingenuity of the younger Napoleon, especially in light of his refusal to accept a more adventurous scheme touted by Marshal Davout. Given the shortness of the Russian line and manifest weakness of its left wing, Davout proposed to launch his own corps – supported by that of Poniatowski – in a powerful encircling movement through the Utitsa woods, while Ney's corps pinned down the Russians at Semeyonovskoye. If it succeeded, the Russians would be cornered between the Kolocha and Moscow rivers and could be hammered into submission. But Napoleon was unusually cautious and told the Marshal: 'No! The movement is altogether too great! It would lead me away from my objective and make me lose too much time.'[153] When Davout tried to argue his point, Napoleon abruptly silenced him: 'Ah, you are always for turning the enemy; this is too dangerous a manoeuvre!'

Napoleon has frequently been criticized for turning down Davout's suggestion. It certainly promised a much more decisive outcome than a direct attack against fortified positions. So what made him reject it? Davout's idea called for detaching two entire corps (I and V) – some 40,000 men – and Napoleon was naturally reluctant to commit half his infantry to this manoeuvre, since it would have weakened his position. In addition, the manoeuvre would have been performed during the night and, as Gourgaud observed, 'it is well known how hazardous such marches are made through a wooded and unknown tract of country, and almost without a guide'. For example, one need only recall Russian troops wandering off-road at night during their retreat from Smolensk. Russian historian Bogdanovich shared this sentiment:

> Considering that Marshal Davout's proposal required [a] nocturnal march in the forested and unfamiliar terrain, one cannot but doubt the success of such enterprise, which promised to be much harder to execute than the failed flanking manoeuvre of Junot at the Battle of Valutina Gora.[154]

Besides, it was probable the Russians would have patrols deployed to detect any such flanking manoeuvre. One historian has also stressed the poor condition of the French cavalry (already giving Napoleon cause for anxiety), which could have limited the extent of the manoeuvre.[155] More importantly, Napoleon was concerned that a flanking movement would induce Kutuzov to retreat. Having pursued the Russians since late June, he was willing to sacrifice some tactical advantage to have the enemy finally accept battle.[156]

# The Battle of Borodino

Although he rejected Davout's *manoeuvre sur les derrières*, Napoleon still planned to utilize a tactical flanking manoeuvre by Poniatowski's Corps.[157]

The French battle plan reveals that Napoleon had concentrated up to 80,000 men – some 60,000 infantry and 20,000 cavalry – on his right wing, and about 40,000 men on the left flank under Prince Eugène. Poniatowski had about 10,000 men, including 8,500 infantry, on the extreme right flank. The French artillery consisted of 587 guns, of which some 22 per cent were 'heavy' 12-pounders and 8-inch howitzers.[158] Guns played a particularly important role at Borodino and many participants would later attest the ferocious nature of the artillery bombardment in this battle. Indeed, the concentration and incidence of artillery at Borodino would not be eclipsed until the carnage of the First World War. Lariboissière, the Inspector-General of the French artillery, would later calculate that the French alone fired 60,000 cannon-balls (Fain claimed as many as 91,000) and 1,400,000 musket shots during the ten-hour battle, which gives 100 artillery rounds and over 2,330 musket shots per minute. If one believes Larionov, that the Russians fired at least as many rounds, the combined average rate of fire would be a staggering 3.4 cannon and 77.6 musket rounds per second.[159]

Napoleon's artillery deployment began late in the evening of the 6th, and Planat de la Faye recalled that:

> the Emperor wanted to know exactly how many musket rounds there were and what munitions in the reserve packs. To get all this information one had to run after units on the march and turn to officers loath to give them, having other things to see to. However, in the name of the Emperor everything became possible. By the end of the day Lariboissière gave him an exact report on the Army's supplies of artillery rounds and infantry cartridges.[160]

During the night two large batteries – those of Generals Foucher du Careil and Sorbier – were set up against the Russian left, while the remaining cannon were arranged in mobile batteries that operated in support of corps. The artillery of the III and VIII Corps was deployed next to Foucher's battery, while General Pernetty (of the I Corps) led a battery organized from sixteen guns from Davout's corps artillery, fourteen from Compans' divisional artillery and eight from the divisions of Friant and Dessaix. Pernetty's orders called for him to coordinate his actions with Sorbier and provide close support for Davout. Thus, Napoleon had about 100–105 guns arranged in the first line, though some scholars estimate their number as high as 120. In total, the French had concentrated up to 382 guns (including the Guard artillery) against the Russian left flank and some 297 of them could engage the Russian positions between Rayevsky's Redoubt and Utitsa. Of the remaining 200 guns, fifty were with the Poles of V Corps, while 152 pieces were spread in the centre and the right wing.

But the artillery deployment had some defects. The officers made a mistake in reconnoitring the terrain at night and placed batteries too far from the enemy positions. Deployment was further confused as units began marching to their positions in the dark. Around midnight, Pion des Loches' reserve

# 6 September: Eve of the Bloodbath

battery was ordered forward and was en route when Napoleon himself came across it and inquired what it was doing. Pion des Loches explained that one of ordnance officers gave him the order to move, to which Napoleon responded:

> 'He is a bloody fool, I have already got too much artillery here. Return to your corps.' That was an order doubtless easily given but where is this army corps I had left at midnight? No point in asking [...] My battery formed in column to retire.

After marching for half an hour seeking his unit, Pion des Loches met Marshal Mortier and explained that the Emperor sent him back. 'Who gave you the order to move?' inquired the Marshal. 'An ordnance officer, speaking in the Emperor's name' – 'Those f****** fools are always speaking in the Emperor's name. Has anyone ever heard of a corps being deprived of its reserve artillery on the eve of the battle?' Mortier instructed Pion des Loches to return to his place and obey no one but him; even if orders came from Napoleon himself, he was to await the Marshal's confirmation.[161]

While there were no major confrontations on the 6th, the day was not as peaceful as it is usually described in books, being full of skirmishes along the entire line.[162] That day, Fedor Glinka, sitting in the bell tower near the village of Borodino, could see as the French 'bands [of tirailleurs] skirmished with our Jägers for almost [the] entire day since our troops did not allow them to get drinking water from the Kolocha'. At one moment, a heated fight began between the tirailleurs of Morand's division and the Russian Jägers near Borodino. Hearing the musket fire, Davout ordered General Dedem, commanding a brigade in Friant's division, 'to ride flat out and stop the firing all down the line'.[163] Still, occasional fire could be heard for the rest of the day and Captain François recalled hearing it as late as 11pm. The 30th Line lost sixty-seven killed that day and François' Company alone had twenty-three casualties, over half of them killed. More important, however, was intensive skirmishing on the right flank, where Polish skirmishers tried to drive back the Russian Jägers and reconnoitre the environs of Utitsa. Later that night, Colonel Kaisarov, who served as Kutuzov's duty general, wrote that 'the enemy occupied us with skirmishes on the left flank', and Kutuzov responded by ordering one of the corps to proceed to the extreme left flank.[164] This was an important development and we will discuss it later in this section.

It is difficult to determine the prevailing sentiment among Allied troops on the eve of the battle. Memoirs, written many years, if not decades, after the event, tend to misrepresent the true emotions felt that autumn day. Ségur tells us that 'there was general rejoicing' at seeing the Russian Army in place:

> This incoherent, sluggish, shifting war in which our best efforts had been fruitless and in which we seemed to be hopelessly, endlessly sinking, was at last cantered in one spot. Here we touched bottom, here was the end, here everything would be decided![165]

# The Battle of Borodino

Bourgogne watched as 'some cleaned muskets and other weapons, others made bandages for the wounded, some made their wills, and others, again, sang or slept in perfect indifference. The whole of the Imperial Guard received orders to appear in full uniform.'[166]

For Raymond de Fezensac

> there was something sombre and imposing in the sight of these two armies preparing to slaughter each other. All the regiments had received the order to put on parade uniforms as if for a holiday. The Imperial Guard, in particular, seemed to be waiting for a procession rather than a battle. Nothing is more striking than the sangfroid of these old soldiers; on their faces were neither anxiety nor exhilaration. A new battle was to them but one victory more, and to share this noble confidence one had only to look at them.[167]

Lieutenant Vossler was among those troops who rejoined the army in time for the battle. Entering the camp he found troops in

> good and sanguine spirits. We were congratulated on all sides upon our timely arrival. If one discounted our men's pale worn faces, the whole army seemed alive with a cheerful bristle. Most of the troops were busy polishing and preparing weapons for the morrow ...

Meanwhile, Griois found it

> difficult to describe what was happening in our camp that night. A raucous joy, inspired by the thought of the battle, reigned here and there was no doubt in the outcome of the fighting. From every direction one could hear cries of soldiers calling each other, the bursts of laughter caused by their merry tales or grotesquely philosophical thoughts on the chances each one of them would face the following day. Innumerable fires, rather disorganized on our side and symmetrically lit along the fortifications on the Russian, lighted up the horizon and gave the idea of a splendid illumination and a true festival.[168]

Captain Girod de l'Ain was among those Bourgogne saw showing 'perfect indifference'. As he recalled:

> after a long walk to reconnoitre the respective positions of the armies, I returned to our bivouac and spent the time in having my first lesson in how to play chess from Major Fanfette [one of General Dessaix's aides-de-camp] who adored the game and always carried with him a little cardboard chess set which folded into eight pieces and which he had himself constructed with great ingenuity.

Their game would be interrupted after Girod de l'Ain was called up later that evening, but Fanfette would record all their moves and, after surviving the horrors of the retreat, they would finish it in Berlin![169]

Still, not everyone shared the joyous atmosphere. For Vionnet de Maringoné and his comrades, 'the night from 6 to 7 September was terrible. We passed it in the mud, without fire, surrounded by the dead and wounded whose cries and moaning tore our hearts.'[170] War weary, hundreds of miles away from home and lacking supplies, many soldiers knew that defeat in battle would be tantamount to death. Meerheim and Roos were contemplating such a possibility, as was Vossler, who observed that 'many a soldier stretched

1. Emperor Alexander I (1777–1825).

2. Mikhail Illarionovich Golenischev-Kutuzov (1745–1813), commander-in-Chief of the Russian Army.

3. General Barclay de Tolly (1761–1818), commander of the 1st Western Army.

4. Count Bennigsen (1735–1826), Kutuzov's Chief of Staff.

5. General Prince Bagration (1765–1812), commander of the 2nd Western Army.

6. Lieutenant General Baggovut (1761–1812), commander of Kutuzov's II Infantry Corps.

7. Lieutenant General Tuchkov (1765–1812), commander of Kutuzov's III Infantry Corps.

8. Lieutenant General Osterman-Tolstoy (1771–1857), commander of Kutuzov's IV Infantry Corps.

9. General Dokhturov (1790–1863),
   commander of Kutuzov's VI Infantry Corps.

10. Lieutenant General Uvarov (1773–1824),
    commander of Kutuzov's I Reserve Cavalry
    Corps.

11. Major  General Korf (1773–1823),
    commander of Kutuzov's II & III Reserve
    Cavalry Corps.

12. General Platov (1753–1818), 'Ataman' of
    Kutuzov's Cossack Irregular Cavalry.

13. General Golitsyn (1771–1844), Cavalry commander of the 2nd Western Army.

14. Lieutenant General Rayevsky (1771–1829), commander of Kutuzov's VII Infantry Corps.

15. Major General Vorontsov (1782–1856), commander of Kutuzov's 2nd Combined Grenadier Division.

16. Major General Sievers (1772–1856), commander of Kutuzov's IV Reserve Cavalry Corps.

17. Major General Karpov (1762–1837), commander of the 2nd Western Army's Irregular Troops.

18. General Löwenstern (1777–1858), Barclay de Tolly's Adjutant.

19. Emperor Napoleon I (1769–1821).

20. Marshal Berthier (1753–1815), Napoleon's Chief of Staff.

21. Armand de Caulaincourt (1773–1827), Napoleon's Grand Equerry.

22. General Auguste de Caulaincourt (1777–1812), killed in the changes against Rayevsky's Redoubt.

23. General Louis-Pierre Montbrun (1770–1812), commander of Napoleon's II Cavalry Corps.

24. Marshal Bessières (1768–1813), commander of Napoleon's Guard Cavalry.

25. Marshal Davout (1770–1823), commander of Napoleon's I Corps.

26. Marshal Ney (1769–1815), commander of Napoleon's III Corps.

27. Prince Poniatowski (1763–1813), commander of Napoleon's V Corps.

28. General Junot (1771–1813), commander of Napoleon's VIII Corps.

29. Marshal Murat (1767–1815), commander of Napoleon's Reserve Cavalry Corps.

30. General Nansouty (1768–1815), commander of Napoleon's I Cavalry Corps.

31. General Grouchy (1766–1847), commander of Napoleon's III Cavalry Corps.

32. General Latour-Maubourg (1768–1850), commander of Napoleon's IV Cavalry Corps.

# 6 September: Eve of the Bloodbath

himself out carefree and contented, little thinking that this would be his last night on earth. But the thought was common to us all ...'

Similar sentiments are revealed by Le Roy, who had

gloomy reflections on the outcome of a battle fought 2,400 miles from France, and about what would become of oneself if wounded. As for death, we did not give it a thought. As to who would win the battle, we were so vain as to believe it would be to our advantage.

Colonel Boulart of the Guard artillery felt that:

if we are beaten at 750 to 800 leagues from France, what terrible risks will we not run! Can even one of us expect to return to his native country again? If we are victors, will peace follow at once? That is hardly likely in the Russian nation's unequivocal state of exasperation!

Julien Combe could see that 'many a mind was anxious, many eyes remained open, many reflections were made on the importance of the drama, which had been announced for the morrow and whose stage, so far from our motherland, allowed us the choice of either winning or perishing'.

Many felt that this was the last evening of their life and they would perish the following day. Biot recalled that Colonel Désirad was overheard remarking to his friends, 'This will be my last battle.' The unfortunate Colonel would be one of the first casualties of this battle. Meanwhile, Westphalian Captain von Linsingen was wondering how many of his comrades would survive the battle when:

suddenly I found myself hoping that this time too the Russians would decamp during the night. But no, the sufferings of the past days had been too great, it was better to end it all. Let the battle begin, and our success will assure our salvation!

Fezensac shared this sentiment: 'Each side had to conquer or perish; for us, a defeat would doom us irrevocably; for them, it would mean the loss of Moscow and the destruction of their main army, Russia's only hope.' Napoleon also had no illusions on this account and Dedem overheard him mutter, 'a big battle [...] lots of people [...] many, many dead ...' but he then suddenly turned to Berthier: 'The battle is ours.'[171]

Some struggled to maintain high spirits since, as Italian Cesare de Laugier lamented, there was 'not a blade of grass or of straw, not a tree; not a village that has not been looted inside out. Impossible to find the slightest nourishment for the horses, to find anything for oneself to eat, or even to light a fire.'

But the Imperial Guard was relatively well supplied, and as Ségur recounted, Napoleon summoned Bessières several times, asking 'whether the needs of the Guards were all provided for. He had a three-day ration of biscuit and rice, taken out of reserve supplies, distributed to these men.'[172]

Many ordinary soldiers, meantime, spent their last night miserable, cold and hungry. But a few tried to make the best of it; for Vossler, this meant that 'a miserable plateful of bread soup oiled with the stump of a tallow candle was all I had to eat on the eve of the big battle. In my famished condition even this revolting dish seemed quite appetizing.' Meanwhile, for Brandt and his comrades:

> the lack of food was bitterly felt that night. We dined on grilled corn and horsemeat. The night was wet and cold and many soldiers and officers, soaked to the skin and prey to forebodings, tried in vain to sleep. They would get up and, like lost souls, walk listlessly before the campfires.[173]

Dumonceau complained about the sufferings of horses whose 'misery was great. Apart from a slender ration of oats brought up from Gzhatsk, they had nothing to eat but a few bits of straw or grass, everywhere disputed on all sides.'[174]

That evening Hubert-Charles Biot, aide-de-camp to General Pajol, was dispatched to receive orders from General Montbrun, commanding the II Cavalry Corps, whom he found 'leaning over his map deep in thought'. Biot introduced himself and Montbrun asked him if he'd dined. Biot replied in the negative:

> whereupon he [Montbrun] added, 'In that case you shall dine with us.' Soon afterwards his manservant came in and announced that a certain Verchére, orderly officer on the General's staff, had returned from accompanying Madame Montbrun as far as Warsaw. 'Bring him in,' said the General. The officer in question handed over a letter and a packet and on taking the latter Montbrun exclaimed, 'I know what this is. You did leave my wife in good health, did you not? As for her letter, we will read it after the battle.'[175]

Alas, Montbrun would be mortally wounded leading his men and the letter would remain unread.

An artillery officer from Württemberg also left an interesting account of the last day before the battle. At about ten in the morning:

> General Beurmann summoned all the officers and made a speech in broken German, in which he informed us that the great battle would begin that very afternoon around 2pm. He stressed that under no circumstances, even if enemy shells tore down whole rows of us, even if Cossacks attacked us in flank and from behind, were we to 'lose our presence of mind'. He expressly forbade the evacuation of the wounded during the battle, because otherwise too many men would be out of the fighting line. The wounded would be taken care of after the battle. He finished by saying, 'I shall load you with decorations because such brave men as you are can never be adequately rewarded.' At 1pm he returned and told us that on account of the thick mist which had only come up at noon, the Emperor had not completed his reconnaissance and therefore the battle would not begin until dawn next day. On receiving this news, we spent the whole afternoon cooking and eating, so that whatever happened we should not have to make the journey into the next world on an empty stomach.[176]

What was happening in the Russian camp across the field? By late evening of 6 September Kutuzov had already deployed his forces in battle positions, with Barclay's 1st Western Army on the right flank and Bagration's troops deployed on the left. On the extreme right were II and IV Corps; behind them were the Cossacks and the 2nd Cavalry Corps. Dokhturov's VI Corps occupied the high ground between Gorki and Rayevsky's Redoubt, with Pahlen's III Cavalry Corps in support. The V Corps and 1st Cuirassier Division were further behind at Knyazkovo. Rayevsky's Redoubt was defended by VII Corps, with the IV Cavalry Corps nearby. The flèches were defended by VIII Corps while, on the extreme left, Tuchkov's corps, reinforced with the Opolchenye, protected the Old Smolensk Road.[177]

Kutuzov set up a convoluted chain of command for the battle. Barclay de Tolly and Bagration continued to command their respective armies, and in a general order Kutuzov stated that: 'unable to be at all points during the battle, I place my trust in the acknowledged experience of the army commanders [Barclay de Tolly and Bagration] and leave it up to them to act as they see fit in the circumstances to achieve the destruction of the enemy'. But in addition to them, General Miloradovich was given command of the *Corps de Bataille* of the right flank, which included the II and IV Corps and the cavalry of Uvarov and Korf; while Lieutenant General Gorchakov led the Corps de Bataille of the left flank, consisting of VII Corps and the 27th Division. Finally, Lieutenant General Golitsyn I was given command of the 1st and 2nd Cuirassier Divisions, which were deployed behind V Corps.

The Russian commanders had contrasting conceptions of strategy, and we have already seen some of their arguments on the eve of the combat at Shevardino. In this respect one can easily disallow Soviet attempts to depict Kutuzov as a great strategist, who anticipated Napoleon's every move and reacted accordingly. Thus, Zhilin and Beskrovny praised Kutuzov's strategy and called him 'the strategist of the world significance', while Garnich claimed Kutuzov had a 'precisely elaborated plan' and he well understood Napoleon's designs, 'seizing the strategic initiative from Napoleon on the eve of the battle, and the tactical initiative during the battle'.[178] With all due respect to the old general, Kutuzov made his share of mistakes and the deployment at Borodino was among them.

We have already discussed the initial Russian deployment – parallel to the Kolocha river, with the right wing near Maslovo and the left close to Shevardino. On 5 September Kutuzov wrote to Alexander that: 'noticing the enemy's main attack against the left flank, I decided to strengthen it and sought it necessary to bend it back towards previously fortified heights'.[179] This 'second position' was anchored on the ridge running from Borodino to the Utitsa woods. It was protected by a series of fortifications on the right flank, a major redoubt in the centre and three flèches on the left flank. Thus, the position was seemingly reinforced all along the line. The problem, however, was in disproportionate deployment of troops. Kutuzov and his advisors remained concerned about their right wing, where they anticipated Napoleon's main attack to cut the New Smolensk Road, which served as the main line of retreat to Moscow. As a result, almost two-thirds of the Russian Army was concentrated in this direction.

Senior officers, including Barclay de Tolly and Bennigsen emphasized the weakness of the left flank. Some officers overheard Bagration arguing at headquarters: 'Why are you so concerned about the right flank [when] the left flank is threatened?'[180] Many shared this view. Captain Alexander Figner told to his comrade-in-arms that 'Napoleon will throw all his forces on this [left] flank and drive us into the Moscow river.' Yermolov could see that 'the left wing was tangibly weak in comparison with other sectors of our position. The fortifications there were incomplete and time was so short that there was nothing we could do to strengthen them.' Bennigsen suggested moving the II and IV Corps to the left flank, where they would serve as powerful reserves to Bagration's army. Barclay de Tolly was even more drastic in his call to shift most of his army to the left.[181] Listening to this proposal, Kutuzov seemingly approved it but, in fact, was reluctant to implement it. Barclay de Tolly scathingly commented that Kutuzov believed the extreme left flank could be 'easily defended by irregular forces alone'.

Such belief seems to have faded away as time progressed and Kutuzov decided to deploy additional troops on the Old Smolensk Road. This brings us to the deployment of Tuchkov's corps at Utitsa. This position was earlier covered by six Cossack regiments, but according to Sherbinin, on 5 September Kutuzov summoned Engineer Captain Folkner and

> instructed him to examine terrain behind the left flank in order to ascertain if it was possible to conceal any troops there. 'When the enemy,' Kutuzov said, 'would commit his last reserves against Bagration's left flank, I will attack with my concealed troops into their flank and rear.'

Folkner soon returned with a report that the location was well suited for such plan: so Tuchkov's III Corps, supported by the Moscow and Smolensk Opolchenye, was deployed.[182] The *Official News from the Army* bulletin asserted that when the enemy concentration against the left flank became obvious, Kutuzov sought

> to enhance the defence of this weak point in our position [...] [and] Tuchkov with the III Corps and part of the Moscow Opolchenye was deployed in *an ambush* [my emphasis] behind thick brushwood on the extreme left flank, with the order to operate along the Old Smolensk Road against the French flank and rear as soon as the enemy starts attacking and seeking to turn our left flank.

Kutuzov's report to Alexander adds further confusion to this issue, since he claimed that he deployed Tuchkov in the south after he 'perceived' Napoleon's 'intention to assault our left flank and, by advancing along the Old Smolensk Road, to separate us from Mozhaisk'. Note that unlike the *Official News* bulletin, there is no mention of the order for Tuchkov to lay in an ambush and attack the enemy and the emphasis lies on the defensive nature of his mission.[183]

This issue became further complicated by the fact that everything was done in great secrecy. The tense atmosphere at headquarters, where various groups intrigued and competed for influence over the commander-in-chief, had a detrimental effect, since Kutuzov and his confidants concealed information from their rivals. Among those unaware of Tuchkov's deployment were

# 6 September: Eve of the Bloodbath

Bennigsen and Barclay de Tolly. The latter recalled that 'an adjutant, whom I sent to find the [III] Corps, informed me of what happened. No one knew under whose command this corps should remain, to whom its commanders should report and receive orders? I informed [Kutuzov] on this account and was told that it was simply a mistake and it would not be repeated in the future.' As for Bennigsen, he examined the Russian left wing during the night of 6/7 September, where he came across Jägers in the Utitsa woods who told him there was a considerable gap between the forces of Bagration and Tuchkov, through which the enemy could drive a wedge. Surprised to hear about troops so far on the left, and unaware of Kutuzov's plan, Bennigsen went to Tuchkov and ordered him to leave his hidden position for open ground closer to Bagration, as traditional histories of the battle inform us.

Thus, for the next 200 years Bennigsen became a scapegoat, bearing the responsibility for the failure of Kutuzov's counter-attack at Utitsa. As years passed, participants and historians began to misinterpret or exaggerate Tuchkov's mission. Sherbinin was convinced that without Bennigsen's intervention, 'the sudden appearance of this hidden detachment in the enemy flank and rear, as it was conceived by Kutuzov, would have been disastrous for the French'. His comrade-in-arms, Bolgovsky, claimed that Tuchkov was supposed to turn the French right flank while Platov attacked the left flank, which would have placed Napoleon in-between a double-pincer movement and delivered the battle to the Russians.[184] Buturlin, Saint Priest and Eugène of Württemberg believed that Tuchkov's orders called for attack against the French right flank.[185] This idea was reflected in the classic work on 1812 by Bogdanovich and then repeated in virtually all subsequent battle histories.

The debate over Tuchkov's mission often centres on its original and subsequent positions, which some believed held the key to the issue. Official documents failed to clarify whether Tuchkov's troops were deployed on the Old Smolensk Road itself or south of it. The official battle plan (see image) showed Tuchkov's troops organized in columns (all other units on the map were in lines) on both side of the road near Utitsa, with Kutuzov's note 'deployed concealed' inscribed nearby. This caused much discussion on whether the position was correctly shown, reflected Kutuzov's plan and could have effectively concealed the troops at such an open ground. Most Russian/Soviet historians tended to support the official thesis, blaming Bennigsen, since this helped justify Kutuzov's actions. Still, some tried to suggest alternative explanations. Gerua argued that Folkner, who examined the terrain, and Traskin, who had drawn the map, both made mistakes that misled Kutuzov, who had not reconnoitred the area in person. Toll, who led the troops to the place, then only confounded the problem by failing to ascertain the flaws of this position. Gerua suggested that Bennigsen's actions could be explained as aimed at correcting Tuchkov's deployment, based on actual terrain.[186] After the battle, Gerua argued, persons responsible for these blunders (that is, Toll and others) tried to suppress information to avoid responsibility. A similar view was expressed by Kolyubakin and Pavlenko, who believed that the problem lay in an improperly conducted

# The Battle of Borodino

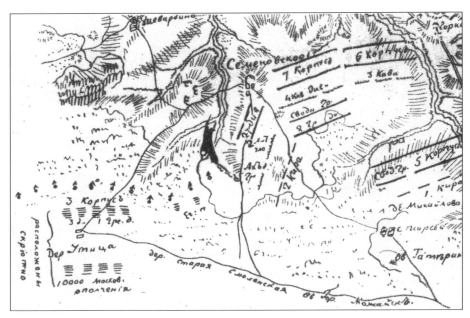

*'Kroki' or official battle plan prepared by Sub Lieutenant E. Traskin for Kutuzov on 6 September. Tuchkov's troops at Utitsa are shown in columns in lower left corner, with Kutuzov's note next to them.*

reconnaissance: Toll, acting in darkness, deployed Tuchkov's troops south of the Old Smolensk Road, facing northward, and Bennigsen corrected him by redeploying these forces westward, closer to the Utitsa Hill.[187] These historians tried to critically assess the mission assigned to Tuchkov and pointed out its limitations, notably the lack of cavalry support for infantry.

Their work was soon forgotten and the official thesis propagated the myth of the well-planned ambush and potentially decisive counter-attack that was undermined by Bennigsen. No one questioned why the Chief of Staff of the entire Russian Army was kept out of loop on such an important tactical decision. Thus, according to Garnich, 'Bennigsen ruined Kutuzov's plan, and if his actions had no substantial effect on the battle, it was only due to Kutuzov who masterly directed military operations and found new solutions to tactical challenges he faced.'[188] Zhilin even claimed that had Napoleon attempted a flanking manoeuvre with the corps of Davout and Poniatowski, they would have been destroyed by Tuchkov's forces, notwithstanding the fact that the French would have outnumbered Tuchkov's men two to one! As one modern Russian scholar remarked: 'The imagination of the Soviet "historians" truly had no boundaries!'[189] Even if Tuchkov's troops remained in their original position, he would not have been able to attack the French right flank because V Corps was marching directly at him and Tuchkov lacked the cavalry and artillery support necessary for any aggressive actions. Furthermore, his force was weakened from the start when Bagration,

78

# 6 September: Eve of the Bloodbath

desperate for help at the flèches, requested one of Tuchkov's divisions to reinforce his command.

The entire Russian position was about 8km long. The 1st Western Army, deployed from the Moscow river to Rayevsky's Redoubt, had concentrated some 80,000 men here, while the 2nd Western Army posted about 34,000 men on the left. This produced relatively close deployment of the troops, which was later criticized by many. Clausewitz noted that: 'the Russian Army fought in so confined and deep a disposition that there is hardly a second example of such'. He disapproved of Colonel Toll, who was:

> fond of deep formations, i.e. of a small extension of front and a heavy reserve [...] The cavalry stood from 300 to 400 paces behind infantry, and from these to the great reserve the distance was scarcely 1,000 paces. The consequence was that both cavalry and the reserve suffered severely from the enemy fire without being engaged.

Indeed, during the battle hundreds of men lost their lives to no purpose because the French artillery had an excellent target in compact masses of Russian troops and the Life Guard Preobrazhenskii and Semeyonovskii Regiments, though in reserve, lost over 500 men without participating in the fighting.[190]

The Russian positions were reinforced by a series of fortifications constructed between 3 and 6 September. Major General Ivashov, commanding the Russian engineer forces, reported that, in three days, his men built 'four bridges and 15 descents [into ravines], many clearings and strong abatis on the left flank, 3 flèches in the centre and one redoubt on the right flank'.[191] Among the earthworks constructed on the right flank were the Maslovo Flèches, located on the heights between the New Smolensk Road and Maslovo. Starting on 3 September, the Russians built here a pentagon-shaped redoubt and two lunettes that were interconnected and defended through a system of retrenchments and clearings. The main redoubt was relatively large, with over 3,500 square metres of internal space and a 2.5m-high *Brustwehr*. The fortifications were guarded by the 4th, 11th and 17th Battery Companies. The two auxiliary lunettes were about 150 paces away from the redoubt and the spaces in between blocked with the abates. Several more earthworks were constructed near Gorki. The first group of fortifications, on the northern edge of Gorki, included a three (some sources say 4 ) gun battery and trenches for infantry. The battery, constructed on 4 September, with a 1.3m-high and 3m-wide Brustwehr, protected the approaches to the right centre of the Russian position and was occupied by three guns of Major Ditterix's Battery Company. The battery is noteworthy because Kutuzov established his command post near it and observed the battle from this vantage point. The trenches – four in total – were dug to protect the northern and western approaches to the battery and Gorki. In the second group of fortifications, the Russians constructed a nine-gun battery south-west of the village. The battery, occupied by the guns from the 17th Battery Company, was, in fact, built, across the New Smolensk Road that

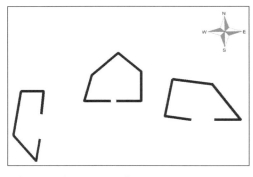
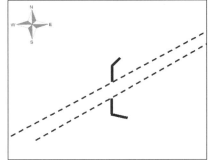

*The Maslovo Fortifications*                    *Gorki Nine-Gun Battery*

cut it in half. After the battle, Barclay de Tolly had assigned some 2,000 militiamen to turn this battery into a redoubt during the night of 8 September but the order was cancelled after Kutuzov's ordered retreat later that night.

The construction of fortifications on the left wing, however, proved a more complicated affair. Kutuzov sought to centralize supervision of such works and ordered to have all regimental tools, including axes, to be placed at the disposal of the main headquarters, where Lieutenant General Trousson was instructed to manage all construction works with his engineer and pontoon companies.[192] This only increased confusion, since Trousson's engineers simply could not handle such an immense task at such short notice and required additional manpower. The regular troops, who had to surrender their equipment to Trousson, soon received Bagration's counter-order to begin work on the flèches, but were unable to comply without their equipment. On 4 September, Bagration, exasperated by the delay in getting his soldiers' tools back, instructed his men 'to take necessary measures to recover all instruments [...] by tomorrow morning'. He then assigned 500 soldiers from each infantry division and 400 men of the Opolchenye to construction work, while some 600 men of the 27th Division were ordered to arm themselves with axes to prepare fascines. The 2nd Grenadier Division was assigned to the northern fortification, the 26th Division to the

*Cross-Section of the Southern Flèche*

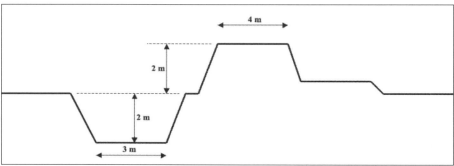

# 6 September: Eve of the Bloodbath

southern, and the Combined Grenadier Division worked on the rear flèche. He instructed his troops to fill in any ravines and ditches between the 'front and back lines' so that they caused no difficulties in manoeuvring.[193]

Three flèche were eventually built between the Kamenka and Semeyonov-skii brooks. To be specific, the two forward fortifications – also known as the northern and southern flèches – were lunettes that had two projecting shoulders or 'faces' and two parallel flanks, while the third fortification, behind the first two, was a flèche: that is a small V-shaped outwork. The lunettes were positioned with their left shoulders facing west and their right shoulders facing north. The shoulders of the northern lunette were each 22m long, with a 1.5m-high parapet or Brustwehr. The southern lunette, with a 2m Brustwehr, was somewhat distorted, its left (western) shoulder being 22m long and its right (northern) shoulder some 63m long. The flanks of both lunettes were about 18m long. The flèche behind them had 18m-long faces and a 2m-high parapet. Its right shoulder was directed westward to cover the gap between the two lunettes, while the left shoulder faced south, in order to prevent any flanking manoeuvres through the Utitsa woods against the southern lunette.[194]

Although seemingly daunting, the flèches were far from perfect. Working in sagging ground and lacking tools, Bagration's troops were unable to complete their construction. Thus, the walls were not properly reinforced, while the outer ditch at the northern flèche was left too shallow. A Russian officer later recalled:

> I have seen Bagration's *shantsy* [flèches] personally [and can tell you that] they were rubbish and it is even shameful to call them shantsy [...] the ditch was too shallow [...] gun enclosures opened to the ground, which made it easy to scale them and through which every soldiers inside could be seen.[195]

According to Clausewitz, 'these works [...] were in a sandy soil, open from behind, destitute of all external devices [...] None of them could hold out against a serious assault ...'

While Bagration toiled over his flèches, construction work had started on another fortification slightly northward, around 5pm on 6 September. It was preceded by a heated argument between Toll and Bennigsen. The former argued that it would be sufficient to construct a simple lunette for eighteen guns, while the latter called for a closed fortification for twenty-four or thirty-six guns, 'capable of defending itself from every direction,

*The Northern Flèche*     *The Southern Flèche*          *The Rear Flèche*

supported by four or five infantry Battalions'. Liprandi, who witnessed this scene, wrote:

> Toll argued that the [French] could attack this protruding site and, having captured it, they would command [a dominating] position over the VI and VII Corps, concentrating numerous artillery that would dislodge [the Russian corps]. If, on other hand, the fortification was integrated with the positions of these two corps, the enemy would have to fight both corps simultaneously [...] Bennigsen countered that if this was done, the enemy could still capture it and then direct the fire along ['anfilirovat'] the line of both corps, forcing them to abandon this position due to heavy casualties.

Liprandi noted that Kutuzov, who was also present, initially 'remained silent, without uttering a word in support or against either of them'. Other generals, probably understanding the futility of their attempts, also remained quiet. Kutuzov eventually sided with Toll, although, as Liprandi admitted: '[the] majority [of officers] shared Bennigsen's view'.[196] So the decision was made to construct a relatively small battery on the Kurgan Heights. Bagration was instructed to move Rayevsky's VII Corps to defend it, which only further weakened the forces at his disposal for the defence of the left wing.

This fortification, later known as Rayevsky's Redoubt (or the Grand Redoubt), was built by the troops of the Moscow Opolchenye, under the direction of Lieutenants Liprandi and Bogdanov. The redoubt was constructed in the shape of a wide 'V' with two 72m-long *épaulments* (shoulders) converging at a 100-degree angle and reinforced by two 19m flanks. According to Bogdanov, by 11pm on 6 September, the fortification was surrounded by '[a] 3.5 *sazhen*-wide [7.3m] and 1.5 sazhen-deep [3.1m] ditch'. Sent to help construct the redoubt, Bogdanov was met by Rayevsky, who told him that 'due to the open and rolling terrain, the redoubt can be attacked by the cavalry ...' So six wolf pits (other sources indicate ten) were dug in a checkerboard formation leading up to the ditch. Bogdanov then spent the entire night working on improving the redoubt's defences. He recalled that

> it was necessary, despite very limited time, to reinforce both flanks with Brustwehr and ditches while the opening in the rear was to be closed by a double palisade, with two openings on the sides [...] We used wood and iron from the nearby villages that were taken apart.

By the time the battle began, Bogdanov's men managed to reinforce the flanks and put up a double palisade with 8-foot-high outer and 6.5-feet-high inner walls. The redoubt was initially defended by twelve guns of the 26th and six guns of the 47th Light companies, though some sources indicate that six guns of the 12th Battery Company might have been deployed here. A Battalion of the Poltava Infantry Regiment was assigned to defend the guns. Inspecting his redoubt a few hours before the battle, Rayevsky turned to his officers: 'Now, gentlemen, we can be assured. Emperor Napoleon saw a simple open battery yesterday but his troops will find a true fortress here today.'[197]

# 6 September: Eve of the Bloodbath

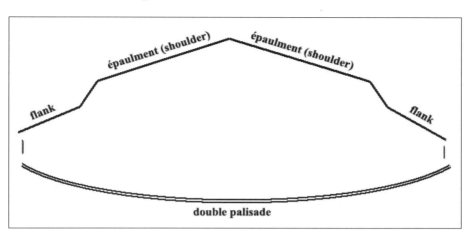

*Rayevsky's Redoubt*

Like their foes, the Russian soldiers spent the day also cleaning their muskets and uniforms, sharpening bayonets, and preparing their parade uniforms. The Russian Army was, by now, well provisioned, and as Bogdanovich noted, 'due to the dedication of the good-hearted Russian people and the proximity of Moscow, our troops had everything in abundance'.[198] Yermolov instructed physicians to prepare sufficient bandages and compresses, and reminded the *general-proviantmaster* to supply each corps with 2 puds [32.8kg] of pepper to spice up meals. Bagration ordered hot meals and alcohol be distributed to his troops but instructed his corps commanders to prohibit setting fires on open places, but rather to prepare meals in 'ravines and other concealed sites'. The Jägers, who spent many hours in the skirmishing line, were allowed 'to rest for [the] entire night, prepare porridge, drink a goblet of wine, and recover; at dawn, they must again cook porridge, drink another goblet of wine, replenish their cartridges ...'[199]

A series of instructions were issued on the eve of battle. Kutuzov urged his subordinates to commit their forces sparingly and advised them that 'the general who retains his reserves remains undefeated'. Any attacks were to be conducted in close columns, 'without firing but quickly using cold steel'.[200] In the intervals between infantry columns, Kutuzov instructed to have some cavalry units in chequerboard formation, while others in columns to support infantry. Yermolov's orders contain an interesting discussion on the use of skirmishers and cautioned commanders that:

> high losses among skirmishers cannot be attributed to the enemy's skilful actions alone but rather to the excessive number of skirmishers deployed against the enemy. In general, avoid skirmishing that will not produce any important results but requires considerable number[s] of men.

Officers were told that, during attacks, the troops should be prohibited from shouting 'hurrah' until a distance of ten paces from the enemy, but drums must accompany the charge. The corps commanders had to pay

# The Battle of Borodino

attention that their troops and artillery did not waste ammunition since 'the enemy might be surprised by the rapid, yet inefficient, fire but it [he?] will soon lose any respect towards it'. Yermolov's order also specified instructions for artillery commanders:

> After deploying artillery in batteries, the remaining artillery in the corps must be kept in reserves with brigades. The artillery in the second line remains in its place. This reserve artillery is commanded by [the] corps commander or the chief of artillery of the entire Army, who will inform only [the] corps commander which battery to deploy and where. The Chief of the Army artillery should not be resisted in his orders, since he is acting on behalf of the Commander-in-Chief and according to the mission assigned to him.[201]

The eve of the battle was a Sunday, and many participants commented on an unusual calmness that descended on their camp that day. To uplift the morale of his troops, Kutuzov had the icon of the Black Virgin of Smolensk paraded through the ranks of the Army. The sight of the famous miraculous icon, accompanied by the robed priests singing Old Russian prayers and swinging their smoking censers and sprinkling drops of holy water, had a remarkable effect on the soldiers. 'It reminded us of preparations for the Battle on Kulikovo Field', noted one officer, referring to the great battle between the Russian and Mongol forces in 1380. Another compared his pious comrades to 'the Puritans of Cromwell'. Glinka described as 'acting upon the call of its heart, the hundred-thousand-strong army fell to its knees and bowed its head to the ground, which it was ready to satiate with its blood'. One soldier shared his feelings:

> Placing myself next to the icon, I observed the soldiers who passed by piously. O faith! How vital and wondrous is your force! I saw how soldiers, coming up to the picture of the Most Holy Virgin, unbuttoned their uniforms and taking from their crucifix or icon their last coin, handed it over as an offering for candles. I felt, as I looked at them, that we would not give way to the enemy on the field of battle; it seemed as though after praying, each of us gained new strength; the live fire in the eyes of all the men showed the conviction that with God's help we would vanquish the enemy; each one went away as though inspired and ready for battle, ready to die for his fatherland.[202]

Soldiers were making the sign of the cross and, in some places, they openly cried. Kutuzov, dressed simply and surrounded by his staff officers, also went to see the icon, bowing low to the ground. Suddenly, as participants recounted, shouts of '[an] eagle is soaring!' were heard, and thousands of soldiers looked up to see the bird gliding through the sky. Kutuzov took off his cap as

> The men around him shouted 'hurrah' and the yell was carried by the entire Army. The eagle was still in the sky and the seventy-year-old commander, taking it as a good omen, stood with his head bared. It was a remarkable sight! [...] A hundred thousand Russians were yelling 'hurrah!' – and the fate of the morrow was placing its dice into a secret urn for us to cast ...

# 6 September: Eve of the Bloodbath

Later that day, Kutuzov reviewed the regiments and spoke to the soldiers. A shrewd and perceptive man, he knew how to inspire his men. One of them later recalled:

> We listened to him, barely breathing and not feeling [the] ground under our feet – What a man the Lord has created! He could sustain us for days with his caring, genuinely Russian and thoughtful words for which he had a ready tongue, he knew well the road to the soldier's heart.

As he passed his troops, Kutuzov was 'accidentally' overheard muttering, 'The French will break their teeth on us! It will be a pity if, having broken them, we cannot finish them off.' Then, stopping at another regiment, he told the rank-and-file:

> Lads! You have to defend the native land, serve faithfully and truthfully, shedding the very last drop of your blood. Each regiment will be used in this battle and you will be replaced every two hours. I lay my hopes on you and may God help you![203]

Sitting in a bell tower of the Church of the Nativity at Borodino, Glinka could see the entire line:

> that narrowed in some places and swelled in another; all these masses seemed to combine to the right, towards the Old Smolensk Road. It was a remarkable sight! The fields, still not harvested, wavered as a golden sea of harvest and were coloured by the rays of the setting sun. In the midst of this golden sea was a steel river of bayonets and muskets that glittered under the evening sun. Due to the height and thickness of the harvest, people almost could not be seen . . .

Bagration toured his positions too, and Mayevsky recalled him showing deep concern for his troops:

> I was napping in the courtyard when [Bagration] passed by with his retinue. Seeing troops asleep, he ordered to move quietly and silently as we usually do while approaching the room of a beloved who is asleep. Such attention to his troops [. . .] only strengthened their feeling of loyalty to this commander.

Bagration talked to soldiers, many of whom had served with him in previous campaigns and believed he had 'not one but a thousand spare lives'. They listened as Bagration spoke: 'As long as we live – we will be the hope of our beloved Fatherland [. . .] It is thirty years now that with the help of your courage I continue to defeat the enemy. I am always with you and you are with me.' The soldiers shouted in response: 'Lead us, father! We will die with you!'[204]

For one artillery officer, the day seemed fleeting as:

> the sun shined brightly and glided with its golden rays over the fatal steel of our bayonets and muskets. It sparkled with brilliant light on the copper of our guns. Everything was getting ready for the bloodshed of the morrow: the Moscow militiamen were completing earthworks on the battery, the artillerymen prepared and distributed ammunition. Soldiers sharpened bayonets, cleaned

# The Battle of Borodino

sword-belts and shoulder-belts; in short, 300,000 men in both armies were preparing for the great, terrible day. As the night approached, the bivouacs of the warring forces flared with numerous fires all around [...] The fires turned the dark clouds in the sky into a crimson twilight and the flames in the sky only foretold a bloodshed on the ground ...

Muravyev claimed that:

there was a remarkable difference in morale between the two sides: the enemy, inspired by the proclamations of its leader, ignited large campfires, revelled in whatever they had and burnt with rage against us; our troops were equally livid about the French and eager to punish them for invading our Fatherland and the destruction they were spreading, but they also abstained from excesses in food and drinking, which they had in abundance [...] and prayed to the Lord to give them courage and strength and bless them for the desperate battle ahead.[205]

As darkness fell, French officer Vionnet de Maringoné could see the Russian fires arranged as an 'amphitheatre in front of us. The fire of their bivouacs created a unique spectacle and presented a contrast to our own.'[206]

That night 'everyone is silent!' wrote Glinka in one of his letters:

Russians, with clear and untarnished conscience, quietly nap around their smouldering fires. Long shouts can be heard periodically in our skirmisher line and echoes often repeat them. A few stars shine through the cloudy sky [...] On the opposite side: bivouac fires shimmer brightly, music, singing and shouts fill the entire camp. Exclamations can be heard at one point! Then more of them! They certainly welcome Napoleon as he reviews them, as it was done before the battle at Austerlitz. What will happen tomorrow? The wind puts the candle out and sleep gently closes the eyes. Goodbye my friend![207]

Not far from Glinka, another officer had a hard time sleeping, as he felt 'that the battle would be a terrible one ...' Mitarevsky's head

was full of things from books about wars – the 'Trojan War' in particular would not leave my thoughts. I was eager to take part in a great battle, to experience all the feelings of being in one, and to be able to say afterwards that I had been in such a battle.[208]

A German captain spent most of that night by a watch fire with the men of the Fanagoriiskii Grenadier Regiment:

The soldiers were in fairly good order, and as they had had a rest during the last few days, they now sat, wrapped in their long grey coats, round the fires – and often joined in chorus to sing the monotonous, melancholy, dirge-like, yet not unpleasing national songs which the Russian people are so fond of. This singing before the battle had a strange effect on me, and I listened to it for several hours until eventually I fell asleep, exhausted, beside my horse ...[209]

The last night before the battle set a sombre mood in the Russian camp. Officers took out their parade uniforms and soldiers dressed in their white shirts, which were prepared for such occasions:

# 6 September: Eve of the Bloodbath

Sacred silence reigned on our line. I heard as the quartermasters called troops, 'Vodka is here, come whoever wants it! Come and take a goblet!' But no one moved. In some places one even could hear deep sighs and shouts, 'Thanks for this honour! But we are getting ready for a different mission: tomorrow is a special day!' At these words, many veterans made the sign of the cross and added, 'Holy Virgin Mother! Help us defend our land!'[210]

Officers also gathered around campfires and shared their feelings and premonitions. Young artillery commander Alexander Kutaisov was drinking tea and laughing with his fellow officers near Rayevsky's Battery, but his mood changed as the darkness fell over the field. He became more sombre and told his comrades: 'I would love to know who among us would survive tomorrow.'[211] At another camp fire, the officers knew that:

> tomorrow will bring a bloody solution to the problem and, naturally, everyone talked only about this. Someone said, 'It cannot be that all of us would survive such a battle unscathed. Some of us will certainly be killed or wounded.' Others responded, 'It cannot be that I will be killed because I do not want to be killed . . .' Another replied, 'I will be only wounded.' One young and handsome *sous-lieutenant* said, pointing to the opening in the tent, 'Look, can you see that large star in the sky? When I will be killed, I want my soul to settle there.' He was indeed killed in the battle but who knows if his soul reached that star?[212]

Not far away, the 27-year-old Captain Ogarev made the last entry in his journal: 'Our hearts are pure. Soldiers put on clean shirts. Everything is quiet. I and Mitkov looked for a long time upon the sky, sparkling with stars . . .'

The night before the battle proved restless for Napoleon as well. Weakened by his urinary problems, he was now tormented by a high fever, a dry cough, and a burning thirst, which he spent the rest of the night trying to quench. Despite his health, he continued to work, issuing various orders and dictating a proclamation. Ségur asserted that:

> with the night came the old fear that under cover of darkness the Russians might escape from the field of battle. This apprehension disturbed Napoleon's sleep. He kept waking up and calling out, asking what time it was, and if anybody had heard a noise, and each time dispatched someone to see if the enemy was still there. He was so doubtful that he had his proclamation distributed with the order that it should not be read until morning, and then only in case there should be a battle.

According to Baron Fain, Napoleon's secretary:

> The Emperor spent most of the night giving out final orders, and only took a few hours' sleep, and even these were interrupted. At first light, he was up and about. He summoned the aide-de-camp on duty. Auguste de Caulaincourt was not asleep, but half lying down on a camp mattress and wrapped in his coat, with his head propped up on his elbow: he was gazing sadly at a portrait of his

# The Battle of Borodino

young wife whom he had been forced to leave almost as soon as he had married her. One would have said he was bidding her eternal farewell.

The young general had only hours to live ...

Jean Rapp spent the night reading reports from various units. 'The Emperor slept very little,' he recalled:

> I woke him several times to give him reports from the outposts which all proved that the Russians were expecting an attack. At 3am he summoned his valet de chamber and had some punch brought in. I had the honour of drinking some with him.

Napoleon told him:

> Today we shall have to deal with this famous Kutuzov. No doubt you remember that it was he who commanded at Braunau during the Austerlitz campaign. He stayed in that place for three weeks without leaving his room once. He did not even mount his horse to go and inspect the fortifications. General Bennigsen, although as old, is a much more energetic fellow. I cannot understand why [Tsar] Alexander did not send this Hanoverian to replace Barclay.

Napoleon then took a glass of punch, read several reports, and added, 'Well, Rapp! Do you think that we [will] have a successful day?' – 'There is no doubt about [it], Sire. We have used up all our resources and have simply got to win.'

A few minutes later, Napoleon contemplated: 'Fortune is a shameless courtesan. I have often said it, and I am beginning to experience it.' Rapp tried to cheer him up, repeating Napoleon's words, 'the wine had been poured out and must be drunk'. He noted that the Army was ready for battle and 'it knows that there are no provisions to be found except in Moscow and that it has only thirty leagues to go'. Listening to Rapp's words, Napoleon added: 'This poor army is sadly depleted, but what remains is good. And my Guard is still intact.' As Ségur recounted, probably apocryphally, Napoleon then contemplated the nature of war and the future of his campaign. 'His fears overwhelmed him again,' Ségur informs us:

> and he sent out to ascertain the Russian position. He was told that their fires were burning as bright as ever and that, judging by the great number of shadows moving about them, it was not merely a rearguard that was keeping them burning, but a whole army. The presence of the enemy soothed the Emperor ...

Napoleon worked until half-past five, when he called for his horse. As trumpets sounded, drums beat and soldiers greeted him, Napoleon turned to Rapp: 'It is the Austerlitz enthusiasm again.' Fain, accompanying Napoleon to a large group of officers outside his tent, heard the Emperor greet them with: 'It is a trifle cold, but the sun is bright. It is the sun of Austerlitz.'[213]

As the Army began to manoeuvre into position, Colonel Seruzier contemplated that

## 7 September: The Battle of Borodino Phase One (6am to 12am)

never has there been a finer force than the French Army on that day, and despite all the privations it had suffered since Vilna, its turnout on that day was as good as it ever was in Paris when it paraded for the Emperor at the Tuileries.[214]

On Napoleon's orders, a special proclamation was read to the troops:

Soldiers! Now comes the battle you have so much desired! The victory now depends on you: we need it. Victory will give us abundant supplies, good winter quarters and a prompt return to our native lands. Fight as you did at Austerlitz, Friedland, Vitebsk and Smolensk and posterity will remember with pride your conduct on this great day. May it be said of each one of us: 'He fought in that great battle under the walls of Moscow!'[215]

The proclamation was laconic and clear in its message but the reaction varied among the troops. According to Robert Guillemard, the opening sentence of the proclamation showed that 'our impatience was known to the Emperor'. Chambray noted that 'its spirit did not dispose for enthusiasm and the proclamation was met coldly'. However, Laugier recalled how

each colonel had the proclamation read out to his regiment, in parade uniform. We of the Italian Guard, formed up in close columns of companies without intervals between our battalions, listened to it on the reverse slope of the hill, where the Italian battery was. Everyone admired the frankness, the simplicity, the imposing force of this proclamation, so well suited to our circumstances.

Another officer saw how 'the soldiers responded with huzzahs'.[216] Indeed, across the field, Russian Lieutenant Bogdanov could hear as 'the stillness of the night was occasionally interrupted by the shouts of Vive l'Empereur!'[217]

## 7 September: The Battle of Borodino Phase One (6am to 12am)

The Monday morning of 7 September dawned gloomy and cold, with thick fog enveloping the ground. Seeking to draw a parallel between Borodino and Austerlitz, the 18th Bulletin later claimed 'it was as cold as [in] December in Moravia [and] the Army accepted the omen'. Despite such an overcast start to the day, General Yermolov was keenly aware of its importance:

The sun, hidden in the mist, maintained the deception of calm until 6am. Its first rays then illuminated the place where the Russians were ready to accept this unequal battle with complete self-sacrifice! Here, oh majestic Moscow, your die will be cast. A few more hours, and if the firm resolve of the Russians fails to avert the dangers threatening you, ruins will mark the place where you once haughtily rose up and prospered!

Meanwhile, Thirion found:

modern battles [were] a strange thing. Two armies gradually turn up on a piece of ground, place themselves symmetrically facing each other [...] All these preliminaries are carried out with calm barrack-square precision. From one army to the other are heard the commanders' sonorous voices. In sombre silence you observe the mouths of the guns being turned on you, which are going to send you death ...

89

## What Time Did the Battle Start?

The exact timing of the first artillery shot varies greatly in both French and Russian literature. Among the French participants, Planat de la Faye, Vionnet de Maringoné and Castellane indicated 5am; Vaudoncourt, Teste, Laugier, Bourgois, François, Pelet, Griois, and Chambray referred to 6am; while Bourgogne, Brandt, Denniée, Kolachkowski and Le Roy argued it was made as late as 7am. On the Russian side, most participants refer to 6am, but some (Bogdanov) also mention 5am. Kutuzov's first (brief) report of 8 September to Emperor Alexander was somewhat confusing, since it stated that the French attacked 'at 4am, at dawn', which is obviously a mistake, since, at Borodino, the sun does not rise so early at that time of year. Kutuzov's later report was corrected by removing the reference to 'dawn' but retaining the '4am' as the start of enemy 'movement'. Bagration's report referred to an enemy attack 'at the very dawn', while Barclay's noted that the enemy 'movement' was noticed 'before dawn'. Both Paskevich and Yermolov gave the specific time of 6am for the start of the battle.

As he left his tent at dawn, Napoleon set up his observation point in front of the Shevardino Redoubt, from where he could observe the Bagration Flèches to his right and Rayevsky's Redoubt to his left. Surrounded by his entourage, he would remain here for the rest of the day, except for a brief excursion in the afternoon, when he visited the left wing. Many participants, and later generations of scholars, were surprised by Napoleon's inactivity, which was blamed both on his age, exhaustion and poor health. Some noted that they could not recognize in Napoleon the hero of Lodi, Arcole, Austerlitz and Wagram. At the opposite end of the battlefield, Kutuzov awoke at Tatarinovo and then travelled with his escort to Gorki, where he established his command post. Bogdanovich acknowledged that:

> since the battle was being decided on the left wing and in the centre, our commander-in-chief [who remained at Gorki on the right flank] had no direct influence on the course of battle, especially because his old age compelled him to remain in one place and limited him to issuing orders, which, due to his distance from the point of enemy attacks, were not always timely. This circumstance deprived our army of the much needy unity of action and had a disadvantageous effect on the course of the battle.[218]

Around 6am the batteries of Sorbier, Pernetty and Foucher welcomed the dawn with a salvo, and as the Russians returned fire, 'thick clouds of smoke curled from the batteries into the sky and darkened the sun, which seemed to veil itself in a blood-red shroud'.[219] The Polish General Soltyk, standing near Napoleon, 'never heard anything like it. At moments, the uproar was so

# 7 September: The Battle of Borodino Phase One (6am to 12am)

## Who Fired First?

Most participants and scholars acknowledge that the French battery fired the first round of the battle. However, several Russian participants provide a different account. D. Danilov of the 2nd Artillery Brigade later claimed that one of his guns made the first shot of the battle and the French round was only made in return. In his memoirs, Danilov wrote: 'At dawn, the first Russian cannon shot was fired by our battery and this round was made by me personally. The noise of the round resounded through the woods and gave a signal. Everything fell silent but several minutes hardly passed when a long line of French guns, deployed in front of Shevardino, erupted in response.'

Bennigsen, however, believed the first shot was made by Raevsky's battery, obliging Bennigsen to go and investigate it in person.

But then Mikhailovsky-Danilevsky – Kutuzov's adjutant and future historian – noted in his memoirs that: 'the first cannon-ball, fired by the enemy batteries, was directed towards the house occupied by Prince Kutuzov'.

This interesting fact is supported by Kutuzov's ordinance officer Dreyling, who remarked: 'It barely dawned when the enemy fired his first round. One of the very first cannon-balls flew above our heads and shattered the roof of the house where Kutuzov was billeted.'

terrible it was more like broadsides discharged from warships than a land artillery engagement'. Meanwhile, Von Roos was even more awestruck, since the cannonade seemed to him: 'as if all Europe's voices were making themselves heard in all its languages'.

Across the field, Radozhitsky was in the midst of the terrible Russian cannonade: 'The rounds were so frequent that there were no intervals between them: they soon turned into one continuous roar like a thunder-storm, and caused an artificial earthquake.' And for Johann von Dreyling, one of Kutuzov's orderlies,

> The thunder of some thousand guns, musket fire – all of this combined into one continuous rumble; one's consciousness faded away and all feelings became numbed [...] in one moment, you can experience a condition that is impossible to describe, as if you are not feeling anything anymore. Then a doubt sets in, 'Are you still alive?'

It was soon noticed that the French cannon shots were falling short of their targets on the Russian left flank; some scholars have argued that peculiar atmospheric conditions (i.e. morning fog) affected the French fire but the truth is more prosaic. As noted above, the terrain was reconnoitred incorrectly and batteries were set up beyond their effective range. So the cannon had to be quickly moved forward. According to Bogdanovich, the

French had to advance some batteries (Sorbier and Foucher) up to '1,600 steps' before the cannonade resumed with greater fury. Lejeune recalled seeing:

> the projectiles ploughing through our ranks with a hissing noise such as it is impossible to describe. As ill luck would have it, our reserves at the beginning of the struggle, even those of the cavalry, were rather too near the fighting, and, either from vainglory or more likely from fear of giving a false impression to the enemy, they would not retire the few hundred paces needed to place them in a position less exposed to useless danger, so that we had the grief of seeing thousands of gallant cavaliers and fine horses struck down, though it was of the utmost importance to us to preserve them.

Captain Biot knew some of these unlucky victims and saw:

> a horse running along our front, its rider thrown on to its cruppers. I recognized poor Colonel Désirad. A Russian round shot had taken off his cranium [...] everything that fell beyond the second line went on to strike the third; not a shot was lost.

On the Russian side, Radozhitsky watched as 'the enemy shot flew towards us in their last bounds or rolled through the grass with their last impetus. Shells burst in the air and showered splinters with a horrid noise.'

## *Northern Sector – The Village of Borodino*

Two hours before the artillery duel began, Barclay de Tolly received 'a report from [Colonel] Bistrom regarding the enemy movement against the village of Borodino'.[220] Yermolov, standing south-east of the village, also noticed a movement 'in the enemy forces opposite our right flank'. Meanwhile, Bistrom reported that his outposts had detected 'the enemy moving in two columns, probably 8,000 men strong – on the right side of the village'.[221] This body of troops belonged to Napoleon's IV Corps, which, 'taking advantage of a thick fog covering the ground',[222] was advancing towards Borodino. It's commander, Prince Eugène later recalled that:

> the Division of General Morand was on the right, and that of General Gérard behind it; farther to the right and in the rear was the cavalry of General Grouchy, in charge of gaining the area which would allow the best use of his arm [...] at the centre and in echelon of Gérard's Division was placed Broussier's division with the [Italian] Royal Guard behind it. Delzon's division formed the extreme left. It was supported by the light cavalry division under the orders of General Ornano.[223]

According to a Bavarian officer, Wiedemann, after Napoleon's proclamation was read at dawn:

> Ornano's cavalry moved again to occupy its position in the battle line. We initially took a direction towards the village of Borodino, but then turned left and reached the Borodino stream that flowed in a deep ravine [...] A battery was set up in this defile and, on the opposite side from it, the 1st Chevau-léger

brigade was deployed, adjacent to an infantry regiment from Delzon's division. The 2nd Chevau-léger brigade stood on the left side of the battery, while [the] Italian Chasseurs à Cheval were nearby ... [224]

Meanwhile, Nikolai Muravyev, standing near Gorki,

> saw a squadron of enemy Horse Jägers that galloped to the valley in front of our right flank. The cavalrymen dismounted and engaged in a skirmish with our Jägers, who had crossed the Kolocha. Count Osterman-Tolstoy ordered a few cannon-balls to be sent into the horsemen ...

Around 5.30am Eugène ordered Delzon's 13th Division to attack the Russian right flank.[225] As Pelet indicates, the French scouts already knew that the village Borodino was 'well protected from the west but had weaker defences from the north', where Delzon decided to attack after crossing the Voina brook near Bezzubovo. Delzon split his division, in order to attempt a two-pronged attack from the north, and moving in a fog, his troops approached the village of Borodino around 6am, halting there to await the signal before advancing further. When the signal came – an artillery salvo – Delzon quickly ordered his troops forward.

Delzon's first column attacked the village from the north, while the second proceeded along the main road. On the Russian side, the soldiers of the 3rd Battalion of the Life Guard Jäger Regiment were stationed on the northern edge of the village, while some their comrades served on patrol duty along the Voina rivulet. Behind them, the 1st and 2nd Battalions were camped out, supported by an artillery battery.[226] The northern approach was blockaded by barricades and various fences, while the eastern side was reinforced by a series of trenches. The bridge across the Kolocha was defended by the Guard Equipage, which had been established from the crews of the court yacht and galleys in St Petersburg only two years before. In 1812 some 500 of these sailors were assigned to the Guard Jägers of the 1st Western Army. At Borodino the Guard Equipage commander, Captain (2nd class) Ivan Kartsev, selected thirty of his most experienced men (led by Midshipman Lermontov) to destroy the crossing over the Kolocha, should the enemy break through the Guard Jägers. The rest of the Guard Equipage was with V Corps.

As the dawn mist hugged the ground, concealing Napoleon's columns, Barclay de Tolly's adjutant, Vladimir Löwenstern, observed that:

> General Barclay, in complete parade uniform, with all his orders and wearing a bicorn with a black feather, was standing with his entire staff at the battery behind the village of Borodino [...] An artillery cannonade was thundering all around. The village of Borodino, located in front of us, was occupied by the courageous Life Guard Jäger Regiment.[227]

And Pavel Grabbe, Yermolov's adjutant, who was standing on the hill behind the Russian right flank – noticed that:

> Everyone's attention was directed to Borodino [...] Barclay de Tolly insisted it was dangerous and futile to defend this village and suggested recalling the

# The Battle of Borodino

Jägers at once. Duke Alexander of Württemberg argued otherwise and Kutuzov silently listened to both of them.[228]

Realizing the futility of persuading Kutuzov, Barclay de Tolly acted on his own, as Löwenstern recalled:

> General Barclay, reconnoitring the entire vale from the hill, understood the grave danger the Life Guard Jäger Regiment was facing and dispatched me with orders to have it immediately withdrawn from the village and the bridge destroyed.

The French 106th Line was first to reach the village. They were met by a bayonet charge, courtesy of the 3rd Grenadier and 9th Jäger Companies of the Life Guard's 3rd Battalion. This action was ordered by Captain Petin, who, though wounded, deployed his companies 'in battle formation under heavy enemy fire and made a second bayonet charge'.[229] The French repelled two further attacks, forcing the Russian battalion to retreat. The Russians were supported by the 2nd Battalion of Colonel Richter – 'a charming lad and brave like a Bayard'[230] – which opened fire before charging with bayonets, in order to delay the enemy. Richter's men even captured two French staff officers.[231]

In the meantime, Bistrom deployed skirmishers under Staff Captain Rall III (from the 1st Battalion), who covered the retreat of the 3rd Battalion and briefly halted the French. The 106th rallied and launched another attack, only to be countered by a bayonet charge from the 2nd Battalion (supported by the troops of the Guard Equipage). Captain Saint Priest III, who saw 'that the enemy was occupying the bridge and trying to cut off the 2nd Battalion from the 1st and the 3rd, which were already under protection of artillery batteries', led his company in a desperate charge that bought enough time for the rest of the battalion to escape. Simultaneously, Colonel Grabovsky's 1st Battalion defended the artillery battery (twelve guns), which the French tried several times to seize. The battery was soon ordered to withdraw from its position.[232]

The initial French success was due to two major factors, one of them being their superiority in numbers. Equally important, however, was the Russian failure to properly prepare for the attack. Yermolov criticized the commanding officers of the Life Guard Jäger Regiment for:

> the disorder in which the Regiment was caught [...] There was such widespread carelessness on the outposts of this battalion that many lower ranks were asleep, having taken off their uniforms. Other battalions were equally careless, but only few were as disorganized.

One-third of soldiers and almost half the officers of the Life Guard Jägers were either killed or wounded in this brief combat. How did this happen? According to Liprandi, the answer lay in the fact that when the Jägers occupied the village, they

> were jubilant to find large bathhouses in this opulent village and decided to use them that night. Thus, when the French attacked, [the] entire battalion was still

in [the] baths. This is why thirty officers and half of the men were lost [in the subsequent fighting]. Many, leaping out from the bathhouses, barely had time to dress and, grasping their muskets, entered the fighting at once.[233]

Liprandi's account (published in the 1860s) naturally caused a scandal and was bitterly criticized for tarnishing the official version of the battle. But other participants also left an unflattering picture of the commanding Jäger officers, especially of Colonel Makarov. According to Mitarevsky: 'Even I, an artillery officer, thought the Guard Jägers abandoned Borodino too hastily, while the infantry officers were even more unforgiving in their assessment.' Indeed, Sherbinin wrote: 'Oh yes, there was indeed a mist that day, not in the air, but rather in the head of the drunken Makarov, who passed out around 6am and could not order his battalion to arms.' Durnovo explained: 'Makarov was in a state of such intoxication that [it] was simply unpardonable for the commander.'[234] It seems the 3rd Battalion was actually commanded not by Makarov but Colonel Dellagarde, whom Bistrom praised for 'greatly assisting with advices in commanding the 3rd Battalion'.[235] Pushin was also critical of the leadership of the Life Guard Jäger Regiment, which resulted in the loss of so many lives:

> Our Jägers, joining us in the morning, earned severe reprimand for their carelessness and inattentiveness on advance posts, as a result of which, the enemy exacted heavy casualties on them; the Jägers lost many men, without inflicting any heavy damage on the French.

Official reports and other materials contain no criticism of the Life Guard Jägers, one of the élite units of the Russian Army, and Makarov, who was accused of such gross ineptitude, was later awarded the Order of St Vladimir (3rd class) and given command of another élite unit, the famous Pavlograd Grenadiers. The whole affair was largely suppressed, but it did find voice in personal memoirs and letters of participants. It also reveals intrigues and personal relations between officers who sought to justify themselves and tarnish their opponents. Thus Barclay de Tolly remains silent on Makarov's incompetence and instead blames Yermolov, 'who suggested to Bennigsen and Kutuzov to deploy this Regiment [at Borodino]'.[236]

In the meantime, Mitarevsky, standing on the eastern bank of the Kolocha, was anxiously listening to the sounds coming from Borodino. 'The smoke of musket fire soon covered the village,' he recalled, 'A confused fighting occurred on the way out of Borodino, near the bridge; although it was in front of us, and so close that some bullets whizzed by us, we could not see what was happening there because of smoke, dust and fog.' Löwenstern, whom, as you may recall, Barclay de Tolly dispatched to withdraw the Jägers, arrived a minute too late:

> I rushed to the commander of the [Jäger] regiment but General Delzon's column, moving on the main road, was already entering the village [. . .] It was marching quickly ['beglym shagom'] and with a drumbeat. The order to retreat was quickly issued but the withdrawal could not be executed fast enough to

prevent the other French column from reaching the riverbank and deploying a chain of skirmishers, who opened fire at [the] Jägers as they were crossing the bridge. The fire was [very] effective and deadly. The second enemy column, moving quickly along the main road from the village, also approached the bridge and opened the longitudinal fire. We were so crammed [on the bridge] that not a single enemy shot missed its target [...] the combat continued no more than fifteen minutes.

The Russian battery of Lieutenant Colonel Yefremov, deployed on the other end of the bridge, opened a canister fire to silence the enemy and help the Jägers to destroy the bridge. The French countered by a battery from the reserve artillery of IV Corps, which fired at the bridge and the Russian positions on the eastern bank of the Kolocha. Their effective fire forced Yefremov to withdraw his outgunned battery, leaving the Russians struggling to dismantle the bridge under the murderous fire of the French skirmishers. Lieutenant Vonogradsky noted: 'The bridge was destroyed and ignited by the marines with the help of Jägers, acting under heavy enemy fire.' However, in reality, the Guard Equipage troops barely managed to ignite and remove half of the bridge flooring when the French carried the bridge and forced them to flee. Major Petrov later described how:

> the enemy infantry from the Italian Corps, supported by reinforcements, made a vigorous attack on the village of Borodino [...] where the Life Guard Jäger Regiment was forced to abandon the village and the bridge, which was still intact, and allowed the enemy to cross to the right bank of the Kolocha, towards the centre of the general position of our armies.

Thus, by 7.30am, Delzon's division achieved its initial goal of seizing Borodino. As Lejeune noted: 'Prince Eugène, who had, of course, not foreseen that this attack would succeed beyond his hopes, had ordered nothing more than the taking of Borodino.' But with the village already seized, the 106th Line, 'carried away by its bravery',[237] crossed the Kolocha by the mill bridge, as the Russians had done before it, and pursued them to the heights beyond, scaling them rapidly. This was a major mistake, since this riverbank was well defended by the Russians. Colonel Vuich's brigade (19th and 40th Jägers) was deployed in a chain from the bridge to the Stonets stream, with its reserves camped out in front of the bridge. The 1st and 18th Jägers held positions between the Stonets and Semeyonovskii stream and their reserves stood in the ravine of the Ognik brook. The position was further defended by twenty-four guns of the 13th, 45th and 46th Light Companies, which were protected by minor earthworks and trenches.

As the French crossed the Kolocha, Colonel Moses Karpenko, commander of the 1st Jäger Regiment, moved his troops to support the Guard Jägers and drive the French back. Karpenko himself recalled receiving such order from Colonel A. P. Nikitin, although he mistakenly referred to Compans' division assaulting Borodino. According to Major Petrov, Bennigsen personally ordered Karpenko to attack with the 1st Jägers Regiment, since he: 'remembered the regiment's celebrated service in the battles of 1806 and 1807 campaigns'.[238] Karpenko marched at once towards the Stonets stream, where he concealed his troops behind a small hill, while he and his senior officers ascended it to reconnoitre the enemy position. He then instructed Bistrom, who led the remnants of the Life Guard Jäger Regiment, and Captain Raal, who directed the skirmishers, to withdraw 'in a column to remain in reserve and clear the battle front around the bridge for the 1st Jäger Regiment's attack'. Barclay de Tolly meantime instructed Vuich to attack the French flank with his Jäger brigade.

The 106th Line soon found itself in the crossfire of Russian batteries. In the immediate vicinity of Borodino there were six guns of the 13th Light Company, six guns of the 12th Light Company and eighteen guns (led by Yefremov) of the 24th Brigade, which engaged the French with a canister fire. They were supported by Major Ditterix III's eight guns of the 7th Battery Company, set up on the heights west of Gorki. General Kutaisov also diverted two Horse Artillery companies to this front, the 22nd Horse Company (Colonel Khoven), and six guns of the 4th Horse Company (Colonel Merlin).[239]

Thus, within a short time, the Russians managed to gather some fifty-six guns against the French regiment, which, obliged to continue its assault across the bridge, consequently suffered heavy casualties. Lieutenant Grabbe described how he was sent 'to Khoven's Horse Artillery Company with the order to occupy the hill overlooking the bridge [...] This was accomplished very quickly and the attacking French were showered with canister.' Nikolai Divov recalled the arrival of Khoven's guns, which were 'deployed with an unusual fearlessness and opened a devastating fire'.[240] Merlin, reaching the bridge with his 4th Company, deployed four of his guns on the right flank, while two guns led by Sub Lieutenant Zhitov were set up near the bridge. Merlin recalled how Zhitov's division, 'through its skilled and targeted fire, greatly contributed to disordering and repelling an enemy column, as well as in the recapture and destruction of the bridge'.[241] Kutuzov seems to have noticed the actions of Merlin's company, since one of his adjutants soon delivered the Commander-in-Chief's word of commendation and rewarded one of the privates with a military cross.

Yefremov's 46th Light Battery particularly distinguished itself and he was later commended for 'defending the crossing under heavy enemy fire [...] and containing the enemy attack with canister, driving [the French] back on several occasions and forcing the enemy columns to flee'. After being wounded in his left thigh, Yefremov was replaced by Captain Bulashevich, who received two severe contusions to his leg and chest but continued commanding. He was assisted by Staff Captain Kharlamov, who skilfully directed the fire of his six guns, and Lieutenant Lukyanovich, who boldly moved a further six guns closer to the French column, 'forcing it to retreat three times'. His comrade, Lieutenant Sestretsov, commanded the licornes ranged against a French battery set up near the village of Borodino. He was later praised for 'twice forcing the battery to retreat and, finally, approaching it at a canister range, he cleared the position from enemy guns, which did not appear there anymore'.[242]

Watching as this massive artillery firepower was directed against his comrades, Adam could see them 'suffering from a devastating fire from the front and flanks. It was horrible to see as the extended line [of French infantrymen] was ravaged and broken by enemy cannon-balls'.[243] The 106th was saved by the 92nd Line, whose soldiers rushed across the bridge to rescue their comrades.[244] General Plauzonne, who commanded a brigade of the 13th Division, led the charge and, as Labaume described, he 'ran to the bridge to recall [the 106th] when a ball struck him in the middle of his body'. The 38-year-old Plauzonne's death threw his men into momentary confusion, allowing the Russians to sweep down on them. Plauzonne was replaced by Adjutant Commandant Boisserolle, who ordered a retreat and, as Eugène reported, 'took some excellent dispositions for the conservation of the village of Borodino'.[245]

Russian participants provide more details on this counter-attack. Colonel Karpenko – whom Yermolov acidly described as a 'fearless commander, but with intellectual abilities limited to a single order, "Forward!" ' – later wrote that he deployed his regiment in columns, instructing the men to lay down and feign hesitancy about attacking: 'The French, not seeing any resistance on my part, rushed with a drum beat across the bridge and began crossing [to the left bank of the Kolocha].' One of his subordinates described the sequel thus:

> the brave Karpenko could inspire the soldiers to march to their death and gain their good will with silence. After issuing orders to staff and junior officers, and having made the sign of the cross, blessing his regiment, which was ready for battle, he rushed forward to set an example in person.[246]

Major Petrov, serving in the 1st Battalion of the 1st Jäger, recalled Karpenko deploying the 1st Battalion in line in the front, while the 3rd Battalion (led by Major Sibirtsev) remained in a column 'some fifteen steps behind the last line of [the 1st] Battalion'. As mentioned above, these troops were deployed behind a small hill near the bridge and were effectively hidden from the French. Karpenko then quickly rushed with the 1st Battalion on this hillock and made a close-range salvo into the French ranks, which became confused and disordered. The smoke barely cleared when the 3rd Battalion, moving in a column, and the 19th and 40th Jägers of Vuich's brigade, attacking from a flank, made a bayonet charge against the French, who found themselves trapped between the attacking enemy and a narrow, half-destroyed bridge. Worst of all, the Jägers brought up artillery, which opened a near point-blank fire that 'destroyed enemy units with their general, staff and junior officers, and forced them to retreat to the left bank of the Kolocha towards the village of Borodino'.[247] Pursuing them, Karpenko's soldiers found the body of General Plauzonne, whose epaulettes were torn off and sent back to Barclay de Tolly.

# 7 September: The Battle of Borodino Phase One (6am to 12am)

Crossing on the heels of the 106th and 92nd Line, the Russians rushed towards Borodino, the 3rd Battalion of the 1st Jäger Regiment entering the village. But many French accounts either dispute or fail to mention this episode. The Russian progress was checked by Yermolov, who, upon reaching the village, realized that 'isolated from the rest of our forces, the 1st Jäger Regiment was now in a dangerous situation [...] of being cut off'. So he ordered them to abandon the village, withdraw across the river, and burn the bridge. A light artillery company, deployed nearby, drove the enemy tirailleurs back and the action in this area was then limited to an occasional exchange of fire. Prince Eugène's troops secured control over the crossing on the Kolocha and Voina and Delzon's brigade, still skirmishing with the Russian Jägers, halted north of Borodino.

General Anthouard de Vraincourt's guns were soon deployed near Borodino to bombard the Russian positions. Eugène later moved the 22nd Light Cavalry Brigade to the left bank of the Voina and had two squadrons deployed near the village of Bezzubovo, where a Bavarian Horse Artillery battery was also set up. French artillery fire covered almost the entire Russian right flank, reaching the third lines, where, as Norov recalled, 'we spread out on a wide distance to present smaller targets for the enemy cannon-balls'.

The opening act of the battle was now over. The French were in control of Borodino, but as Löwenstern remarked, 'it ceased to play any role in the great drama that would be soon named after it'.

The seemingly futile engagement around the village claimed numerous lives. The Life Guard Jäger Regiment alone lost twenty-seven officers killed and wounded, while its rank-and-file suffered forty-six killed, 527 wounded and 101 missing.[248] After the battle, the men of the Life Guard Jäger Regiment were awarded two Orders of St George (4th class), three Orders of St Vladimir (3rd class), three of St Anna (2nd class) with diamonds, fourteen Orders of St Vladimir (4th class) with ribbon, three Orders of St Anna of 2nd class and sixteen of third class, and nine officers received golden swords for courage.[249] Ninety-four private soldiers were rewarded with the medal of the Military Order, also known as the soldiers' Order of St George. On the French side, the 106th Line had twelve officers killed, six died of wounds and thirty-eight wounded, while its overall casualties reached almost 1,000 men. The 92nd Line lost eight officers and seventy-six soldiers in its attempt to rescue the 106th. Certainly the greatest loss was the death of General Plauzonne, first of the many generals to die that day.

The attack on Borodino had important consequences, since it kept Kutuzov's attention diverted from the left flank. The actions of the 106th Line, which rushed across the Kolocha without orders, were perceived by Kutuzov's staff as part of Napoleon's battle plan and further operations were expected in this direction. As a result, when he received urgent appeals for reinforcements from Bagration on the left flank, Kutuzov delayed sending them until it was clear that there was no immediate threat to his right flank.

# The Battle of Borodino

## *Southern Sector – The Bagration Flèches*

While Eugène made a diversion on Borodino, the main French assault began to the south. Through the dissipating mist, the Russians could see the masses of enemy troops around Shevardino, where Napoleon had concentrated approximately 60,000 infantry, 20,000 cavalry and 297 guns. Davout was destined to carry the burden of the attack, aimed at seizing Bagration's flèches. He was instructed to have

> Compans' Division arranged in brigade columns [...] with 16 guns of the corps' reserve artillery and 14 guns of the Divisional artillery deployed ahead of it. Dessaix's division should be deployed in similar fashion between the captured redoubt and the forest, with 14 guns arranged on its left flank. Friant's division should be placed in brigade columns on the same level as the redoubt.[250]

In total, Davout had about 22,000 men and over 70 guns in the three divisions destined to lead the assault. Marshal Ney was told to deploy his three divisions (about 10,000 men) behind the redoubt, arranging them in brigade columns with the artillery on the left wing. Behind them were two divisions (about 7,500 men) from VIII Corps.[251] Ney's forces were supposed to move around 7am, attacking the village of Semeyonovskoye and supporting Davout's assault to their left. The infantry would be supported by almost 300 guns, which would be gradually employed, while Murat reported that his

> I, II and IV Corps of Cavalry Reserve [about 18,000 men in total] were in columns of each brigade [...] The I Reserve Corps was to support the attack of the I Corps [Davout], the II that of the III Corps [Ney]. The IV [Reserve Cavalry] marched in reserve at the centre and was to support either of those corps according to the need.[252]

On the Russian side, the flèches were occupied by Vorontsov's 2nd Combined Grenadier Division, with one battalion in each flèche and the remaining eight battalions deployed in the second line beyond the redoubts. The southern flèche was protected by twelve guns of the 32nd Battery Company, while the 11th Battery Company had eight guns in the northern flèche and four cannon in the middle flèche. The grenadiers were also supported by the 1st Don Cossack Artillery Company and four guns of the 21st Light Company, and some sources suggest that 2nd and 12th Battery Companies might also have had some guns near the flèches. Behind the grenadiers was Neverovsky's 27th Division, arranged in battalion columns and reinforced by the 3rd Battery Company. Bagration deployed the 2nd Grenadier Division (Prince Mecklenburg-Schwerin) at Semeyonovskoye, where a small redoubt (with six guns of the 1st Battery Company) was constructed on the north-western edge of the village. The 31st Battery Company was set up on the opposite corner of the village. Closer to Rayevsky's Redoubt was the 12th Division and, behind it, IV Cavalry Corps. Duka's 2nd Cuirassier Division (twenty squadrons) was south-east from Semeyonovskoye.

# 7 September: The Battle of Borodino Phase One (6am to 12am)

To further strengthen his defences, Bagration had moved his artillery reserve closer to the first line, bringing as much firepower as possible to bear upon the advancing French. While the precise number of guns employed is difficult to establish, it is possible to ascertain that 172 cannon were gathered in this direction, with over 50 deployed in and around the flèches, some 40 at Semeyonovskoe and the rest in the reserve. Bagration took advantage of thick brushes and woods on the western side of the Semeyonovskii ravine to deploy there the six battalions of the 6th, 49th and 50th Jäger Regiments, while the 5th, 41st and 42nd Jägers were extended in a skirmisher line along the Kamenka brook as far as the Utitsa woods. Shakhovsky's detachment (20th and 21st Jägers, and two Combined Grenadier Battalions of the 3rd Division) was concealed in the Utitsa woods. In total, Bagration had about 25,000 infantry and 2,500 cavalry in the vicinity of the flèches. By the end of the day, this number would increase to some 40,000 infantry and over 11,000 cavalry.

Around 6.30am, following the artillery bombardment, Davout ordered the advance. One of the French officers could see the effect the artillery barrage had on the vicinity, where

> the peaceful plain and silent slopes erupted in swirls of fire and smoke, followed almost at once by countless explosions and the howling of cannon shot ripping through the air in every direction.[253]

Mayevsky recalled that:

> The dawn of 26 August turned into a real hell! Our wretched corner, that is, the left flank [...] drew the fire from the entire artillery of the French Army. Bagration was correct in saying that there was no place for a coward there that day.

As Compans' men advanced towards the woods, they 'disappeared into a cloud of dust infused by a reddish glow by the radiant sun...' as Dumonceau recalled, adding: 'The deafening din of our cannonade was interspersed with a sound that seemed like a distant echo.'[254]

Compans had two objectives, securing the flèches and clearing the nearby woods of Russian Jägers that might harass the French flank. His troops moved in two columns: the one on the left (57th and 111th Line) moving towards the southern flèche, and the one on the right (61st and 25th Line) advancing against Russian Jägers from the brigades of General Shakhovsky and Colonel Glebov. To the left, and slightly behind Compans, the 4th Division of Dessaix (except for two battalions of the 85th Line, left behind to protect battery) was also advancing in column. Friant's division remained in reserve.[255]

Entering the woods, the French came under the Jägers' fire and their progress was delayed. As Shakhovsky reported, his adjutant Stepanov, 'observing an enemy column marching towards our battery, gathered about thirty skirmishers ['strelkov'] from various regiments', who engaged the enemy at once.[256] Thus, Ney's warning to Compans, that the march through woods would delay the attack, began to materialize, as there were more Jägers in this thick woods than Compans had expected. Compans' men became involved in the protracted skirmishing and precious time was wasted. In order to proceed with the attack, Colonel Charrière sent the 1st and 2nd Battalions of the 57th Line through the forest to engage the Jägers, while the 3rd, 4th and 6th Battalions turned left to flank the southern flèche.[257] Yet, as the French emerged from the forest, they encountered devastating canister fire, which caused frightful casualties to their dense columns. Löwenstern, on the Russian end of the guns, recalled that:

> The execution wrought by our batteries was frightful and the enemy columns faded away perceptibly despite the continual reinforcements which arrived. The more effort the enemy put into the attack, the higher their casualties piled up.[258]

As the French regrouped for a new assault, Compans, who had suffered an injury to his arm two days before, again fell wounded 'along with the bravest of his soldiers' (Ségur). General Teste replaced him and rallied the troops, supported by the 1st Battalion of the 111th Line.[259] The French demonstrated magnificent courage during this assault, especially the 57th Line, which living up to its nickname 'Le Terrible', advanced steadily with muskets levelled, but withholding fire despite growing casualties. Impressed by the courage of these soldiers, Bagration clapped his hands several times and yelled 'Bravo, bravo!'[260]

Through the deafening artillery thunder, Dutheillet de Lamoth, of the 57th Line, was still able to discern the command to assault the flèche. Running with his comrades from the 6th Battalion, he followed in the wake of the 3rd and 4th Battalions, which were already fighting on the parapets of the flèche. According to Löwenstern: 'the enemy impetus against the [Russian] battery was so powerful that it was forced to retreat'.

As the Russian gunners began to quickly remove the guns from the flèche, the grenadiers deployed in support engaged the French in bitter hand-to-hand combat, but it was an unequal struggle. One French soldier looked on as 'a brave [Russian] officer, seeing his men about to fall back, placed himself across the entrance to the redoubt and did everything he could to prevent them leaving it but was shot through the body'. Almost all the Russian grenadiers were killed.

Some French troops pursued the retreating Russians and Dutheillet de Lamoth later recounted, with a certain swagger, that he and his companions of the 6th Battalion advanced over 'two hundred paces' beyond the flèche before Major Yager ordered them to immediately return. Even so, the soldiers 'resisted his orders, wanting to pursue the enemy and telling the officer he had sent to us, "Have us supported by other troops."'[261]

As the left column (57th Line and a battalion of the 111th Line) of the 5th Division entered the flèche, the right column – General Guyardet with the 61st and 25th Line – was fighting the Russian Jägers in the woods. Informed of the capture of the flèche, Guyardet initially dispatched two companies of voltigeurs to secure the woods close to the flèche and then led the rest of the 61st and 25th Line towards the flèche itself. Meanwhile, the 1st and 2nd Battalions of the 57th and the 5th and the 6th Battalions of the 111st Line were still engaged in the forest. Two other Battalions (2nd and 3rd) of the 111th Line were kept back to defend artillery battery.[262]

The 4th Division of Dessaix was, by now, in the heat of the action and General Friederichs moved his 85th Line by quick march through the woods, which only exhausted the troops, while Dessaix himself, accompanied by his adjutants du Bourget, Girod de l'Ain and Marquiaut, rode forward to assume command of the 5th Division after Compans was wounded.[263] Dessaix was now in formal command of both divisions but General Friederichs exercised actual command of the 4th Division, while General Teste led the 5th Division.[264] Girod de l'Ain, riding a white horse:

> got there just as the first redoubt had been taken by storm. They were nothing but redans, that is chevron-shaped campaign works not closed at their throat, in such a way that the enemy's second line swept their interior with the sharpest musketry and grape. So it was a lot harder to gain a foothold and stay there than to have stormed them.

Dessaix 'remained a few instants totally exposed beside one of the redoubts, examining the Russian units' position and movement', when a musket ball smashed a bottle of brandy, which Dessaix carried in his saddle holsters. 'It was more than he could take not to exclaim angrily, turning to [Girod de l'Ain]: "I owe that to your damned white horse!"' General Teste was less lucky, as a canister shot soon shattered his right hand.[265] His adjutant, Mouchon, was mortally wounded and Dutheillet de Lamoth, short of footwear, 'stripped the unfortunate, still not cold, of the boots he had on his feet to put them on my own!' Soon after, Major Yager, of the 57th, was killed as well.

Meantime, Vorontsov, 'noticing that one of the redoubts on my left flank was lost', charged with the 2nd Battalion of the Grenadier Division to reclaim it. Bagration also ordered Neverovsky to counter-attack with several battalions of his division.[266] The Russian infantry attack and artillery fire soon prevailed and forced the French out of the flèche. This is, however, a very contentious issue since, as we will see later in this section, both sides claimed success in the fighting around the flèches.

As for Poniatowski's supporting assault on the extreme Russian left, this had now been delayed. In effect, the Poles could not now threaten Bagration's wing to support Davout's charges. Furthermore, Marshal Davout, riding forward to rally Compans' men at the very beginning of the attack, had his horse shot from under him, throwing him to the ground and inflicting a severe contusion.[267] The rumour quickly turned Davout's concussion into a violent death, the news of which stunned Napoleon. Davout had to send his aide-de-camp to assure the Emperor that he was still alive. According to Murat:

upon receiving the word the Prince of Eckmühl [Davout] had been [only] wounded, [Napoleon] gave me orders to go and take command of the I Corps if the Prince was not in condition to resume his command. I returned to inform His Majesty that the Prince had told me his wound was only a contusion and that he was able to continue to command.[268]

Considering the less-than-friendly relations between these two marshals, Davout's response was hardly surprising. Still, Napoleon sent Rapp, his aide-de-camp, to assist Davout. Then, 'observing the enemy's movements through his telescope', the Emperor ordered Ney to advance.[269] That first hour of waiting must have been nerve-wracking for the men of the III Corps as they stood awaiting orders. Pelleport, of the 18th Line, recalled 'complete silence reigning in our ranks [...] Everyone was deep in thoughts and emotions.' But not everyone was in such sombre mood. Lossberg, sitting on his horse, was writing letters (he managed to finish three of them) home. The Westphalian troops mainly consisted of young conscripts and Captain Franz Morgenstern of the 2nd Westphalian Line described a fascinating scene as the battle developed:

> We had already suffered casualties when my senior sergeant, who had seen much action in his past service [...] delighted me with his sense of humour when he came up to me and suggested that I order the three flankers next to me to stick out their tongues. This I did and was surprised to see that all their tongues were as white as their uniforms! I at once ordered others to do the same; theirs, too were white. The sergeant assured me that this was the case with all men who were going into action for the first time. Of course, I had to put this to the proof and demanded that he show me his tongue; he obliged immediately – it was lobster-red! 'And yours, captain?' he grinned. 'We will just let that remain my secret,' I replied. The 'tongue test' spread quickly to neighbouring companies and caused considerable hilarity as they were all white.

Around 7am, as Suckow described, the troops were told that the Russian fortifications were already seized. The III Corps, inspired by the news, was then ordered to advance. The 10th Division marched first, arranged 'in attack columns, with its last regiments in battalion columns deployed at the distance of a division, ready to form square and to serve as reserve'. It was followed by the 25th and 11th Divisions and the 8th (Westphalian) Corps, which was moving in two columns.[270] Count Ségur could see as 'Rapp galloped up to replace Compans and led the troops at a run with levelled bayonets against the redoubt.'[271] As he reached the flèches, Rapp placed Dessaix's 4th Division in the first line and moved the worn out 5th Division into the second. Rapp himself was at the head of the 61st Line, 'whom I had known in Upper Egypt [in 1798]; there were still a few of the officers from that period and it was very strange to meet them again'. It is unclear if Rapp's attack was successful but he himself described that 'the firing was still terrible; cannon-balls and shells rained down all round me'.

Noticing the French reinforcements, Bagration also began to concentrate his forces. He rallied the 27th Division and Vorontsov's grenadiers around the flèches and requested four battalions of the 12th Division, then assigned to the 27th Division. The artillery was told to concentrate its fire on the narrow front around the flèches. Bagration then ordered the 2nd Cuirassier Division to cross the Semyenovskii stream and instructed Sievers to 'dispatch some cavalry to support the infantry deployed inside the two flèches on forward positions'. The Novorosiiskii Dragoon and the Akhtyrskii Hussar Regiments were ordered to move forward at once.[272]

Unaware of events unfolding further south, Bagration asked Lieutenant General Tuchkov, who formally was not under his command, to send the 3rd Division of the III Corps. However, Tuchkov himself faced an attack and barely had troops to spare. Furthermore, his relations with Bagration were somewhat strained. Mayevsky was quite outspoken when he noted:

> [Bagration's] two requests to Tuchkov remained unanswered because of Tuchkov's dislike of Bagration. The third dispatch was entrusted to me and I delivered it to Tuchkov, telling him, in decisive terms, the will of [Bagration]. The 3rd Division [...] [was] then sent back with me ...

Mayevsky also complained that Konovnitsyn was 'ridiculously pedantic' and 'acting under the Yellow Book, interrogated me and then took me as a captive, fearing deception or treason'.[273] According to Vistitsky, 'Bagration sent several requests to [Tuchkov] to attack into the rear and the flank of the enemy from Utitsa but the latter, sadly, brushed him off noting that "he is an experienced general and knows what to do."'[274]

Bagration then appealed for help to Kutuzov, who initially refused it, since his attention was diverted by Eugène's attack on Borodino. But as the combat in this sector died down, Kutuzov realized there was little chance of a major French attack from this direction and the weakness of the left wing became more apparent. Bagration was promised the II Corps, which started a long march from the extreme right to the left. Yet it would take at least one hour before it would arrive, thereby providing the French with time to prepare and launch another attack.

Bennigsen had travelled to the left wing that morning and, despite the early morning mist, he was able to observe French forces advancing against Bagration. As he recalled

> I rushed back to Prince Kutuzov and told him, 'If you do not want to have your left wing routed [...] you need to hurry up with dispatching your troops from the right flank. If only they could arrive there in time.'[275]

Kutuzov listened to him and ordered General Lavrov to move part of his V Corps closer to the left flank. Bennigsen's testimony should be seen in light of Lavrov's subsequent battle report, which claimed that he was acting on the orders of Colonel Toll, who was sent by Barclay de Tolly.[276] Yet the Guard regiments were moved from reserve without Barclay de Tolly's knowledge. Kutuzov issued the order on his behalf and Toll delivered it to Lavrov. Furthermore, Bennigsen also instructed Lavrov, circumventing Barclay de Tolly, to send the Life Guard Izmailovsk and Lithuanian Regiments, and the Combined Grenadier Brigade [...] to the left wing.[277] The precise timing of the Guard units' departure is hard to determine. Lavrov claimed it was around 5am, but this would not explain Bagration's urgent appeals for more troops. Colonel Kutuzov of the Life Guard Izmailovskii Regiment reported that: 'around 6am, Colonel Khrapovitsky ordered to arrange Battalion columns for attack and leave the reserve, where we remained until then, to assume position in the front line'.[278] One can assume that the troops would have taken about an hour to change their position and reached Semeyonovskoye after 7am.

It remains unclear which units were dispatched in this first wave of reinforcements. Toll noted that Kutuzov dispatched three regiments of the 1st Cuirassier Division, eight guns of the Guard Horse artillery, the Life Guard Izmailovskii and Litovskii Regiments, and two artillery companies. However, Toll's information seems incomplete. Buturlin, based on Lavrov's report, acknowledged all of these units, plus a brigade of combined grenadiers. Mikhailovsky-Danilevsky referred to Borozdin II's brigade, the Life Guard Izmailovskii and Litovskii Regiments, and three artillery companies. Bernhardi referred to the Izmailovskii, Litovskii and Finlyandskii Regiments, eight battalions of combined grenadiers and two Guard battery companies.

Neither Kutuzov nor Bennigsen took the trouble of informing Barclay de Tolly of these changes. That morning, as 'cannon-balls and grenades literarily exploded the earth all around', Barclay de Tolly rode southward to inspect the troops, coming across the Life Guard Preobrazhenskii and Semeyonovskii Regiments from Lavrov's V Corps. The soldiers greeted him:

> calmly, standing with a true military bearing. Enemy cannon-balls already began to devastate their ranks but they remained steadfastly and silently with their muskets and quietly closed their ranks as soon as cannon-balls hit their victims.

After directing the artillery fire, Barclay de Tolly dispatched his adjutant, Löwenstern, to tell Lavrov 'not to dispatch any units of his corps under any pretext and let the troops rest as much as possible, and remain ready to advance at the first order'. Löwenstern was surprised to find Lavrov 'in [a] most miserable condition: he was paralysed and could not move his legs, move or ride a horse. In [a] physical sense, he embodied powerlessness itself'. Lavrov told him that he could not carry out Barclay de Tolly's order since Toll had already moved regiments to support Bagration. Learning of this, Barclay de Tolly 'lost his usually impassiveness, his eyes burning with anger', and he exclaimed:

> So, Kutuzov and Bennigsen consider this battle already lost while it is just starting. At nine o'clock in the morning, they already commit reserves that I wanted to commit no earlier than 5 or 6 o'clock in the evening.

Incensed, Barclay de Tolly spurred his horse towards Kutuzov's encampment. The Russian Commander-in-Chief, surrounded by a 'numerous and glittering suite', was sitting on a horse near the village of Gorki. Löwenstern could see from a distance that

> Barclay de Tolly told him something in [a] passionate manner; I could not hear what they discussed but it appeared that Kutuzov tried to calm Barclay. A few minutes later, the latter galloped back, telling me, 'At least, they now will not waste the rest of the reserve.'

The fact that Kutuzov committed his reserves – and élite Guard units at that – right at the very beginning of the battle was later concealed. As one Russian historian argued:

> a firmly established legend that the Russian Guard units entered the fight for the village of Semeyonovskoye only around noon was invented in order to conceal the time when it became necessary to use this 'privileged force'; at the same time, questions could have been raised at Kutuzov's complete 'carelessness' towards the most exposed sector in the Russian position.[279]

Ney's troops reached the Russian positions between 7.30–8am. Ney let the 11th Division (Razout) carry the northern flèche while he turned the 10th and 25th Divisions south to support Davout's already fatigued soldiers in securing the southern flèche. Ney's decision to divert two divisions south to support Davout and the entire VIII Corps to assist the Poles was of great importance. As a result, he weakened his forces marching towards their main goal of Semeyonovskoye. In addition, the troops of I and III Corps became intermingled and, with many officers disabled, the command structure became increasingly confused. Rapp warned Ney of the danger of having his 'troops mixed up with my own'. Meanwhile, with two marshals and an imperial aide-de-camp present, the overall chain of command also became convoluted.

As Pelleport described, Ledru's division advanced through thick brushwood on the right flank of III Corps, and then turned right to meet up with Davout's men. As it turned out, Ney arrived in time to drive the Russians back from the southern flèche, which 'was attacked at the same time by the troops of the I Corps'.[280] According to Bogdanovich: 'Ney, at the head of the 24th Light, and supported by the 57th Line [from Compans' Division] seized the outmost [left] flèche. Meantime, other regiments of Ledru's division broke into the right flèche.'[281]

But the French now discovered there was a third fortification built behind the front two. The flèches occupied by the French were open in the rear and afforded no protection from the heavy artillery directed against them. Ney himself reported that the Russians, 'recovering from their first shock, turned around and went back to retake the flèche. But the 25th Division marched at that same moment to support the 10th Division and the enemy was repulsed'. He also acknowledged the bitter fighting around the right flèche, which was seized by Razout's troops: 'The enemy's renewed efforts, although making successively several charges of infantry and cavalry, were in vain ...'[282] Captain Bonnet (4th battalion of the 18th Line) provided further details:

> By a movement to our right, we passed through some bushes and came close to the first flèches, which was carried by our leading troops. Whereon the regiment marched on the second [rear] flèche, its four battalions in line one behind another and the leading battalions seized the flèche together with four damaged guns. Half-way between the first and the second redoubts Commandant Fournier was wounded and I took command of the battalion, reforming it into column on the ditch of the redoubt we have just taken. I have got the flag and was awaiting the moment to act. The colonel [Pelleport] approached me on foot and I asked his permission to send the flag back to that part of the regiment which was close to the first redoubt and in sight of the copse from which we emerged. It was done.

Musket and artillery fire combined with hand-to-hand combat to create carnage all around the flèches, inflicting heavy casualties on both sides. The scene appalled a Russian participant, who exclaimed:

> A hellish day! I have gone almost deaf from the savage, unceasing roar of both artilleries. Nobody paid any attention to the bullets, which were whistling, whining, hissing, and showering down on us like hail. Even those wounded by them did not hear them: we had other worries![283]

Dreyling, standing amidst Kutuzov's suite, could observe from a distance as the French 'advanced with reckless courage against our batteries [flèches]; drenched in blood, they were seized by the enemy and then recaptured by our troops on several occasions'.[284] Bagration later reported: 'The battle was the most savage, desperate and murderous that I have witnessed. Enemy corpses were piled [in front of us] and this place became a graveyard for the French. We, however, suffered equally heavy casualties ...'[285]

Bonnet, whom we just saw proudly holding the flag of the 18th Line, soon saw the Russian sharpshooters 'arriving in good order to the left and a dense infantry column to our right. I deployed my battalion and, without firing, marched strait at the column. It recoiled.' However, the French were now exposed to the Russian artillery and Bonnet's battalion was soon 'failing and being breached like a crenulated wall. But we still went on.' The 18th Line soon run into another Russian column that was 'marching gravely and without hurry' and had to turn around and slowly withdraw back into the flèche. Yet, as Bonnet tells us, 'the place, being open on its side, was untenable. I was the last to jump up on to its parapet, just as a Russian was about to grab my greatcoat. In one leap, I jumped the ditch. They must have fired 20 shots at me, without hitting anything except my shako. We withdrew as far as to the bushes near the first redoubt.' But even here the 18th Line could not find a safe spot. It was charged by the Russian cuirassiers and driven further back to the woods. With his men scattered all over the field, the regiment could rally no more than one battalion by late morning.

# 7 September: The Battle of Borodino Phase One (6am to 12am)

Meantime, on the Russian side, Vorontsov, leading his battalions in a desperate charge to reclaim the flèches, was seriously wounded in the leg and would later declare that 'my resistance was not of long duration but it stopped only after my division ceased to exist'.[286] Neverovsky recalled 'leading several bayonet charges', while his division 'performed its duty of honour and gallantry here, thwarting several enemy attempts to recapture the flèches'.[287] The continuous attacks indulged in by both sides only increased the butcher's bill. As one officer of the 27th Division described: 'Our division was virtually annihilated [...] When the remaining troops were rallied, only 700 men gathered [...] Just 40 men survived from my regiment ...'[288] Vorontsov summed it up:

> Fate cast me the lot of being the first in the long list of generals who were disabled that dreadful day [...] An hour after the fighting began my division ceased to exist. Out of about 4,000 men, there were less than 300 at the evening roll-call and out of eighteen staff officers only three survived, and only one of them was not wounded [...] We did not perform any great feats but there was not a single man amongst us who fled the battle or surrendered. If I were asked the following day where my division was, I would have responded as did Count [Pedro Henriquez d'Azevedo y Toledo] of Fuentes at the Battle of Rocroi [in 1643], pointing my finger to our position and proudly declaring, 'Here it is.'[289]

As Vorontsov's and Neverovsky's men were dying around the flèches, the Novorosiiskii Dragoon and the Akhtyrskii Hussar Regiments, which Bagration earlier ordered Sievers to commit, arrived in time to engage the French.[290] The French quickly countered Bagration's cavalry charge with the 14th Light Cavalry Brigade of Beurmann, who formed his troops into three ranks, with the 4th Chasseurs à Cheval in the first, followed by the 2nd Leib Württemberg Chevau-léger and 1st Prinz Heinrich Württemberg Chevau-léger. The Russian cavalry routed the 4th Chasseurs à Cheval – already in disorder due to the Russian canister fire – and as the French troopers quit, they spread disorder to 2nd Leib Württemberg Chevau-léger Regiment behind. But Colonel von Falkenstein of the 1st Württemberg Chevau-léger Regiment, standing in the third line, quickly opened intervals to let the chasseurs through, and then supported the 2nd Württemberg Chevau-léger to repel the Russian charge. Sievers observed that: 'our infantry did not support this attack and [the cavalry] was forced to retreat beyond the rearward flèche'.[291] As the French chasseurs rallied behind them, the Württemberg cavalry charged the Russians. Their speed and thrust was strong enough to drive the Russian cavalrymen off the field and gain time for the French infantry to arrive.

Vasilchikov's cavalrymen were rescued by the arrival of Duka's 2nd Cuirassier Division, which attacked the Württembergers in rear and flank. Facing five fresh cuirassier regiments, the Württembergers had no choice but to abandon their trophies and fight their way out. The 3rd Württemberg Horse Artillery Battery was still moving forward to support its compatriots when the Russians suddenly overwhelmed it and seized six guns.[292] Girod de l'Ain, marching with Dessaix's troops between the southern flèche and the woods, described the Russian attack on Pernetty's battery:

> We had advanced a certain distance and were standing in column on the edge of a wood stretching away to our right, when we saw a charge of Russian cuirassiers coming at us like a tempest. They were not exactly aiming at us, but at a battery [...] which under cover of our advance, had come and taken up position a little to our left rear. Although this charge suffered from our fire as it passed us, it did not slow it down [...] sabring those gunners who were not able to throw themselves down between the wheels of the guns and ammunition wagons.

Lieutenant Vossen also watched as the 'enemy cavalry soon counter-attacked and penetrated our ranks, capturing both guns and men'.

Duka's troops then split up into groups that pursued the enemy and engaged Dessaix's 4th Division. The 85th Line managed to organize itself against the cuirassiers but the 108th Line suffered from the charge. The fortunes of the battle swung back and forth as both sides sustained many casualties. Louis Planat de la Faye described the horrors of the fight:

> The struggle which developed was one of the most murderous I have ever seen [...] The cannon-balls and shells rained down like hail, and the smoke was so thick that only at rare intervals could one make out the enemy masses.

The 24th Light and survivors of the 57th Line, deployed inside the southern flèche – which, as noted above, was open at the rear – was exposed to the Russian canister fire and barely held ground. The redoubt was soon occupied by the fleeing Württembergers and the pursuing Russian cuirassiers, who trapped some of their enemies inside the fortification. Heavily armoured and with straight-bladed swords, the cuirassiers inflicted heavy casualties on the French, forcing some of them to flee over the shattered ramparts.

The French inside the southern flèche were rescued by the arrival of the three Württemberg battalions, led by Lieutenant General von Scheeler. The 1st Württemberg Battalion, joined by survivors of the 57th Line, stormed the flèche, driving the cuirassiers out of it. The 72nd Line of the 10th Division also supported this attack. The newly arriving 2nd and 3rd Württemberg Battalions then took up positions to the left and right of the flèche. According to regimental reports of the 61st and 111th Line, some Russian cuirassiers did charge beyond the flèches to threaten a French battery (probably Pernetty) and the 61st and 25th Line, led by Guyardet, deployed between the flèche and the Utitsa woods. The French troops, protecting the battery, opened fire, forcing the cuirassiers to turn left and retreat between the flèche and Guyardet's troops, who deployed in squares and fired upon them. According to reports, the Russians made several more charges before they were forced to retreat.[293]

Falling back before Nansouty's cavalrymen, some Russian cuirassiers were charged by the 6th Polish Lancer Regiment, and as they retreated, came across the 2nd Württemberg Battalion, deployed outside the flèche.

# 7 September: The Battle of Borodino Phase One (6am to 12am)

They would have overwhelmed the Württembergers had it not been for the swift reactions of their commander, Colonel von Stockmayer, who ordered his third rank to turn and face the enemy. This crucial manoeuvre was executed with remarkable order and precision and disaster was averted. Meanwhile, the 3rd Württemberg Battalion, deployed nearby, formed square against the Russian horsemen, who now had to endure close-range fire from front and left – courtesy of the Württembergers – while Nansouty's cavalry charged them from the rear. Girod de l'Ain claimed that out of 1,500 cuirassiers, 'scarcely 200 got back to their lines. All the rest, men and horses, remained on the ground. I do not recall our taking a single prisoner'. Still, there were some Russians taken, including Colonel Sokovnin, commander of the Novgorod Cuirassier Regiment, who was wounded and captured.

As the Russian cavalry retreated to regroup, Dessaix's men could see 'a mass of infantry' that had advanced behind the Russian cavalry:

> Left exposed and isolated after the cuirassiers' retreat, it had halted. And in the same instant we saw it as it were swirling around itself and then retiring in some disorder. As it did so, however, it, in turn, unmasked a battery, which sent us several volleys of grape, causing us considerable losses.

Among the many dead and wounded was Rapp, as he described:

> Within the space of an hour I was hit four times, first quite slightly by two shots, then by a bullet in my left arm [...] Soon afterwards I received a fourth wound, when grapeshot hit me on the left thigh and threw me off my horse.

This was the twenty-second wound of Rapp's military career! Forced to retire from the field, Rapp was replaced by General Dessaix, who, for the second time, took command of the 4th and 5th Divisions. When Rapp reached headquarters his wounds were dressed by Napoleon's surgeon and the Emperor came to see him: 'So it is your turn again,' he said, and then inquired about the situation around the flèches. 'Sire I think you will be forced to send in your Guard,' Rapp replied, but Napoleon paid no heed to it: 'I shall take care not to. I do not want it destroyed. I am certain to win the battle without the Guard becoming involved.'

Meantime, suffering from the Russian fire, the 108th and 85th Line slowly withdrew towards the woods. However, Dessaix was wounded in process after grapeshot shattered his right forearm.[294] The command of the 4th Division now passed to Friederichs, who wisely kept his men in the woods to protect from the canister. The casualties, however, continued to mount. When Girod de l'Ain, who accompanied Dessaix to an ambulance, returned to the line, Colonel Anchard of the 108th Line, already wounded several times, pointed towards a handful of men grouped around a regimental eagle, telling him: 'That is all that is left of my regiment.' Behind the 4th Division, Compans' troops (25th, 57th, 61st and 111th Line) continued to lose men and, as Vossen testifies, 'the enemy deployed guns and howitzers on the edge of the woods and opened fire against our lines. Generals and staff officers appeared at the front and we could hear them yelling, "Advance intrepidly, comrades! Soldiers, forward!"' The 61st and 57th Line moved into the woods but were still unable to avoid the Russian skirmishers. Nearby, at the edge of the woods, the 111th Line fought off the Russian cavalry while simultaneously trading shots with Jägers, still harassing them from behind the trees.

The fighting around the flèches was chaotic and the precise course of events in this section remains difficult to ascertain. Thus, Russian/Soviet and Western historians differ on the number of attacks on the flèches. The latter usually acknowledge three major assaults by the French divisions, while some Soviet scholars – in an attempt to embellish Russian exploits – refer to eight epic assaults on Bagration's positions. The honour of capturing the flèches was later bitterly disputed by the troops of Davout and Ney. Some participants, especially from the regiments engaged in this combat, argued that the southern flèche was seized during the initial attack and retained for

## A Cantinière at Borodino

During the bloody combat around the flèches, voltigeur corporal Dumont of the 61st Line, wounded in the upper arm, struggled to conceal his injury, in order to lead his soldiers. But the pain soon forced him to seek an ambulance.

As he quit the battle, he saw Florencia, a Spanish *cantinière* of his regiment, who 'was in tears [since] some men had told her that nearly all the regiment's drummers were killed or wounded'. Despite his anguish, Dumont agreed to help her find these unfortunate men. And so under canister and musket hail, 'we were walking amidst wounded men. Some moved painfully and only with difficulty, while others were being carried on litters [...] When she caught sight of all the drums of the regiment strewn on the ground [Florencia] became like a mad-woman. 'Here, my friend, here!' she yelled, 'They are all here!' And so they were, lying with broken limbs, their bodies torn by grapeshot. Mad with grief, she went from one to the other, speaking softly to them. But none of them heard her. Some, however, still gave signs of life, among them one drum-major she called her father. Stopping by him and falling on her knees she raised his head and poured a few drops of brandy between his lips.'

As she mourned her comrades, Florencia was suddenly struck by a musket ball in her left hand, which 'crushed her thumb and entered the shoulder of the dying man she was holding'. Dumount tried to carry the unconscious Florencia to the ambulance but, with his agonizing wound, it was more than he could do. Fortunately, a French cavalry-man came by and 'without much ado he lifted up the young Spaniard and carried her like a child' to the Guard artillery ambulance, where Larrey himself operated on her, amputating her finger.

the rest of the day. Thus, Colonel Charrière of the 57th Line claimed that his regiment seized and remained inside the southern flèche for hours, despite repeated Russian attacks. He did, however, acknowledge that he had appealed for help to General Ledru, because the 57th Line was running out of ammunition and could not retain the flèche unless reinforcements were received at once.[295] Murat and Rapp recalled seeing flèches captured and then 'two of them relinquished' by the Russians but it is unclear which two and when. Suckow believed that the redoubt changed hands many times before being captured by his comrades from the 25th Division. Scheler's report claims the honour of seizing the flèches belonged to his Württemberg troops. Pelet and Chambray described how the French succeeded in seizing the flèches only to be driven back by the Russians. In his report, Ney described the capture of the flèches as follows:

> The 10th Division, driving back the enemy skirmishers and advance elements, approached the left redoubt with great valour. This redoubt was then attacked by the troops of the I Corps, and the 24th Light and the 57th Line entered inside it, getting mixed up in the process. The enemy, having recovered from the first blow, returned to reclaim the redoubt but the 25th Division arrived in time to support the 10th Division and the enemy was repelled.[296]

According to General Marchand, 'the fortifications, which were abandoned by the 57th and 72nd Line, were reclaimed by the Württemberg soldiers'.[297]

Meanwhile, the reports and memoirs of Bagration, Vorontsov, Löwenstern, Eugène of Württemberg, Konovnitsyn and Saint Priest, show that the flèches were repeatedly recaptured and lost for several hours, although the precise timing of events remains uncertain.

Marshal Murat recalled arriving at the flèches just as 'our light troops entered the second redoubt, from which they were then repulsed. Some Russian cuirassiers were charging our light infantry ...'[298] Seeing these charges, Murat then personally led the two Württemberg Chevau-léger regiments: a fact borne out by the Russian officer, Fedor Glinka, who testified that: 'a horseman in gaudy uniform led the attack followed by a stream of cavalry. It seemed as if knights from the Medieval Age were attacking! The mighty cavalrymen, in yellow and silver armour, merged into a single column [...] and followed Murat.'[299] The French charge, which was led by the 2nd Württemberg Chevau-léger, recovered the guns that the Russians had captured moments before. Murat reported that the Württemberg charge 'was made with great success upon the Russian infantry that was marching at the first redoubt and was entirely sabred. Then I ordered a charge at the second Redoubt which was definitely taken.'[300]

But Murat's men then got carried away in the heat of action and were showered by Russian canister fire. Isolated and without support, the pursuers, in a moment, became the pursued, as Russian cuirassiers, supported by the 2nd Grenadier Division, counter-attacked. The Russians soon reached the southern flèche, where the French infantry, already wavering under canister fire, abandoned the flèche, which was then occupied by the 2nd Württemberg

# The Battle of Borodino

Battalion, supported by the 3rd Battalion deployed outside the walls. So, as the Württemberg chevau-léger – pursued by the Russian cuirassiers – approached the southern flèche, they were protected by their compatriots. According to Suckow, the Württembergers initially withheld their fire since they mistook the Russian uniform for the Saxon. But they confusion was quickly resolved after the Russian colonel shouted his order in German (!?), 'Kill these German dogs!' In response, he received a salvo from the Württembergers.

Murat – barely escaping Russian attempts to capture him – sheltered inside the flèche, where he was able to rally the troops and fight off the Russian cavalry.[301] In order to encourage the Württembergers, Murat, 'knowing little or no German, cried out, "Ah brav Jäger, brav Jäger, scheuss, scheuss, Jäger!" He meant to encourage the troops but the effect was merely comical.'[302] Still, the Württemberg soldiers managed to repel the Russian charges and protect the Marshal. Faber du Faur, the Württemberg artist who produced a memorable engraving of this incident, noted that:

> A vigorous fire from our light infantry, and from the line infantry in their support, soon repulsed the enemy's cavalry and assured the safety of the King [i.e. of Naples, meaning Murat]. He, Murat, threw himself upon the retreating foe with the cavalry of Bruyère and Nansouty and, after a number of attacks, forced them back off the heights.

In the centre of this cauldron, Bagration – dressed in his parade uniform adorned with his favourite Order of St George (2nd class) – remained calm, since, as Glinka recalled, 'he always drew inspiration at such moments of despair. It seemed that the flames of the battle awakened something deep inside his soul [...] His eyes were full of sparkle.' With the units of General Konovnitsyn's 3rd Division approaching and the Life Guard Izmailovskii and Litovskii Regiments already near Semeyonovskoye, Bagration decided to counter-attack with available forces to gain ground and time. The precise moment of this counter-attack – and Bagration's subsequent injury – remains a matter of debate, largely due to the many attempts at embellishing Russian exploits. Uncertainty surrounds not only the timing of the attack but its place in the overall sequence of events during the battle. Some participants (Yermolov, Glinka, Grabbe) and scholars (Zhilin, Beskrovny, Garnich, Troitsky, Mikhailovsky-Danilevsky, Neyelov, Mikhnevich) have asserted that Bagration was wounded around noon, *after* the first French attack on Rayevsky's Redoubt (discussed in the next section). Others, among them Jomini, Bogdanovich and Skugarevsky, have argued that Bagration was wounded around 11.30am, *before* the French attack on the Grand Redoubt. Finally, some participants (Eugène von Württemberg, Vistitsky, Saint Priest, Clausewitz) and the new generation of Russian historians (Vasiliev, Zemtsov, Popov, Ivchenko etc.) have suggested that Bagration was injured prior to the arrival of II Corps: that is, between 9 and 9.30 am. This latter interpretation is supported by French memoirs and, to this author, it seems closer to reality, considering the overall course of events.

# 7 September: The Battle of Borodino Phase One (6am to 12am)

Recent research by Russian scholars reveals that Colonel Toll, the Quarter-master General and Kutuzov's right-hand man, can be held responsible for the confusion outlined above.[303] In the decades after the battle, Toll tried to cover up some of the miscalculations and errors the Russian command (i.e. Kutuzov and Toll himself) made in the initial deployment at Borodino, as well as later battle decisions. Toll was well aware of the scathing criticism voiced in the memoirs of Barclay de Tolly, Bennigsen, and other participants, which placed a hefty slice of responsibility on his shoulders. In response, Toll, taking advantage of his reputation and connections at the imperial court, published his *Opisaniye*, an account of the battle, which justified his actions and revised the sequence of events on the left flank and centre. Thus, in the official reports – complied immediately after the battle – Toll wrote that the flèches were defended from 7am to 10am, which placed Bagration's counter-attack and injury around 9am. But a decade later, as he completed his *Opisaniye*, Toll added a line claiming that Russian grenadiers drove the French out the flèches after 10am, pursuing their foes as far as the Utitsa woods.[304] By this device, Toll extended the fighting at the flèches until noon, when, by his account, the fortifications finally fell to the French and Bagration received his wound. Toll's sleight of hand allowed other historians – especially Soviet – to claim eight major assaults on the flèches, which, they claimed, remained embattled until the afternoon. This was the version espoused in Russian studies of the battle until well into 1990s.

Around 9am–9.30 am Bagration issued orders for all his immediate forces to launch a counter-attack and, after directing the artillery fire of his batteries towards the flèches, he personally led the charge of the 2nd Grenadier Division and the 1st Combined Grenadier Brigade. The vigorous Russian offensive seized two flèches, while the French stubbornly held out in the third, southern, flèche. According to a witness:

> Observing the menacing movement of the French forces and grasping their intentions, Prince Bagration conceived a great design. Under his orders, the entire left wing in all its length moved quickly forward with fixed bayonets! Thousands became split into single beings, each of whom whirled around, acted and fought! This was a personal, private struggle of a man against man, of a warrior against warrior, and the Russians refused to surrender even an inch of their soil.[305]

Buturlin described the Russian attack thus:

> [the] entire line of the left flank suddenly moved in a bayonet attack. The assault was dreadful [...] a desperate and savage fighting followed at which both sides demonstrated marvellous and superhuman courage.

Meanwhile, Dushenkevich looked on as

> the Grenadiers, whose units were preceded by the priests holding the crosses, marched instilling fear in their enemies – they moved heroically and [the] eyes of each of them sparkled with tears of pure faith, while their faces showed the willingness to die fighting [...] This was not a battle but a true slaughter. A

previously flat valley now resembled a ploughed field due to [the] cross ricochet fire from batteries; clusters of cannon-balls, grenades and canister pierced our columns or ploughed [the] ground in front of us.

According to another officer:

> [We made a bayonet attack], and the French ran around like mad. The Frenchmen [were] courageous, as they remained firm under [our] artillery fire [...] [and] even made a stand against the cavalry, and no one could best them as skirmishers. But they could not resist [our] bayonet [attacks].[306]

Murat admitted that the French had to abandon one of the flèches, while, according to Rapp and Pelet, the Russians were able to carry two of the flèches. Ségur described the attack as 'violent, impetuous, with infantry, artillery and cavalry all joining in one great effort. Ney and Murat, whose concern now was not to complete the victory, but just to hold what they had gained, braced themselves against this onslaught.'[307] Pelet, who was with his 48th Line, witnessed this Russian attack:

> As Bagration's supporting troops arrived, they were fed into the action, boldly advancing over the bodies of the fallen to retake the lost redoubts. The Russian columns moved in accurate response to the orders from their commanders and were, themselves, living bastions. As soon as they emerged into the open terrain, our canister knocked them down, but these brave warriors let nothing bother them and continued to come at us as before.

The attack brought a temporary relief and gained precious time for the Russian reinforcements to arrive, but it was bought at a terrible price. Hundreds of soldiers were killed or wounded and the officer corps was decimated.

On the Russian side, Colonel Kantakuzen managed to recover several Russian guns before being mortally wounded, while Buxhöwden, commander of the Astrakhanskii Grenadier Regiment, was wounded three times but continued commanding his men before receiving his final, mortal, injury. Not far from him, Colonel Monakhtin tried to inspire his men by yelling: 'Lads! This is Russia so defend her with your warrior chests!' but a moment later the French canister ripped through his own ribcage.[308] Generals Borozdin, Gorchakov, Mecklenburg, Saint Priest and Colonel Shatilov were all wounded. The French lost Generals Marion and Komper dead and Gengoult wounded.

The greatest casualty, however, was Prince Bagration himself. As the attack developed, a shell splinter struck Bagration's left leg, smashing his shinbone. For a few minutes he made a valiant effort to conceal his wound, in order to prevent panic or discouragement among his troops. Yet he bled profusely and began to slip from the saddle. His adjutants bore him away, but the thing Bagration most feared soon occurred. A mistaken report of his death spread through the 2nd Army and, as Yermolov recalled, 'in an instant the rumour spread that he was dead [...] it was impossible to check the confusion of the troops [...] There was one common feeling – despair.'

# 7 September: The Battle of Borodino Phase One (6am to 12am)

Barclay de Tolly later noted that after Bagration's injury, 'The 2nd Army was in a state of utter confusion', and his sentiments were echoed by Mayevsky: 'Prince [Bagration] was taken behind the line and his retinue accompanied him. The fighting now was waged in such confusion that I did not know whom and how I should join.' Meanwhile, Butenev saw 'the troops shocked [by Bagration's injury]; they believed he was invulnerable because he was never wounded, despite participating in numerous battles over a quarter of century'.[309] Another participant described how, following Bagration's wound, 'the soul of courage and defiance itself had departed from the entire left wing'.

Soon a remarkable frenzy to avenge their commander spread among Bagration's soldiers. As he was carried away, Bagration's adjutant, Adrianov, ran towards his stretcher: 'Your Excellency, you are being taken away and I am no longer of use to you!' Then, as a witnesses recalled: 'Adrianov, in the sight of thousands, moved like an arrow, cutting his way through the enemy, dealing blows at many before dropping dead.'[310]

In the midst of the battle, Bagration was carried to the surgeons at a nearby station. Muravyev saw him 'with heartbreaking appearance and constantly looking around, taking [with] lively interest in the bloody carnage [around him] ...' Glinka recalled seeing Bagration, surrounded by his adjutant and physicians

> his linen and garments soaked in blood, his uniform unbuttoned, one leg bare, and his head spattered with blood. A large wound was obvious above his knee. His face, covered with dark patches of gunpowder was pale but calm. Despite his agonizing pain, Bagration gazed silently into the distance, listening to the rumble and din of the battle.

Bagration soon saw Barclay's adjutant Löwenstern approaching him and, despite pain, told him: 'Tell General Barclay that the fate and salvation of the Army depends on him. So far everything has been going well, but now Barclay ought to come to my Army in person.' Seeing that Löwenstern was himself wounded, Bagration told him, 'Get yourself bandaged.' A few minutes later, Norov of the Guard Artillery, saw

> a small group [of officers] who half-carried a general, whose one leg barely touched the ground [...] Who was he? He was the man who until now held the entire left flank with some supernatural power – Bagration! [...] It is difficult to express the sorrow that seized us at that moment ...[311]

So, between 9.30am and 10am, the Russian counter-attack was repelled and the flèches were lost once again. The loss of so many officers, and especially of Bagration, spread confusion among the Russian troops and the left flank appeared to be on the verge of collapse. The French counter-attack sought to pierce the Russian defences and seize Semeyonovskoye, and it might have succeeded if not for the arrival of Russian reinforcements. The 3rd Infantry Division, which Bagration requested from Tuchkov at the start of the battle, finally appeared and the Chernigovskii, Muromskii, Revelskii and Selenginskii Regiments [. . .] despite the devastating enemy fire, made a bayonet attack shouting 'hurrah,' over-whelmed the superior enemy, spreading confusion into his columns and occupy-ing the position that was bitterly contested from the start of the battle.[312]

According to Konovnitsyn, 'after this fairly successful attack I was informed that Bagration and his chief of staff Saint Priest were wounded [. . .] and Bagration left me in charge as the senior ranking officer'. Konovnitsyn defended the flèches for some time before the French seized the fortifications again. However, he counter-attacked with his 3rd Division, which was sup-ported by the Kievskii, Astrakhanskii, Sibirskii and Moskovskii Grenadiers. The Russian success, however, proved fleeting, since they were driven out of the flèches. Colonel Toll, accompanied by Sherbinin, was examining troops near Semeyonovskoye when he witnessed the attack of the Muromskii and Revelskii Regiments: 'Cannon-balls were raining upon Semeyonovskoye, trees were falling all around and houses were destroyed as if theatrical production sets. The air itself howled constantly and the earth trembled.'[313] Sherbinin and Glinka saw the charge of Major General Alexander Tuchkov IV with the Revelskii Infantry Regiment and the death of this gallant officer near the rear flèche. According to Glinka:

under a terrible artillery fire, Tuchkov shouted to his troops, 'Lads, follow me forward!' His soldiers, whose faces were lashed by a storm of lead, hesitated. 'So you are going to stand here? Then, I will attack alone!' [Tuchkov yelled] and, grasping the regimental flag, he rushed forward. A moment later, a canister shot shattered his chest [. . .] [and] numerous cannon balls and shells, resembling a boiling cloud, fell on the very place where the dead General lay and ploughed the earth burying the General's corpse.

Tuchkov's body was never found. As Mikhailovsky-Danilevsky observed:

Three kin [Tuchkov] brothers, all of general's rank, ended their lives this fateful campaign: one, wounded, was captured near Smolensk, while two others had fallen at Borodino. Their mother lost vision from her tears while the youthful wife of one of the fallen brothers later established a cloister on the Borodino battlefield and left the secular life.[314]

The Westphalian troops of Napoleon's VIII Corps, meantime, were moving southwards to support the Poles and flank the Russian positions. As Borke and Lossberg described, the Westphalians initially followed Ney's III Corps but then turned right towards the Utitsa woods. Lieutenant Colonel Conrady recalled moving along the ravine that protected them, but barely did his troops emerge on the plain above the ravine when they came under devastating artillery fire. Captain Zakharov's 1st Life Guard Horse Company was especially effective, as it opened a canister fire at the approaching enemy masses. As one Russian officer recalled: 'the head of the enemy column was literally mowed down'. Zakharov continued commanding his battery until he suffered a mortal wound. His last words, reputedly, were: 'I envy your fortune, my friends, since you still can fight for

## General Alexander Tuchkov and the Borodino Saviour Monastery

The death of General Alexander Tuchkov shattered the life of his wife, Margarita Mikhailovna Tuchkova, née Naryshkina. Even more devastating was the fact that the General's body was never found, precluding a proper burial. Tuchkova spent years trying to preserve the memory of her husband on the battlefield and, in 1818, she was finally able to lay the foundation of a church with the help of Emperor Alexander, who donated 10,000 roubles for the construction.

The Church of the Saviour ('Spasa Nerukotvornogo'), built on the spot where General Konovnitsyn believed Tuchkov to be killed, became the first monument constructed on the battlefield and laid the foundation for the eventual memorial. Tuchkova barely recovered from her husband's death when she experienced two more tragic events, as her only son died in 1826 and her brother was exiled for his involvement in the Decembrist Uprising.

Abandoning the secular life, she organized a recluse for women at the Church of Saviour, living in a small house, which was destroyed by the German Army in 1942 but reconstructed as a memorial exhibition in 1994.

The Church of Saviour was eventually turned into the Borodino Saviour Monastery ('Spaso-Borodinskii Monastyr') in 1838, with Tuchkova as its first mother superior. It was surrounded by a brick wall and four towers and gates in 1837–39. Over the next decades it came to include a bell tower (1840), the Cathedral of the Vladimir Icon of the Mother of the God (1851–59) and the Church of John the Baptist (1874). Its Pilgrim's House became famous after novelist Leo Tolstoy lived there while studying the battlefield for his masterpiece *War and Peace*.

In 1912, on the centennial of the battle, Emperor Nicolas II and his family visited the monastery and attended the unveiling of the monument to the 3rd Division. In 1929 (following the October Revolution of 1917) the monastery was closed. It sheltered a hospital during the World War II and was damaged during the battle at Borodino. Restored in 1962, the monastery was included in the Borodino Military Historical Museum-Reserve in 1975. After the fall of the USSR, it was returned to the Russian Orthodox Church and became active again in 1992.

the motherland.' Zakharov's company was reinforced by eleven guns collected from various companies, which halted the Westphalian advance, allowing the Russians to bring up cavalry. Amidst smoke, noise and confusion, as Conrady, Lossberg, Morgenstern and Boedicker acknowledged, the Westphalians initially mistook the Russian cuirassiers for the Saxons, who wore similar uniforms, but quickly realized their mistakes and organized squares from the 2nd Line, 3rd Light and the 6th Line. The Russians called off their charge but the Westphalians suffered from an artillery fire that caused havoc amidst their tight formations. Suckow's memoirs complained about an enemy battery of twenty guns bombarding his men, while, according to Scheler, 'defending the flèches required immense determination and courage because the enemy showered them with grenades, cannon-balls and canister ...' Planat de la Fay observed that the

> the Westphalian Corps was deployed in a column behind the flèche and was from time to time hit by shells that threw shakos and bayonets into the air. With every such explosion, these poor soldiers threw themselves to the ground but not all of them managed to raise to their feet afterwards.[315]

After the French seized the flèches for the final time, a brigade of the 24th Division moved closer to the fortifications but suffered under the Russian guns firing from Semeyonovskoye. Ney then repeated his order for the VIII Corps to proceed south to assist the Poles (see page 138).

As the French began to regroup, Konovnitsyn faced the challenging decision of continuing to fight for the flèches, which by this time were largely destroyed, or withdrawing his troops to a new position, where they could regroup. Some participants recall overhearing the General's murmur: 'My Lord, what should I do?' He even called upon Rayevsky to come in person to Semeyonovskoye, but Rayevsky was himself under attack and replied that he could not abandon his position. Thus Rayevsky 'advised him [Konovnitsyn] to act according to circumstances'.[316] After some thought, Konovnitsyn decided to withdraw his troops to Semeyonovkoye, which meant the Russians effectively gave up battle for the flèches and took up new positions along the ravine of the Semeyonvskii brook.

The Russian headquarters was stunned by news of Bagration's wound. Kutuzov, initially appointed Prince Alexander of Württemberg to lead the 2nd Western Army but then replaced him with the more experienced Dokhturov, who reached the left flank between 10.30 and 11.00 am.

Dokhturov's arrival was witnessed by Glinka, who saw 'a horseman wearing [a] worn out general's uniform, with stars on his chest, small but [with] strong features, and [a] genuinely Russian face.' Dokhturov, 'calmly riding amidst the raining death and horrors', saw the entire left wing in disarray and requested reinforcements. He supposedly appealed to the troops: 'Moscow, the mother of all Russian cities, is behind us!' and began redeploying his forces. The Life Guard Litovskii and Izmailovskii Regiments were in a chequerboard formation south of Semeyonovskoye, while survivors of the Combined Grenadier Brigade, the 12th and 27th Divisions were nearby in support. The 3rd Division was deployed to their right, while the remnants of the 2nd Grenadier Division occupied the village ruins. Borozdin's cavalry brigade stood behind the Guard Regiments, while the 2nd Cuirassier Division was rallied behind the 3rd Division. Neverovsky spread a chain of

# 7 September: The Battle of Borodino Phase One (6am to 12am)

skirmishers in front of the Guard Regiments and assumed command of the Combined Grenadier Battalions and the Don Cossack Horse Artillery Company. Parts of the IV Reserve Cavalry Corps were deployed further to the south, to maintain communications with Shakhovsky's Jägers.

## *Central Sector – The First Assault on Rayevsky's Redoubt*

While Ney and Davout attacked the flèches, Prince Eugène prepared to assault the Russian positions in the centre. By now, Delzon's 13th Division was around Borodino, Ornano's light cavalry brigade was to the north of the village, while the Italian Guard, Morand's 1st, Gérard's 3rd and Broussier's 14th Divisions and Grouchy's III Cavalry Corps were on the banks of the Kolocha, preparing for the attack. Morand's skirmishers were already fighting the Russian Jägers that were spread in the bushes along the Semeyonovskii stream. As Zemtsov calculated, Prince Eugène's forces included about 33,000 men and 7,000 cavalry but he could commit about 24,000 infantry and 4,000 cavalry for the attack on the redoubt. They would be supported by over 135 guns

Rayevsky's Redoubt was occupied by the 26th Battery Company (twelve guns) of Lieutenant Colonel Shulman (the Russian troops thus called the redoubt the 'Shulman Battery') and six guns of the 47th Light Company, under protection of VII Corps; additional batteries were deployed to the north of the redoubt and, according to Larionov, the total number of guns between the New Smolensk Road and the redoubt was close to 110. Rayevsky initially deployed his troops in two lines, with 'the right wing anchored on the incomplete redoubt [...] while the left was in the direction of Semeyonovskoye'. The 12th Division (Vasilchikov) was deployed with the Narvskii and Smolenskii Regiments in the first line, in the Semeyonovskii ravine, and the Ingermanlandskii and Aleksopolskii Regiments in the second line on the hill's southern slope. As for the 26th Division, a battalion of the Poltavskii Infantry Regiment was deployed in the trench in front of the redoubt, while another Poltavskii battalion, with the Ladozhskii Infantry Regiment, was on the southern side of the redoubt. The Nizhegorodskii and Orlovskii Regiments were placed in two battalion columns on the northern side. The Jägers were spread as skirmishers in the brush, west of the redoubt.[317]

Rayevsky's forces were considerably reduced when Bagration, hard pressed at the flèches, requested reinforcements and, as Rayevsky noted, 'took the entire second line from me'. Rayevsky deployed the remaining troops in columns and placed the remaining four battalions of the 12th Division on the left, behind the Poltavskii and Ladozhskii Regiments, while four battalions from the 26th Division were on the right side of the redoubt. Vasilchikov and Paskevich were instructed: 'in case of enemy attack on the redoubt, to attack him from both flanks'.[318] Rayevsky also appealed for reinforcement to Barclay de Tolly, who sent him 18th, 19th and 40th Jägers, which were transferred from the northern sector after the combat at Borodino died down. These troops were placed in battalion columns in the reserve behind the redoubt.[319] The 6th, 49th and 50th Jägers were spread along the

Semeyonovskii stream on the left side of the redoubt, while the 5th, 41st and 42nd Jägers were arranged along the Kamenka stream. Further northward, the VI Infantry Corps, and the III Cavalry Corps behind it, supported Rayevsky's right flank, while IV Cavalry Corps was arranged behind the 12th Infantry Division on the left. Thus the Russians had approximately 27,000 infantry and 8,500 cavalry and forty-six guns concentrated in and around the redoubt.[320]

The number of guns initially set up inside the redoubt varies in sources. French scholar, Tranié, and the Russian, Larionov, estimated as many as twenty-four, while Bogdanov, who helped construct the fortification, referred to nineteen. Yermolov, Toll and other Russian participants reported eighteen guns, which is usually acknowledged to be closer to the truth. Still, historians Gerua, Palmer, Thiers, Holzhausen and others argued there were twelve pieces in the redoubt, while Skugarevsky claimed as few as eight. Rayevsky instructed his artillerymen to defend their guns to the last and ordered draught horses and ammunition caissons to be sent away, in case there was a real threat of the enemy seizing the redoubt.[321] He remained on foot inside the fortification, since he was suffering from a wound sustained few days before, when he accidentally impaled himself on a bayonet protruding from a stack of hay on a cart. As he recalled: 'I could barely ride a horse and even then with unbearable pain ...'

Barclay de Tolly, noticing French movement towards the redoubt, ordered Creitz's Dragoon brigade of III Cavalry Corps to the redoubt. 'Under heavy artillery and musket fire,' Creitz recalled, '[I] deployed [the] Sibirskii and Orenburgskii [Dragoon] Regiments in the first line and placed the Irkutskii Regiment, which was much weaker, in reserve. Smagin's Horse Artillery Company with twelve guns was deployed next to it.'[322] However, Army roll-calls do no identify anyone by the name of Smagin commanding a Horse Artillery Company and, as Larionov suggested, it might be that Lieutenant Colonel Girsch's 22nd Light Company was deployed there and, after Girsch's death, it was probably commanded by Lieutenant Smagin.[323]

As the battle began in other sectors, the French made a reconnaissance in force but avoided attacking the fortified battery. This movement is sometimes (especially in Soviet literature) described as a major attack and the first of the three assaults on the redoubt. The memoirs of many participants, however, do not describe this charge and the first Russian histories of Buturlin and Mikhailovsky-Danilevsky are also silent on this count. Bogdanovich simply states that: 'around 10am, Broussier tried to seize the battery but was repelled and retreated to the ravine to rally his forces'.[324] Gerua was more specific in defining this event as an attack and his sequence of events seems to have influenced subsequent generations of Russian/Soviet historians, who began to describe this first assault in increasingly embellished terms. Even such prominent Russian historians as Tarle, Larionov and Troitsky claimed that Broussier's division made a major assault, which was beaten back with heavy casualties.[325] Western historians generally acknowledge some action on Broussier's part but describe it as an

# 7 September: The Battle of Borodino Phase One (6am to 12am)

'assault' or 'reconnaissance'. Chuquet and Rivollet describe such movements taking place around 9am, Popov and Zemtsov between 9am and 10am, Riehn, Duffy, Tranie and Carmigiani at 10am, while Kukiel suggested between 10.30am and 11am. Finally, Elting and Nafziger argued in favour of 11am.

It seems plausible that, between 8am and 9am, Broussier crossed the Semeyonovskii brook and appeared on the plateau in front of the redoubt. His appearance caused the Russian defenders to assume the French were preparing for an attack, but Broussier was far from launching an unsupported assault, and probably made a reconnaissance in force against the Russian Jägers spread in front of him, before withdrawing his troops to the safety of the ravine. This course of events seems to be supported by Paskevich, who recalled that:

> the skirmishers of my division, lodged in bushes, which the enemy had to pass through, met the enemy [Broussier's troops] with fire. The French had to make tremendous efforts to pass the bushes and the Jägers of my division halted them for over an hour [...] Broussier's division then remained in the ravine [...] while Morand's and Gérard's divisions, having deployed in the ravine, suddenly appeared above it and prepared for attack ...[326]

Glinka also described 'Broussier's division crossing the Kolocha but unable to endure the Russian fire, it took cover in the ravine ...'

The first major assault – attempted by Morand's division – was preceded by an artillery bombardment to soften the Russian defences and probably continued until after 9am. At that time, Bagration dispatched Mayevsky to see what was happening at Rayevsky's position:

> Rayevsky took me to the battery, which was to the battlefield what a belvedere is to a town. A hundred guns bombarded it. Rayevsky, with an elated face, told me, 'Now go back and tell the Prince what is going on here.'[327]

Shortly afterwards Rayevsky received a message from Konovnitsyn, who had just assumed command of the entire left wing after Bagration's injury, asking Rayevsky to come to Semeyonovskoye to help. Rayevsky politely refused in light of impending attack against his own position.

Morand's division of some 6,000 men (with twenty-six guns) consisted of three brigades, each containing a single regiment. The division advanced in mixed order with the leading 30th Regiment[328] deployed in line and the 13th Light and 17th Line following in battalion columns.[329] Prior to the attack, Captain François of the 1st Battalion of the 30th Line tells us that Morand personally reviewed the 30th Line. Then the French advanced across the plateau under a hail of artillery fire and began falling into the wolf pits. Mitarevsky described: 'besides us, fire was maintained by the batteries to the left of us, as well from the lunette itself and from behind it; musket fire could not be heard at all since it was overpowered by the deafening cannonade.'[330] François remembered as entire files and half-platoons fell under the enemy fire, leaving great gaps. General Bonnamy, who was at the head of the 30th, made us halt in the thickest of the canister fire, and after he rallied us we went forward again at the *pas de charge*. A line of Russian [skirmishers] tried to halt us but we delivered a regimental volley at thirty paces and passed over the wreckage.

Rayevsky wrote:

This was a decisive moment [...] My guns began to thunder out when the enemy came within range and the smoke hid the French so completely that we could see nothing of their array or ascertain what progress they were making. There was one of my orderly officers standing a little to the left of me, and after another volley[331] he cried out, 'Your Excellency, save yourself!' I turned around and fifteen yards away I saw French grenadiers pouring into my redoubt with fixed bayonets.

Rayevsky, with a wounded leg, managed to mount his horse and galloped to the nearby hill to observe the area.[332]

The 30th Line was first to reach the redoubt, charging with bayonets. According to François:

We dashed towards the Redoubt and climbed through the embrasures [...] The Russian gunners tried to beat us back with spikes and ramrods and we found them truly formidable opponents as we grappled with them hand-to-hand. At the same time a large number of French soldiers fell into the wolf pits and landed on Russian troops who had already tumbled in. Once inside the redoubt, I fought the Russian gunners with my sword and cut down more than one of them ...

Yermolov noted:

Our feeble fortification with just a few troops had withstood the concentrated fire of superior enemy forces for [a] long time but there was not a single caisson for any of its eighteen guns and their feeble fire facilitated the French advance. Due to limited space inside the fortification, only [a] small number of infantry could be deployed there at any one time and any troops outside the redoubt were mowed down by canister and scattered.

In a bloody combat, the French swept through and beyond the redoubt, chasing the survivors before them. Cesare de Laugier, standing on a hill at a distance from the redoubt, could observe it all 'as a spectator at a circus might make out what is going on in the ring below him'. Seeing the dashing attack of the 30th Line, he was seized with an 'indescribable anxiety' and cheered his comrades. Not far from him, von Muraldt (from the Bavarian troops) saw Prince Eugène excited by this initial success and 'waving his hat in the air and crying 'The battle is won!'

This was indeed an important moment in the battle. With the Russian left wing in tatters after the loss of the flèches and Bagration's wound, the French success in the centre threatened to break the Russian Army into two parts. Pelet reasoned: 'Had Morand been supported or had he managed to hold ground, the battle would have been lost for the Russians. Their centre would

have been pierced and the forces of Barclay and Bagration separated ...'
Griois, standing with his guns near the ravine, saw as 'a grenadier, who had
been wounded in this attack, came back, covered in blood and drunk on
glory, to confirm for us the happy success, which, by opening the enemy
centre and separating his two wings, seemed to decide the victory for us'.
The Russian centre was indeed in chaos and Yermolov tells us that he saw
crowds of soldiers in complete disorder running from the front line.

But Morand was not supported and Rayevsky himself later criticized the
enemy attack because 'the [French] became the very cause of their defeat
since they had no reserve to support the attacking column'. Bonnamy's
troops could not take advantage of the guns captured inside the redoubt
since first, they hardly had time to do it, and second, on Rayevsky's orders,
no caissons were left nearby to supply the guns. Bonnamy's troops were
overextended and unsupported. Morand's other units were still moving on
the plateau in front of the redoubt when they came under attack from the
Russians (unclear what units) and Morand himself was wounded in the chin
by grapeshot, which briefly halted the advance.[333]

According to Gérard's report, three battalions of the 12th Light were sent
forward to protect Morand's right flank while, on the left, the 7th Light
advanced in 'an open order to the base of the redoubt, where a fierce fighting
developed'.[334] Thus, only a battalion of the 13th Light was close enough
to support Bonnamy's troops inside the redoubt. It is unclear how long
Bonnamy's troops remained in control of the redoubt, but it could not have
been longer than half an hour, since Russian reports imply the counter-
attack was launched immediately after the redoubt was seized. Thus,
Laugier's elation at seeing the redoubt fall was soon replaced by 'a feeling of
pity as this unfortunate regiment [30th Line] which I had just been admiring
was [being] massacred ...'

Rayevsky remembered as 'Vasilchikov and Paskevich, acting on my
earlier instructions, attacked the enemy at once'. Simultaneously, Yermolov
happened to be passing in the vicinity of the redoubt. He was sent by
Kutuzov to rally the troops on the left wing following Bagration's injury
and was accompanied by his adjutant, Pavel Grabbe, and young General
Kutaisov. The latter, Yermolov recalled

> eagerly desired to join me. I pleaded with him to return to his command and
> reminded him of Prince Kutuzov's earlier angry reproach that he was never
> around when he was needed; however, Kutaisov did not accept my advice and
> stayed with me ...

Divov, who served at the headquarters, also remembered that 'Kutaisov
did not follow Kutuzov's order to remain with him and went with Yermolov
towards the battery ...' Pavel Grabbe, who, as noted, also accompanied
Yermolov, was aware of the Russian Commander-in-Chief's reluctance to
let Kutaisov go, and 'for a long time Kutuzov did not allow Yermolov and
Count Kutaisov to leave him, although both of them were bursting to go to

Bagration. When Kutuzov finally ordered Yermolov to go there, Kutaisov [defied Kutuzov] and followed him.' Denis Davydov added:

> Kutaisov decided to accompany Yermolov despite the latter's arguments to dissuade him, 'You always rush where you are not supposed to be, do not you remember the Commander-in-Chief's recent reprimand that no one could find you. I am going to the 2nd Army to act on behalf of the Commander-in-Chief, but what will you do there?'[335]

Approaching Rayevsky's Redoubt, Yermolov found it

> covered with thick smoke and the troops protecting the heights scattered. Many of us knew and, it was indeed obvious, that leaving this important point, as General Bennigsen described it, in the enemy's possession would result in the most disastrous consequences for us. Therefore, I immediately rushed to this place. Any minute lost could have been fatal for us.

Yermolov ordered the 3rd Battalion of the Ufa Infantry Regiment to follow him in open order, hoping to halt the fleeing troops. He then directed the 18th, 19th and 40th Jägers forward as well:

> Despite the steepness of the slope, I ordered the Jäger Regiments and the 3rd Battalion of the Ufimskii Regiment to attack with their bayonets, the Russian soldier's favourite weapon. The combat was fierce and terrible, and continued for no more than half an hour: we faced tenacious resistance, but seized the Heights, [and] recaptured the guns ...

To motivate his men, Yermolov resorted to a peculiar means of inspiration:

> I happened to have a bunch of the medals of the Military Order with St George ribbons that I threw several at a time and each time throngs of our soldiers went after them. These soldiers showed examples of incredible fearlessness. Suddenness of this incident left not time for thoughts, while we could not ponder retreat once this feat was accomplished. My encounter with the Jäger Regiments was completely unforeseen. The venture was no more a reckless audacity and many were jealous of my luck!

This incident, as recounted by Yermolov, proved to be quite controversial after the war was over, as some participants disputed its veracity while others supported it. The account itself is quite unabashed in taking the sole credit for the recapture of the redoubt and fails to mention other units that contributed to this success. So lets explore other accounts.

As the redoubt was seized by the French, Barclay de Tolly, who was riding south from Gorki after a heated argument with Kutuzov (discussed in the previous section), noticed a commotion around the redoubt but, as Löwenstern recalled, 'due to smoke and dust, we could not see what was the cause of this movement.' Dispatched by Barclay de Tolly to investigate, Löwenstern was surprised to find it in the hands of the French. He sent Lieutenant Vardenburg to notify Barclay de Tolly, who dispatched two infantry battalions and the Orenburgskii Dragoon Regiment to charge the

French left flank, and 'ordered all artillery located in the vicinity to concentrate its fire on the enemy column'.[336] Löwenstern, meantime, noticed a battalion of the Tomskii Infantry Regiment to the right side of the hill and, acting on behalf of Barclay de Tolly, ordered the battalion commander to follow him. Löwenstern continued:

> I forbade the soldiers to yell 'hurrah' without my order since they had to ascend the hill and had to preserve their breath. The battalion commander moved on foot; he was a stocky short man but he was burning with a sacred ardour.

Halfway through their climb, Löwenstern ordered the battalion to give a hearty – and intimidating – 'hurrah!', and the soldiers of the Tomskii Regiment 'charged with a reckless abandonment against everyone they encountered. They made a bayonet charge and a ferocious fight had begun. [By now] General Yermolov, with his entire staff, rushed to this point ...'

As Yermolov and Löwenstern led their battalions in a frontal attack, the 12th and 26th Divisions charged from the flanks. Paskevich later recalled that the 'combat on the main battery presented a terrifying sight. The 19th and 40th Jäger Regiments attacked the enemy from the left flank while Vasilchikov, with several Regiments of his 12th Division, moved from the right flank.' The Sibirskii and Irkutskii Dragoons charged the fleeing enemy while the Orenburgskii Dragoon Regiment was moved against the French forces trying to rescue the 30th Line.[337]

The artillery played a major role in repelling the French attack. As soon as the redoubt was captured, the Russian command diverted the 5th, 9th and 10th Horse companies and six guns of the 4th Horse Company, a total of forty-two guns, to assist in recapturing it. Toll later dispatched the 1st, 2nd and 5th Light companies, totalling thirty-six guns, from Knyazkovo. As Dokhturov reported, Lieutenant Kliber of the 1st Artillery Brigade, commanding the 2nd Light Company, was brought by Colonel Toll to the centre. He was supported by Captain Shishkin's 1st Light Company and seven guns of the 5th Light Company led by Lieutenant Nagibin. The 48th Light Company, located at Semeyonovskoe, also directed its fire against the French forces. Lieutenant Colonel Sablin commanded the 23rd Light Company, which joined Nagibin's guns. To the left of the redoubt, Creitz's cavalry was assisted by twelve guns of the 22nd Light Company; its commander Lieutenant Colonel Karl Girsh was killed in action and the company was led by Lieutenant Smagin. On the right, the Russians had ten guns of the 24th Battery, six guns of the 45th Light, twelve guns of the 12th Light and six of the 13th Light Companies. As Larionov calculated, the Russians managed to concentrate the firepower of a staggering 197 guns on this small sector.

General Charles-Auguste Bonnamy's troops were 'attacked from both flanks and from the front', as Rayevsky recalled. They fought gallantly but were routed. In less than half an hour, the 30th Line had lost two-thirds of its strength and Bonnamy was captured after receiving thirteen (some claim fifteen or even twenty-two) bayonet wounds. Aleksei Nikitin, who

# The Battle of Borodino

commanded one of the artillery companies, watched as the French 'filled the trench and wolf pits with their corpses, allowing us to move beyond the battery'. Wolzogen praised the Russian attack, which was

> executed in astonishingly good order. The various columns approached the foot of the hill in an even step to the time of the drum, and not a single cry arose from the troops. All of this so intimidated the French that we could clearly see that many men were fleeing from the ranks and that the garrison of the redoubt was diminishing perceptibly. The French kept up a fire on the advancing columns only from their cannon, which they had not managed to bring forward in any great quantity. Our troops reached the hill and then to a general hurrah they carried the summit and the fortification.[338]

As the remnants of the 30th Line fled back, Paskevich 'took the remaining regiments of the 12th Division and marched beyond the lunette in order to cut off any French troops that still remained around it'. Rayevsky reported that: 'Vasilchikov and Paskevich pursued the enemy troops into the brushwood so vigorously that barely any of them survived.'[339] Although some French sources, including the 18th Bulletin and Prince Eugène's report, describe a major Russian counterattack, in reality the Russian command was concerned about overextending itself and Yermolov recalled his infantry:

> I feared that, if we were counter-attacked, the enemy would bring strong forces in the wake of our beleaguered crowds [sic] and deprive us of our recently acquired success; so I dispatched my adjutants with a few other officers to recall our troops and, to clear a valley lying in front of us. Following this fierce combat, my battalions were reduced in strength and there was not a single caisson for the guns inside the fortification, yet an enemy attack was imminent.

Yermolov was soon reinforced by Barclay de Tolly, who, 'attentively observing the action, saw my perilous position, and, without waiting for my appeal for reinforcements, he immediately dispatched a battery company and two infantry regiments, so that I soon had everything prepared to meet an attack and everything supplied in excess.'[340]

The Russian Dragoons engaged Morand's division and Creitz – leading the Sibirskii, Orenburgskii and Irkutskii Regiments and supported by the 5th Horse Artillery Company of Lieutenant Colonel Kandyba – made several charges against French troops.[341] Creitz's troops had already suffered from the French bombardment and Lieutenant Smagin's Horse Artillery Company was soon so hard-hit that it was sent back. Nevertheless, Creitz reported: 'neither the courage of the commander not the precision of its fire could save the company from destruction. Horses and men were struck down, the ammunition boxes blown up and the guns wrecked.'[342] Still, his dragoons charged the upcoming French troops, who tried to rescue their comrades but were forced to withdraw.

Prince Eugène, meantime, saw several lines of Russian infantry advancing 'to reclaim the redoubt and [...] approaching the right of General Morand. Immediately I had Gérard's division start to form a little beyond and to the right of the first; the 7th Light was placed on the left and I arranged the division of General Broussier to support them.'[343] Paskevich also recalled the arrival of Gérard's division, which 'revived the combat'.[344] Laugier could see the 7th Light form square, 'and after letting the Russian Dragoons [...] advance, it opened a well-nourished fire by files, which, in the twinkling of an eye, covered the terrain with men and horses, dead or wounded, forming a new barrier around these brave battalions'. Sergeant Bertrand was marching with the 7th Light and experienced the carnage of Russian canister first-hand. The regiment barely began its movement when a cannon-ball shattered the head of [the] company commander, while the Russian canister injured several other officers. Bertrand took command and the led his troops forward:

> We were at the bottom of the redoubt [...] two battalions seemed to be retreating while two other made a flanking move. The colonel ordered me to remain in place [...] [suddenly], a peloton of Russian Dragoons charged from the redoubt shouting 'hurrah!'

Bertrand quickly ordered his men to organize a square around him and opened fire at the charging dragoons, who were driven back.

The role of the Russian cavalry in the fighting around the redoubt became a matter of dispute soon after the battle. Rayevsky disputed Buturlin's claim that the cavalry supported him. Yermolov's account, cited above, over-looks the cavalry as well. Other participants do acknowledge the involve-ment of the dragoons but their contradictory reports only further confuse the picture. Although the details on the French cavalry charges south of the redoubt are sketchy, it is possible to recreate a general sequence of events.

As the fighting raged around Semeyonovskoye and Rayevsky's Redoubt, Baggovut's II Corps was still marching from the right flank to the left. Baggovut personally led the 17th Division, while Eugène of Württemberg commanded the 4th Division. Both divisions initially moved on a local road to the right of Knyazkovo but then the 17th Division proceeded through the woods towards the left flank (see page 139 for its arrival at Utitsa), while the 4th Division was diverted to the centre.[345] Duke Eugène of Württemberg was informed about the French attack on Rayevsky's Redoubt and ordered to assist in recapturing it. He recalled:

> Toll led me and my four line infantry regiments through the forest near Knyazkovo to the centre, where we were to plug the gap which had opened up in the Russian line. Some cannon-balls reached us even as we were marching through the woods but when we emerged from their cover we found ourselves in the most dangerous of spots.

The Duke led the 2nd Brigade of Pyshnitsky (Kremenchug and Minsk Regiments) in attack columns (with music and drums beating) but, before it reached the redoubt, he was told that the redoubt had been recaptured. Eugène of Württemberg was then ordered to cover the position south of the redoubt, which was threatened by an approaching enemy column. It is unclear what units were in that 'mass of enemy infantry' but most probably troops from Gérard or Morand's divisions. The Duke directed his troops there but, as he recalled, 'it was like marching into a hell'. The depth of the French formation could not be seen while 'their frontage alone was imposing enough'. The French had a battery of artillery moving to their right side but, due to smoke and confusion, Eugène could not count the guns in it. He deployed the Volhynskii Infantry Regiment in line, followed by the Tobolskii Infantry Regiment in columns on both flanks. The 2nd Brigade, in columns, formed the second rank at some distance. 'We advanced towards the enemy through a hail of artillery fire,' he recalled, and forced the enemy infantry to fall back. Yet the 1st Brigade suffered heavy casualties from the French artillery fire: both regimental chefs, Major General Rossi and Colonel Schroeder, being wounded. The Duke himself had three horses shot from under him and 'as the last one fell, a battalion adjutant who had just jumped from his horse to offer it to me, was also killed. The entire horrific, bloody scene was like a nightmare except for such events which convinced me that it was reality'.

Eugène of Württemberg hardly managed to regroup his men when 'enemy cavalry in superior numbers' attacked his troops. He immediately issued orders for the Volhynskii and Tobolskii Regiments to organize battalion squares, while the two other regiments were kept nearby in reserve. Allowing the enemy to approach at close distance, the Russians then opened volley fire and repelled several enemy charges. During this combat, Lieutenant Kiselev of the Tobolskii Regiment was dispatched 'with the skirmishers to halt the enemy skirmishers, followed by several Horse Artillery guns and cavalry that sought to flank our squares. He accomplished this task with exemplary gallantry, arresting the enemy until the arrival of our cavalry'.

Simultaneously, Sub Lieutenant Popov I of the Volhynskii Regiment was sent with

> a squad ['vzvod'] to recapture a gun that was seized by the enemy and which the enemy cavalry was already moving away. However, Popov's commendable courage recaptured this gun from the enemy's hands and delivered it to Colonel Glukhov's Company [Half Company of the 1st Battery Company].

Despite its heavy losses, the 4th Division held its grounds against the enemy charges and was soon supported by Creitz's Dragoons. Eugène of Württemberg saw Barclay de Tolly in the heat of the action and was surprised by 'his utter resignation and the conduct of this most chivalrous of men, who had been completely misjudged by Russian public opinion'. Barclay de Tolly soon ordered him to halt and deploy the 2nd Brigade more to the right-hand side, where General Miloradovich needed support. As Barclay de Tolly was conversing with Eugène of Württemberg, General Miloradovich's adjutant, Bibikov, rode up and asked him to ride at once to his commander. The Duke asked which way and, as Bibikov raised his arm to point it out, a cannon-ball ripped it off. Ignoring his agonizing pain, Bibikov pointed again with his remaining arm and responded, 'There! Hurry!'[346]

As Barclay de Tolly and Eugène travelled to meet Miloradovich, who awaited them near the 2nd Brigade of the 4th Division, an eyewitness recalled that: 'a cloud of dust swept down on us from the left like an avalanche and the closer it rolled the more monstrous its dimensions appeared'. Almost as soon as the command 'Battalions form squares!' rang out, the French cavalry came charging. The Russians organized squares where Barclay de Tolly, Miloradovich and Rayevsky sought shelter. 'We were completely surrounded', recorded a survivor,

> and each of our squares was left to work its own salvation like some warship driven before a storm [...] The yell of 'En avant!' rang in our ears and the force of the onslaught of these mighty masses almost took our breath away [...] The French cavalry emerged from the dust with a gleam of armour, a rattling of their scabbards and a flashing of the sun on the metal of those helmets of theirs with the horsetail switches. Drunk with victory, this majestic, heroic horde of cavalry pressed home its attack against our iron wall ...[347]

Although the enemy cavalry charges were repulsed, the 4th Division suffered severely from artillery fire and some 300 men of the Volhynskii and Tobolskii Regiments alone were killed. Around noon, the IV Corps of Osterman-Tolstoy finally arrived to support Eugène of Württemberg. One brigade of the 4th Division, commanded by the only surviving staff-officer, Major Wolf, was moved slightly to the south, while the Duke himself, acting on Barclay de Tolly's order, led his other brigade (Kremenchug and Minsk Regiments), on a roundabout road running to the right of Psarevo, to help Baggovut on the extreme left flank.[348]

Eugène of Württemberg's memoirs contain interesting details on this episode of the battle but fail to identify who the French horsemen were. Bogdanovich referred to 'carabiniers' (probably those of the 4th Cuirassier Division of II Corps), Nafziger and Duffy to the III Cavalry Corps, while Bleibtreu thought it was Subervie's 16th Light Brigade of Pajol's Division. Dittfurth and Kukiel argued that the horsemen belonged to Montbrun's Corps.[349] Thiers, Tranier, Popov and Zemtsov describe the involvement of Latour-Maubourg's troops in the attack, which seems reasonable, since neither the III nor II Cavalry Corps operated east of the Kamenka brook at that moment; Grouchy's corps also had no cuirassiers that are mentioned in reports and memoirs.

The IV Cavalry Corps spent the morning near the Kamenka brook and 'was ordered to advance and cross the ravine and charge the cannon of the infantry, which were at [Semeyonovskoye], a very important position for the enemy ...'[350] During this attack, some cavalry units came across the infantry of Eugène of Württemberg. Russian historian Popov argued that the attack also involved Rozniecki's Polish Lancers and Lepel's Westphalian

Cuirassiers. This supposition is supported by the nomination reports for Colonel Nikitin's two Horse Artillery companies operating south of the redoubt. Documents on the 10th Horse Artillery Company commend bombardiers Savelyev, Inozemtsev, Kolesnyuk, and others for their gallantry in repelling the charge of 'enemy Uhlans'.[351] It is also possible that some troops of Burthe's 8th Light Brigade were involved in some of the charges, since the history of the 5th Hussar Regiment maintains that the hussars seized two guns here. Russian historian Zemtsov argued that some Westphalian Hussars of von Hammerstein's cavalry could have been involved as well and tried to explain Bogdanovich's note about 'carabiniers' attacking the Russian troops by suggesting some Russian participants may have confused the uniforms of the Westphalian Cuirassiers, who wore white collets resembling those of carabiniers (for more details, see page 168).

Thus ended the first major attack on Rayevsky's Redoubt. The fighting had been intense in and around the redoubt and both sides suffered high losses. The French artillery, after Morand's division entered the redoubt, was forced to cease its direct bombardment of the position, in order to avoid injuring its own troops, which allowed the Russians to utilize their firepower. Russian reports are packed with commendations for artillery officers, nominated for awards due to their effective actions against the French infantry. The combat inside the redoubt was vicious and, according to Yermolov, 'not a single prisoner was taken, and few managed to escape out of the entire French brigade'. Rayevsky reported that 'barely anyone escaped from the French'.[352] The 30th Line had less than 300 survivors after (as Laugier puts it) the regiment 'was literally shot to pieces'. François' Company alone lost sixty-eight men. And Griois could see 'the whole esplanade in front of the entrenchment covered by the dead'. The gallant General Bonnamy was spared but, as Yermolov noted, he was 'so badly injured that one may say he was impaled on the points of our bayonets'. Bonnamy was captured by Feldfebel Zolotov of the 18th Jägers, who was promoted to sub lieutenant after the battle.[353]

Some participants claimed that to save himself from a certain death, Bonnamy cried out that he was Murat, King of Naples. Radozhitsky described how he heard a major of the Yeletskii Regiment, who had a slight speech defect, yelling as loud as he could 'Lads ['byatsy']! Muyat [sic] is captured!' which made the soldiers laugh. 'This false Murat,' Radozhitsky noted with embellishment, 'was grabbed by the scruff of the neck by a Russian grenadier with big moustaches and dragged to the Commander-in-Chief'.[354] The news of Murat's capture was celebrated at headquarters but Kutuzov showed a cautious optimism. Mikhailovsky-Danilevsky writes: 'An adjutant at once rushed with the news to Kutuzov's headquarters. On hearing this, the Prince's entire entourage broke out in cheers, he, however, said, "We will await confirmation."' According to Clausewitz:

> several voices proposed to make this news known to all the troops, but some
> calmer heads among the general officers thought the fact so improbable as

to require further confirmation: it was, however, believed for half an hour, although no King of Naples made his appearance, which was accounted for by the supposition of his being severely wounded.[355]

Glinka described in his memoirs as 'Murat' (*alias* Bonnamy) was finally brought to Kutuzov in

a frightfully battered state and reeling from side to side, whether from wounds or other causes. 'Doctor!' was Kutuzov's cry on seeing him, and after exchanging a few words with the wounded man, he had him carried away. Under the uniform of the French hero were found two undershirts and, beneath them, his whole body was ripped with wounds.[356]

Mikhailovsky-Danilevsky reminisced that news of 'Murat's capture' spread through the Russian Army like wildfire. Major von Heideggen of the 4th Jägers heard it from a Cossack, and Major von Wolf, of Eugène of Württemberg's staff, heard it, too. Wolf then told the Duke: 'It will all be over before they call us up ...'

The Russians suffered high losses, but probably the most important of them was General Kutaisov, 'a young hero, well known for his gallantry, good heart and intelligence' as one Russian officer described him. Yermolov recalled that: 'Kutaisov parted with me in the very beginning of the attack on that hill and I never saw him again ...' It was said that Kutaisov and Paskevich had been seen together amidst the crowds of soldiers who pursued the French beyond the redoubt. In the words of Mikhailovsky-Danilevsky, 'It fell on Kutaisov's lot to lead our infantry against the French [...] Shaking hands with Paskevich, Kutaisov moved forward in a bayonet attack – and no one saw him alive anymore.' Meshetich, probably based on rumours, wrote that Kutaisov 'led the nearest cavalry regiment, yelling "Forward, attack, defend your battery!"'[357]

Some time later, Kutaisov's horse returned to camp with its saddle covered with blood and bits of human brain and, as Grabbe noted, 'there was no uncertainty about the fate that befell on him, though his body was never found and the circumstances of the last minutes of his life remain unknown to us'. According to Divov:

[During the attack, Kutaisov] noticed that the guns of Colonel Veselitsky [who commanded the 24th Battery Company] were wasting its ammunition and sent me there to deliver his request [to preserve ammo.] Upon my return, Kutaisov was already gone from the place I left him. Despite all our efforts, [we] were unable to find [him]. Later we saw his brown battle horse, standing idle not so far from the battery where we were standing. We approached it and saw that it was covered with blood and splatters of brain, which convinced us in irreversible loss of this admirable commander.[358]

Still, many cherished a hope that Kutaisov was alive, perhaps wounded and captured by the French. Later that month, Nikolai Durnovo, in St Petersburg, recorded in his diary that: 'a courier brought the news about the decisive battle [at Borodino]. Kutaisov has disappeared and it is believed that he was captured.'[359] Yet, with no reports on Kutaisov's fate, such hopes gradually faded. It was in early October that Kutuzov finally decided to write a letter to Kutaisov's father, whom he'd known since the days of Tsar Paul I: 'I dare not to take my quill so as not to become the first herald of this heartbreaking news,' Kutuzov wrote. 'If the mourning of the entire army at the grave loss of your esteemed son on the battlefield of honour can somehow alleviate your grief, please accept my sincere condolences.' Thus, Kutaisov's 'life ended still in the age of the blossoming youth, enjoying a brilliant career and occupying important position,' Yermolov lamented. 'His loss was mourned not only by his friends: gifted with valuable abilities, he could have rendered great service to his Fatherland in the future.' Glinka shared the grief:

> Looking at him, it was easy to imagine the young Paladin [one of the twelve legendary knight retainers of Charlemagne] from the Middle Ages! And it was even easier to contemplate this due to the fact that the grand Battle of Crécy where the knights, cast in iron, contested each other, was also fought, as was our Borodino, on 26 August of the year 1346! Youth, stature, gallantry, everything combined in Kutaisov, this vivacious and cheerful warrior!

Describing Kutaisov's actions in the battle, Mikhailovsky-Danilevsky later wrote that: 'this talented and fearless artillery commander moved with composure from one battery to another. Several times during the battle, Kutuzov summoned him and they discussed the course of the battle.' When Kutuzov suggested reinforcing the troops with guns from the reserve artillery, 'Kutaisov was so convinced we would hold the ground that he told Kutuzov, "I see no need in sending for the reserve artillery."'[360] As the battle intensified, Kutaisov visited one of the batteries and, while standing there

> a cannon-ball flew above him and several gunners ducked their heads: 'Shame on you for ducking,' Kutaisov told them loudly but a moment later, another cannon-ball whizzed by and this time it was Kutaisov who ducked his head. 'This one does not count,' he said laughing, 'It was my acquaintance, they cast it right in front of me.'[361]

Yet, the assessment of Kutaisov's role in the battle was not unanimously positive. Almost a month after the battle, Lieutenant General Ferdinand Winzegorode wrote to Alexander I: 'No matter what is claimed, the aftermath shows that the battle was lost [. . .] And one of the causes of this defeat lays, as I am assured, in the disorder that spread in the artillery after the death of Count Kutaisov.'[362] A similar sentiment is expressed by Kutuzov's ordinance officer:

> As a result of uncertainty about instructions left by Kutaisov, we had less artillery than [the] French in all directions and, in many cases, our field pieces

had to operate against enemy battery guns. Kutuzov frequently downplayed this incident but he said this only out of politics.[363]

Mikhailovsky-Danilevsky highlighted that Kutaisov's

death had important consequences for the course of the battle, since it deprived the 1st Army of the artillery commander in a battle where artillery played a leading role. Ambiguity about Kutaisov's orders produced incidents when some companies, having exhausted their ammunition, were unaware where to replenish them, while in other cases our light artillery was engaged against the French heavy guns. When the Battle of Borodino was later discussed, Prince Kutuzov frequently said that if we failed to achieve a complete success [...] one of the reasons was the death of Kutaisov.[364]

Among other participants, Grabbe, Norov and Bolgovsky were both critical of Kutaisov's actions, with the latter observing that: 'after the loss of General Kutaisov, our artillery operated disjointedly and without any coordination'.[365] Such arguments were shared by Bogdanovich, who wrote in his classic account of the battle:

Without a doubt, the death of Kutaisov was the reason why many [of] our batteries remained uselessly in the reserve and our artillery failed to show its full capacity [...] Kutuzov himself believed this and later often remarked that the battle would have had a more favourable outcome for us if Kutaisov remained alive.[366]

Although similar opinions can still be found in modern publications (both Russian and Western), Kutaisov should not be held solely responsible for the perceived failure of the Russian artillery. Back in the 1860s, Liprandi – himself an artillery officer at Borodino – campaigned against such attempts to question Kutaisov's actions, justly arguing that:

it is inconceivable to assume that on the eve of the decisive battle [...] [Kutaisov] would have made no arrangements on supplying any battery in need of replenishing its ammunition [...] The secret or uncertainty of such arrangements could not have died with him. His entire staff and regimental commanders were still alive and in place [...] Their location was well known and, in such cases, every battery commander knows what to do [to get ammunition] without consulting with corps artillery commanders, who also must have received instructions either the day before or earlier in the battle.

Liprandi's observations were further elaborated by Larionov, who produced a meticulous study of the Russian artillery at Borodino. It showed that

all 296 guns of the reserve artillery took part in the Battle of Borodino. The main artillery reserve was under direct control of Kutaisov and all of its companies were committed to the battle on his orders. The Russian artillery, in the most vulnerable places, was continuously reinforced from the reserves, which ensured solid defence of these directions [...] Of the artillery companies of the 1st Western Army, only 2nd Don Cossack Horse Artillery and the 8th and 44th Light Companies, which were left on the extreme right flank, did not participate in the battle.[367]

Thus, evidence suggests that Kutaisov's death, although a serious blow to the Russian Army, did not have as serious a consequence as claimed later.

By 11am the first assault on Rayevsky's Redoubt was repelled. The French setback resulted due to a number of factors. There was virtually no coordination of action between the French forces in the centre (Eugène) and right flank (Murat, Ney and Davout), which led some scholars to suggest that Napoleon was responsible for the loss, since he should have provided better direction. Both sides suffered considerable losses, but the French casualties were particularly high. Barclay de Tolly estimated them at 3,000 men, since 'the heights and the valley surrounding it were covered with enemy corpses for a distance of several hundred paces'.[368]

## Extreme Southern Sector – The Old Smolensk Road and Utitsa

On the extreme right flank of the French Army, Poniatowski's Corps of some 10,000 men had advanced with the first rays of light. Although the shortest route to the Old Smolensk Road was through the woods, the Poles had earlier ascertained that it would be impossible for them to transport their artillery through the dense and marshy Utitsa forest, which was also defended by enemy Jägers. As a result, they had to backtrack to Yelnya, where they turned eastward. This march took longer than expected and the Polish attack was delayed when Davout's forces assaulted Bagration's positions. Leading the way was the 16th Division, followed by the reserve artillery of forty guns and the 18th Division. Sébastiani's cavalry was moving in squadron columns south of the road.

The Old Smolensk Road sector was the weakest spot in the Russian positions. Tuchkov commanded about 23,000 men, almost half of them irregular troops. The Opolchenye men, although ardent in their enthusiasm, lacked proper training and were largely armed with pikes and axes. Tuchkov's initial position was four lines deep, with the first two lines occupied by the 1st Grenadier Division (deployed in line) and the two rear lines occupied by the 3rd Division, which was arranged in battalion columns. The Moscow and Smolensk Opolchenye were deployed further behind. However, on the morning of 7 September, Tuchkov's position was weakened by the departure of two Jäger regiments (20th and 21st), which were assigned to Shakhovsky's detachment in the Utitsa woods, and four regiments (the Chernigovskii, Muromskii, Revelskii and Selenginskii) of the 3rd Division, which had been sent to help Bagration around the flèches. Thus, Russian grenadiers carried the brunt of the initial attack of the Polish Corps.

As they approached Tuchkov's position, the Poles – 'superb men, with genuine martial attitude and excellent horses' as one officer described them[369] – engaged the Russian skirmishers near Utitsa. Lieutenant General Stroganov reported that:

33. French Tirailleur and Voltigeu.    *(Bellangé)*

34. French Fusilier-Grenadier.    *(Bellangé)*

35. French Chasseur à Cheval.    *(Bellangé)*

36. Polish Lancer (Ulan) of the Vistula Legion.
*(Bellangé)*

37. Horse Artillery of Napoleon's Imperial Guard. *(Bellangé)*

Carabinier.
1812.

38. French Carabinier. *(Bellangé)*

39. Red (Dutch) Lancer of Napoleon's Imperial Guard. *(Bellangé)*

40. French Chevau-léger. *(Bellangé)*

41. Icon procession on the eve of battle. *(Ivanov)*

42. Counter-attack of the Life Guard Lithuanian Regiment near Semeyonovskoye. *(Samokish)*

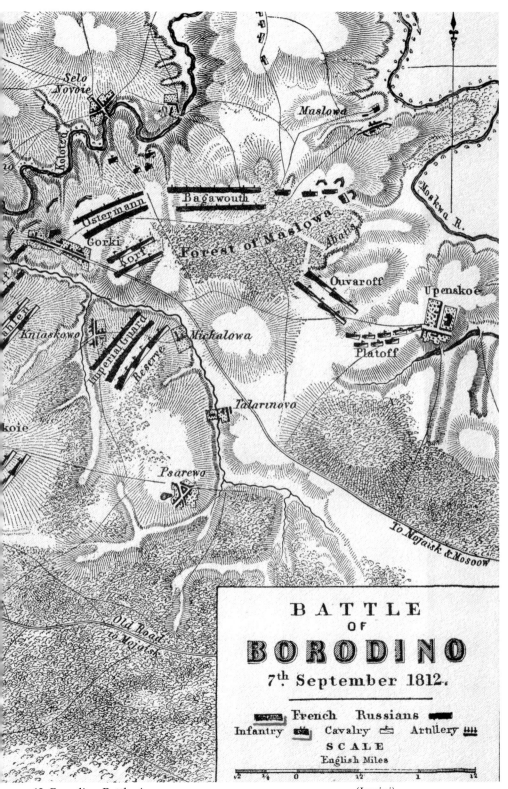

Selo Novoie

Maslowa

Kolord

Moskwa R.

Bagawouth

Ustermann

abatis

Gorki

Forest or Maslowa

Korr.

Ouvaroff

Upenskoe

Kniaskowo

Imperial Guard

Reserve

Michalowa

Platoff

koie

Talarinovo

Psarewo

To Mojaisk & Mosoow

Old Road To Mojaisk

## BATTLE
### OF
# BORODINO
### 7th September 1812.

French — Russians ▬

Infantry ▦  Cavalry ⬦  Artillery ⧢

SCALE

English Miles

½⁄₂   ¼   0   ½₂   1   1½₂

43. Borodino Battle-Array  *(Jomini)*

44. Kutuzov at his command post at Gorki. *(Shepelyuk*

45. Napoleon views the Battle of Borodino from the Shevardino Heights. *(Vereschagin*

6. Combat at the Bagration Flèches.

*(Averyanov)*

7. Battle of Borodino.

*(Desarno)*

48. Bagration wounded.
(Hesse

49. During one of the Allied attacks, General Kostenetsky, a tall man of extraordinary physical strength, seized a ramrod and led a counter-attack against the Lancers. *(painting by A. Averyanov)*

as soon as the French columns began to appear out of woods, the first line of the 1st Grenadier Division, deployed behind the village on the Old Smolensk Road and, commanded by Major General Fock, deployed its skirmishers against the enemy. However, the terrain facilitated the enemy advance. Tuchkov then ordered to retreat behind the 2nd line, commanded by Major General Tsvilenev, and set the village on fire.[370]

Colonel Yegor Richter, commander of the Pavlovskii Grenadier Regiment, travelled to the front line to direct the skirmishers but was soon wounded and replaced by Major Nikolai Musin-Pushkin.

'At the debouch of the woods, in the plain,' Poniatowski reported, 'we saw a strong column of infantry near the village ...' Judging from its size, Poniatowski certainly realized he would face a more resolute resistance than he expected. He ordered up Colonel A. Gursky's battery to a hill on the left side of the road and engaged the Russians in an artillery duel. 'After striking upon the [Russian] column for some time,' as his report described it, Poniatowski sent the 16th Division against the village, which it seized after a brief combat.[371] The official Russian report declared that 'despite a rigorous fire of our artillery' the Polish tirailleurs, supported by advance elements of the 16th Division, emerged in a valley behind the village, where they came across the first line of the 1st Grenadier Division, which repelled their first attack.[372]

Receiving reinforcements, the Poles soon resumed their attack, forcing Tuchkov to withdraw his troops eastward to a more advantageous position near a hillock, known as the Utitsa Kurgan. In his report, Konovnitsyn noted that Tuchkov retreated well before the Polish troops attacked because 'the terrain was disadvantageous to us'. Stroganov, however, described his division deploying sharpshooters ('vislala svoikh strelkov'), after which Tuchkov had to beat a retreat because 'the terrain was advantageous to the enemy'.[373] Yet Poniatowski described the terrain as 'full of woods and thickets, from the small wood to the top of the knoll which dominates the whole plain and which was strongly occupied by the enemy'.[374]

Covered by Stroganov's grenadiers and the smoke of the burning Utitsa, the Russians redeployed to the new position. The Leib Grenadier and Count Arakcheyev's Grenadier Regiments were moved to the right at the bottom of the mound, with the Pavlovskii Regiment placed in reserve behind them. On the left side of the hill, Tuchkov arranged the Ekaterinoslavskii and St Petersburgskii Regiments, which protected six guns of the 1st Battery Company. The Tavricheskii (Taurida) Regiment was located to the north, where it supported the Jäger regiments of Shakhovsky's detachment, which protected the Utitsa woods.[375] The Opolchenye troops were arranged behind the regular troops on both sides of the road. Tuchkov also appealed for reinforcements to Kutuzov and Barclay de Tolly.

But Poniatowski did not press his attack. Instead he dispatched 'three battalions in extended order into the brushes that were full of a great number of Russian chasseurs on foot. A lively fusillade was at once engaged as well as a very strong cannonade, which lasted until noon.'[376] Indeed, considerable time was spent in this skirmishing, and hesitation marked Poniatowski's actions. He could see that the Russian forces exceeded his own and his original mission of turning the Russian left flank could not be easily accomplished without additional forces. After Utitsa was occupied, he dispatched his aide-de-camp, Lieutenant Rostworowski, to inform Napoleon of the situation and request his decision on further operations. Rostworoski was seriously wounded on his way and Roman Soltyk saw him arriving

> pale and with his coat covered in blood. He could hardly keep his horse [. . .] He was losing a lot of blood. Yet, he had had the courage to carry out his mission. Scarcely had he arrived at the ambulance to have his wound attended to than he fainted . . .

As a result, Rostworowski could not timely and sufficiently apprise the Emperor of the situation on the extreme right flank. Almost two hours were wasted in such vacillation, which was of importance, since Poniatowski could not turn the Russian flank and threaten Bagration, who was, by now, heavily engaged with Ney and Davout. Napoleon finally made his decision, ordering Poniatowski to renew his efforts and instructing Ney to divert VIII Corps southward to help the Poles.[377]

As VIII Corps progressed southwards, Tharreau's 24th Division engaged Shakhovsky's Jägers in the Utitsa woods and was later charged by the Russian cuirassiers. Poniatowski, meantime, prepared to resume his advance and take the Russian-controlled Utitsa Kurgan. The Polish divisions deployed in attack columns and a large battery – estimates vary from twenty-two to forty pieces – was set up near the main road. The artillery duel between the Polish and Russian batteries (Glukhov's six heavy guns and Ditterix IV's twelve light guns) continued for some time and participants attested to a relentless cannonade. The Polish artillery did enjoy numerical superiority and used its firepower and skill to suppress the Russian batteries. Stroganov acknowledged that 'our [six-gun] battery continued to operate until it lost most of its men and exhausted [a] large portion of its ammunition and was compelled to reduce its firing, operating with four guns only.' After the battle, Stroganov also noted that Colonel Glukhov 'forced the enemy batteries to withdraw several times', while Ditterix IV was commended for 'maintaining an effective fire against the enemy'.[378] According to General Karpov: 'Both sides maintained such a petrifying fire that salvos of guns arranged in line resembled battalion volleys of infantry, while the artillery thunder suppressed any other sounds.'

The Poles finally launched an assault and in a bitter hand-to-hand fighting, seized the Kurgan. The Russians managed to remove their guns from the hilltop and retreated eastward to regroup. Poniatowski, standing on a hill, could now see the Russian forces, including the Opolchenye troops extending further eastward, and the sight probably further convinced him of the difficulty of his mission.

The Polish success proved short-lived, since Russian reinforcements were already on their way. In response to Tuchkov's earlier request, Barclay

# 7 September: The Battle of Borodino Phase One (6am to 12am)

de Tolly dispatched the 17th Division of Baggovut's II Corps to the Old Smolensk Road. Passing behind the Semeyonovskii ravine, Baggovut noticed a large number of enemy troops massing in the valley to his right. These were the Westphalians, dispatched to help Poniatowski, but who had became bogged down en route. Baggovut immediately diverted four battalions of the Brest and Ryazan Regiments and the 17th Battery Company to help local Russian forces, and receiving Tuchkov's message that 'the enemy was attacking and seeking to seize the hill on his left flank', he instructed Lieutenant General Olsufiev to hurry there with the 2nd Brigade of Major General Yakov Vadkovsky. For greater firepower, Baggovut replaced the six light guns of the 39th Light Company, which was assigned to Olsufiev's division, with six heavy pieces of the 17th Battery Company.[379] Paskevich also referred to Russian Cuirassiers attacking the Westphalians, who 'tried to break through between the Russian left flank and Tuchkov's troops'.[380]

Olsufiev arrived just as Tuchkov was rallying his troops after the loss of the Utitsa Kurgan. Taking advantage of reinforcements, Tuchkov launched a counter-attack, personally leading the Pavlovskii Grenadier Regiment up the hill. Olsufiev was told to turn the left flank of Poniatowski while Stroganov, with the St Petersburgskii and Ekaterinoslavskii Grenadiers (supported by the Leib-Grenadier and Count Arakcheyev Regiments), flanked the Polish right. The outcome of this attack hardly could have been surprising since, as Polish historian Kukiel noted, six Polish battalions (of the 16th Division) faced fourteen Russian battalions.[381] The Moscow and Smolensk militiamen also took part in the charge.

As Baggovut reported, the Poles maintained

> a heavy fire on our battery, sending forth skirmishers supported by a strong column which sought to prevent us from [re]capturing the Heights that were of great advantage to them. Canister and cannon-ball fire, produced by the enemy batteries, could not contain the swiftness of movement with which Lieutenant Shepotiev, acting with remarkable sangfroid, led his artillery company to his location and acted with such incredible skill that rarely was there a round that did not inflict heavy damage on the enemy; in short time, the enemy columns, advancing against our battery, were forced to retreat. However, the enemy battery, despite two of its caissons being blown up by Shepotiev's actions, continued its powerful fire against our batteries and infantry columns.[382]

The Russian infantry assault, meantime, reached its destination on the slopes of the Kurgan.[383] Poniatowski dispatched reinforcements – 'another column, more powerful than the first one', as Baggovut described it – but Olsufiev directed Lieutenant Colonel Kern with the soldiers of the Belozerskii Infantry Regiment against them. Supported by the Pavlovskii Grenadiers, Kern halted the Polish advance, earning praise from the newly arrived Konovnitsyn, who told him: 'If it were up to me, I would have taken off my Cross of St George and given it to you!' The Russian infantry was supported by gunners who 'hastily pulled six battery guns up the hill and, deploying them at reduced intervals', opened a canister fire that forced the

# The Battle of Borodino

Poles to withdraw towards the woods in the rear. As Stroganov described, the Polish skirmishers, meantime, tried to 'force their way into the brushwood that separated our right flank from the left wing of the 2nd Army, but the Tavricheskii Grenadier Regiment, led by Colonel Sulima, was sent against them'.[384]

Prior to the attack of the 18th Division, Poniatowski joined the 5th Polish Chasseurs à Cheval south of the road and intended to flank the Russian left. However, Sébastiani prevented him from doing this, telling him: 'Where are you going, my Prince, do not you know that there are masses of Russian infantry on your left? You will be cut off from the Grand Army and destroyed ...'[385] Poniatowski then called off his attack and moved some of his cavalry to the left flank. He reported that

> it became impossible for [Polish infantry] to sustain their efforts against a force infinitely superior. We were repulsed from the knoll, but we managed to maintain position in the undergrowth [...] I had my batteries continue to strike the summit of the knoll where the enemy had twelve large-calibre pieces.[386]

Thus the Russian attack was successful in both recapturing the important height and containing the Polish flanking manoeuvre. However, it cost the Russians the life of their commander, Nikolai Tuchkov, who was seriously wounded on the hilltop when a Polish bullet pierced his chest. Unbeknown to him, his brother, Alexander, had died shortly before, leading a charge near the flèches. Nikolai would live for another two months after the battle before dying in Yaroslavl on 11 November 1812. With Tuchkov wounded, Baggovut assumed command of the Russian troops on the Old Smolensk Road. He regrouped his forces, deployed a battery on the Kurgan and requested reinforcements. In response, the Kremenchugskii and Minskii Regiments of the 4th Division marched to the Old Smolensk Road.

It was noon already. Poniatowski's troops remained on defensive for the next couple of hours, although their artillery occasionally engaged the Russians. Back at Shevardino, Brandt of the Vistula Legion met Captain Desaix, who 'paused briefly before us, saying, "I have just come from the right and your Prince Poniatowski is not making any progress. The Emperor is not very pleased with him. Our losses are enormous; the Russians are fighting like madmen."'[387]

## The Battle of Borodino Phase Two (12am to 6pm)

We left the village of Borodino shortly after the attack by Delzon's division in the opening act of the battle. The village was recaptured by the counter-attacking Russian troops, who were then ordered to abandon it to the French. For the next several hours, one brigade of Delzon's division was engaged in intermittent skirmishing with the Russian Jägers along the river, while the second brigade was deployed north of the village. The 21st and 22nd Light Cavalry Brigades were moved to the left bank of the Voina to cover the left flank of the French troops at Borodino. Not far from them was the 84th Line, while two squadrons of the 4th Bavarian Chevau-léger

# The Battle of Borodino Phase Two (12am to 6pm)

were left behind near the village of Bezzubovo.[388] General Anthouard de Vraincourt deployed his and Colonel Millot's batteries on the heights east of Borodino and maintained fire against the Russian right flank. Sources disagree on the number of French guns involved, estimates varying from twenty to almost 100. Labaume and Laugier indicate that, in addition to his own battery, Anthouard de Vraincourt was also assisted by the reserve artillery of the 15th Division and the Italian Guard. Russian participants agree that the French had set up 'large batteries' near Borodino, which waged an efficient fire. Memoirs of Bavarian officers reveal that their cavalry was dismounted until noon and observed the ongoing battle from a distance. By late morning, as the fighting at Semeyonovskoye and Rayevsky's Redoubt escalated, Napoleon had only about 10,000 men, including some 2,000 cavalrymen, covering his extreme left flank while the majority of his forces were shifted to the centre and the right flank. As a result, his left wing became weakened and, as Pelet noted, 'attacking with its right shoulder forward [the French] gradually subsided from the New Smolensk Road, which served as their line of communication'.

## Northern Sector – The Cavalry Raid
Around 7am, shortly after the combat for Borodino ended, Ataman Platov, with the Ilovaisky V, Grekov XVIII, Kharitonov VII, Denisov VII, Zhirov and parts of the Ataman and Simferopol Horse Tartar Regiments, departed his camp and began moving along the right flank of the Russian Army.[389] Clausewitz, who was at the Russian headquarters, recalled that Platov

> was astonished where he had expected to find the entire left wing of the enemy to meet with few or no troops. He saw the left wing of [Eugène] moving against Borodino and it seemed to him that nothing would be easier to fall on its left flank, et cætera [...] In short, Platoff [sic] dispatched the Prince of Hesse-Philippsthal who was with him as a volunteer, to General Kutuzov to acquaint him with the discovery he had made and to make the proposal to throw a considerable body of cavalry over the river by the ford and fall on the exposed flank of the enemy.[390]

Colonel Ernst Constantine Hesse-Philippsthal was forty-one years old and, although Clausewitz describes him as 'a young officer without experience', he did serve in the Hessian Army for many years before enlisting in the Russian military in 1808, fighting the Turks and suffering two serious wounds in as many years. Platov's idea appealed to him and he presented it to Colonel Toll 'with so much liveliness that at first it really had a winning appearance'. Clausewitz noted that Hesse-Philippsthal reached headquarters at an important moment, when Toll just returned with an exaggerated report that

> all was going on favourably [on the left wing], Bagration having repulsed every attack. At the same moment arrived an account that in the redoubt of the centre, which had for a moment been regained from the French who had stormed it, the King of Naples had been taken prisoner.

# The Battle of Borodino

The reader certainly remembers that situation was far from favourable on the left wing, where Bagration's troops were in the midst of a bloodbath, and that 'the King of Naples' was none other than the unfortunate General Bonnamy. But the truth is in the eye of beholder and, as Clausewitz recalled, 'the enthusiasm blazed up like lighted straw' when Toll and Hesse-Philippsthal laid before Kutuzov the idea of attacking the French left flank. Clausewitz was cautious of the idea and he criticized Toll, who was 'too much carried away by the pervading feeling, believed that a lively diversion with a corps of cavalry on the enemy's left would strike an effectual blow and perhaps decide the battle'.

Bennigsen, who was present at this scene, later wrote in his memoirs:

> After the enemy launched an attack, as I predicted, against our left wing, I hurried to Prince Kutuzov and told him the following, 'If you do not want to have your left wing shattered, you must reinforce it with the troops from the right flank; if only they would arrive in time there.' Kutuzov listened to me and then ordered to send some troops to strengthen our left flank.

Bennigsen then listened to Toll's report on the cavalry raid and witnessed Kutuzov's approval of it.[391] Löwenstern, Barclay de Tolly's adjutant, reached headquarters to find Kutuzov

> standing still, surrounded by a large suite. Throughout the day, General Bennigsen and Colonel Toll explored the battlefield on the orders of Kutuzov. Bennigsen briefly stopped to talk to Barclay de Tolly, and when he left, Barclay told me, 'This man would spoil everything – he is very envious. His self-esteem makes him think that only he is capable to give a battle and conduct it with success. There is no doubt that he is talented but he seeks to use his skills only to satisfy his ambition; he is disinterested in this great and sacred matter [and] I consider his presence with the army as a great adversity. Kutuzov shares my opinion. Let us see now how he would execute a cavalry movement on our extreme right flank, which I count on to move forward with all my reserves. This should deliver a powerful blow to the enemy.'[392]

Memoirs suggest that the proposal for launching a cavalry raid came from Platov, via Prince Hesse-Philippsthal and Toll, to Kutuzov. However, subsequent battle histories sought to mitigate the awkward fact that such a 'great' idea did not emanate from the Commander-in-Chief. So attempts were made to correct it. Thus, according to Alexander Mikhailovsky-Danilevsky, receiving reports on casualties on the left flank, Kutuzov

> desiring to personally confirm their veracity, ascended a nearby hill that was showered by grenades and their fragments [...] The life of a man on whom Russia placed her hopes was now hanging by a hair. In vain did his adjutants try to persuade him to come down from the hill and, when no arguments convinced him, the adjutants simply took the reigns of his horse and led him out of the fire. After this personal observation, Kutuzov made two orders [...] [and under the second order,] Platov, with Cossacks, and Uvarov, with the I Cavalry Corps, were to ford the Kolocha upstream from Borodino and attack the enemy

left wing. With such movement, Prince Kutuzov sought to distract Napoleon's attention and divert some of his forces from our left wing.[393]

This account leaves no doubt who came up with the idea of the cavalry raid and then made a decision to act upon it. It was Kutuzov, without any input from other generals. However, Clausewitz left a drastically different account of how Kutuzov arrived at his decision. After Toll presented Platov's suggestion, the Russian Commander-in-Chief simply replied 'C'est bon, prenez le!' Kutuzov 'had been listening to all the reports and discussions like one who did not exactly know whether he stood on his head or his heels, and only from time to time said "C'est bon, faites le!"' This version is plainly critical of Kutuzov, who shows no initiative and passively observes the flow of the battle.

These contrasting accounts eventually produced feuding factions, which sought to correct the historical record. Mikhailovsky-Danilevsky's attempt to embellish Kutuzov's reputation was certainly due to his status as a court historian, whose writings were regularly censored. However, the historian also had a personal feud with Colonel Toll, which probably made him seek ways to erase his rival from the annals of history. Among participants of the battle, Bennigsen, Wolzogen and Toll were highly critical of Mikhailovsky-Danilevsky and tried to correct Kutuzov's role in making the decision.[394] On the opposite side, Liprandi objected to Clausewitz's account and called for Russian historians to rely on memoirs of 'genuine' Russians rather than of 'some foreign German'. Liprandi argued that if the cavalry raid idea was first suggested by Platov, he would have been appointed to command it, especially considering the fact that Uvarov was a lieutenant general, while Platov was a full general. He also disputed the notion of Toll being able to influence Kutuzov and instead portrayed Kutuzov as a strong-willed and independent leader.[395]

This approach was later taken by the Soviet historians and can be traced through virtually all Soviet-era publications. Beskrovny, in his 1951 study, asserted that Kutuzov was the person behind the manoeuvre and it was due to his 'anticipating Kutuzov's counter-manoeuvre' that Napoleon refused to commit his Imperial Guard elsewhere. Tarle repeated Mikhailovsky-Danilevsky's account and described the raid as Kutuzov's 'sudden and truly ingenious decision' and 'cunningly conceived and brilliantly executed diversion'. Garnich went as far as to claim that Kutuzov 'planned this manoeuvre before the battle' and was supported in this assertion by Beskrovny, who, in his 1968 study, believed that 'Kutuzov seized [the] initiative from Napoleon by dispatching M.I. Platov and F.P. Uvarov's cavalry on flanking raid'.[396] To support this official version of history, special artworks were commissioned, depicting Kutuzov actively directing Platov (who was not at Gorki at all) and Uvarov to launch the raid. All these claims were far-fetched. Kutuzov could not have conceived the raid prior to the battle, since he was still concerned that Napoleon would make his main attack against the Russian right flank so Platov, acting with Cossacks only, could produce no tangible results. Instead, Kutuzov's initial order simply instructed Platov to make a reconnaissance of the enemy left flank and the Cossack Ataman's six regiments were more than enough for forceful scouting.

So, the decision to launch a raid was made. Kutuzov agreed to assign half of Platov's Cossacks (up to 2,700 men) and Uvarov's entire I Cavalry Corps (about 2,440 men with twelve guns) for this mission.[397] The strength of the Russian cavalry committed to this manoeuvre varies between Russian and Western studies, mainly because the latter often include Platov's total Cossack force, when in reality he led only six regiments.[398] The attacking body consisted entirely of cavalry, without infantry support, and as such could hardly have achieved serious results. Clausewitz lamented that 'a due estimate of the magnitude of the undertaking was wanting ...'

The area between Bezzubovo and Borodino was intersected by several marshy rivulets with steep banks. Just south of Bezzubovo was a small lake, created by a dam on the Voina stream. The banks of the stream were steep, as Lieutenant Heilbronner attested. A small mill with a bridge was situated near the dam. The Allied 21st Light Cavalry Brigade was moved to the left bank of the Voina around 10am, while the 22nd and 13th Brigades were on the opposite bank along with the Bavarian battery of Captain Wiedemann. The French infantry was also deployed along the banks: the 84th Line being near the mill, while the 92nd and 106th further south. There were additional French forces available at the confluence of the Voina and Kolocha, where Chastel's 3rd Light Cavalry Division, La Houssaye's 6th Heavy Cavalry Division, and the Italian Guard with artillery were located.

As his cavalry began moving, Uvarov forded the Kolocha near Maloye Selo and deployed the Yelisavetgradskii Hussars and the Guard Cossacks in the front line, with the Guard Dragoons, Uhlans and Hussar regiments behind them. The Nezhinskii Dragoons and the 2nd Horse Artillery Company were moving further in the rear. According to Clausewitz, 'it was between 11[am] and 12[noon]' when Uvarov's troops finally reached the Voina stream. Löwenstern, standing near Gorki, was dissatisfied the way Uvarov handled the attack, noting that 'either orders were not particularly precise or the General, who was entrusted with this attack, was not sufficiently skilled; in any case, the movement was carried out quite clumsily. General Uvarov, who directed it, showed himself as an incompetent man.' Uvarov's slow movement can be partially explained by the rough terrain, but one can agree with Löwenstern's lament that the Russians 'could have achieved completely different results if the cavalry, delegated to turn the enemy left flank, were commanded by someone of Vasilchikov's, Pahlen's, Lambert's or Chernyshev's stature'. Instead, the Russian cavalry advance was 'remarkably slow-paced and [...] seemed to tell the enemy "Beware!" [instead of attacking] [...] the entire manoeuvre was executed methodically and unhurriedly .'[399]

Lieutenant Heilbronner of the 4th Chevau-léger was with his company, assigned to patrol duty along the stream, where he could see such steep banks that it seemed impossible to me that a cavalry could cross the river here. So I calmly watched the opposite bank that suddenly became alive with enormous masses of enemy cavalry. Numerous horsemen appeared seeking a ford. Suddenly, a long cavalry column approached [the brook] and, descending into the ravine, it crossed it. I quickly turned back to withdraw my company but it was too late and a moment later I was in a tight circle of attacking Russian cavalrymen and all of us galloped in confusion through the woods. These were the troops of the [Russian] Guard light cavalry under [the] command of Uvarov, who decided to launch this attack to turn our left flank. I noticed that the enemy cavalry was in disarray and, it was a bit slighting that the enemy cavalrymen did not even notice my small detachment. And so I moved amidst a glittering escort of Guard Hussars and Cossacks, completely unnoticed by them ...[400]

Platov, informed of Uvarov's advance, ordered his Cossacks to spread along the valley and harass the enemy lines. Cossacks made several charges to probe the French defence and the Ataman reported that he 'acted offensively against the enemy cavalry and infantry, which was in the woods, and after numerous charges, we routed [the French] cavalry and captured up to 200 [men].'[401] With a mass of blue and red uniformed Cossacks moving towards the enemy, Glinka recalled that

the entire valley suddenly flushed brightly with Don Cossacks. They began making circles and flaunting their tricks. The French forward patrols quickly fled [but] the Cossacks sat on their shoulders! The French and Germans tried in vain to fend them off with their long swords and spurred their heavy horses [to escape]: yet, the Don Cossacks, braced to their saddles, flew like arrows on their small horses, circled around, rushed forward and stung them with their lances like incensed wasps. It soon began to resemble a hunt on hares. Russian soldiers, standing near the Gorki Heights [...] saw the Don Cossacks' valour and cheered them: they waived their hands, laughed aloud and yelled, 'Look at them, look at them! Well done Cossacks! Bravo Cossacks! Show no mercy to the French!'

As soon as the Russian cavalry was noticed, Ornano sent an urgent message to Eugène, which was received as the Viceroy was preparing for a new assault on Rayevsky's Redoubt.[402] Concerned about the flanking manoeuvre, Eugène halted his attack and, sending his adjutant to inform Napoleon, rushed himself to the new theatre of action. As Clausewitz described:

the village [of Borodino] lay on [Uvarov's] left, in which the troops of [Eugène] had established themselves; before him was the brook, which runs through swampy meadows. On his side of it stood a couple of regiments of cavalry and a mass of infantry [...] The French cavalry retired immediately over a dam, which crossed the brook at about 2,000 paces from Borodino; the infantry, however, was bold enough to remain and form square with the dam in their rear.[403]

Among the French Regiments were the 84th Line, which organized square in front of the dam, while the 1st Croatian Provisional Regiment, the 92nd Line and 8th Light deployed into battalion squares further downstream.[404] Mitarevsky, standing near Rayevsky's Redoubt, claimed the enemy troops were in confusion, 'running on the right side from the village [Borodino] and moving into the field, where they organized several squares a few moments later'.[405] Meanwhile, Glinka recalled that:

> The commotion at Borodino did not escape the eyes of [Russian] spectators [...] 'Look! Look! The Frenchies ["Frantsuzishki"] are making a square: they are in trouble. We are winning!' [the soldiers shouted] and many of them clapped and yelled 'Hurrah!'[406]

According to Prince Eugène, Delzon's troops

> rapidly formed into squares but this formation was not yet accomplished when the Croats received a charge that they repulsed with their fire. The enemy cavalry, reinforced by new squadrons, came to charge the 84th, which received it in the same manner. The forces of this cavalry were increasing each moment, it renewed successfully its charges on the square of the 8th Light and the Croats, of the 84th and the 92nd.[407]

Eugène got to the front line during one of the Russian cavalry attacks and, as Lejeune described, he 'was going about amongst his battalions' when the Russians, 'who had probably recognized him, ordered a considerable body of Cossacks to charge and try to carry [Eugène] off'.

Prince Eugène had no other recourse but to take refuge inside the square of the 84th Line, where Colonel Jean-Gaudens-Claude Pégot, who commanded the regiment, assured him that he was as safe inside the square as in one of his palaces. At the same time, General Anthouard and Colonel Millot redeployed their batteries to face the new threat and began firing upon the Russian cavalry. Eugène also dispatched orders to Grouchy to send additional cavalry from his corps against the Russians. 'It was about 11am,' wrote Lieutenant Combe of the 8th Chasseurs à Cheval, 'when General Grouchy's adjutant reached us ordering us to move to the left and cross the road upstream from Borodino ...' Anthouard noted that a large part of the III Cavalry Corps was deployed at that time, while Griois referred to just one brigade (the 11th) and Cerrini acknowledged only the Chasseurs à Cheval regiments of Chastel's division.[408] According to Laugier of the Italian Guard

> at that very moment, we were fording the Kolocha, and, while preserving the greatest calm, were hastening our steps, the more ardent for a rumour that the Prince himself was in danger. Meanwhile, the Russian cavalry, growing more numerous, renewed its charges against the squares of the Croat's 8th Light, of the 84th and the 92nd Line ...[409]

Clausewitz, accompanying Uvarov

> suggested in vain that the artillery should first open upon the [enemy in squares]'. But, Uvarov and 'the Russian officers feared that they would then retire and escape capture. The Hussars of the Guard were therefore advanced, and ordered to charge. They made three ineffectual attacks; the infantry lost neither their composure nor their ranks and returned a steady fire. The Hussars retired, as usually happens in such cases, some thirty paces, and withdrew out

# The Battle of Borodino Phase Two (12am to 6pm)

of fire. General Uwarow [*sic*] then discontinued these not very brilliant attempts and caused the artillery to open; at the first discharge, the enemy retired over the defile [and] the whole affairs then came to an end.[410]

Uvarov's report adds some details to Clausewitz's account. The attack was made

despite disadvantageous terrain since we had to cross a deep ravine and a rivulet and, after ascending the opposite bank, to engage the enemy, with the [enemy occupied] village [of Borodino] to our left and the woods full of enemy troops to the right. Despite these difficulties, the attack was carried out in front of the entire army with an unexpected success. The enemy was routed and the battery barely managed to escape, but its two guns were seized by the Yelisavetgradskii Hussars; if not for such unfavourable terrain, they would have been removed at once. The enemy suffered considerable losses during the pursuit.[411]

Further research reveals that the first attack was entrusted to Major General Vasili Orlov-Denisov, who led the Life Guard Hussar and Cossack Regiments and the Yelisavetgradskii Hussars; they were followed by the Life Guard Dragoon, Uhlan, and Nezhinskii Dragoon Regiments, supported by the 2nd Horse Company.[412] The Russian charge, however, faced stiff resistance. Ornano's cavalry crossed the dam across the Voina, which was protected by several squares organized by the 8th Light, 1st Croat Regiment, 84th and 92nd Line. The 6th, 8th and 25th Chasseurs à Cheval of Chastel's division were moved to the left bank of the Kolocha, later followed by additional troops from Grouchy's III Cavalry Corps and the Italian Guard.

During their attacks, the Russian cavalrymen suffered high casualties attacking the squares. Bavarian officer von Muraldt saw

the enemy cavalry [. . .] implementing its plan. By the time the voltigeurs reached us, the wood was already in enemy hands. And hardly had the voltigeurs drawn up to our left, within range of it than individual sharpshooters from the Guard Cossacks were already visible on its fringe. As soon as the enemy facing us saw we had been outflanked, he crossed the Kolotcha [*sic*], everywhere shallow and easily forded, and, protected by his artillery, attacked our front. Every moment we were waiting for the order to advance against him; but whether our general's attention was mainly directed towards the attack threatening our flank or for some other reason no such order came; and we could only wait the enemy, who was coming at us flat out. Not until the Russians were 200 paces away did the order come: 'Carbines up! Fire!' And hardly had we fired out carbines – mostly without effect (as is usual with cavalry) – than we were attacked and over-thrown by two hussar regiments [. . .] At the same time, the Guard Cossacks were advancing out of the wood, overriding both our voltigeur companies, and striking into our flank. Attacked from front and in flank, and on such utterly unfavourable terrain, the many of us took to our heels. For a moment, generals, officers and soldiers swirled around in a single confused mass. Everyone was spurring his horse to get out of this jam as quick as ever he could . . .

Uvarov's charge forced Bavarian commander Preysing to order 'one of my brigades to move forward onto a near hill to support the infantry. My troops barely reached it when they were charged by several enemy Regiments'. Bavarian officer Wiedemann recalled 'several Cossack sotnyas that made a feint attack, brandishing sabres and firing, against the [2]1st Chevau-léger Brigade'. Another participant saw

> several sotnyas of Cossacks and Dragoons attacking the 21st Brigade and, although they were fired upon by Captain Wiedemann's battery and another French battery deployed behind this brigade, they executed a vigorous charge against it. They were hardheartedly met by carabiniers, who opened fire at a close range and forced them to retreat.

The Yelisavetgradskii Hussar Regiment was repelled and it was pursued by the Bavarian regiments, who were, in turn, charged by the Life Guard Uhlan Regiment, which was later commended for 'halting enemy cavalry and infantry columns that sought to attack and pierce the [Russian] line'.[413]

Artillery officer Radozhitsky, watching from the vicinity of the Gorki Heights, was

> thrilled to see as our cavalry moved on the opposite riverbank in long lines of red and blue Hussars and Uhlans and then charged the French cavalry, driving it beyond Borodino; then it made an attack on an artillery battery and the Yelisavetgradskii Hussar Regiment seized two guns. But four enemy infantry regiments, deployed in squares, moved against our cavalry, which attacked each of them but was forced to retreat after being unable to break them.

Not far from Radozhitsky, Mitarevsky also observed the fighting but his recollections are less favourably towards Uvarov's men. Mitarevsky observed as

> our cavalry quickly advanced and then charged forward [...] A thought flashed in my mind – as squares would discharge their muskets, our cavalry would charge and overwhelm them, and then it would be easier to deal with them. Yet, it proved quite different in reality: the cavalry approached [squares] to a musket range and then quickly turned back, without the [enemy] squares even firing. 'Did you see that? asked our staff officer, who just approached us, 'And there goes their attack!' We then made a few disparaging comments about them.

Notwithstanding Mitarevsky's criticism, the Russian cavalry did make several charges and sought to cross the river over the dam, but its efforts were thwarted by the French squares and the canister fire which thwarted two Russian crossing attempts.

Uvarov and Platov then deployed the 2nd Horse Company of Lieutenant Colonel Goring to engage 'the enemy battery that was set up on the edge of the woods and acted against our Corps'. After a short artillery duel, that battery was forced to retreat but this minor success failed to bring any breakthrough for the Russians.[414]

A few miles south of the fight, Roth von Schreckenstein was initially concerned by the enemy move that 'seemed to be a serious flanking attack'. He saw several officers of the 7th Cuirassier Division, among them

# The Battle of Borodino Phase Two (12am to 6pm)

Colonel Leyser (of the Saxon Gardes du Corps) and brigade commanders Thielemann and Lepel, discussing this new development. Noting that no enemy infantry or artillery was committed to the attack, they quickly agreed that 'this movement, which initially was quite threatening, would have no serious effect'.[415] Clausewitz, who was 'convinced from the beginning that this diversion could produce no result', noted in his memoirs that

> a diversion by 2,500 horse could not possibly have a decisive influence on a battle delivered on one side by 130,000 men; it could at best put a spoke in the wheel of their plans for a moment, and astonish them more or less.[416]

It was already afternoon and the Russian Army – struggling to hold ground on the left flank and the centre, and with most of its reserves already committed – was in urgent need of respite. Uvarov's raid might have delivered it but, as we have seen, it quickly stalled. Still, as Clausewitz suggested, 'the Russians could contemplate no offensive movement other than that confided to General Uwarow [and so] all eyes were now turned to that officer'. Kutuzov sent several adjutants and staff officers to 'see whether anything could possibly be done in this quarter',[417] and Colonel Toll, together with General Ozharovsky, also visited Uvarov 'in order to find means so that the raid, or to be precise, diversion, attempted by [Uvarov's] forces, had more noticeable effect on the events of that day. However, everyone came to conclusion that it was impossible to do.'[418] Clausewitz agreed with Toll that

> all rode back with the conviction that General Uwarow could effect nothing. It both seemed no trifling matter to pass this brook under the fire of the enemy and so many troops were seen standing idle as reserves on the other side that it was plainly impossible for 2,500 horse to affect the result of the battle by any effort in that quarter.

The Russian cavalry forces, meantime, became split after Platov continued his movement westward to threaten the French rear and baggage train. As the Russian regular cavalry made its futile charges on a dam, the Cossack Ataman 'was a quarter of a league to the right of Uwarow, and looking for a passage over the marshy stream [Voina]'.[419] Around noon, his troops had at length found a passage not far from Loginovo and quickly moved across the Voina, where Platov ordered his men 'to proceed to the right, and, attacking the enemy flank and rear, make a rapid attack against the enemy'.[420] Lieutenant Flotow soon saw some Russian troops

> secretly moving towards a village [Bezzubovo] on our left flank; the village was defended by four companies and additional troops were sent to support them. But they were not sufficient to repel a superior enemy [...] and were forced to retreat beyond defile.[421]

The Cossack manoeuvre threatened the left flank of Prince Eugène's troops opposite Uvarov's squadrons near the dam, and Platov reported that 'the enemy [probably Italian Chasseurs], located beyond the woods, was routed by the rapid attack of the [Cossack] Regiments and fled leaving many casualties behind'. Among those fleeing were the Italian Chasseurs à Cheval of Villata's 13th Brigade, who were rescued by the Bavarian troops of Major General von Preysing-Moos' 22nd Light Cavalry Brigade. The 4th and 5th Chevau-léger engaged the Cossacks and were supported by a two-gun battery under Lieutenant Belli de Pino that fired canister at the charging Cossacks. However, General Ornano soon ordered the battery to withdraw, fearing the enemy might capture it.[422]

It is unclear how far Platov's Cossacks advanced into the rear of the French Army. Platov reported that 'Colonel Balabin, acting on the flank and partially in the rear of the enemy, harassed and slew the enemy, capturing plenty of prisoners ...' Soviet scholars claimed the Cossacks went as far as Valuyevo, which was in the rear of the Grand Army.

The news of the Russian appearance on the western bank of the Voina reached Napoleon just as he was about to order his Young Guard to advance in support of troops fighting near Semeyonovskoye and the Grand Redoubt, but 'a heavy fire beyond the stream [Voina], out of the brushwood, upon the left wing'[423] made him postpone this decision. The Russians across the field could see 'commotion on the heights extending from Borodino to the Kolotsk Monastery [...] and it was remarkable to see how hastily were many of the camp tents removed!'[424] Unaware of the strength of the enemy raiding party, Napoleon realized that it could spread confusion among his troops and threaten his baggage train and lines of communication. On his orders, troops were dispatched to support Eugène, though it is unclear exactly which units were involved. Russian scholar Popov suggested the 1st Chevau-léger Lancier de la Garde Regiment, but Chlapowski noted that the unit did not participate in the fighting that day, while Krasinski and Zaluski argued that Napoleon sent only a squadron of this regiment, which was assigned to his escort. Furthermore, Dautancourt referred to Colbert's brigade, consisting of the 2nd Chevau-léger Lancier de la Garde Regiment (Dutch), while General Anthouard mentioned the chasseurs à cheval units. Napoleon then went himself to investigate what was happening on the left flank. Although many French memoirs fail to record this trip, Dautancourt and Pelet tell us that Napoleon travelled to the Kolocha river and, after making a quick observation, returned to his headquarters near Shevardino.

One can contrast this testimony with the claims of many Russian/ Soviet historians that Napoleon personally led one of the Guard divisions to reinforce his left flank and remained there for hours to stabilize it. Mikhailovsky-Danilevsky claims that Napoleon remained with Eugène on the left flank until 3pm and his absence from the headquarters at Shevardino gave the Russians a breathing space in the centre and on the left. Danilevsky wrote: 'Those who fought at Borodino certainly remember that minute when the determination of enemy attacks declined along the entire line and the firepower became considerably weaker and we, as someone justly noted, "could breath freely [at last.]"' Eugène Tarle, described Napoleon 'flying like an arrow' to the left flank, where, as Garnich and Beskrovny agreed, he remained for two hours.[425]

# The Battle of Borodino Phase Two (12am to 6pm)

Back at the dam, Clausewitz saw that, with Platov attacking their left flank, the French troops

> immediately in our front feared to be locked in the morass and made a side movement. The Cossack Regiment of the Guard attached to Uwarow's Corps could stand it no longer: like a rocket with its tail, they were over the dam like lightning and into the wood to join their brethren.

They were followed by the Yelisavetgradskii Hussars. Opposing them, Colonel Seyssel led his 4th Chevau-léger to help the Italian Chasseurs against the Cossacks, while Colonel Gaddum's Bavarians of the 5th Chevau-léger hurried to protect the battery. The front lines of Seyssel's troops became disordered after the fleeing Italians passed through them, and were soon under Cossack attacks from left flank and rear. To face them, Major Sigmund Bieber of the 4th Chevau-léger recalled seeing

> the second line of his division, which consisted of the squadrons of Zandt and Hörtling, turn back and fire their carbines. However, this did not help and Seyssel's entire brigade was soon forced to retreat behind a square of the Italian Guard. It quickly rallied there and charged the [Russians] who reached the square, and drove them back across the stream with heavy casualties.[426]

Flotow also recalled that 'to avoid being isolated, [Bavarian] brigades had to retreat towards the approaching infantry square', while the artilleryman, Captain Wiedemann, saw 'the Italian chevau-léger regiment driven back to [his] Bavarian battery', thus preventing him from opening fire. 'After the [Italians] passed between the guns,' Wiedemann recalled, 'it was already too late for us to open fire against the enemy, who was so at such close distance that the battery had to retreat immediately.' As his subordinates began to remove their guns, one of the limbers broke down and Wiedemann rushed to help remove it. However, as he brought new limber

> a cannon-ball fired by a French battery, which bombarded the Russian cavalry, killed the horse and made it impossible to save the gun. The soldiers, who remained with me to remove the piece, were now too close to the cavalry mêlée as the mass of the Russian cavalry advance against us on a wide front.

Captain Wiedemann's men quickly retreated but were caught up by the Yelisavetgradskii Hussars (some of them armed with lances) and Cossacks, some of whom charged the Captain himself: 'One Cossack would have certainly pierced me with his lance if not for an Italian Chasseurs à Cheval who threw him off the horse at the very moment when the [Cossack] aimed his deadly lance at me.' Wiedemann then moved his guns towards the units of the Italian Guard and Delzon's division, which formed squares to repel the enemy charges. His battery had several guns damaged and Wiedemann could utilize only two remaining pieces, which he quickly led to support the counter-attacking Bavarian cavalry.[427]

Among the Italian guardsmen Wiedemann observed was Laugier, who found himself 'face to face with the enemy cavalry. Formed in squares, we advanced in echelon to meet the Russians, who by now reached the Italian batteries, extinguished their fire and overthrown Delzon's regiments'.[428] Supported by the Italian Guard, the Bavarian and Italian cavalrymen counter-attacked. Combe saw the 6th Hussars and the 8th Chasseurs making successful charges against the Cossacks, who quickly retreated, while Dautancourt had his men search thick bushes and woods to capture any remaining Russians and his men did seize several Cossacks.[429] Platov's men retreated across the dam on the Voina and were protected by a Russian battery that engaged the pursuing Bavarian cavalry. Prince Eugène, realizing that the enemy raid was effectively over, turned his Guard units back to prepare for the assault on Rayevsky's Redoubt.

On the Russian side, Uvarov understood that the French would soon try to divert some of their forces from the left flank to the centre, so he sought to maintain pressure on Napoleon's flank. Uvarov later reported: 'I sought to remain in my position and, through my movements, to trick the enemy into believing that I would make another attack.' He continued his feint attacks until 3pm when he finally received Kutuzov's order to return to his initial battle position. Clausewitz recalled that the Russian cavalry retreated between 4pm and 5pm and assumed its position behind the Gorki Heights. As for Platov's Cossacks, some of them seem to have returned to their initial position, while others remained on the western bank of the Kolocha, since Platov reported that his troops harassed the enemy until late that night.[430] Liprandi, who seems to have consulted some Cossack participants, noted that as Platov was withdrawing his troops, he ordered his regimental commanders to take note of the terrain and surroundings, in case they had to operate there at night.[431]

Thus ended the Russian cavalry raid against the French left flank. Compared to other sectors, the fighting here was less intense and both sides lost a couple of hundred men. The Life Guard Hussar Regiment had twelve killed and seventeen wounded, the Yelisavetgradskii Hussars had five killed, fourteen wounded and twenty missing, the Life Guard Cossacks lost three killed and thirty-two wounded, the Life Guard Uhlan and the Nezhinskii Dragoons had no losses at all.[432] On the French side, the most substantial loss was the death of General of Brigade Léonard Huard de St Aubin, commanding the 1st Brigade of the 13th Division, who was killed by a canister shot while commanding his infantry.

The purpose and outcome of the raid have been debated, often bitterly, for the past 190 years. Russian generals and staff officers were more disapproving of the whole enterprise than junior officers and the rank-and-file, and participants were, in general, more critical than later historians, especially those of the Soviet era. Although poorly implemented, it should be said that the raid did produce an important result: it diverted French forces at a crucial moment, when they were preparing for the assault on the Russian centre. The two or three hour delay it caused allowed the Russians to rally and regroup, while the French troops, especially Latour-Maubourg's cavalry, suffered under the fire of the Russian artillery.

# The Battle of Borodino Phase Two (12am to 6pm)

Among those praising the raid, Friedrich von Schubert went as far as to claim that the manoeuvre 'produced tremendous results and added certain indecision to enemy attacks. Napoleon's own tent was quickly removed and his Guard was organized into square. The Kolotsk Monastery, where the main [French] hospital and infirmary was established, was taken over by panic.' On the opposite side, Clausewitz, as we have seen, was very critical of the entire venture.[433] Many senior Russian officers believed the raid had the potential for tremendous success but was mishandled. They shared Clausewitz's and Löwenstern's accusations against Uvarov for sluggish performance and failure to take full advantage of the manoeuvre. Barclay de Tolly believed that: 'if this attack were carried out with greater firmness and not limited to only wearing out the enemy, it would have had brilliant consequences'. Nikolai Muravyev was certain that, if well executed, this 'surprise attack could have decided the battle outcome to our favour' and a similar opinion was voiced by Norov, among others. Furthermore, Golitsyn, who served as ordinance officer to Kutuzov, recalled that Kutuzov coldly greeted Uvarov upon his return from the raid and, hearing his report, told him: 'I know everything and may God forgive you for it!'[434] The fact that Platov and Uvarov were the only generals *not* nominated for rewards after the battle speaks volumes about the Commander-in-Chief's dissatisfaction with their actions. In December 1812, Kutuzov even wrote to Alexander, stating that he could not recommend Uvarov for any rewards, since he failed to carry out the raid successfully. As for Platov and his Cossacks, Kutuzov told the Emperor that 'they did not fight that day as such'.[435]

A gallant officer, Uvarov saw his reputation somewhat tarnished at Borodino. Nevertheless, he served with distinction in the 1813–14 campaigns and was promoted to the rank of general for his actions at Leipzig. Platov's case is interesting because participants criticized him for failing to break through to Napoleon's baggage train, which would have had a major impact on the course of the battle. The Ataman had already established himself as a capable leader of Cossacks, but was also known for arrogance, a tendency to bicker with other generals, and a fondness for alcohol. A. Muravyev noted that one of the reasons for Platov's poor performance at Borodino was his hatred of Barclay de Tolly, to whom he was formally subordinated. Yet, other participants reveal that there was also one more, often overlooked, factor. Nikolai Muravyev blamed the failure of the raid on the

> inept orders and intoxicated condition of Count Platov [...] who was drunk that day [...] [and] Kutuzov refused to give him overall command [of the raid]; the abilities of Uvarov, who was [the] next senior officer after Platov, were mediocre and well known to everyone ...

Similar testimony can be found in the personal journal of Mikhailovsky-Danilevsky, who recorded that Platov was 'in a drunken stupor [...] which, among other things, made Kutuzov to tell me [...] that this was the first time he had seen a full general dead drunk in the midst of a decisive battle.

# The Battle of Borodino

It was natural, then, that when the first histories of the battle were written, attempts were made to gloss over these awkward and unpleasant incidents. Historians and some participants tried to suppress or falsify the events of the Platov–Uvarov raid. Thus, Liprandi argued that Uvarov retreated, not because he could not break through the French squares, but because 'he was twice ordered to retreat' by Kutuzov, who was too cautious to continue this attack. Justifying Platov's actions, he argued that the Ataman purposely kept his troops in the bushes because he wanted to keep Napoleon believing that the Cossacks were supported by infantry (hiding in shrubs) thus forcing him to divert more forces to the left flank. Liprandi was supported in his effort by Bolgovsky, who also suggested that some Cossacks dismounted, acting as infantry in order to deceive Napoleon. Bolgovsky believed that

> had Platov acted strictly in compliance with the orders he received [...] the defeat of our army would have been imminent, since while he remained with his men in the defile, he continued to threaten the enemy; had he attacked with his inferior forces, the threat would have disappeared at once.[436]

Bolgovsky was the first to provide a specific number of troops (23,000) that Napoleon allegedly had to divert to reinforce Eugène. Later, Soviet historians came up with the even higher number of 28,000 men. Neither calculation had any factual basis, but these figures were utilized by historians to portray the raid in a favourable light.

## Southern Sector – The Fight for Semeyonovskoe

We left the southern sector shortly after Bagration was wounded, Dokhturov was sent to shore up the left flank and the survivors of the 2nd Western Army began taking up a new position along the Semeyonovskii ridge around 11am. The Bagration flèches were occupied by the French for the final time and preparations were made for a further advance. The village of Semeyonovskoye was the next target, as it was located immediately behind the flèches, protected by a relatively steep ravine. Its fall would have led to the collapse of the Russian left wing and exposed the centre, allowing the French either to break through and split the enemy army in two or drive the entire Russian host into a tight space between the Kolocha and Moscow rivers. The village initially came under attack early in the morning, when some troops from Razout's division tried to cross the Semeyonovskii Brook and enter the village but were driven out by the Russian grenadiers and the cavalry. Now, with the flèches secured and the Russians driven back, it became obvious that Davout and Ney would require reinforcements for the attack on Semeyonovskoe to succeed.

The circumstances leading to, and surrounding, the fighting at Semeyonovskoe are confusing, so the precise course of events is difficult to determine. For example, it is unclear when the French charged the village and how many times they did so. Chambray, Kukiel, Pelet and Cate argued that the village was, in fact, briefly seized by troops from Razout's division early in the morning. Buturlin described the fighting taking place around

# The Battle of Borodino Phase Two (12am to 6pm)

10am, Bogdanovich thought it occurred after 11am, while according to Thiers, the village fell around noon. So lets examine what happened.

We know that, after the flèches were secured, French forces were significantly weakened. Napoleon's I and III Corps became intermingled in the fighting, while VIII corps was diverted south from its original goal (Semeyonovskoye) to assist Poniatowski's Poles. To help Davout and Ney, Napoleon gradually moved forward additional infantry and heavy cavalry, while hundreds of French guns (some sources claim as many as 400) had begun bombarding this sector by noon. According to Pelet, 'Napoleon kept the divisions of Friant and Claparède at hand in reserve. He wanted to preserve reserves for the army and conserved his forces to act as the battle developed.' After 9am the Polish Vistula Legion was ordered to advance and assume positions near the Kamenka stream. Brandt recalled as his troops

advanced, in two columns [...] and came to a halt in a slight depression. Cannon-balls were striking the lip of the depression and ricocheting over our heads. Chlopicki, as impassive as he had always been in Spain, moved as far forward as possible to get a view of the enemy's position. Claparède came over to us and gathered the officers of the 2nd Regiment of the Vistula around him in a circle and impressed upon them the need to uphold the good reputation of the regiment [...] We could hear the relentless whistle of cannon-balls and yet not one man was hit, as the General had deliberately chosen this position to shield his men from needless casualties.

Around 10am, the Vistula Legion was ordered to advance further and, 'moving obliquely, heading to the left, and marching over meadows', it began to suffer from the Russian fire.[437] Dedem, who commanded a brigade in General Friant's 2nd Division, recalled seeing Napoleon

approach the troops of my brigade [in the morning] and the soldiers began to ask him to send them into the battle; the left flank and centre were already in the heat of the action. However, he replied, 'regiments like this are not committed in battle unless to decide the victory'.[438]

Between 10am and 11am, Napoleon ordered the 2nd Division to move forward and, as the Journal of Friant's division informs us, its main goal was Semeyonovskoye.

Besides the 2nd Division, Napoleon also allowed Murat to move the II and IV Reserve Cavalry Corps to the front line. Colonel Seruzier's battery was deployed on the bank of the Kamenka brook, with the 2nd Light Cavalry Division of Pajol behind it. To their right, II Cavalry Corps was deployed in two lines, with the 2nd Heavy Cavalry Division of Wathier in the first and the 4th Heavy Cavalry Division of Defrance in the second. Further south, the position was occupied by Latour-Maubourg's IV Cavalry Corps. The I Cavalry Corps of Nansouty was regrouping around the southern flèches.

On the Russian side, Dokhturov deployed the remnants of the 2nd Grenadier Division in the ruins of Semeyonovskoye. He arranged Konovnitsyn's 3rd Division southeast of the village, while the Life Guard Izmailovskii,

# The Battle of Borodino

Litovskii and Finlyandskii Regiments were organized in squares on its left flank. Dokhturov placed the survivors of the Combined Grenadier Brigade, and the 12th and 27th Divisions in-between them, to protect and help operate the batteries. Borozdin's cavalry brigade stood behind the Guard regiments, while the 2nd Cuirassier Division was rallied behind the 3rd Division. Neverovsky spread a chain of skirmishers in front of the Guard regiments and assumed command of the combined grenadier battalions and the Don Cossack Horse Artillery Company. The Russian IV Cavalry Corps was deployed nearby, with some units further to the south to maintain communications with Shakhovsky. Some 300 cannon defended the village and its vicinity. The new Russian position had both its advantages and disadvantages. Bogdanovich noted that the

> Russian troops, deployed to the right of Semeyonovskoye, were partly protected by a slight crest on which the village was located but, after retreating behind it, they were unable to maintain effective fire in the area in front of them which helped the enemy to cross the ravine. Meantime, the Russian troops to the left of the Semeyonovskoye were completely exposed and suffered from the fire of enemy batteries ...

The French cavalry assault began around noon, when the Saxon and Westphalian cuirassiers from IV Cavalry Corps charged from the north, while Nansouty's cavalrymen attacked south of Semeyonovskoye. Lieutenant von Meerheim could see

> the whole extent of the battle in the central sector [...] though everything was shrouded in a dense cloud of smoke and all we could make out were the thick masses of our troops, who were swaying backwards and forwards in front of the enemy held ridge.

The Allied cavalry advanced in columns of half squadrons, and faced the daunting challenge of ascending a slope

> so steep that some riders, who did not appreciate the advantage of climbing obliquely, tumbled over backwards and were trampled by the horses behind. On the top of the hill, about sixty yards from the edge, we saw the burnt out village of Semeyonovskoye, whose side was marked only by glowing logs.[439]

Latour-Maubourg's corps moved in two columns, with Lorge's cuirassier division in the right column and Rozniecki's Lancer division in the left. The crossing over the Semeynovskii stream proved marshy, which delayed their passage, but the Allied troops were concealed from Russian batteries and thus escaped their murderous fire. The Saxon cavalrymen were the first to reach the ridge, where, a few hundred paces away on the edge of the village, Thielemann saw a Russian battery protected by grenadiers. He immediately sent the leading squadrons of the Saxon Gardes du Corps against it, while the remaining squadrons were formed in echelon to the left. The Saxons rode over the grenadiers and drove back the Russian dragoons that rushed to their aid. Lieutenant Stolypin, of the 2nd Light Company of the Life Guard Artillery Brigade, tried to stop the Saxon charge but his fire proved futile as the enemy troopers pushed forward. General Lepel, however, had his hand torn off by a Russian round.

Thielemann's man pressed beyond the village, where they threatened the rear of Russian Guard regiments fighting off the charges of Nansouty's corps. As the Saxons thundered onto the plain behind the village, they were attacked by Borozdin's cavalry brigade (the Astrakhanskii, His Majesty's and Her Majesty's Cuirassier Regiments), supported by the Akhtyrskii Hussars (some of them armed with lances) struck the Saxons in the flank. Borozdin's report provides numerous details of individual exploits in these attacks before succinctly noting: 'In one word, the enemy cavalry was routed and suffered heavy losses.'[440] Indeed, Lorge's division was forced to retreat from the crest back into the ravine. Rozniecki's Polish Lancers, who advanced to the left of the Saxons, had become involved in the fighting with Duke Eugène of Württemberg's 4th Division south of the Grand Redoubt, and were of little help to the Saxons.

In the south, Nansouty's cavalrymen suffered from the Russian batteries but maintained order as they charged. Their attack, however, proved unsuccessful as they faced the Russian élite regiments. The Life Guard Izmailovskii and Litovskii Regiment were deployed south of the village and suffered from artillery bombardment. As Colonel Kutuzov of the Izmailovskii Regiment reported, 'although the enemy artillery fire devastated our ranks, it failed to produce any disorder among the men. The ranks were simply closed up again and soldiers maintained their discipline as coolly as if they had been on a musketry exercise.' Konovnitsyn, who was in one of the squares, recalled:

> The clouds of dust ascending from the ground to the heavens showed me the advance of the enemy cavalry. I arranged the Izmailovskii Regiment in squares in chess [i.e. chequerboard] order and awaited thus the enemy cavalry that attacked like a tempest. I could not comment on how many paces separated the enemy from the squares but rather note that the enemy was so near that practically every bullet toppled over a horseman. The terrible cross-fire from the lateral faces of the squares sped thousands [*sic*] of men to their deaths and filled the rest with terror ...

Despite the sight of the terrifying *hommes de fer*, the Russian Guard regiments proved resilient as they withstood several charges. Furthermore, they even counter-attacked in places. Konovnitsyn described how

> The Izmailovskii grenadiers, without any disorder, charged the giant armoured cavalrymen and brought them down with their bayonets [...] The Litovskii Regiment, which was to the left of me, showed incredible resilience and courage as well.

Colonel Kutuzov provides further details on the exploits of his regiment: 'The enemy cuirassiers made a vigorous attack but quickly paid a heavy price for their audacity. All squares, acting with remarkable firmness, opened fire and waged battalion volleys from the lateral faces.' The Russian infantry was supported by the 1st Light and two Guard batteries, whose artillery crews often found themselves fighting off the French cuirassiers with their ramrods.

Colonel Udom of the Life Guard Litovskii Regiment deployed his battalions in squares against the cavalry. He later reported that:

> despite being surrounded by a superior enemy, they met him gallantly and courageously, allowing him to approach to close range before opening a battalion volley, and, yelling 'Hurrah!', disordered and drove the enemy back to the heights, inflicting heavy losses both in killed and wounded; our soldiers were so incensed that no prisoners were taken.

The Russians repelled two cavalry charges in this manner and Lieutenant Colonel Timofeyev, commanding the 2nd Battalion of the Litovskii Regiment, described as

> a column of enemy cuirassiers charged directly at us [...] I ordered the battalion, which was in a square, 'ready' and prohibited firing without my orders. Instead I instructed my men to move their muskets from side to side, knowing from own experience that horses would never charge [a wall of] sparkling bayonets; if any cuirassiers forced their horses close to the front, I ordered my men to thrust into the animals' faces [...] The cuirassiers surrounded the square from all sides and, unable to disorganize it, they formed a column some 30 steps in front of us with the obvious intention of charging *en masse*. To prevent this, I took advantage of their commotion as each horseman was seeking his place, and, shouting 'Hurrah!', my battalion charged with bayonets. The front ranks of cuirassiers still had not organized a firm front and, upon being attacked with bayonets, they could not hold ground but the rear ranks prevented them from escaping. They suffered heavy casualties and only after hearing their desperate shouts did the rest of the cavalry column flee.

The French regrouped and attacked again but, as Colonel Kutuzov noted, they were 'dealt in a similar manner, routed and forced back ashamed. Some enemy horsemen still dared to reach the squares but our bayonets punished them for their boldness ...'[441]

According to A. Marin of the Life Guard Finlyandskii Regiment, his battalion also allowed the cuirassiers to approach before firing and engaging them. Many of the attackers remained on the field while 'the few survivors were captured, disarmed and placed in the middle of the square'. Lieutenant General Lavrov reported that the Finlyandskii Regiment advanced 'with drums beating and meeting the enemy cavalry with bayonets'. Glinka described the

> enormous enemy cavalry spread out as a sea while our squares floated like islands that were washed by the copper and steel waves of enemy cuirassiers [...] [However,] the Russian wind of lead met and repelled these *hommes de fer* ...

Russian sources describe three major French cavalry charges that were repelled by the Guard units. Nansouty's men were then attacked by the Yekaterinoslavskii and Voyennogo Ordena (Military Order) Cuirassier Regiments, which pursued them across the Semeyonovskii ravine.

# The Battle of Borodino Phase Two (12am to 6pm)

While the Allied cavalry was charging around the village, Friant's 2nd Division attacked Semeyonovskoye proper. General Dufour led the charge with the 15th Light and his immediate goal was to seize the Russian earthworks on the north-eastern corner of the village, from where the Russian artillery continued to fire. Dufour was assisted by the 48th Line, followed by two battalions of the Spanish Joseph Napoleon Regiment. The 33rd Line was kept in reserve. The French infantry crossed the ravine and climbed uphill only to be repelled by the Russians. Lejeune, sent by Napoleon with a message for Davout to attack, recalled that the Marshal, upset about having to assault this position, commented angrily: 'It is a confounded shame to make me take the bull by the horns.' Meanwhile Ney, 'admirable to see, quietly standing on the parapet of one of the redoubts and directing the combatants, was also unsatisfied with the situation and repeatedly requested reinforcements'. According to Roth von Schreckenstein, after the first attack, the French rolled back, regrouped and attacked again, targeting the earthworks. This assault proved more successful as the French seized the earthworks and then carried the village as well. It remains unclear if the Russians managed to save their guns, which apparently continued operating until the very last moment. As Friant's troops entered the smouldering ruins of Semeyonovskoye, Chambray observed that:

> the Russian army quickly regrouped behind the village. Its right flank was anchored on the [Grand] Redoubt, the left was adjacent to the woods behind the [Bagration] redans [flèches]. Enemy batteries, deployed on the plateau that dominated above Semeyonovskoye, maintained heavy fire.[442]

Friant, awaiting the Russian counter-attack, placed the 15th Light to the left of the village and moved the 48th Line on the hill behind it. The 33rd Line was deployed amidst the village ruins; the location of the Spanish Joseph Napoleon Regiment is unclear, since its regimental history describes it protecting the Pernetty battery, while Jean François Friant – the General's son and adjutant – recalled that some Spanish troops were with the 48th Line near Semeyonovskoye.[443] On the Russian side, the men of the 2nd Combined Grenadier and the 27th Infantry Divisions were supported by several battalions of the Life Guard Litovskii Regiment.[444]

Colonel Udom described how, after the Allied cavalry pulled back, he noticed that the French skirmishers began appearing on nearby heights. He dispatched Lieutenant Colonel Timofeyev with the 2nd Battalion of the Litovskii Regiment to drive them back and recapture the heights. He later reported that:

> although this was accomplished with considerable success, the enemy was reinforced with several columns in this direction and supported the skirmishers, which made it impossible for my regiment to capture the heights.

Furthermore, Timofeyev and Udom were both wounded and Lieutenant Colonel Schwartz took over command of the Life Guard Litovskii Regiment. Schwartz charged with the 1st Battalion and seized the hillock, although he suffered a mortal wound in the fighting.

# The Battle of Borodino

Colonel Kutuzov of the Izmailovskii Regiment also described the fierce fighting that developed for a hillock on his left flank. On Konovnitsyn's order, Colonel Musin Pushkin dispatched the 2nd Battalion (of the Izmailovskii Regiment), under Captain Martinov, to seize the heights, which it quickly accomplished. Kutuzov described that:

> sending forth its skirmishers, the battalion held ground there until Staff Captain Katenin, who replaced the wounded Captain Martinov, received an order and made an oblique forward movement, marching to protect the batteries that were some 200 paces away on the battalion's right flank. The fire of enemy artillery, directed against this battery, did not prevent our column from accomplishing its task in complete order.

Although Russian reports are silent on cavalry involvement, according to General Dufour, the 15th Light repelled several Russian cavalry charges, while the 33rd Line repulsed a few more, each celebrated with shouts of 'Vive l'Empereur!' Murat himself took shelter in the square of the 33rd Line on several occasions and encouraged the troops to fight. According to Ségur, at one moment Friant's men began to give way under musket and canister fire and one officer even gave order to retreat:

> At that critical moment, Murat ran up to him, and seizing him by the collar, exclaimed, 'What are you about?' The Colonel [most probably Groisne of the 48th], pointing to the ground, covered with half his troops, answered, 'You see well enough that it is impossible to stand here.' – 'Very well, I will remain!' exclaimed the King. These words stopped the officer: he looked at Murat steadily in the face, and turning round, coolly said, 'You are right! Soldiers, face to the enemy! Let us go and be killed!'

Ney was appalled by the exposed position of the 33rd Line, which suffered heavy losses from a barrage of Russian cannon-balls and canister: 'Who is the imbecile who placed you here?' he exclaimed at one point, and, apparently realizing the answer, he turned to Murat, shouting, 'Why don't you charge with your cavalry or have this infantry advance, since you seem so bent on getting it killed off?' Friant barely escaped death when a canister shot struck him in the chest: he refused to leave the battlefield and continued commanding the troops.[445] As a Russian officer Lubenkov described:

> It was a fight between ferocious tigers, not men, and once both sides had determined to win or die where they stood, they did not stop fighting when their muskets broke, but carried on, using butts and swords in terrible hand-to-hand combat, and the killing went on …

The fighting for Semeyonovskoye continued throughout the afternoon and the French made repeated attempts to advance beyond the village. Between 2pm and 3pm, Ney ordered the I, III and VIII Corps (see page 000 for discussion) to resume the attack, and as Pelleport, Pelet, Girod de l'Ain and Le Roy described, the French troops managed to gain some ground.

On the Russian side, Lieutenant General Lavrov was ordered to shift his Guard regiments to the left, following reports that the French were seeking to turn the Russian left flank and their skirmishers, lodged on the edge of the woods there, were harassing the Russian cavalry. Lavrov dispatched a battalion of the Life Guard Finlyandskii Regiment, under the command of Colonel Zherve, to support the cavalry, but was soon informed that enemy forces were increasing in this direction. As a consequence, he sent two more battalions of the same regiment, led by Colonel Kryzhanovski. Zherve, meantime, deployed a thick screen of skirmishers and engaged the French for half an hour before reporting additional enemy columns arriving. Kryzhanovski then led a bayonet charge with the 2nd and 3rd Battalions, which succeeded in driving the French back. The Russians took up position inside the woods but could not advance further, due to effective fire from the French artillery.

Both Davout and Ney requested additional reinforcements but their appeals fell on Napoleon's deaf ear. By now, almost all of the Grand Army was committed to the battle, except for the Imperial Guard, and its involvement might have had a crucial effect on the battle. According to Ségur, Murat sent one of his officers (Borelli) to the Emperor and upon reaching Napoleon:

> that officer pointed to the clouds of dust which the charges of the cavalry were raising upon the heights [...] Borelli insisted [on reinforcements], and the Emperor promised his Young Guard. But, scarcely had it advanced a few paces, when he himself called out to it to halt. The Count de Lobau [Mouton], however, made it advance by degrees, under pretence of dressing the line. Napoleon, perceiving it, repeated his order.

Soon after, Ney, Davout, and Murat again called for the Guard. Murat sent Belliard, his chief of staff, to the Emperor. Belliard declared that, from their position near Semeyonovskoye, the French could see confused crowds of Russian soldiers and carriages retreating and only a single effort was required to win the battle. Napoleon hesitated and ordered Belliard to have another look. Belliard soon returned, reporting that the Russians were rallying and 'the opportunity was about to escape; that there was not a moment to be lost, otherwise it would require a second battle to terminate the first!'

But Bessières, whom Napoleon also had sent him to examine the Russian positions, argued that the Russians, far from being in disorder, were in their second position, and seemed to be preparing for an attack. Confused by two contradicting reports, Napoleon murmured that 'nothing was yet sufficiently unravelled [and] he wanted to see more clearly upon his chess-board'. Belliard, in consternation, returned to Murat and complained about finding the Emperor 'still seated in the same place, with a suffering and dejected air, his features sunk, and a dull look; giving his orders languishingly, in the midst of these dreadful warlike noises, to which he seemed completely a stranger!' At this account, Ney supposedly exclaimed:

> Are we then come so far, to be satisfied with a field of battle? What business has the emperor in the rear of the army? [...] Since he will no longer make war

# The Battle of Borodino

himself, since he is no longer the general, as he wishes to be the emperor every where, let him return to the Tuilleries, and leave us to be generals for him!

Back at the command post, Count Daru, the Secretary of State, supported by Count Mathieu Dumas, Intendant-General of the Grand Army and Marshal Berthier, again approached Napoleon with a request to send in the Imperial Guard. Napoleon replied: 'And if there should be another battle tomorrow, where is my army?' No further attempts were made to urge Napoleon to commit his élite force to the battle.

Napoleon's refusal to commit the Guard became one of the most debated issues over the 200 years following the battle. Participants and scholars argued that this was surely one of the decisive moments of the campaign and envisioned what would have happened if the Imperial Guard had attacked. This issue is directly connected with Napoleon's overall conduct during the battle. Unlike his other battles, Napoleon was unusually passive at Borodino – a fact noted by many. During the morning he rarely mounted his horse to observe the front line and stir up his troops. Instead he spent hours sitting near the Shevardino Redoubt, periodically pacing up and down with his hands clasped behind his back, occasionally looking through his telescope, and quietly listening to reports. It seemed that poor health – cold, sore throat and urinary problems – had an effect on his mental state and put him in some kind of depression. He was seen taking cough drop pills from a little box in his pocket and did not eat breakfast or lunch, except for 'a slice of bread and a glass of Chambertin wine, without diluting it with water'.[446]

Napoleon's apologists often use his ill health to explain the indecisive outcome of the battle. His health does much to explain his passivity that day but cannot be used as the sole factor in Napoleon's meagre performance at Borodino. The tactical situation he was facing was no more difficult than earlier battles he had successfully fought. During the Italian Campaign of 1796–97 he was often struck by fever, but that did not prevent him from waging a victorious campaign against a numerically superior enemy. One can admit that cold and exhaustion had hindered his physical performance but it would difficult to explain the collapse of will so evident at Borodino. Chambray could not recognize in this tired old man the warlike commander of the past, who would gallop about the field encouraging his troops and spotting the right moment to launch the decisive attack. 'Previously it was above all on the battlefield that his talents had shone with the greatest *éclat*; it was there that he seemed to master fortunate itself.' Lejeune was surprised to find the Emperor always seated in the same attitude, following movements with his pocket telescope and giving his orders with imperturbable composure:

> We all agreed in wondering what had become of the eager, active commander of Marengo, Austerlitz, and elsewhere [...] We were anything but satisfied with the way in which our leader had behaved, and passed very severe judgments on his conduct.

162

# The Battle of Borodino Phase Two (12am to 6pm)

There is certainly some justice to the critique of Napoleon's decision to keep the Guard in reserve. Such an attack probably would have delivered a more decisive victory but one can only speculate if the Russian Army would have been routed as a result of this. The Guard would have certainly suffered losses – maybe even significant losses – in the process. Besides, it is often forgotten that Napoleon did commit the Young Guard and the Guard artillery, so the only force remaining in reserve was the Old Guard. As prominent British historian David Chandler argued, Napoleon's 'refusal to commit the Old Guard was probably correct in the long term view; he never forgot that 1,200 miles separated him from the French frontier and consequently was well-advised to retain his last major formation intact'. Napoleon himself was well aware of the disapproval surrounding his actions. After the battle he summoned Dumas and Daru to discuss the battle results and, among other things, told them:

> People will be surprised that I did not commit my reserves in order to obtain greater results, but I had to keep them for striking a decisive blow in the great battle which the enemy will fight in front of Moscow. The success of the day was assured and I had to consider the success of the campaign as a whole. That is why I kept my reserves in hand.[447]

The sporadic battle around Semeyonovskoye continued well into the evening. According to Colonel Kutuzov, the Allied cavalry, after exhausting itself charging the Russian squares, was moved back and the French infantry made repeated attempts to advance but was repelled. During one such attack, shortly after 4pm, General Friant was wounded again and Dufour took over the command of the 4th Division; some French scholars (Thiry, Tranié) suggest that Friant was replaced by Gallichet, but other sources do not be substantiate their argument. According to Murat's report, one of the French attacks, taking place around 5pm, shattered the Russian position, drove the enemy further into woods and cleared the valley behind Semeyonovskoye. However, Murat's claims are not supported by the Russian sources and even some French participants contradict him. Thus, Pelleport complained about disorder and lack of coordination between the French forces and noted that the Russians, although suffering heavy losses, held ground.

The French artillery, however, hardly missed its target and, as Colonel Kutuzov lamented, 'wreaked havoc among us'. This forced the Russians to redeploy to a new line of defence. Between 6pm and 7pm the soldiers of the 33rd Line noticed that the Russian troops, near the woods, were changing position. Led by Captain Michel, the French skirmishers approached them but, fearing an ambush, they were reluctant to proceed into the woods. They were later recalled by General Dedem. Russian Colonel Udom described that, after hours of enduring the bombardment, his regiment, leaving skirmishers for cover, finally retreated towards the nearby woods, where it joined a battalion of the Izmailovskii Regiment. Lavrov also described how, late in the evening, the French made several attempts to seize woods where the Life Guard Finlyandskii Regiment was deployed with orders to 'defend it at any cost'. The enemy was repelled and, to prevent future attacks, the Russian skirmisher chain was reinforced with two companies. Lavrov reported: 'the skirmishers held ground on the edge of the woods for the rest of the evening and around 9pm the fire began to die down, and completely ended by 10pm'.

## Central Sector – The Second Assault on Rayevsky's Redoubt

After the first French assault failed, Prince Eugène planned to utilize his Italian Guard to launch a new attack on the redoubt, while artillery bombarded the Russian troops massing in the centre. But French preparations were interrupted by news of the sudden appearance of the Russian cavalry on the extreme left flank, which compelled Eugène to postpone his attack for a couple of hours and take reinforcements to the threatened positions. The French cavalry, meantime, was redeployed to plug the gap between Ney and Davout around Semeyonovskoye and Eugène's forces near Borodino.

The delay in attacking the redoubt proved costly for these cavalrymen, as they remained exposed to the Russian artillery for the best part of three hours. Polish Colonel Malachowski lamented that:

> our cavalry was exposed to the fire, without taking any precautions against it. Cannon-balls were like an autumn wind [. . .] a hail of cannon-balls reaped men and horses from our lines. The gaps were filled in with new soldiers, who assumed places of their fallen comrades.

Griois was amazed at the sight of 'cannon-balls, bullets, shells and canister raining down from every direction and creating large gaps in our cavalry, which remained exposed and motionless for several hours.' He could see that

> the plain was covered with the wounded men making their way back to ambulances and of riderless horses galloping around in disorder. I noticed a Württemberg [Westphalian?] cuirassier regiment, which was particularly hard hit with the enemy cannon-balls and their helmets and cuirasses kept flying apart in shattered fragments.

Combe complained that

> The enemy redoubt directed its main fire against the artillery deployed on our right flank but some of its guns also targeted us. Cannon-balls hit us and ricocheted through our ranks, as we stood at attention with our sabres raised to our epaulettes. We remained in this terrible position for six hours.

The carabiniers of the II Cavalry Corps bitterly complained at having to suffer these casualties. At one moment, the exasperated Sergeant-Major Ravat shouted, 'Either we charge or we leave the field!' but was quickly silenced by Captain du Barail's response: 'One more word and I will break your gob, you miserable *Jean-Foutre* [good for nothing]!'[448] The Saxon Prinz Albert Chevau-léger lost almost half its men without even engaging

# The Battle of Borodino Phase Two (12am to 6pm)

the enemy. One officer of the Vistula Legion close to II Cavalry Corps described seeing 'long lines of French cavalry, in whose ranks the enemy artillery blasted bloody lanes at every moment'.[449] Among the killed and seriously wounded officers were Colonel Désirat of the 11th Chasseurs and Daubenton, Pajol's aide-de-camp.[450] Subervie, of the 16th Light Cavalry Brigade, escaped death by a hair's breadth when a shell exploded close to him, ripping off the legs of two soldiers nearby. Major von Werder, of the 1st Prussian Uhlans, had his horse killed under him but, to the surprise of all around him, immediately stood up, calmly smoking his pipe. As Thirion de Metz explained:

> In a charge [...] everyone is excited, everyone fights and parries if he can; there is action, movement, hand-to-hand combat; but here our position was quite different. Standing still opposite the Russian cannons, we could see them being loaded with the projectiles which they would direct at us, we could distinguish the eye of the gunner who was aiming at us and it required a great dose of composure to remain still.

After waiting patiently for reinforcements, Thirion de Metz saw 'poor Westphalians, partly recruits, surprised to find themselves so close to thundering guns and to see us moving, shouting, 'Wir bleiben nicht hier! Wir bleiben nicht hier!' ['We are not staying here! We are not staying here!']'[451]

Around noon, Captain Biot – who served as adjutant to Pajol – saw General Montbrun approaching Pajol and witnessed their conversation. After exchanging greetings, Pajol complained that he was so exposed that 'not a single shot misses my troops'. Montbrun suggested moving to the left and the two generals travelled to take a look at the terrain there. Biot goes on to recount:

> And there we were, passing along the front of our line [...] Montbrun was to our right, flanking us toward the enemy, Pajol in the middle, and I was to on the left [...] Suddenly I heard a dull thud. 'Someone has been wounded,' I exclaimed. At the same instant General Montbrun rolled off his horse ...

A Russian round-shot had pierced Montbrun from side to side, leaving a gaping wound that proved deadly. Officers rushed to help the wounded general but the injury was too severe. Physician Roos, who was among the few who witnessed the scene, watched as Montbrun 'quickly turned pale and then yellow. His very lively look had been extinguished and we saw his strength gradually fail'. Still, the General somehow found strength to mutter, 'Excellent shot,' before losing conscience. Montbrun was quickly taken to the celebrated surgeon Dominique Larrey but he could do nothing to rescue him. 'A round shot passed through the region of his kidneys from side to side,' Larrey noted, 'There was little to be done. Death was certain and not far off. I applied a dressing, and had him carried to a little village nearby.' There, in the shadow of trees and under the thunder of guns, the 42-year-old Montbrun breathed his last around 5pm.[452]

# The Battle of Borodino

## A Hero's Death

The death of Montbrun was a grave loss for Napoleon and the Grand Army. A talented cavalry general, he was in his prime and would have accomplished much in the years to come. There was even a talk of him eventually becoming a marshal.

After the battle, Marshal Lefevbre had him buried near the northern flèche and had a small wooden tablet erected over his grave. A year after the battle, an Englishman (J.T. James), visiting the battlefield, described:

> a small wooden tablet, attached to a rough stake, erected over the place where [Montbrun] was interred, bearing an inscription to his memory. It had been penned in ink after the hurry of the day was past; but the simple and classical turn of its style well entitles it to record:

> Here lies
> General Montbrun
> Passer-by of whatever nation
> Honour his Ashes
> They are the remains of
> One of the Bravest of the Brave,
> Of General Montbrun.
> The Marshal of the Empire and Duke of Danzig
> Has erected this modest monument in his honour
> His memory will live for ever in the hearts of the Grand Army

Tensions were running high among the soldiers and officers. Travelling along the ravine, General Thielemann barely survived after a Russian shell exploded nearby, wounding his horse. He was already irritated by considerable losses among his troops and by what he perceived as Latour-Maubourg's repeated instructions. This brush of death, and the subsequent death of his favourite adjutant, only further incensed him. As bad luck would have it, one of Latour-Maubourg's adjutants arrived with new orders at that moment and, failing to notice Thielemann, delivered orders to the regimental commanders, who, apparently, began to move. Thielemann immediately stopped them and, finding Latour-Maubourg's adjutant, demanded to know why the order had not been delivered to him. The adjutant blurted that the General was not at his spot, which threw Thielemann into a rage. Chasing the adjutant with his drawn sword, he galloped directly to Latour-Maubourg, where he brusquely explained to him that he was not one of those who could be pestered with instructions and ordered about by adjutants. Before leaving, Thielemann also warned Latour-Maubourg against sending that adjutant again, since next time he would run him through with his sabre![453]

166

# The Battle of Borodino Phase Two (12am to 6pm)

The Russians fared no better and to Barclay de Tolly, 'it seemed as if Napoleon decided to eliminate us with his artillery'. Paskevich recalled the horrors of artillery bombardment:

> My division lost half of its men under that dreadful artillery fire that wiped out entire ranks but, as the French acknowledged themselves, we held ground with remarkable courage. Showered by canister, my division suffered such heavy casualties that we had to remove it from the first line ...

And according to Rayevsky, 'my corps [...] sustained so many killed and wounded that it turned into a complete nothingness ['sovershennoye nichtozhestvo'] ...' Indeed, Rayevsky's troops had to be replaced with the 24th Division of Major General Likhachev, which was moved from Dokhturov's 6th Corps.

Yermolov anticipated a new round of enemy assaults and tried to quickly mobilize forces at his disposal. Although the redoubt initially counted eighteen guns, many of them were damaged and Yermolov had to replace guns at least twice, drawing artillery pieces from nearby batteries. The loss of artillery personnel also caused him to employ the 3rd Battalion of the Ufimskii Regiment to man the pieces. He continued to direct men until 'a canister shot, which killed a non-commissioned officer [in front of me] [...] pierced a collar of my overcoat and tore a lapel of my coat, but a silk scarf on my neck softened its impact'. Yermolov fell down as his 'neck turned blue, a large tumour quickly appeared and all neck muscles were seriously damaged'. Meanwhile, Mikhailovsky-Danilevsky described the shells

> exploding in the air and on the ground, cannon-balls whistling through the air and raining on the ground from every direction, ploughing the ground and shattering everything on their path. Artillery rounds were made so frequent that there were no intervals between explosions and they persisted continuously like a relentless thunder.[454]

The French artillery fire even reached Russian units standing in reserve behind the front line. The Life Guard Preobrazhenskii and Semeyonovskii Regiments lost dozens of men killed and wounded without firing a single shot. 'Our brigade – the Life Guard Semeyonovskii and Preobrazhenskii Regiments – remained under the heavy bombardment of the enemy batteries for hours. It withstood this ordeal with incredible composure which is characteristic to the élite troops,' wrote Captain Pushin in his diary. Muravyev-Apostol described conditions in these regiments:

> The 2nd Battalion of the Life Guard Semeyonovskii Regiment was deployed on the right flank of the 1st Battalion. Peter Olenin, as an adjutant of the 2nd Battalion, was mounted on his horse. Around 8am, a cannon-ball whistled near his head and he fell down to the ground, everyone assuming he was dead. Prince Trubetskoy, who visited the wounded in infirmary, assured the elder [Nikolai] Olenin that his brother only suffered a contusion and would survive his wound. Olenin was beyond himself with joy. The officers gathered in a circle in front of the battalion to ask about his wounded brother. However, as the enemy fire intensified and the cannon-balls rained down on us, Colonel

# The Battle of Borodino

Baron Maxim Ivanovich de-Damas, the commander of the 2nd Battalion, ordered, 'Gentlemen, return to your places.' Nikolai Olenin took his place in front of his squad while Count Tatishev was standing in front facing him. They were both delighted by the good news about [the younger Olenin]. Suddenly, a cannon-ball shattered Count Tatishev's back, then pierced Olenin's chest and tore off an NCO's leg ...[455]

The Russian command massed considerable forces in anticipation of the next attack. Likhachev, who was in poor health and, unable to stand, was sitting on a campaign stool inside the redoubt, deployed his 24th Division in two lines, with the Butyrskii, Tomskii and Combined Grenadier Regiments in the first line, and the 19th and 40th Jäger Regiments behind the ravine of the Ognik stream, supported by the Ufimskii and Shirvanskii Regiments. The survivors of the VII Corps were moved to the rear, though some were organized by Vasilchikov to reinforce the left flank. The 4th Division was deployed south of the redoubt, with the 2nd Brigade, supported by Creitz's cavalry, in the immediate vicinity of the redoubt, while the 1st Brigade was closer to Semeyonovskoye. Around noon, the IV Corps replaced the 2nd Brigade of the 4th Division (which was sent to the II Corps on the Old Smolensk Road) and took up new positions, with its 11th (Bakhmetyev I) and 23rd Divisions (Bakhmetyev III) facing southwest. To the north of the redoubt, the 7th Division was holding positions extending to Gorki, while in the south stood the 1st Brigade of the 4th Division and remnants of the 12th Division and the Combined Grenadier Brigade of the V Corps. The Life Guard Preobrazhenskii, Semeyonovskii and Finlyandskii Regiments were arranged behind the left flank of the IV Corps. The II and III Cavalry Corps were also ordered to proceed towards the redoubt, but were delayed due to terrain and heavy fighting on the left flank.[456] It is difficult to estimate the precise number of Russian troops concentrated at the redoubt by late afternoon, but they must have numbered about 30,000–33,000 men. The strength of the Russian artillery is less definite and Larionov argued that some 'artillery companies, having exhausted their ammunition, left the positions'.[457]

While Eugène coped with the Russian cavalry raid, the French finally seized Semeyonovskoe after a bitter combat and were now able to shift some of their troops to the centre. Lorge's 7th Cuirassier Division and Rozniecki's 4th Light Cavalry Division moved about 1,000 paces northwest of Semeyonovskoe, where they assumed a new position. Thielemann's brigade was deployed in the first line, with the Saxon Gardes du Corps in front, the 14th Polish Cuirassiers in rear and the Zastrow Cuirassiers in the middle. The second line, located about 100m behind Thielemann's men consisted of Lepel's brigade of Westphalian cuirassiers in columns. To their right were Rozniecki's Polish Lancers, also in columns. To their left, and slightly behind, was the II Cavalry Corps, with Wathier's 2nd Cuirassier Division in the first line and Defrance's 4th Cuirassier Division in the second. Pajol's division was on the left flank of the II Cavalry Corps and the Vistula Legion assumed position to the left of Lorge's men. Additional light cavalry brigades (the 8th, 9th, 14th and 24th) were deployed between the II and IV Cavalry Corps. In the afternoon, the 1st and 2nd Chevau-léger lancier de la Garde Regiments were moved forward in support.[458]

The French also gathered substantial infantry. Eugène's troops were north of the II Cavalry Corps. Gérard's division was organized with the 21st Line and two battalions of the 12th Light in the front. Behind them was the 7th Light and the remaining battalions of the 12th Light. Morand's division was north of Gérard and had the 17th Line in the first line, followed by the 13th Light and the survivors of the 30th Line. The 14th Division (Broussier) was next to the Kolocha, with the 9th and 35th Line in the front and 53rd Line in the second line, followed by the two battalions of the 18th Light and two battalions of the Joseph Napoleon Regiment.[459] Further upstream was Grouchy's III Cavalry Corps, though some troops from Chastel's light cavalry division were near Broussier's men.[460] The total number of French guns concentrated at this sector is naturally difficult to determine due to battle confusion. Estimates vary from as many as 400 to as few as 170, though some 200 guns actively engaged in the attack seems more plausible.

About noon, the French cavalry made several charges on the Russian positions around the redoubt, mainly towards the village of Semeyonovskoye. Beurman's Westphalian chasseurs were involved in several such attacks south of the redoubt, where they were engaged in a bitter mêlée with the Russian cavalry – probably Creitz's dragoons (see pages 130–1). At one moment the Westphalians began to suffer heavy losses and turned back to their positions, pursued by the Russians. Pajol noticed these troops fleeing in 'great disorder' and personally went to rally them. After regrouping, the Westphalian chasseurs drove the Russians back, but the see-saw action continued for some time. Observing another Russian cavalry charge, Pajol was prompted to counter-charge with his troops but was stopped by Murat, who told him to allow the heavy cavalry of Wathier and Defrance to prepare for attack. Still, Pajol moved forward two carabinier regiments and three squadrons of lancers.[461]

It is difficult to find reliable information on this charge in Russian battle reports, which often lack details and concentrate on the decisive cavalry charge that took place later that day. The report of Korf, who commanded the II and III Cavalry Corps, mentions this attack in vague terms:

> The Sibirskii and Irkutskii Dragoon Regiments were deployed to protect the grand battery, located in the centre, and they remained under a dreadful artillery fire between 8am and noon, when a strong column of the enemy cavalry and infantry thought to seize the battery. They quickly charged and routed the enemy.[462]

Colonel Creitz distinguished himself commanding his dragoons in these back-and-forth charges; already twice wounded, he now suffered a third injury. Disregarding his pain, he continued to fight until a canister shot dislodged him from his horse, which was killed. Changing his mount, Creitz led another counter-charge against the French and sustained three more wounds (making a total of six), which finally forced this indomitable warrior to seek medical assistance. But while Kutuzov and Barclay praised the Russian cavalry, Creitz was more critical, noting that:

> The Irkutskii Regiment, under [the] command of Lieutenant Colonel Yuzhakov, failed its duties and the Sibirskii and Orenburgskii Regiments were rescued by Colonel Emanuel, who led the Kievskii Dragoon Regiment in a gallant charge against the enemy flank and halted its advance.

Creitz's memoirs also note that this French attack seized eight guns of Kandyba's 5th Horse Company, but could not remove them because of a valiant effort by the 2nd Squadron of the Sibirskii Dragoons, which recovered them.[463]

Friedrich von Schubert attested to the chaotic nature of the fighting, writing:

> Someone who did not see it with his own eyes can have no idea of what this disorder was like. One could no longer speak of general order or leadership. Each regiment, as soon as it had been halfway regrouped by a new bugle call, immediately returned to the attack [...] In the midst of it all there were the remains of our infantry division, which the officers were trying to reorganize; Paskevich, who in desperation was tearing out his hair, cursing and swearing; and Barclay, whose horse had just been killed and who quite calmly was trying to restore order on foot.

Wolzogen could see as, 'each canister shot kicked up a tiny cloud of dust from the surface of the ground, which had been trampled into a fine powder, and as everywhere these tiny clouds were curling over on themselves, they looked like moving waves'. He had his horse shot under him and had to carry his saddle, in the midst of fighting, to the rear. Behind the Grand Redoubt, he was halted by a special cordon that Yermolov had established to turn back soldiers who claimed they needed to escort a wounded comrade to the ambulances.[464]

Löwenstern was wounded in the hand and received medical assistant at an ambulance in the rear: 'My hand was in a sling,' he recalled, 'I could not hold a sabre but I still could do something and that was enough for me. I was in a state of extreme agitation and felt as if some kind of fever took over me.' Returning to the front line, he found Barclay de Tolly in the midst of the battle and was sent to Osterman-Tolstoy, who was wounded earlier but refused to stay in the dressing station and returned to his post, which he 'defended like a lion'. According to Löwenstern: 'After spending only 8 or 10 minutes with Osterman, I saw a number of men of his suite being killed and wounded ...'

Russian battle reports are vague on the exact development of events leading to the fall of the redoubt. Barclay de Tolly was personally directing the defence of this important location, always cool and collected, providing a striking example to his troops. It was evident to him that

> the enemy was preparing one more decisive attack; enemy cavalry was moved forward and organized in various columns. I anticipated that our II and III

# The Battle of Borodino Phase Two (12am to 6pm)

Cavalry Corps, having suffered greatly in previous attacks, would not be able to withstand this new and powerful blow, and sent for the 1st Cuirassier Division. Unfortunately, someone had moved it to the left flank and my adjutant could not find it where I intended to keep it; all he could do was to find the Chevalier Guard and Life Guard Horse Regiments, which rushed to my assistance. However, by then, the enemy had charged the 24th Division ... [and] strong enemy columns attacked the hill from both sides ...

Back at French headquarters, Napoleon was informed of the capture of Semeyonovskoye and contemplated a decisive blow against the redoubt in the centre, which, as Pelet described it, served as an anchor for the Russian Army. If successful, this attack would shatter the Russian defences, bringing the decisive victory Napoleon was seeking. According to Ségur, it was about this time that Napoleon received Murat's complaints about the losses his cavalry was sustaining, accompanied by a request for the Guard cavalry to attack. Napoleon seemed to give his consent and sent in search of Bessières, who could not be found. 'The Emperor waited nearly an hour without the least impatience, or repeating his order ...' Ségur noted. Told about Montbrun's injury, Napoleon replaced him with General Auguste de Caulaincourt, younger brother of his Grand Equerry. Caulaincourt had a distinguished career in Spain and, as he instructed this general, Napoleon told him: 'Do what you did at Arzobispo' – referring to a daring attack Caulaincourt carried out in Spain in August 1809, when he forded the Tagus with his dragoons to seize a fortified bridge across the river.[465]

Before leaving, Caulaincourt had a meeting with Belliard and Murat to discuss this important attack. Murat seems to have reconnoitred the Russian positions earlier, since Griois recalled seeing Murat at his battery:

We were quite sure he [Murat] would put an end to a murderous cannonade which was leading to nothing and even slowing down for lack of ammunition, and that he would dispose of enough troops at one point to make a fresh and decisive attack. Indeed, having examined the situation and ridden over the terrain, where, for several hours now, our cavalry was being devastated, he noticed that the parapets of the Grand Redoubt had almost been razed to the ground by our gunnery.

According to Murat's report, he ordered Caulaincourt 'to charge on his left all that was there of the enemy and attempt to reach the Grand Redoubt, which, taking us in the flank, caused us a lot of mischief each time it found a favourable occasion'. Pelet is more specific on Caulaincourt's mission, which was 'to clear the area between the redoubt and the Semeyonovskoye [...] then turn left and assault the redoubt from the rear, while Eugène's columns attacked from the front'. Ségur confirms that the main target was 'the terrible redoubt whose front fire was mowing the ranks of the Viceroy'.

It was a do or die mission and Caulaincourt knew this well. Whether from a premonition or a realistic appraisal of his chances, he told his brother before leaving: 'The fighting is so fierce that I shall doubtless not see you again. We will triumph or I will get myself killed.' According to Ségur,

171

# The Battle of Borodino

Caulaincourt 'found the aides-de-camp of the unfortunate Montbrun in tears for the loss of their commander. "Follow me," said he to them, "weep not for him, but come and avenge his death!"' Captain Coignet of the Imperial Guard – not always a reliable source – provides additional details on the preparations for this decisive charge. He writes that Caulaincourt summoned the regimental colonels and informed them of orders to take the redoubt: 'There is not a moment to lose! Trot when I give the command, and charge as soon as you are within musket-shot ...' The assault was launched around 3pm and it involved almost the entire Allied cavalry force. Caulaincourt led the first wave, charging at the head of the 5th and 8th Cuirassiers, which were followed by Defrance's carabiniers. Some time later, the IV Cavalry Corps charged as well.[466]

Covered in dust and smoke, the Grand Redoubt presented an almost surreal sight, which one German participant (Leissnig) compared to a 'hellish concert' as the fortification was regularly illuminated by the 'reddish, aurora-borealis glow' of its firing guns. The redoubt was so badly damaged that its parapet was all but razed to the ground. Behind the redoubt, a French round ignited a barrel of resin, with which the Russians lubricated the axles of their guns, and Lejeune could see 'the purple flames rolling along the ground like an infuriated snake, then climbing upwards in columns of smoke, throwing broad shadows on the ground'. Indeed, it would have been stunning to observe hundreds of Allied cavalrymen – with gleaming cuirasses, resplendent uniforms and tall, gaudy plumes – charging up the slopes leading to the redoubt. Labaume was dazed to see 'the eminence of a mass of moving iron: the glitter of arms, and the rays of the sun reflected from the helmets and cuirasses, mingled with the flames of the cannon that on every side vomited forth death, to give the appearance of a volcano in the midst of the army.' Across the field, a Russian artillery officer was also fascinated as 'the brilliant rays of the half-hidden sun were reflected from the sabres, swords, bayonets, helmets and cuirasses, making a dreadful yet sublime picture ...'[467]

According to Murat, the cavalry charge was

> executed with as much rapidity as bravery. Caulaincourt, at the head of the 2nd Cuirassier Division [...] overthrew everything he met in front of him, and finding he had gone past the Grand Redoubt on the left, came back and fell upon it and, with the 5th Cuirassiers, took it from the enemy.

Griois saw as the cuirassiers

> started to gallop, overthrowing everything in front of them, turning to the redoubt, entering it by the throat and by the place where the earth that had rolled down into the ditched made it easier of access. At the same time, [Eugène], with his infantry, attacked the redoubt from the left ...[468]

The impetus of the heavily armed cavalrymen carried the charge beyond the redoubt. Some cavalrymen jumped over the ditches and the half-destroyed parapet into the redoubt, where the remaining Russians fought to their last breath. Lejeune described how 'in the struggle, the wind, which was blowing strongly, raised clouds of dust, which mingled with the smoke from the guns and whirled up in dense masses, enveloping and almost suffocating men and horses'. Meanwhile, Colonel Griois, watching the attack from the rear, was elated to see the charge:

> It would be difficult to convey our feelings as we watched this brilliant feat of arms, perhaps without equal in the military annals of nations. Every one of us would have liked to give a helping hand to that cavalry which we saw leaving over ditches and scrambling over ramparts under a hail of canister, and a roar of joy resounded on all sides as they became masters of the redoubt.[469]

However, the French attack was far from being as successful as Murat, Lejeune or Griois would have us to believe. In reality, the Russians managed to hold onto their position, despite Caulaincourt's initial charge. The French cavalry was exposed to the fire of the Russian regiments on both sides of the redoubt. Although some cuirassiers broke into the redoubt, they were soon repelled and Caulaincourt himself was mortally wounded, either by a Russian bullet or canister ball. Some time later, an officer of the Vistula Legion saw 'Caulaincourt, mortally wounded, being carried away in a white cuirassier cloak, stained deep red by his blood ...' News of Caulaincourt's death quickly travelled to Napoleon's headquarters, where Lieutenant Wolbert, one of Caulaincourt's adjutants, arrived sobbing to relay the grisly news. A moment later Coignet arrived, declaring: 'the brave Caulaincourt fell dead beside me'. Ségur, standing nearby, observed as Armand de Caulaincourt, brother of the unfortunate General

> listened, and was at first petrified; but he soon summoned courage against this misfortune, and, but for the tears which silently coursed down his cheeks, you might have thought that he felt nothing. The Emperor, uttering an exclamation of sorrow, said to him, 'You have heard the news, do you wish to retire?' But as at that moment we were advancing against the enemy, the Grand Equerry made no reply; he did not retire; he only half uncovered himself to thank the Emperor, and to refuse.

'He has died as a brave man should,' Napoleon told Caulaincourt, 'France loses one of her best officers.'[470]

As Caulaincourt's men were fighting around the redoubt, Latour-Maubourg's IV Cavalry Corps came charging around the southern side of the redoubt.

Von Leissnig recalled as:

> an order was given to attack redoubt with several regiments of French, Westphalian and Saxon cuirassiers (La Garde du Corps Royal et le Regiment von Zastrow) whose men were well defended by their armour against the grapeshot. At the same time, several French regiments, two Bavarian units of light cavalry as well as the Saxons light horsemen were to be held ready for attack and diverting the attention of the enemy [...] But the Russians, who had guessed this manoeuvre, opened on us a well-nourished fire of grapeshot at a distance of eleven hundred steps. Our batteries responded with strength: a

# The Battle of Borodino

dense, thick smoke then covered all space between the Russians and us: one could not see in this dimness the flashes of the blows of gun. It could be said that the hell opened its doors and plunged us in the darkness of chaos: the sabres themselves emitted a dull light [...] This darkness, unbearable by itself, was still reinforced by clouds of dust akin to sandstorms in the deserts of Arabia [...] Suddenly the enemy batteries fell silent, smoke and dust dispersed and the light lit the plain. I then saw several regiments of cavalry (of which the two were Saxon) throwing themselves against the batteries of the redoubt and forcing the Russians to abandon the ground.[471]

Rozniecki's 4th Polish Light Cavalry Division, in two ranks, formed the right flank of this assault, while the Saxon and Westphalian cuirassiers were on the left; Latour-Maubourg placed his horse artillery batteries in the centre. The Saxon Gardes du Corps, and the nearest squadrons of the Zastrow Cuirassier Regiment, were first to reach the redoubt, which Caulaincourt's cuirassiers failed to secure. Some of the Saxons jumped over the parapets while others fought through one of the entrances into the redoubt. Sources disagree on how many Russian troops the Saxons found inside the fortification. Considering the size of the redoubt, and losses sustained in the earlier fighting, it can be assumed that there were few infantry inside it and the garrison largely consisted of artillery crews.

Meerheim, who took part in the attack, shared his experiences:

The combat was frightful! Men and horses hit by lethal lead, fell down the slope and thrashed around among the dead and dying foe, each trying to kill the enemy with their weapons, their bare hands or even their teeth. To add to this horror, the succeeding ranks of assaulting cavalry tramped over the writhing mass as they drove on to their next targets, the infantry squares, who greeted them with well-aimed volleys ...

The Russians fiercely defended their guns and, as Meerheim described, 'inside the redoubt, horsemen and soldiers, gripped by a frenzy of slaughter, were butchering each other without any semblance of order'. The Russians managed to remove several of their guns (most sources acknowledge six) but, as Roth von Schreckenstein claimed, two more were abandoned at the northern entrance and a third in the ditch behind the redoubt.[472]

At the same time, Prince Eugène attacked as well, with the 35th Line on the extreme left, the 21st Line (supported by the 12th and 7th Light) on the right and the 17th and 9th Line in the centre.[473] Sergeant Bertrand of the 7th Light saw as

a round shot took my Captain's head off, killing or mortally wounding four men in the first rank. The Lieutenant took the Captain's place, but scarcely was he at his post than he was himself hit by a piece of grape, which shattered his thigh. At the same time, the Sous-Lieutenant's leg was shattered by another splinter. With the officers *hors de combat* and the Sergeant Major absent, I, as senior sergeant, took command of the company. We were at the foot of the redoubt, two of the regiment's battalions seemed to be retiring by echelons, and the two others making an oblique movement. The Colonel ordered me not to budge. The reasons for his order were beyond me, but I was proud to be commanding an élite company. My musket on my shoulder, facing the redoubt and under grapeshot, I was addressing my comrades when suddenly a platoon of Russian dragoons emerged from it shouting hurrah ...

However Bertrand's men quickly organized a defence and 'opened a rolling fire, which cost the horsemen, already almost on our bayonets, dear'. Labaume informs us that 'in the midst of this scene of carnage I discovered the body of a Russian gunner decorated with three crosses. In one hand he held a broken sword, and with the other he firmly grasped the carriage of the gun at which he had so valiantly fought'. As the redoubt was captured, General Likhachev continued to fight until, as Cesare de Laugier described, Chef de Bataillon Del Fante, 'recognized a Russian general [...] threw himself at him, disarmed him and snatched him from the fury of the men ...'[474]

The Russian sources indicate that some troops of the 35th Line, which crossed the Kolocha at its confluence with the Stonets stream, were engaged by the 1st Jägers. According to Petrov, after the initial attack on Borodino in the morning, a company of Jägers under Captain Zubko was left along the river and skirmished with the French until late afternoon, when it

> moved to the right side of Stonets stream to prevent enemy attempts to cross to our side at the stream's confluence with the Kolocha and to threaten the rear of [Rayevsky's Redoubt]. Our regiment repelled four such attempts and inflicted considerable losses on the enemy each time.

Petrov also noted that his regiment was later supported by the Libau Infantry Regiment to 'fend off the decisive attacks of the enemy, who was assaulting [the redoubt]'. Gulevich's 23rd Battery Company seems to have played an active role in this area. Deployed on the left bank of the Stonets stream, it engaged the attacking French columns in their flank but suffered greatly from the returning fire of the French batteries. Petrov tells us that Gulevich's battery lost

> [The] larger part of its men, halted its fire and wanted to withdraw to the right bank of the stream. Colonel Karpenko dispatched me with two officers and forty soldiers, who were specifically trained for such incidents at the division quarters in Slonim before the war. I replenished the battery's crew with these men, which allowed it to continue firing ...[475]

Karpenko's memoirs provide a few more details on the fighting along the Stonets stream:

> Around 4pm, the French columns rushed across the rivulet [...] As they approached my positions at pistol range, I opened murderous volleys at them. They and us both held the ground with intrepid gallantry for the next quarter of hour before the enemy was deprived of his victory again. However, the casualties were great and both sides, as if on command, seized the fire and retreated from each other ...[476]

Back at the redoubt, facing cavalry charges, the Russian infantry contracted into formidable squares behind the redoubt and their volleys mowed down the successive waves of cavalrymen. Meshetich, although confusing the sequence of attacks on the redoubt, still left an interesting account of the charge:

> The French cavalry charged like a whirlwind against the battery, making what seemed a splendid charge [...] The Russian infantry was driven back but they organized in squares and put up resistance [...] One could soon hear the rumbling noise and sound of weapons – this was the tempest of the Russian cavalry attacking the French horsemen; the success of the [French] attack was denied and they were forced to flee back, without seizing our artillery and with considerable losses.[477]

The Russian casualties also mounted. General Bakhmetyev I was wounded while his brother, Bakhmetyev III had his leg torn off by a cannon-ball. Among the wounded were also Generals Aleksopol and Osterman-Tolstoy. Yet, even in the midst of this cauldron, some men still thought of vying for recognition. Seeing Barclay de Tolly standing intrepidly under fire, Miloradovich exclaimed: 'Barclay wants to top me!' and, as participants recalled, he chose a spot closer to the French lines, where he demanded to be served lunch![478]

## Leo Tolstoy and Borodino

Leo Tolstoy's *War and Peace* is considered one of the masterpieces of world literature. This massive novel, published between 1865 and 1869, tracks the destinies of several characters – Andrei Bolkonsky, Pierre Bezukhov, Natasha Rostova – throughout the Napoleonic Wars, and contains a detailed description of the Battle of Borodino. Tolstoy's account of the battle, and his conclusions and general views on history, had a profound effect on how the Battle of Borodino was – and still is – perceived by the general reader. A compelling work of fiction, it generates a powerful mythology that, in fact, overshadows historical reality and assumed the authority of a historical document.

For Tolstoy, Borodino was a titanic battle and the turning point in the war between France and Russia. In describing the overall pattern of events, the novelist argued against the role and free choice of individuals in history. Thus, the battle is shown as part of the 'irresistible tide of history', which enveloped both Kutuzov and Napoleon, who hardly manifested any will of their own. Tolstoy suggests that Kutuzov acted merely as a catalyst, allowing the forces of destiny to work through him, while he, through intuition and emotion, not sentiment or intellect, understood the Russian state of mind. The battle itself is described as a national struggle and a moral victory of the Russian people against the invaders. Napoleon not only had no control over the course of the battle but his ambition prevented him from understanding the actual insignificance of his role. The Emperor is shown as helpless under the tide of destiny as any soldier in the ranks of his army. His orders are inevitably delayed, or made irrelevant by unforeseen developments.

But *War and Peace* did not assume its present-day iconic status at once. At its publication, it caused a stir among contemporaries, since the novel challenged the prevailing views of the battle. Veterans of 1812 questioned its authenticity and the legitimacy of this genre, which seemed to supplant history with fiction. They were particularly incensed by Tolstoy's depiction of various mundane and irreverent details of the battle, which, veterans felt, distorted the heroic atmosphere of the battle as they remembered (or wanted to remember) it.

Several veterans of Borodino were particularly vocal in their criticism. Prince Peter Vyazemsky saw *War and Peace* as a lampoon of 1812. Avraam Norov and Parmen Demenkov were insulted, among many other things, by Tolstoy's suggestion that Kutuzov, this genuine Russian, would be reading a cheap French novel while assuming command of the Russian armies at Tsarevo-Zaimishe. Ironically, it was later discovered that Norov himself was not shy of savouring a French novel during the Russian retreat from Moscow, causing one Russian writer to note that: 'what had happened to the artillery lieutenant in September of 1812 was forgotten by the venerable dignitary, since it did not fit the notion which he subsequently formed about 1812'.

This explains well why many veterans were so upset by Tolstoy's work – it directly contradicted their cherished memories of this memorable event. Tolstoy's attempt to debunk the place and role of historical individuals struck a particular chord with the veterans, who argued that this would make history meaningless. Norov complained that Tolstoy painted a 'picture without actors [in which] everything occurs by chance, which is hardly in accordance with the high purpose given to man by God. Since there are no human agents, there is no history either.'

Despite such criticism, Tolstoy's novel gradually became perceived by the public as an authoritative account, on a par with historical reports of the campaign. Objections from veterans were disregarded on the suspicion that they mythologized history.

Barclay de Tolly, informed of the fall of the redoubt, intended to recapture it with available sources. 'The 24th Division fell back in great confusion but was immediately rallied and regrouped,' he later wrote. These troops hardly moved out of the ravine behind the redoubt when they were attacked. 'The enemy continued his attack, with part of his cavalry tying down our forces while the other part attacked the 24th Division.'[479] The charge was beaten back but Barclay de Tolly realized that the redoubt was lost and ordered further withdrawal. The Allied cavalry regrouped amid clouds of dust and smoke and Latour-Maubourg then ordered an attack on the Russian squares on the plateau behind the redoubt.[480] The Allied cavalry attacked the Pernovskii, Kexholmskii and the 33rd Jäger Regiments and, as Kutuzov's report described:

> the enemy cavalry, consisting of cuirassiers and Lancers, attacked the IV Corps in many points but our courageous infantry, allowing the enemy to a close range, opened such devastating battalion volleys that the enemy was routed and fell back in disorder and with heavy casualties.[481]

At one moment, the Polish Lancers attacked a Russian battery, which was commanded by General Kostenetsky, chief of artillery of the VI Corps, himself. As the Poles began cutting down the gunners, Kostenetsky, a tall man of extraordinary physical strength and gallantry, seized a rammer and alone attacked several Lancers. Inspired by their General's heroism, the Russian gunners rushed to his assistance and repelled the Poles.[482]

Barclay de Tolly's report contains a few more details about the 'attacks of enemy cavalry, cuirassiers and Uhlans' against IV Corps. The infantry, showing 'remarkable firmness', allowed the cavalry to approach as close as 'sixty paces' before opening a fire that mowed down the enemy ranks. The Pernovskii Infantry and the 33rd Jägers were commended for their actions and Barclay de Tolly rewarded each company of these regiments with three medals of distinction.[483] According to Saxon sources, the Russian infantry fell back following the initial cavalry attack and was deployed in squares in chequerboard formation on the plateau behind the redoubt. Thielemann's men charged in-between them but found Russian cavalry deployed behind the infantry; the Russian soldiers allowed the enemy to approach as close as 20 paces before opening fire which devastated the Zastrow Cuirassiers.

The Russian cavalrymen initially hesitated because, seeing the Saxon uniforms, they mistakenly assumed they belonged to fellow Russians. But moments later their true identify was revealed and a cavalry mêlée followed. According to Barclay de Tolly, the Sumskii and Mariupolskii Hussars, supported by the Irkutskii and Sibirskii dragoons, counter-attacked and pursued the retreating French to 'their very reserves', but had to fall back after encountering 'strong artillery and musket fire'. It was now the Russian turn to flee as the French cavalry, 'receiving reinforcements from its reserves, pursued ours, and, breaking through the intervals between our infantry squares, got into the rear of the 7th and 11th Divisions'. Barclay de Tolly also reported that 'our incredible infantry, without showing any slight disorder, received the enemy with a strong and effective fire [...] Our cavalry, meantime, regrouped, and the enemy was driven back from this point ...'[484]

Some Russian infantrymen sought shelter in a ravine further behind, where, as Löwenstern notes, 'the enemy cannon-balls and canister did not reach them'. Barclay de Tolly sent his adjutant to rally these troops and lead them out of the ravine. However there was nothing that could have animated these men. They suffered too much and lost their spirits, choosing to die in this trap rather than to leave it. I left them there and do not know what happened to them since the French soon appeared and surrounded them from every side. I only escaped because of my admirable steed.

The French carabiniers (from Defrance's division) were also actively engaged in charges on the Russian squares but could not break through them. After one of the charges, Sergeant Major Ravat, with his right sleeve soaked with the Russian blood, which was also dripping from his sabre, approached Captain du Brail, who scolded him earlier for inappropriate talk. 'Well Captain,' Ravat yelled, 'am I still a miserable *Jean-Foutre?*'[485] The 1st Carabinier Regiment suffered considerable losses in these attacks and had to retire. As he was galloping back, the Carabiniers' Captain Marceau suddenly heard someone yelling behind him and, turning around, saw his comrade lying with an eagle in hand under his dead horse. With the Russians charging, Marceau turned back to rescue him but could only retrieve the eagle. Not far from the redoubt, Karl Schell, a fourteen-year-old trumpeter of the 2nd Carabinier Regiment, came across his squadron commander, von Bruckheimer, who was lying in a pool of his own blood but refused to be taken to a dressing station, saying, 'Let me be, I feel I must die today.' The young trumpeter sat beside von Bruckheimer and, seeing his commander die, wept.[486] One carabinier's fate, however, became more famous than all the others, largely due to French artists producing masterful paintings of his death. Although only a sous-lieutenant in the 1st Company of the 1st Squadron of the 1st Carabiniers, Ferdinand de Lariboisière seemed destined for a great career, being the son of Napoleon's Inspector General of Artillery and a former page to the Emperor. At Borodino, as his brigade was deploying for a charge on the redoubt, the 21-year-old Lariboisière saw his father nearby and left the ranks to bid him farewell. Moments later he was mortally wounded by a Russian cannon-ball and was carried by his comrades to his father's tent. Napoleon sent his personal surgeon to attend him but Ferdinand died a few days later at Mozhaisk. His grief-stricken father survived the retreat only to die of exhaustion at Königsberg in December 1812. Young Lariboisière was buried on the battlefield, while his father was laid to rest in Paris: but both their hearts were removed before entombment and buried together at the family crypt of their château.

Meanwhile, facing the Allied cavalry, Barclay de Tolly

already could foretell the terrible blow dealt to our destiny. My cavalry was insufficient to contain the massive enemy and I could not risk committing it because I anticipated that it would be routed and driven back in disorder onto my infantry. My only hope was on the courageous infantry and artillery who immortalized themselves that day; both of them met my expectations and the enemy was halted.[487]

According to Löwenstern, Barclay de Tolly watched the French movements attentively and 'called me asking if I knew where was the reserve

# The Battle of Borodino

Guard cavalry. Hearing my affirmative response, he instructed me to order General Shevich, who temporarily commanded it, to move his troops forward, without endangering them too much, and be prepared to charge when needed. This order caused a widespread elation among the courageous and élite cuirassiers, who were burning with desire to take part in this memorable battle. When I told Shevich about the order to place his troops in such a manner as not to expose them to artillery fire, he responded smiling, 'This would be difficult to do. For hours now we are closing our ranks to conceal the loss caused by the enemy cannon-balls. Let us advance, this is the best we can do at the moment.'

As Shevich's troops were moving to their new location, they were attacked by Latour-Maubourg's cavalry but, as Löwenstern observed:

> the men of Chevalier Guard, Horse Guard and Cuirassier regiments charged them with a remarkable composure. Salvoes followed one another. Our gallant cuirassiers covered themselves in glory but the Saxon and French cuirassiers were valiant opponents indeed ...[488]

Barclay de Tolly was delighted to see Guard cuirassiers arriving 'at this challenging moment'. He supported them with the Sumskii and Mariupolskii Hussars and the Sibirskii, Irkutskii and Orenburgskii Dragoon Regiments. He complained that 'The Pskovskii Dragoons and Izumskii Hussars were earlier moved without my knowledge but they arrived under command of General Korf and I placed them in reserve.' Barclay de Tolly describes the sequel:

> A cavalry mêlée, one of the fiercest ever to have been fought, then ensued. The enemy and our cavalry charged and drove back each other in turns, regrouping under cover of artillery and infantry and attacking again.[489]

From the Allied side, Leissnig recorded how

> attacked by Russian dragoons, we had to withdraw behind a ravine under a terrible artillery fire [...] But suddenly, the dragoons had disappeared and through smokes el dust, we saw all of the Russian cavalry moving against us, a truly unique spectacle [...] The grenades burst above our heads, sometimes flying over the points of our sabres [...] and covering us with ground and dust [...] It was a terrible quarter of an hour to pass. Our ranks quickly thinned out [...] Suddenly, the plain around us was filled with the French cavalry: the closest were the *grenadiers à cheval* and the cuirassiers. We were ordered to remain on the spot in support while the French threw themselves furiously on the Russians. The enemy grapeshot bounced off their armour and their helmets. Soon, they drew their long swords against the lines from the Russians and the enemy cavalry was forced to yield. But the Russian infantry had had time to regroup in thick masses ...[490]

Meanwhile, for Löwenstern

> There was a moment when the battlefield reminded me of one of the battle paintings [...] The battle developed into a hand-to-hand combat: warriors of both sides became mixed, there were no precise lines or close columns, but

# The Battle of Borodino Phase Two (12am to 6pm)

rather more or less numerous masses of men that collided with one another. The men were fighting in the front and rear [...] the infantry deployed in a square was firing with every side at once. Personal courage and aptitude were fully revealed on this memorable day.

In the middle of this cauldron, Barclay de Tolly had three horses shot under him. As his last horse was wounded, he found himself charged by several Polish Lancers. His adjutants rallied to his rescue and, as Löwenstern tells us, 'we gathered several cavalrymen from various regiments, who helped us in defending Barclay. We charged the Polish Uhlans, some of whom were cut down while others fled.' Among Barclay de Tolly's six adjutants, two would be killed by the end of the day, while the four remaining would be wounded.

As Caulaincourt's and Latour-Maubourg's troops were fighting south and south-east of the redoubt, one part of Prince Eugène's infantry, supported by the divisions of Chastel in first line and Lebrun La Houssaye in the second, led the charge to the north of the fortification, where they engaged the 7th Division of Kaptsevich. As Eugène reported:

> the enemy had formed in the rear on several lines and was covered by a ravine. I had it attacked; my troops crossed the ravine, overthrew the enemy and established themselves on the opposite plateau: the Russians, crushed, retreated [...] Grouchy executed a great charge with the division of cavalry of General Chastel, who at that moment supported the left of the infantry. General Grouchy was slightly wounded by a splinter of a shell.[491]

According to Griois, the wounded Grouchy ordered him to inform Eugène that he had to leave the battlefield and Lebrun La Houssaye was now in charge of the cavalry.[492] Grouchy was not the only casualty, however, as La Houssaye himself was wounded shortly after, followed by Generals Dommanget and Thiry and Colonels Ledard and von Wittgenstein among others.

The Allied attack faced stiff resistance as the Russians organized squares and fired upon the approaching cavalry. The French, however, broke through a square of the 19th Jäger Regiment. At that moment, Sub Lieutenant Korf, commanding the 2nd Division of the 2nd Guard Horse Artillery Battery, realized the danger the Jägers were facing and, without waiting for orders, moved his guns out of the reserve, advancing within 200m before opening a canister fire. Chastel's light cavalrymen quickly charged the battery, which could not remove its guns in time. Running to a nearby hill, Korf shouted as loud as he could to the commander of the 1st Division of the right-wing squadron of the Chevalier Guard Regiment, 'Bashmakov! Save my guns!' The Russian cavalrymen attacked at once and drove off Chastel's troops, saving the battery.[493]

The ever-present Barclay de Tolly arrived moments later and ordered Colonel Löwenwolde, Commander of the Chevalier Guard Regiment, to charge again. Löwenwolde formed his unit by squadrons and, advancing through the intervals of the squares of the 19th and the 40th Jägers, attacked Latour-Maubourg's cavalry. Bogdanovich informs us:

> Löwenwolde intended to charge the enemy front with his 1st Squadron, while the 4th Squadron, moving on his left, would attack the Saxons' flank. Ordering 'Gallop!' Löwenwolde then shouted to Rotmistr Davidov, who commanded the 4th Squadron, 'Evdokim Vasilievich, command the left wing.' He barely finished the sentence when he fell off his horse, killed by a canister ball to the head. His death, at such decisive moment, slightly disheartened our élite cavalrymen, but the Chevalier Guardsmen, now led by Colonel Levashov, made repeated charges against Latour-Maubourg's cavalry, preventing it from resuming its attacks on our infantry.

The Saxon Gardes du Corps, Zastrow Cuirassiers and the Polish 14th Cuirassiers were by now exhausted from repeated charges and could not hold the Russians back. Löwenstern later saw Levashev 'at a critical moment, as he, accompanied by several trumpeters, tried to rally his regiment [. . .] [and] was able to do this through his composure and skill'. The Life Guard Horse Regiment assisted the Chevalier Guard Regiment in these attacks. Its Colonel Arsenyev was seriously injured when a cannon-ball struck his left shoulder and he was replaced by Colonel Leontyev.[494] More details about this can be gleaned from Korf's report:

> Around 3pm, the enemy, directing all his attacks against the centre of our army, began to drive back our infantry. On [Barclay de Tolly's] orders, I rushed with the II Cavalry Corps to reinforce this point. On my arrival, I saw that the enemy had a strong infantry column moving in the centre, with cuirassiers and carabiniers to its left and the horse grenadiers on the right. Supported by its artillery batteries, the enemy vigorously attacked our infantry and forced our skirmishers to retreat in disorder.

Korf ordered the Izumskii Hussar and the Polskii (Polish) Uhlan Regiments, commanded by Major General Panchulidzev II, to move forward at a trot and, having deployed for attack, charge the enemy carabiniers and cuirassiers. But these regiments had barely prepared their attack when they were assaulted in turn (Nafziger suggests they were charged by the '1st Cuirassier Regiment and a half-squadron of chevau-léger lanciers') and disordered. Korf's adjutants, Captain Yakovlev and Ober-quartermaster Captain Schubert, distinguished themselves by rallying the chaotic cavalrymen, while Rotmistr Loshkarev charged with a squadron of the Izumskii Hussar Regiment to gain some time. Korf continues:

> After these two regiments regrouped they repelled the quick thrust of the enemy cuirassiers and carabiniers and allowed our infantry, which was also in disorder, to regroup and move forward. In the meantime, I ordered the Pskovskii Dragoon Regiment to move to the right while the Moscovskii Dragoon Regiment was left behind in reserve. Colonel Zass, commanding the Pskovskii regiment, noticed that the enemy infantry and horse grenadiers were forcefully attacking and threatening the left flank of the Izumskii Hussar and the Polskii Uhlan Regiments, which were not ready to repel them. He immediately led his regiment

at a trot against the enemy cavalry, then charged it and, despite the enemy's numerical superiority, forced it to retreat in disorder. After this attack, Colonel Zass regrouped his regiment under the enemy fire and this manoeuvre was carried out in great order; one can only hope that every cavalry regiment could act with such excellence.[495]

The French cavalry (from Grouchy's III Reserve Cavalry Corps) was still attacking, however, and Zass's men had to charge again. This time they also hit 'the left flank of the enemy infantry, which directed all of its firepower against our regiment'.[496] The Pskovskii Dragoons were supported by Colonel Kozen, of the Life Guard Horse Artillery Brigade, who had recently arrived from the left flank and personally directed the fire of the 1st Division of the 2nd Guard Horse Battery. Colonel Kudashev soon advanced with four guns and made a few canister rounds before the French countered with a larger battery, which inflicted considerable losses on Kudashev's crew: including the mortally wounded Captain Rall, Commander of the 2nd Horse Battery. Among those commended for their actions was Lieutenant Gelmerson of the Life Guard Horse Artillery, whom General Osterman-Tolstoy praised for 'defending for a half an hour, with his six guns of the Guard Horse Artillery, a position that was supposed to be held by an entire battery. He preserved the honour of my infantry and allowed the battery artillery to assume its position.' The 2nd Horse Battery was later replaced by the 29th Battery Company, which was supported by the 30th Battery Company. The nomination rosters reveal that

> Lieutenant Colonel [Bogdan] Nilus, commanding a company [...] was deployed in the centre and forced an enemy battery to withdraw by blowing up one of its caissons. He was then drawn on at other directions as well and skilfully operated against enemy columns and batteries.[497]

Among other batteries, the 2nd Battery and the 4th Light companies were attached to the 11th Division, while the 3rd Battery and the 3rd Light Companies were with the 23rd Division, which was later also supported by the 6th Horse Company as well. The 44th Light Company remained in reserve throughout the battle. Some batteries sustained heavy casualties and Nikitin's horse company alone lost ninety men and 113 horses.[498] Staff Captain Alexander Figner's 3rd Light Company was initially kept behind, remaining a passive observer of the action in front of it. As the French stormed the redoubt, Miloradovich's adjutant ordered the company to move forward, but the joy of its artillery crew turned sour when 'the Adjutant brought us near dragoons and left us there'. Radozhitsky and his comrades could see 'many dead Russian soldiers and one blown-up ammunition cart, which was surrounded by a patch of burnt grass and the charred remains of the horses and drivers'. To his right, Radozhitsky saw four horse artillery guns that were still firing, although their crews were largely killed and wounded and only three gunners were manning each piece. According to Radozhitsky, the dragoons standing in front of his company were constantly falling down hit by artillery rounds and musket balls. Shot, shell, canister and even musket balls flew through the files of the dragoons and among our gunners, striking down several men and horses [...] Here I appreciated the truth that nothing is less pleasant on a battlefield than to stand inactive under enemy fire: almost every soldier followed the flight of the cannon shot with his eyes and paid them a degree of involuntary respect.

Moments later he himself became a victim of one of these rounds. Suffering from a severe concussion, he was taken to the rear and saw:

> a great number of other unfortunates, with various wounds, who were emitting groans and yells. There was a [Cossack], who was a particularly horrifying and pitiable case. As I came in the surgeons were extracting a bullet from his back, causing him to writhe and scream in a frightful manner ...[499]

By 4.30pm, Eugène's troops were firmly in control of the Grand Redoubt, and the Allied cavalrymen, after being in the saddle for almost ten hours, withdrew to their lines. The Russians were also considerably weakened and Barclay de Tolly preferred to slowly withdraw his men across the ravine and take up a new position some 800m from the redoubt. As Löwenstern recalled, Barclay de Tolly 'was not particularly distressed by the loss of the great battery, [saying] "It is unfortunate [that we lost it] but we will recapture it tomorrow or maybe even tonight after the French abandon it."' As Meshetich described:

> the grand sight of the Russians troops arranged in three lines of infantry and artillery in between, was gone. The infantry line of the IV Corps stood now and then on the left flank, thinning out but withstanding the last attack of the enemy [...] One could see here the bloody sweat of the battle exhaustion, the tears and laments of the lost commanders, comrades and acquaintances. The field of the battle was covered with the numerous corpses, the ravines and brushwood were full of the moaning wounded asking for one thing, to put them out of misery. Human blood flowed in small streams ...[500]

The subsequent combat in this sector was limited to an artillery duel and skirmishing between advance elements. With the sound of gunfire still coming from the left flank, it seemed all that was needed for a complete French victory was a final blow from Napoleon's reserves. The Emperor seemed satisfied with the capture of the redoubt but, as Lejeune recalled, he 'was still hesitating whether, as many amongst us wished, he should follow up this success with a grand charge from the whole of the brilliant cavalry of the Guard'. At this moment Napoleon was told about Likhachev, captured defending the Grand Redoubt. Likhachev was initially taken to Prince Eugène, who met him amiably and had him escorted to Napoleon. After talking to him for a few minutes, Napoleon instructed his adjutant to bring the General's sword. As Soltyk and Lejeune tell us, a sword was at once brought and the Emperor graciously offered it. However, the Russian General refused to accept it. The French and Russian sources disagree on the reasons for this refusal. French participants claimed that Likhachev refused the sword because it was not his but that of Napoleon's adjutant and, as Soltyk described, the General

> persisted in refusing it from the Emperor's hand [...] shaking his head and saying 'Niet, niet.' Napoleon smiled disdainfully, handed the sword back to the French aide-de-camp who had brought [Likhachev] in, and with a gesture ordered the Russian General to be taken away.

According to Lejeune, Napoleon 'was astonished at this want of tact in a general, shrugged his shoulders, and turning to us said, loud enough for the General to hear him, "Take the fool away!"'

But the incident is described differently in Russian sources. Mikhailovsky-Danilevsky, thus, explained that Likhachev 'declined the magnanimity of the victor and told him in a weak voice, 'I am grateful, Your Majesty. The captivity deprived me of the sword that was granted to me by my Emperor [Alexander] [...] and I can accept it only from his hands.'[501] Likhachev was well treated in his captivity and was later sent under escort to France, only to be liberated by the Russian troops in Königsberg in December 1812: but privation and exhaustion had a detrimental effect on his health and he died five months later.

---

## Borodino Military Historical Museum-Preserve

The Borodino Military Historical Museum-Preserve was established in 1839 and initially included Rayevsky's Redoubt, General Peter Bagration's grave and central part of the battlefield. In 1859, the house of Margarita Tuchkova, wife of General Alexander Tuchkov, became the memorial museum of the battlefield while in 1903, the Borodino railway station was turned into the historical museum of the 1812 Campaign. Nine years later, the centennial celebration resulted in the construction of a new museum near the Rayevsky's Redoubt and erection of thirty six monuments dedicated to the units of both sides. In 1923, the Borodino museum was attached to the Military Historical Museum and later the famous State Historical Museum of the USSR. Its exhibition was evacuated during the Nazi invasion in the fall of 1941 and the museum building and some monuments were destroyed during the subsequent battles in the region in 1942. However, the museum was restored only two years later and was expanded over the years. In 1961, it received the status of the museum-preserve and, by 1990s, it came to include the entire battlefield with some 200 monuments as well as the Kolotsk Monastery, the Mozhaisk complex and 75 acres of land around them.

The Borodino Museum, designed by architect V. Voyeikov, houses an impressive collection of some 40,000 items, including personal items of Emperors Napoleon and Alexander, Generals Kutuzov, Barclay de Tolly, Bagration and others, uniforms and weaponry of both armies and trophies captured during the French retreat. Among its exhibitions are 'Borodino – The Battle of Giants' in the central building of the museum, 'Leo Tolstoy and the Battle of Borodino' and 'House-Museum of Mother Superior Maria' at the Borodino Saviour Monastery. The museum-preserve also showcases events of World War II and houses display 'Borodino during the Great Patriotic War.' Among its minor but illuminating expositions are 'Russian and Western European Uniforms of the early XIX century' and 'Military Portraiture in Russia in the first half of the XIX century.'

With one of the best-preserved battlefields in Europe, the Borodino museum-preserve is visited by some 300,000 persons every year. It organizes annual celebrations and re-enactments, including the Day of Borodino (1st Sunday in September) that draws hundreds of re-enactors and thousands of spectators. The museum also hosts several historical conventions, including international conference 'Patriotic War of 1812: Sources, Monuments, Problems.'

After Likhachev was taken away, Napoleon decided to survey the results of the charge on Rayevsky's Redoubt. 'He mounted his horse with difficulty, and rode slowly along the heights of Semenowska,' wrote Ségur. After observing the redoubt, Napoleon crossed the Kamenka and travelled towards the flèches in the south. Von Roos saw him, surrounded by a large entourage, slowly moving with calm appearance. According to Pelet, the Emperor inspected the flèches and visited Semeyonovskoye. The Russians noticed a group surrounding a small figure in a grey coat in the centre of the battlefield, and directed their fire towards it. Concerned about the safety of the Emperor, his adjutants persuaded Napoleon to leave. According to Pelet, a few moments after Napoleon left this spot, the Russian canister ploughed the ground thereabouts. As Lejeune informs us: 'The Emperor, satisfied with all that had already been accomplished [...] now thought the right moment had come to send his whole Guard to complete the victory.' However, he was advised against it. According to Ségur, Bessières, 'continuing to insist, as he always did, on the importance of this *corps d'élite*', objected, noting the lack of reinforcements and the necessity to safeguard some reserves. Berthier argued that: 'it was too late [and] the enemy was strengthening himself in his last position; and that it would require a sacrifice of several more thousands, without any adequate results'.[502] Thus, the option to commit the Guard was declined.

Instead of his Imperial Guard, Napoleon turned to artillery and instructed Lejeune to order Sorbier 'to extend sixty guns at right angles with the enemy's line, so as to crush him by a flank fire'. Lejeune quickly delivered the order to Sorbier, who, 'incredulous of my message, did not give me time to explain it, but broke in with the words, "We ought to have done that an hour ago!"'

# The Battle of Borodino Phase Two (12am to 6pm)

Sorbier's battery ascended the Semeyonosvkoye ridge, where it took up a new position and began 'to pour out volleys of grapeshot, shells, and balls on the enemy's lines ...'

Meanwhile, in the distance, Lejeune could see

> King Murat caracoling about in the midst of the mounted skirmishers well in advance of his own cavalry, and paying far less attention to them than to the numerous Cossacks who, recognizing him by his bravado, as well as by his plumed helmet, and a short Cossack mantle made of goat's skin with long hair resembling their own, surrounded him in the hope of taking him prisoner, shouting, 'Hurrah! Hurrah! Murat!' But none of them dared even venture within a lance's length of him, for they all knew that the King's sword would skilfully turn aside every weapon, and with the speed of lightning pierce to the heart the boldest amongst his enemies.

As Armand de Caulaincourt noted:

> Success was hardly won, and the fire was so murderous that generals, like their subordinate officers, had to pay in person for victory. We did all we could for the wounded whilst the battle was raging and during the night that followed, but most of the houses in the vicinity of the battlefield had been burned during the day, and in consequence many casualty stations passed the night without shelter. There were very few prisoners. The Russians showed the utmost tenacity; their fieldworks, and the ground they were forced to yield, were given up without disorder. Their ranks did not break; pounded by the artillery, sabre by the cavalry, forced back at the bayonet point by our infantry, their somewhat immobile masses met death bravely, and only gave way slowly before the fury of our attacks. Several times the Emperor repeated that it was quite inexplicable to him that redoubts and positions so audaciously captured and so doggedly defended should yield us so few prisoners. Several times he asked, of the officers who came with reports of our successes, where the prisoners were who ought to have been captured. He even sent orderlies to the various positions to make sure that more had not been taken. These successes, yielding neither prisoners nor trophies, made him discontented. Several times he said to the prince of Neuchâtel and me, 'These Russians let themselves be killed like automatons; they are not taken alive. This does not help us at all. These citadels should be demolished with cannon.'

To support Sorbier's battery, Napoleon ordered Mortier 'to make the Young Guard now advance, but on no account to pass the new ravine which separated us from the enemy'. He specified that Mortier was 'to guard the field of battle [and] that that was all he required of him'. Napoleon even recalled the General shortly after to ask if he had properly understood him.[503] As the Vistula Legion of the Young Guard advanced, one of its officers saw:

> the redoubt and its environs [which] presented a ghastly sight more horrible than anything one could possibly imagine. The earthworks, the ditches and the inside of the redoubt had all disappeared under a mass of the dead and dying

# The Battle of Borodino

piled seven or eight men deep one on top of the other. I shall never forget the sight of a middle-aged staff officer, with a massive head wound, slumped against a Russian howitzer.

Brandt could see that 'after unsuccessfully pursuing the Russians, the French cavalry fell back and the Russian infantry began to advance towards us. They paused or hesitated, perhaps overawed by the sheer scale of the fighting.' To Ségur

> It was impossible to pursue the fugitive Russians; fresh ravines, with armed redoubts behind them, protected their retreat. There they defended themselves with fury [...] From this second range of heights, their artillery overwhelmed the first which they had abandoned to us. [Eugène] was obliged to conceal his panting, exhausted, and thinned lines in the hollows of the ground, and behind the half-destroyed entrenchments. The soldiers were obliged to get upon their knees, and crouch themselves up behind these shapeless parapets. In that painful posture they remained for several hours, kept in check by the enemy, who stood in check of them.

Brandt was in the midst of this bombardment and personally felt

> the terrible artillery duel, of which all historians speak [...] The redoubt, which to some extent sheltered us, was torn up by shot and shell. Shots soon began to fall amongst our ranks and our losses began to mount. The soldiers received the order to lie down while the officers 'awaited death standing,' as Rechowictz put it. He had just finished speaking when we were both splashed by the blood and brains of a sergeant who had his head blown off by a cannon-ball just as he had stood up to go and talk to a friend. The horrible stains on my uniform proved impossible to remove and I had them in my sights for the remainder of the campaign as a *memento mori*.[504]

Despite the fire of the French batteries, which as Brandt described were 'extended from the Grand Redoubt as far as the eye could see', the Russians still tried to counter-attack:

> Suddenly the enemy's ranks showed movement and it seemed as if the Russians now intended to launch a fresh assault despite the massive weight of artillery deployed against them. They came on in superb order and almost reached the redoubt before we counter-attacked, when they fell back, this time for good, after a violent and murderous infantry battle in which my regiment suffered heavily.

As the Russian attack was repelled, Berthier himself approached the redoubt, where he briefly talked to Prince Eugène and ordered to cease firing. According to Labaume, the Russians also decreased the intensity of their fire and then ceased firing altogether. Paskevich described that 'the terrifying artillery fire' continued until after 6pm, when it began to cease.[505]

One last note should be made on the assault on the Grand Redoubt. Almost immediately after the battle was over, the image of the French cuirassiers, led by Caulaincourt, charging over the parapets of the Russian redoubt and seizing it while their young and gallant commander was killed

# The Battle of Borodino Phase Two (12am to 6pm)

became firmly established in popular memory and later in participants' memoirs, negating contributions made by non-French forces. The issue of who seized the redoubt turned into a bitter dispute between the French and their allies, later inflated by national sentiments.

Napoleon naturally attributed the final capture of the redoubt to the French cuirassiers. Marshal Murat, writing his report two days after the battle, described the charge of the 2nd Cuirassier Division and noted that 'this brave general [Caulaincourt] died gloriously in that redoubt, which was held until the troops of Gérard's division arrived'. On 10 September the 18th Bulletin further determined the matter. It mentioned the IV Cavalry Corps, which 'penetrated the breaches that our cannon-shot had made in the condensed masses of the Russians and the squadrons of their cuirassiers', and then credited the French cuirassiers with the capture of the redoubt:

> Général de division comte Caulaincourt, Governor of the Emperor's Pages, advanced at the head of the 5th Cuirassier Regiment, overthrew everything, and entered the redoubt on the left by its gorge. From this moment there was no longer any uncertainty. The battle was gained [...] Caulaincourt, who had distinguished himself in this fine charge, has terminated his destiny. He fell dead, struck by a bullet. A glorious death, and worthy of envy ...

This version was repeated in the memoirs of almost all French participants, the most influential of them being Vaudoncourt and Chambray. Published in 1817 and 1823 respectively, these works influenced subsequent publications and laid the foundation for the exaltation of Caulaincourt. According to them, Caulaincourt, at the head of the 2nd Cuirassier Division, penetrated the Russian line and then, wheeling left, charged through the troops behind the redoubt, entering it from the rear. After it was seized, Prince Eugène's troops stormed the redoubt in a frontal assault. Thus, neither Chambray nor Vaudoncourt acknowledged the contribution of the Saxon, Polish or Westphalian troops, who also shed blood in this combat. Thiers, writing a relatively detailed account of the charge in mid-19th century, described Caulaincourt at the head of the 5th, 8th and 10th Cuirassiers, followed by General Defrance with two regiments of carabiniers. According to Thiers, Caulaincourt

> debouched beyond the ravine and overwhelmed some remains of Rayevsky's corps, which were still upon this part of the field, together with the cavalry of Korf and the Baron de Kreutz, he passed the Grand Redoubt. At this moment, General Caulaincourt, perceiving Likhachev's infantry, which guarded the redoubt, fell upon it by a sudden movement to the left and sabred it at the head of the 5th Cuirassiers.

Thiers then described the assault of Prince Eugène's troops, which secured the redoubt for the French. Non-French troops were ignored once more. Decades later, modern historians Thiry, Tranié, Hourtoulle, Palmer, and Chandler showed their pro-French bias when they repeated this version of the charge in their books.

# The Battle of Borodino

But several other versions describe the fall of Rayevsky's Redoubt. The most vocal and thorough critique of the 'French version' came from German participants. One of the first to challenge the official version was Cerrini, who served on the Saxon General Staff and published his works in the early 1820s. Cerrini argued that it was the troops of the Saxon General Thielemann, not the French cuirassiers, who seized the Grand Redoubt. His findings were supported by Burkersroda, who served as an officer in Latour-Maubourg's corps and published his memoirs (*Die Sachen in Russland*) in 1846. Most damaging to the official version, however, proved to be Roth von Schreckenstein's *Die Kavallerie in der Schlacht an der Moskva*, which appeared in 1856. Based on his own recollections, as well as those of his comrades, Roth von Schreckenstein criticized French claims in detail, making a case in favour of the Saxon capture of the redoubt. He directed his ire mainly at the work of Chambray, which popularized the French version of the attack. He argued that 'it was only Defrance's division that assaulted on the right of the redoubt' and that Wathier's division 'attacked it from the direction of Borodino [north-west], while the Saxon cavalry penetrated it from the direction of Semeyonosvkaya [south]'. He also disputed the claim that Caulaincourt overthrew a line of Russian infantry behind the redoubt and criticized Murat's report, which did not mention the role of Latour-Maubourg's men. Roth von Schreckenstein suggested that 'perhaps sections of [Murat's] report were removed at Napoleon's instructions to glorify Caulaincourt . . .' And noted that:

> According to an eye-witness who related the following to us the next morning, Napoleon was standing by Berthier [at Shevardino] when the latter, squinting through his telescope, said, 'The redoubt is taken, the Saxon cuirassiers are in it!' Napoleon took the telescope, peered through it and said: 'You are wrong, they are dressed in blue; they are my cuirassiers.' What Napoleon *may* have seen through his telescope, from his distant vantage point at Shevardino through all the smoke and confusion, was the 14th Polish Cuirassier Regiment, which at that point formed the third rank of Thielemann's Saxon brigade, as it followed the two Saxon regiments into the battery. The uniform of the Polish cuirassiers was almost identical to that of their French comrades. Or they may have been the Westphalian cuirassiers [of Lepel's brigade, 7th Division] who followed us.

Despite these possibilities, Napoleon chose to attribute the capture of the redoubt to Caulaincourt. 'Latour-Maubourg was extremely angry at this misinterpretation of the true events,' Roth von Schreckenstein noted.

Roth von Schreckenstein was not the only German officer to come up with such conclusions. Dittfurth noted that Caulaincourt's initial attack was unsuccessful and the Saxon Gardes du Corps brought the charge to its successful conclusion. According to Meerheim:

> Despite all the perils and obstacles, we were unstoppable and burst over and into the battery, inspired by the examples of our commanders, Generals

# The Battle of Borodino Phase Two (12am to 6pm)

Latour-Maubourg, Thielemann, and our brigade adjutant von Minkwitz. The interior of the battery was an indescribable mess of infantry and cavalry all intent on killing one another. The [Russian] garrison fought to the last ...

Minkwitz was also quite vocal in denouncing the French attempt to claim the glory of capturing the redoubt. Naturally, such views found their way into the works of many German scholars, especially during the late 19th century and early 20th century, when Franco-German rivalry was at its height. More recently, English-speaking historians – among them Duffy, Cate, Smith and Nafziger – argued in support of the Saxon capture of the redoubt. Duffy noted that: 'posterity is still wider of the mark when it attributes the whole of the charge to Caulaincourt, who at the most functioned as a brigade commander in Wathier's division'.

A lesser known account is that offered by the memoirs of E.F.C.A. Heckens, who served with the 6th Chasseur à Cheval in the 3rd Light Cavalry Division. Heckens highlights the role of Grouchy's troops in the episode, recording that:

Caulaincourt's corps, in the first line, crossed the first ravine but, as it approached the second, it was attacked by the Russian cavalry. The carabiniers, who were moving on [Caulaincourt's] right flank, charged this cavalry, allowing the cuirassiers to reach the redoubt, which they, however, failed to seize.

At that moment, Grouchy's cavalry, moving in the second line, charged forward and seized the Grand Redoubt, which it 'maintained until the arrival of Viceroy's troops'.

The Russian historians rejected the French version of the events almost from the very beginning. Buturlin wrote:

The French cavalry of the II Corps carried out its orders in most brilliant manner. It daringly crossed the Semeyonovsk ravine and charged the Russian lines. However, the infantry of the IV Corps, especially the Pernovskii, Kexholmskii and 33rd Jäger regiment fearlessly met this cavalry and opened continues volleys at it, which it could not withstand. General Caulaincourt, with Wathier's cuirassier division managed to reach the lunette and even break into it with the 5th Cuirassier Regiment, but was killed there while the cuirassiers had to abandon this fortification.

Mikhailovsky-Danilevsky's account is largely based on Barclay de Tolly's above-cited report, and, in itself, is quite confusing. Thus, the Russian historians described the failure of the initial French attack by Caulaincourt and noted that, after multiple attacks, 'the Saxon cavalry of Thielemann broke into the redoubt [and] it was followed by the entire corps of Caulaincourt'.

Another famous Russian historian, Bogdanovich, utilized some German memoirs, which led him to downplay the role of the French cuirassiers in the assault on Rayevsky's Redoubt. Instead, he directly stated that Thielemann, with the Saxon Gardes Du Corps cuirassiers, broke into the redoubt and seized it. Other Russian imperial historians accepted this account in their studies as well. The Soviet historians largely concentrated on Russian experiences of the battle and described the Allied charge in general – and erroneous – terms. For example, in *Borodino, 1812*, leading Soviet historians claimed that Thielemann's Saxon troops were 'the advance elements of Caulaincourt's corps'. Unlike them, modern Russian historians, notably Zemtsov, Popov and Vasiliev, are more thorough in their research and highlight the role of the Saxon and Polish troops, who are credited with the capture.

It should be noted, however, that the Allied cavalry could not hold the redoubt for long and the honour of retaining it belongs to the infantry of Prince Eugène. Eugène reported that his troops 'attacked the redoubt in front and in the flank, and seized it . . .' And Laugier credited one of Eugène's Italian officers with the capture of General Likhachev, who commanded the defenders of the redoubt. Fezensac de Montesquiou argued that 'the large redoubt was taken by a regiment of cuirassiers, retaken by the enemy, and then seized anew by the 1st Division of the 1st Corps detached for service with the Viceroy'. Labaume also noted that the cuirassiers' attack on the redoubt was unsuccessful and credited Eugène's infantry with its capture. Some participants (Lieutenant Flotow, Almeras, etc.) went even further, ignoring the cavalry charges altogether, simply noting that the infantry of IV Corps seized the fortification.

## Extreme Southern Sector – The Old Smolensk Road and Utitsa

By late afternoon, the extreme southern sector remained the scene of active battle as Poniatowski and Baggovut continued to face each other. The first round of fighting ended in a stalemate and both sides spent the next few hours preparing for the resumption of hostilities. The fighting, meantime, was largely limited to an artillery duel. The Utitsa woods, however, proved to be more action-filled, although it is often ignored in studies of the battle.

As we already discussed, Junot's VIII Corps was supposed to assist Ney's troops in the attack on Semeyonovskoye but was diverted south to clear the Utitsa woods and support the Polish V Corps. However, stiff Russian resistance in the woods delayed its advance and, as Borcke noted:

> the first division of General Tharreau was sent forward to attack the woods where the enemy was firmly lodged and fired upon the flank of the seized fortifications [Bagration's flèches]. Because it took [a] long time to dislodge the Russians from the shrubs, we suffered high losses in defending them [. . .] Simultaneously, the second division under the command of General Ochs was left to cover and defend the fortifications.

Another author (Linsingen) noted that the 23rd Division (Tharreau) was sent to the right, to make contact Poniatowski, while the 24th Division (Ochs) remained to strengthen Davout's right flank. As Tharreau's men advanced, they fought Shakhovsky's Jägers and Linsingen acknowledged that 'our division suffered from heavy fire from the woods on the right side. General von Borstel marched there with his 2nd Brigade and seized the woods on the first attempt. Russians, French, Poles and others now became intermingled in this dense forest ...'

Sievers reported that:

> When our troops abandoned the two forward flèches, I anticipated the enemy's intention to proceed with several infantry and cavalry columns under cover of tirailleurs to turn our left flank, threatening the rear of our positions and cutting off Baggovut's corps. Therefore, I took two heavy and three light guns from the nearby artillery battery and set up a battery on the hill near the wood, slightly ahead of the position of the 2nd Army. Our canister fire had such effect that columns were routed ...

However, the battery soon exhausted its ammunition and attempts to obtain additional caissons proved futile until a clerk of the Lithuanian Uhlan Regiment, 'through his dedication and enterprise' managed to bring caissons. So when the French resumed their attack, the Russian battery was able to meet them with a devastating fire, which 'forced it to hastily retreat in complete disorder'.[506]

Yet lack of ammunition limited the effectiveness of the Russian artillery. When Baggovut passed this position on his way to Tuchkov with his II Corps, he diverted some of his troops to support Sievers. Baggovut saw the dire conditions near the flèches, where, according to his report, Sievers' artillery, deployed on a hill

> was, due to its calibre, too weak to inflict serious damage on the enemy so I replaced it with the 17th Battery Company of Colonel Ditterix II and left the Ryazan Infantry Regiment to defend it. Also, to prevent the enemy from occupying the shrubs on the left side of the battery, I ordered the Brest Regiment to spread its skirmishers and keep the enemy at bay.[507]

As soon as the 17th Battery Company began to operate, the French returned fire and 'moved forward their batteries under cover of three strong infantry columns'. But as Baggovut reported, '[the] successful actions of our artillery quickly thwarted their undertaking and the enemy columns and artillery immediately retreated into the woods'. Sievers confirmed this story and noted that 'the enemy failed in his attempts to seize a battery I deployed near the woods and it, with support of other units, inflicted heavy losses on the enemy battery and the troops'.[508] During this battle, Ditterix II was supported by the 33rd Light Company of Bashmakov, who was wounded but 'skilfully and successfully operated against the enemy batteries and defeated several infantry columns and the French cavalry'. Twelve guns from the 4th and 17th Battery companies were sent to Tuchkov, while the remaining twelve guns stayed near the flèches, where they were supported by the 32nd and 7th Light companies. Later that day, Colonel Taube brought his 2nd Life Guard Battery Company, which was deployed south-east of the flèches and maintained effective fire against the French. Almost all its officers were killed or wounded. Not far from it, Staff Captain Bazilevich commanded the 1st Life Guard Battery Company, deploying his guns north-east from the flèches:

# The Battle of Borodino

> The company maintained fire from the right side of the lunettes, facing a twice superior enemy battery [...] Increasing its fire against the enemy batteries and skilfully directing our guns, [Bazilevich] was able to silence the enemy guns and moved forward, halting the enemy columns with canister fire.[509]

Conrady, standing with his Westphalian troops on the receiving end of this fire, confirmed its deadly results as the 'Russian forces drove us from our positions which we earlier fought hard to seize. Only after retreating across the ravine in our rear did we manage to halt and regroup our battalions.' General Damas was killed, while Lossberg saw Tharreau being wounded in his stomach and replaced by von Borstel, who was later wounded himself.

The ravine provided some shelter to the Westphalians since, as Conrady noted, the Russian artillery fired above their heads. The situation improved for the Westphalians when the French forces seized Semeyonovskoye, diverting the Russian attention. According to Lossberg:

> our VIII Corps was ordered to resume its advance to the right flank to support the V Corps. After a tenacious combat, we finally seized the woods, deployed in a line, with a few battalions in the reserve. However, the right portion of the woods, which was more dense, remained in the Russian hands ...

Later that afternoon Soltyk, who was on his way to observe situation on the Old Smolensk Road, encountered the Westphalian Division extended in a line and waging a resolute fight against the Russian infantry. Conrady described the orderly retreat of the Russians (probably Shakhovsky's troops) and the heavy casualties his Westphalian troops suffered. Finally, about 2pm, the Westphalians established contact with the V Corps and preparations began for a coordinated assault on the Russian position. Meantime, the Russians also received reinforcements as the 2nd Brigade of the 4th Division arrived from the centre and filled the gap between Baggovut's corps and Sievers' cavalry in the north-western corner of the Utitsa woods.

Around 2pm the Poles and Westphalians resumed their attack through the woods, which would have turned Baggovut's left flank. The 23rd Division [Westphalian] engaged the troops of the 4th Division [Russian], while General Ochs led the 24th Division to secure the plain north of the road, with Major von Rauschenplatt's 1st (Westphalian) Light Battalion leading the way. The Westphalians barely advanced when they were met with volleys, obliging them to fall back with losses. To silence the Russian artillery, which maintained a devastating fire, a battalion of the Westphalian chasseurs-carabiniers, armed with rifles, was dispatched to approach the Russian battery and kill its artillery crew. However, as one Westphalian soldier (Fleck) recalled, when the Westphalian chasseurs were passing the 1st Westphalian Light Battalion, its commander Major von Rauschenplatt, failed to recognize them through smoke and confusion and, seeing their green uniforms, assumed they were Russians and ordered his troops to fire. Fortunately for the chasseurs, they were beyond effective range of muskets, although several soldiers were wounded nevertheless. Lossberg and Conrady also described the complete confusion that reigned in the woods, where most

# The Battle of Borodino Phase Two (12am to 6pm)

## *Museum-Panorama 'Battle of Borodino'*

Located on the Kutuzov Avenue in Moscow, Museum-Panorama 'Battle of Borodino' was opened on the 150th anniversary of the battle in 1962. It includes a large panorama displaying Francois Rubeau's famous painting the Battle of Borodino (1910–21), the Kutuzov watchtower, Kutuzov monument and an obelisk from the grave of the common grave of soldiers killed at Borodino from the Dorogomilov cemetery; the museum also operates the Kutuzov hut, where Kutuzov stayed after the battle of Borodino. The panorama complex has a cylindrical shape with a height of 23 meters and diameter of 42 meters. It contains two wings with various exhibitions, including trophy guns moved from the Arsenal of the Kremlin. At the very heart of the building is a round hall with Rubeau's enormous painting (15 meters in height, 115 meters in length) of the battle that shows one of the crucial moments of the battle, the French attacks on the Semeyonovskoe village. The museum complex, renovated in 1991–1995, had its display halls expanded and contains over 30,000 items, many of them on display.

of the fighting took place. Officers found it difficult to oversee their troops, who were often fighting in small, isolated groups. This naturally resulted in many deaths and injured due to friendly fire.

The Russian resistance caused the initial Westphalian advance to falter, but new orders were received as Girod d'Ain delivered Ney's orders to press forward. While Friederichs complied, Junot seemed reluctant to follow orders, again demonstrating the lack of initiative that had surfaced three weeks previously at Valutina Gora. Instead, Junot forwarded the order to the 5th Division (from Davout's corps), where General Guyardet, according to his report, received it close to 2.30 p.m. The order required Guyardet to assist the Westphalians troops, who were fighting in the woods. The exhausted soldiers of the 5th Division carried out the order over the next hour or so.

Around 4pm the Westphalians made a new attack, which proved successful, since the Russian batteries lacked ammunition and retreated. 'On my orders,' Sievers reported

> five guns of the battery were withdrawn under cover of the Lithuanian Uhlan Regiment, which charged an enemy column. However, another enemy column, advancing in the ravine on the edge of the woods, forced the Uhlan Regiment to retreat. After passing through the brushwood, the Ulans took up position near the batteries on the left flank of the [2nd] Cuirassier Division.[510]

In the meantime, the four companies of the Brest Infantry Regiment, commanded by Major General Ivelich, engaged the Westphalians but

# The Battle of Borodino

struggled to contain their attack. Ivelich was soon wounded and appealed to Baggovut for help, who dispatched Vadkovsky with the Willmanstrand and Ryazan Infantry Regiments and some 500 militiamen of the Moscow Opolchenye. The joint Russian counter-attack succeeded in stopping the Westphalian assault. Conrady tells us that 'all generals of the 23rd Division were killed or wounded', and when Ney repeated his order to clear the woods, Ochs requested permission to leave his 24th Division to take command of the 23rd. As the 1st Brigade of the 23rd Division advanced, Ochs led the way with the 6th Line (commanded by Lieutenant Colonel Jungkurt) and cleared the woods and the hill, where a small Russian battery was set up. 'The Russians were so consumed by the [Polish] attack from the front, that they noticed our attack only after we charged with yells. Although they resisted [...] they were forced to retreat,' wrote Conrady. To reinforce the 3rd Battalion of the Tavrida Grenadier Regiment fighting the Westphalians, Baggovut dispatched Shakhovsky with his Jägers and the Minsk Infantry Regiment, who halted the enemy advance but suffered heavy losses in process.

Baggovut was also attacked on his left flank by the Poles. The 13th Polish Hussars flanked the Russians and engaged the 1st Battalion of the Tavrida Grenadier Regiment, which was supported by the Cossacks and a battalion of the Belozersk Infantry Regiment, which Olsufiev hurriedly dispatched there. The Polish cavalry, Baggovut reported, attacked the Russian battery on the Kurgan and was about to seize it when

> the courageous Colonel Pyshnitsky charged with the Kremenchug Infantry Regiment, showing remarkable gallantry [...] in a moment, the enemy was driven back from the battery and the Russian bayonets punished him for this audacity as the hill became covered with enemy corpses ...

Baggovut then dispatched a

> strong group of Cossacks of Major General Karpov's Regiment to assess the enemy on the [extreme] left flank [...] where the Cossacks found the enemy troops deployed in several columns and artillery concealed in the woods. The enemy considered this appearance [of Cossacks] an attack and immediately moved his guns forward, dispatched skirmishers and opened fire.[511]

Around 5pm Poniatowski launched an attack coordinated with the Westphalians. The 2nd Brigade of the 23rd Division, led by Junot himself, made a frontal attack with the 3rd Line in the front and two battalions of the 7th Line in the second line; the 2nd (Westphalian) Light Battalion of Lieutenant Colonel Bödicker was deployed in a skirmisher line on the left, near the woods. Bödicker later recalled that his battalion lost ten officers and some 340 men, and the rest of the division also suffered heavy losses. As Lossberg described, the 2nd Brigade charged under canister and musket fire but the Russians slowly retreated and Junot halted his men. Ochs, leading four battalions of the 24th Division and the 1st Brigade of the 23rd Division, was more successful, as he forced the Russians to abandon the heights to the north of the Old Smolensk Road.

Baggovut then decided to abandon the Kurgan and retreat along the Old Smolensk Road. As Mikhailovsky-Danilevsky explained, this decision was occasioned by the news that the Russian left wing was moving behind the Semeyonovskii ravine, as well as by the successful advance of the Westphalian Corps, which could cut him off from the main army.[512] As Baggovut described, after his guns were removed from the hilltop, Poniatowski, noticing the Russian retreat, attacked at once, forcing Baggovut to deploy his troops on both sides of the road. The Russians took up a new positions 'near the heights in front of Psarevo', where they set up a small battery to cover their retreat. When the Poles assaulted it, the Kremenchug and Minsk Regiments counter-attacked but were mown down by Polish canister. They also suffered greatly under the lances of the 12th Polish Lancers of Colonel Józef Rzyszczewski.[513] Nevertheless, neither Poniatowski nor Junot pressed further attacks but rather kept their forces at bay, and Baggovut was able to maintain his new position until late that night.

The role of the Opolchenye in this combat is often overlooked, although Soviet studies tend to exaggerate it. As mentioned above, the Moscow militiamen were directly involved in the fighting against the Westphalians. Morkov also described the 6th Dismounted Cossack Regiment fighting alongside the Pavlovsk Regiment during the assault on the Kurgan, while according to Kutuzov, the 7th Dismounted Cossack Regiment 'demonstrated exemplary gallantry, being constantly in the midst of relentless fire and ignoring all dangers ...' Battle reports also praise the 1st and 3rd Jäger Regiments, which participated in several charges. The Smolensk Opolchenye seems to have played an auxiliary role. Thus Vistitsky described these militiamen removing hundreds of wounded in the midst of the combat and 'Kutuzov, with tears in his eyes, [later] thanked the Smolensk Opolchenye for its dedication and gallantry'. After the battle, the militiamen would receive five roubles each, while fifty-two of them would be awarded the Military Order medal.

## The Battle of Borodino Phase Three (6pm to 12pm)

Around 6pm the battle began winding down. Clausewitz observed that it was

> striking how the action gradually reflected the weariness and exhaustion of the armies. The masses of infantry had melted away so drastically that perhaps less than one third of the original number was still in action: the rest of the troops were dead, wounded, engaged in carrying away the casualties or rallying in the rear. Everywhere there were wide gaps. The mighty artillery [...] now spoke only by sporadic shots, and even these did not seem to ring out in the old strong and thunderous style, but sounded languid and muffled. The cavalry had almost everywhere taken the place of the infantry and it moved up and down in a tired trot.

# The Battle of Borodino

Meanwhile, Petrov noted that

> As the day began to wane, the fervour of the Battle of Borodino faded away and the bloodshed ceased; musket fire could be seen occasionally through the darkness of the night. Now and then, artillery guns, as if snorting off their exhaustion, covered the battlefield with the thunder of their fearsome sighs. The moans of those dying from their wounded could be heard among the piles of dead, which covered the entire field and filled up ravines. To us, they were the sacred shadows of our courageous comrades, who bid their farewell after falling in glory defending their Fatherland.

Wolzogen recalled that:

> Barclay could not understand why Napoleon did not exploit his victory; for he had in fact already gained possession of the principal points of the battlefield [...] [and] a fairly general weariness had gripped the Russian Army. Many of the generals were dead or wounded, and almost all the regimental commanders too [...] I had met a lieutenant with thirty to forty men behind the front line, and when I ordered him to rejoin his regiment at once, he replied, 'This is my regiment!' All the rest of the men were dead, wounded or missing. Nearly all the Russian reserves had already been committed, whereas [...] Napoleon's Imperial Guard had not been seen in any attack. Therefore the Guard could in any case either continue the fight against the Russian centre or reinforce the Emperor's right wing and, by overthrowing Baggovut's corps, could attack the Russian Army in the rear. However, neither move occurred.[514]

Observing the situation on the front line, Barclay de Tolly sent Wolzogen to Kutuzov to obtain further orders. Knowing Kutuzov's character well, he instructed Wolzogen to 'get his reply in writing because one has to be very careful with Kutuzov'. Wolzogen found Kutuzov on a hill near the Moscow Road, surrounded by a suite of 'rich young noblemen, who indulged in all kinds of pleasures and had taken no part whatever in the terrible and earnest events of the day. Colonel Toll was with them and was busily eating a *capon*'. Wolzogen reported on the state of the Russian Army with his German directness, noting that 'all important posts had been lost' and 'the regiments were all extremely tired and shattered'. Such depressing reports naturally infuriated Kutuzov, who felt embarrassed in front of his suite. 'With which low bitch of a sutler have you been getting drunk that you come giving me such an absurd report?' he yelled at Wolzogen. Ever aware of the power of propaganda, Kutuzov then quickly gathered his thoughts, hinting at what he expected from others:

> I am in the best position to know how the battle went! The French attacks have been successfully repulsed everywhere, and tomorrow I shall put myself at the head of the army to drive the enemy without more ado from the sacred soil of Russia.

At this, Kutuzov looked challengingly at his entourage, which applauded him with enthusiasm. Wolzogen was offended by such a 'disgraceful reception' and especially because 'I had only reported what I had seen with my own eyes during the turmoil of battle, whereas I knew that Kutuzov had spent the whole day in rear of the army among champagne bottles and delicatessen.' Understanding Kutuzov's 'sly, unfair motives' at treating him thus, Wolzogen went on to note:

> Certainly, I said to myself, his associates will not realize the true state of the Army and, so as not to be able to condemn his prepared bulletin on the battle as lies, will leave him in the belief that the Russians have won a glorious battle. Besides, he assumed correctly that Napoleon [. . .] would not renew the battle; consequently, the Russians would remain in control of the battlefield overnight.

Wolzogen was correct in his reasoning. The Russian Commander-in-Chief knew well what had happened that day but, always a shrewd diplomat, he could not allow news of the failed battle to spread. This is why he reprimanded Wolzogen for an 'inappropriate' report but welcomed Rayevsky, who, arriving moments later, brought positive news. As Rayevsky recalled, Kutuzov

> received me more kind-heartedly than usually because a few moments earlier somebody described our state of affairs in negative light [. . .] He told me, 'So you believe we should not retreat?' I responded that, on contrary, I believed we should attack the enemy the very next day, since in such inconclusive battles the side that is most tenacious always wins. This was not bragging on my side. It might be that I was mistaken but at the time I sincerely believed in this.

Kutuzov then talked to Toll and dictated a plan of attack for the following day, while Toll prepared another order for Barclay de Tolly. Rayevsky was told to deliver oral instructions to Dokhturov, currently commanding the 2nd Army, while Wolzogen received a written order for Barclay de Tolly. The order stated that:

> from all the movements of the enemy I [Kutuzov] conclude that he [Napoleon] has been weakened no less than us during this battle, and that is why, having started with him, I have decided this night to draw up the Army in order, to supply the artillery with fresh ammunition and in the morning to renew the battle with the enemy.[515]

After reading the order, Barclay de Tolly 'shook his head' and told Wolzogen that he did not know where he was going to find enough men for this disposition:

> If we could attack the French on the spot and straightaway, this might perhaps be feasible; but next day the troops, who had exerted themselves for twelve hours without any food and could still not get anything to eat during the night, would be so exhausted that a further attack would be out of question.[516]

Barclay then travelled to meet Kutuzov and talked to him for a quarter of an hour before returning to Gorki Hill. Accompanied by three of his adjutants (including Löwenstern, who described these events), he dismounted on the hill and admitted that he was starving. He had a small glass of rum and a piece of bread, while still calmly observing the enemy movements in the distance. The battle had a remarkable effect on the soldiers' perception of Barclay de Tolly, who was seen galloping into the thick of the action in a full-dress uniform adorned with numerous decorations and orders, and directing troops in one dangerous spot after another. As he inspected his worn-out regiments, he was greeted by spontaneous 'Hurrahs', which, as one Russian officer justly noted, 'greatly contrasted with the insulting and unfair accusations that had been heaped upon him up till then'.[517]

But what kind of solace could this afford to the General amid the battlefield covered with his dead troops? 'A fog soon covered the battle field ...' Löwenstern wrote,

> and complete stillness descended. Only now we were able to calmly discuss the events of this memorable day. None of us considered the battle lost. Trophies were equal on both sides. It is true that the main battery (of Rayevsky) was in the enemy's hands but Barclay was still hoping to recapture it the following day as well as to recover the ground lost on the extreme left wing and launch an offensive movement.

That night, Kutuzov issued orders congratulating his troops with a victory and ordered to prepare for another round of fighting. The Russian troops remained eager to resume the battle, albeit largely unaware of the actual condition of the Army. Muravyev-Apostol recalled receiving 'the order that the troops should not take off their knapsacks since the battle would be continued the following day'.

Generals, meantime, were busy rallying their troops. Barclay de Tolly regrouped the remnants of his army at what is often described as the 'third Russian position', the Army having moved about 1,500m to the rear. The VI Corps was near Gorki, with the IV Corps behind it, while the cavalry and the V Corps were in the reserve. Barclay de Tolly also ordered a reconnaissance of the French position and, upon hearing the Grand Redoubt was occupied only by 'scattered groups that were busy withdrawing', he instructed Miloradovich to seized this important location with several battalions and establish a battery by dawn. The night-time sortie, however, was unsuccessful. Barclay de Tolly then suggested to Dokhturov that he should 'reinforce the troops of the 2nd Army, gathered on the left flank of the IV Corps and [...] occupy the area between him and Baggovut's corps'. To strengthen his position, Barclay de Tolly also ordered the construction of a redoubt on the heights near Gorki and some 2,000 Opolchenye troops were ordered to start building it. Kutuzov confirmed these arrangements.[518]

Meantime, on the Russian right flank, the soldiers of the 1st Jäger Regiment were still guarding the banks of the Kolocha. As Petrov recalled:

> During the night of 27 August [8 September], the patrols dispatched from our regiment reported every hour that the French advance posts were withdrawal further and further. Finally, around the midnight, our patrol officer, returning from his watch, reported to the regimental commander that the enemy was not detected in the area between Rayevsky's Battery and the Stonets Redoubt and

50. Death of Auguste de Caulaincourt.                    *(Lithograph by Motte)*

51. General Tuchkov leading the charge on the Old Smolensk Road.         *(Safonov)*

52. Battle of Borodino.   (*Lejeune*)

53. Ney leading III Corps against the Bagration Flèches. *(Jean-Charles Langois)*

54. Napoleon directing his troops at Borodino. *(Lithograph by Martinet)*

5. Council of War at Fili. Kutuzov, seated left, addresses his generals. *(Kivshenko)*

6. Napoleon on the heights overlooking Moscow. *(Vereschagin)*

57. Earthworks of Rayevsky's Redoubt, restored in 1912. *(Robert Mosher*

58. View of the northern flèche from the direction of the French attack. The flèche was restored in 1912 and 1962. The remains of an unknown soldier were buried inside in 1962. *(Robert Mosher*

9. View of the left flèche. Restored in 1912 and 1962, General Neverovsky's remains were buried nearby in 1912. *(Robert Mosher)*

0. Shevardino Redoubt, seen from the location of Napoleon's subsequent command post: the view is to the north-west. The redoubt was reconstructed in 1912 during the centennial celebration of the battle. *(Robert Mosher)*

61. Russian veteran with medal for service in 1812.

# The Battle of Borodino Phase Three (6pm to 12pm)

to the right to the Kolocha river. To gather more intelligence and explain the whereabouts of our enemy, one NCO and ten Jägers were ordered to take off their boots, swim across the Kolocha, and determine if the French were still in the village of Borodino. The patrol returned in an hour reporting that the enemy was not in Borodino but on the hill behind the village on the right bank of the Voina, where a thick chain of their cavalry was noticed. Our commander [Karpenko], an experienced staff officer with advance post service in various campaigns, quickly realized the importance of this news and sent his regimental adjutant to apprise Barclay de Tolly. In the meantime, [Karpenko] assumed that the next day would certainly start with an order to attack and instructed his company commanders to increase the number of cartridges issued. After this, the troops were allowed to place their weapons in trestles ['na kozly'] and rest; the men lay down on the ground and had a quiet sleep on the steep bank of the Kolocha [...] Around 5am on 27 August, we dispatched a company of artisans to gather woods from bivouacs to the bank of the Kolocha, where a floating bridge was constructed in order to facilitate the crossing to the village of Borodino as everyone eagerly awaited the order to attack. Instead, we are ordered to remove our advance posts and proceed to Mozhaisk following the army as it began retreating to Moscow; the Cossacks were told to observe the enemy whose cavalry pickets could be seen on the position that the enemy occupied on 25 August [6 September].[519]

Late that evening, Kutuzov returned to his headquarters at Tatarinovo, where he convened a council of war to decide what to do next. According to Bennigsen, 'That evening we were still not aware of the huge losses we had suffered during the day. We therefore considered, for a while, retaking our central battery during the night and continuing the battle on the morrow.'[520] Toll and his staff officers were instructed to inspect the army and their reports began arriving around 11pm. They brought the frightening news of Russian casualties and the full picture of the Army's condition was gradually revealed. Tens of thousands were killed, wounded and missing, entire regiments destroyed and divisions reduced to hundreds. Kutuzov still had six regiments (four Jäger units and two Life Guard Semeyonovskii and Prebrazhenskii Regiments) remaining in reserve but they were certainly insufficient to shore up the Russian positions. After a discussion with his generals, Kutuzov, realizing the futility of remaining on the battlefield, ordered a retreat to a new position, several miles away, near Mozhaisk. The Russian Army was divided into three columns led by Dokhturov, Miloradovich and Platov, with a fourth consisting of artillery. Barclay de Tolly was initially unaware of these arrangements and learned about it only after midnight.

The Russian headquarters was, meantime, discussing the direction of further retreat. Should it be to Moscow? Or maybe to Vereya or Borisov, which might compel Napoleon to follow the Russian Army towards Kaluga instead of advancing to Moscow? Kutuzov argued that the Army should withdraw along the Moscow Road, and so it did.

Kutuzov knew that he was now on dangerous ground. This very action – a reprehensible retreat – had brought down his predecessor just ten days ago, and Kutuzov was certainly not willing to share Barclay's fate. So he carefully calculated his next steps. A shrewd propagandist, he turned to preparing the Russian public for news of another retreat. The fact that Napoleon had ordered his troops to pull back to their original positions played into Kutuzov's hands, since he could foster the illusion that the Russians had really won the day and remained in firm control of the battlefield. The battle was hardly over when one of the first letters was sent to Rostopchin, Governor of Moscow:

> Today was a fierce and bloody battle. With divine help, the Russian Army refused to concede a single step, even though the enemy was in much superior numbers. Placing my faith in the Lord and the Moscow saints, I hope to resume the battle with fresh forces tomorrow.[521]

Then came the first of a series of letters to Alexander, in which Kutuzov highlighted Russian gallantry and resolve. He explained that the heavy loss suffered in the battle reduced the number of troops at his disposal and made the position at Borodino too vast to be defended. Therefore, he decided to withdraw to Mozhaisk, where he hoped to received reinforcements and fight another action. He assured Alexander that he was not interested in 'the glory of merely winning battles but rather in achieving the goal of destroying the entire French Army'. The official army bulletin reiterated these points, claiming the French 'were driven back at all points and forced to retreat while we remained the masters of the battlefield'. It even noted that Platov 'chased [the French] rearguard to a distance of 11 verstas [11.7km] from Borodino'. Knowing that even his private letters would eventually become public, he penned a letter to his beloved wife Ekaterina, telling her 'I am well my dear, and am not beaten: I have won the battle with Bonaparte.'[522]

Most Russian sources suggest that the Russian Army spent the night on the battlefield, while the French withdrew to their initial positions. The rank-and-file certainly did not feel vanquished and participants, who later wrote memoirs, reflected this prevailing opinion. It was further strengthened by official reports, especially Kutuzov's, which portrayed the battle as a victory. The fact is, both armies spent the night on the battlefield, although some Allied units had to withdrew in order not to bivouac amongst the dead bodies that covered the ground. These withdrawals were seen by the Russians as a general retreat by the Grand Army and this 'legend', as some Russian historians describe it, quickly spread. Witmer, a prominent Russian historian, justly commented that 'this legend gained such deep roots and entered [popular] history because it flattered our national self-esteem'.

# Aftermath

The night after the battle proved breezy and rain drizzled over the thousands of bodies lying in the open fields. That night the distraught Konovnitsyn listed losses in his private letter

> Numerous are wounded and killed. Tuchkov is wounded in his chest, Alexander Tuchkov is killed [...] Ushakov's leg was torn off. Driezen is wounded, Richter as well [...] My division is virtually non-existent [and] there is hardly a thousand men in it ...[523]

Barclay de Tolly was shaken by his experiences: 'I searched for death and did not find it,' he told another general. Three horses had been shot from under him and still his life was spared. 'My ardent wish to die did not come true,' he wrote to Tsar Alexander. The troops remaining in the front line, although high in sprits, suffered from exhaustion and hunger. In the 1st Jäger Regiment, the officers 'fell to the ground from exhaustion and hunger'. After a few minutes of this 'half-dead condition' as Petrov described it,

> Our courageous and adroit Captain Tokarev [...] stood up and asked our Colonel to leave the regiment for ten minutes to go to the battery that was deployed not far from us. The Colonel gave him permission and Tokarev, mounting his horse, galloped at once. A few minutes later he returned with a triumphant appearance and holding a small bundle in his hand. Jumping of the horse in front of us, he quickly opened it on the ground [...] There was an indescribable treasure inside – five or six biscuits and two ordinary herrings [...] 'Gunners gave it to me.' [Tokarev explained] 'I told them, 'Gentlemen! Spare something edible for the staff officers of the 1st Jäger Regiment, who are exhausted to death after the battle but still remain at their spot ahead of the entire army.' And they gave me almost everything they had, including this ...' – he said as he revealed a flask filled with alcohol.

And so the three Russian officers shared this 'magnificent' meal on the banks of the Kolocha, remembering the experiences of the bloody day gone by.[524]

## Kutusov Retreats

The Russian retreat began soon after midnight when the artillery was moved to Mozhaisk. Around 3am the remaining forces proceeded in its wake. By dawn, only Platov's rearguard remained on the battlefield. Learning of the

Russian withdrawal, Murat 'again came to ask [Napoleon] for the cavalry of his Guard. "The enemy's army," said he, "is passing the Moskwa in haste and disorder; I wish to surprise and extinguish it." The Emperor repelled this sally of immoderate ardour ...'[525]

During the night, the Russian outposts harassed the French lines and some Russian sources suggest that Cossacks might have recovered (albeit briefly) the Grand Redoubt, which was all but abandoned by the French. Ségur's memoirs tell of Russian 'unseasonable clamours' that hassled the French: 'There was an alert, close to the Emperor's tent. The Old Guard was actually obliged to run to arms; a circumstance which, after a victory, seemed insulting.'

Many Russians were unhappy over the abandonment of the battlefield, especially in light of Kutuzov's order congratulating them with victory. Grumbling, they obeyed, and many French officers noted the care with which the retreating Russians took the time to bury their dead along the road. Fantin des Odoards wrote in his diary: 'In all fairness, it must be said that these people whom we call barbarous take great care of their wounded and have the piety to bury their dead ...'[526]

Still, hundreds of Russian wounded were gathered in Mozhaisk, where they found themselves stranded due to lack of transportation. As Mikhailovsky-Danilevsky described:

> the civil administration of the Moscow province explained the lack of carts by noting that the districts closest to the theatre of war were placed under the authority of the Ministry of War, while the military administration found very few people remaining in the villages, since the majority had escaped to the woods fearing the enemy invasion.

Kutuzov's repeated pleas to Governor Rostopchin for carts and horses had gone unheeded and many wounded were eventually abandoned in Mozhaisk.

The Russian Army was spared the sight of the carnage that reigned on the battlefield, vividly recorded in the memoirs of Allied soldiers who stayed behind. 'Nothing could have been more depressing than the appearance of the battlefield covered with groups occupied in carrying away the thousands of wounded, and in taking from the dead the few provisions remaining in their haversacks,' noted Lejeune, adding that

> Some of the wounded dragged themselves towards Kolotskoy, where Baron Larrey had set up an ambulance, whilst others were carried thither by their comrades in one way or another. Very soon an immense number were waiting attention, but, alas, everything needed for them was wanting, and hundreds perished of hunger, envying the happier lot of those who had been killed on the spot.

## A Pyrrhic Victory

On the morning after the battle, Napoleon reviewed the field, which as Armand de Caulaincourt described, was 'thickly strewn with dead'. Napoleon

# Aftermath

carefully examined every portion of this battlefield and, as Caulaincourt wrote, 'at each point he demanded minute details of everything that had happened, dealt out praise and encouragement, and was greeted by his troops with all their wonted enthusiasm'. Ségur also accompanied the Emperor on his tour of the battlefield:

> Never did [a battlefield] present so horrible an appearance. Every thing concurred to make it so; a gloomy sky, a cold rain, a violent wind, houses burnt to ashes, a plain turned topsy-turvy, covered with ruins and rubbish, in the distance the sad and sombre verdure of the trees of the North; soldiers roaming about in all directions amidst the dead, and hunting for provisions, even in the haversacks of their dead companions; horrible wounds, for the Russian musket-balls are larger than ours; silent bivouacs, no singing or story-telling – a gloomy taciturnity!

According to Ségur, Napoleon observed the surviving officers and soldiers gathering around their eagles,

> their clothes torn in the fury of the combat, blackened with powder, and spotted with blood; and yet, in the midst of their rags, their misery, and disasters, they had a proud look, and at the sight of the Emperor, uttered some shouts of triumph, but they were rare ...

Approaching the Grand Redoubt, Caulaincourt was overwhelmed with emotion and could not describe

> my feelings as I passed over the ground which had been dyed by my brother's blood. If the eulogies and the justice rendered by an entire army to the memory of a brave man could have consoled me, I ought to have had peace in my heart ...

Bausset, standing nearby, could see as 'M. de Caulaincourt and M. de Canouville, with tears in their eyes, turned away from the spot that contained the glorious remains of their brothers.' Meanwhile, Ségur noted that:

> it was impossible, no matter how careful one was, always to walk on the ground. The Emperor, I saw, was still ill, and the only animated gesture I saw him make was of irritation. One of our horses, striking one of these victims, had drawn a groan from him, albeit it was I who had caused it. Upon one of us remarking that the dying man was a Russian, the Emperor retorted, 'There are no enemies after a victory!' and immediately had Roustam [Napoleon's manservant] pick the man up and give him to drink from his own flask, which the Mamluk always carried on him.[527]

Dedem could barely contain himself while observing 'the most disgusting sight' he had ever seen. 'Mountains of dead on both sides,' he reminisced, 'the wounded calling for help ...'

The Württemberg Captain von Kurz, saw the wounded, both the French and Russian, lying 'one on top of the other, swimming in pools of their own blood, moaning and cursing as they begged for death'.

Brandt, who spent the night 'surrounded by the dead and dying', witnessed how the agonized and tormented wounded began to gather until they far out-numbered us. They could be seen everywhere like ghostly shadows moving in the half-light, creeping towards the glow of the fire. Some, horribly mutilated, used the last of their strength to do so. They would suddenly collapse and die, with their imploring eyes fixed on the flames. Others retained some stamina but still seemed more like ghosts than living men.

Brandt observed Napoleon's examination the Grand Redoubt:

I saw him deep in conversation with one of his staff officers who then went into the redoubt with some of the Guard Chasseurs. They marked out a square and then counted the number of corpses in the square. They repeated this at a number of different points and I understand that using this mathematical technique, they got an approximate idea of the number of victims. Whilst all this was going on, Napoleon's face was quite impassive but he did look a little pale.

The number of the dead also stunned Boulart, who found it 'hard to move without stepping on corpses [...] whole squares were traced by the dead or wounded left there'. Labaume could see 'mounds of cadavers, and the little spaces where there were not any were covered with debris of arms, lances, helmets or cuirasses, or by cannon-balls as numerous as hailstones after a violent storm'.

In some places, soldiers gathered in groups to discuss the exploits of previous days or search for missing friends. Le Roy managed to reunite with his son and as thy were speaking, surrounded by a few officers, he felt a soft pinch in the back. It was a Russian bullet and fortunately for Le Roy, it was already spent 'after flying for over quarter of a lieue' [approximately half a mile]. Less fortunate was Vossen's friend (a sergeant in the 111th Line) who was killed by a stray bullet late at night, while preparing roll-calls of surviving troops.

Meanwhile, Dumonceau lamented the loss of thousands of horses:

One could see some which, horribly disembowelled, nevertheless, kept standing, their heads hung low, drenching the soil with their blood, or, hobbling painfully in search of some pasture, dragged beneath them shreds of harness, sagging intestines or a fractured member, or else, lying flat on their sides, lifted their heads from time to time to gaze on their gaping wounds.[528]

Soltyk recounted a conversation between Murat and Ney after the battle:

The two heroes of the battle greeted each other amicably, and the King [Murat] said to the Marshal, 'Yesterday was a hot one. I have never seen a battle like it for artillery fire. At Eylau the guns fired as many rounds but it was cannon-balls. Yesterday the armies were so close that most of the firing was with grapeshot.' The Marshal responded, 'We did not break any eggs. The enemy's losses must be huge and his morale has undoubtedly been seriously damaged. We must pursue him and exploit our victory.' 'However, the Russians retired in good order,' added the King. 'I find that hard to believe,' replied the Marshal. 'How could they, after such a pounding march?' Yet, Ney was mistaken and the Russians indeed made an orderly withdrawal.[529]

# Aftermath

After his 'sombre review', Ségur recorded that Napoleon

in vain sought to console himself with a cheering illusion, by having a second enumeration made of the few prisoners who remained, and collecting together some dismounted cannon: from seven to eight hundred prisoners, and twenty broken cannon, were all the trophies of this imperfect victory.[530]

The Allied wounded were gathered and tended in several hospitals organized on the battlefield, the main ones being set up at the Kolotsk Monastery and in Mozhaisk. Conditions were appalling and hundreds died over the next few weeks. Generals Teste and Compans were placed in the same room with about a dozen other wounded; the next day, everyone except for generals, was dead. Captain François spent the night in a room with twenty-seven wounded, seven of whom died that same night and many more followed them over the next two weeks. The wounded General Dessaix refused surgeons' suggestions to amputate his hand, which eventually healed itself quite well. Yet, General Romeuf was less fortunate and, as Larrey describes it, he died of his horrendous wounds caused by a round-shot later than night.

Conditions in hospitals quickly deteriorated and Lejeune was stunned to see 'our troops using horseflesh as food' in Mozhaisk two days after the battle. According to Ségur:

The Russians were seen dragging themselves along to places where dead bodies were heaped together, and offered them a horrible retreat. It has been affirmed by several persons, that one of these poor fellows lived for several days in the carcase of a horse, which had been gutted by a shell, and the inside of which he gnawed. Some were seen straightening their broken leg by tying a branch of a tree tightly against it, then supporting themselves with another branch, and walking in this manner to the next village. Not one of them uttered a groan.

And yet, a more gruesome picture awaited Alexandre Bellot de Kergorre, a young *commissaire des guerres* at Mozhaisk, who left a vivid description of thousands of wounded lying throughout the town and dying of hunger and thirst.[531]

Napoleon remained in Mozhaisk for three days, quartered in a house near the main square. His sore throat quickly turned to laryngitis and the Emperor could no longer speak or dictate his orders, which forced him to scribble down all his instructions. This brief respite also allowed him to regroup his troops after the bloodletting at Borodino and gather more ammunition and supplies. His advance guard, meantime, pursued the Russian Army.

## Casualties

Battle reports revealed immense casualties on both sides, placing the Battle of Borodino among the bloodiest combats in history. In his letter to Alexander, Kutuzov described it as 'the bloodiest of all the battles known in modern times'.[532] One Russian officer, who went on to serve in the 1813–14 campaigns, reflected the prevailing opinion on Borodino when he noted: 'In my

207

# The Battle of Borodino

life I participated in a whole series of general engagements as well as a variety of other operations, and I discovered that they stood in the same relation to Borodino as peacetime manoeuvres did to the realities of war itself.'

The precise number of casualties is hard to establish and estimates vary between sources, causing one modern historian to note that casualty estimates oftentimes are 'guess-timates'.[533] Many French documents perished during the dreadful winter retreat of 1812, while Russian roll-calls and battle reports are often incomplete or vague, while some have been lost.

Besides the problem of sources, there is an issue of contrasting viewpoints of the battle – the French (and English) participants and then scholars considered the battles of Shevardino and Borodino as separate actions, while the Russians believed, and still do, that they constitute parts of one major engagement. Thus, Russian studies often refer to Borodino as a two-day battle fought on 24–26 August (5–7 September). This is an important distinction, since the French data on casualties usually includes only those suffered on 7 September, while the Russians combined losses sustained in the actions of 5 *and* 7 September.

Two days after the battle, in a letter to his father-in-law, Emperor Francis of Austria, Napoleon acknowledged 8,000–10,000 French losses and '40,000–50,000 Russians killed and wounded, sixty guns and many prisoners'. The 18th Bulletin, issued on 10 September, claimed that

> 12,000 to 13,000 men, and from 8,000 to 9,000 Russian horses, have been counted on the field of battle: sixty pieces of artillery and 5,000 prisoners have remained in our power. We have had 2,500 killed and thrice that number wounded. Our total loss may be estimated at 10,000, that of the enemy at from 40,000 to 50,000. Never was there seen such a field of battle. Out of every six dead bodies, there were five Russians for one Frenchman.

That same day, however, Kutuzov penned his own report and, after claiming victory, he acknowledged his heavy losses (without specifying them) and estimated Napoleon's loss at 40,000. The official battle account, prepared after the battle but not made public until many years later, recognized 25,000 killed and wounded in the Russian Army and over 40,000 in the French.[534]

Russian imperial scholars estimated between 44,000 and 55,000 Russians losses and 28,000–50,000 French casualties. Bogdanovich's figures – 44,000 Russian and over 28,000 French casualties – were largely accepted by later historians until the establishment of the USSR. Soviet scholars produced figures driven by ideological concerns and claimed some 58,500–60,000 French losses. Scholars deviating from this line were pressured to adhere to it. Thus, in 1943, Eugène Tarle referred to some 50,000 French and 58,000 Russian losses, but was then forced to revise his figures to 58,500 on the French side and 42,000 on the Russian for his 1962 study.

The figure of over 58,000 French casualties was first made public in 1813, when a Swiss officer Alexander Schmidt defected to Russia and claimed that he had served under Berthier. Schmidt, remarkably, could recall the precise

# Aftermath

number of losses Napoleon's troops suffered at Borodino, though his reliability should have been doubted after he claimed that Reynier VII Corps was present there! Despite such fraudulency, Governor Rostopchin of Moscow utilized Schmidt's figures in his propaganda publications, hoping to boost Russian morale. In subsequent decades, some scholars, seeking to embellish Russian actions, based their estimates on Rostopchin's pamphlets, gradually making the figure of over 58,000 French losses seem genuine. Modern Russian historians revised these figures and their current estimates place Russian losses between 45,000 and 50,000 and those of the French at approximately 35,000. Each side had about 1,000 men captured.

The Allied participants give significantly different estimates. Dominique Larrey believed that the French lost 12–13,000 'hors de combat' and 9,500 wounded. Girod de l'Ain estimated some 15,000 losses, Soltyk – 18,000, while Berthezene, noting that some colonels tried to conceal the real figures, referred to 22,600 casualties. Chambray, Meneval and Dedem estimated between 28,000 and 30,000 losses while Lejeune gave the highest estimate with forty-eight generals, ten colonels and some 40,000 soldiers killed or wounded. At the time, the most detailed analysis of French losses was done by Baron Denniée, Inspector of Reviews of the Grand Army, who prepared initial reports for Berthier, but due to the high number of losses they revealed, he was told to keep them secret. Denniée finally made them public in his *Itinéraire de l'Empereur Napoléon* in 1842, revealing the loss of forty-nine generals (ten killed), thirty-seven colonels (ten killed), 6,547 officers and soldiers killed, and 21,453 men wounded. Denniée's figures, despite their shortcomings, had a lasting influence, since virtually all subsequent authors accepted and repeated them. Currently, most Western accounts give Napoleon's losses at 28,000–30,000 men and estimate between 44,000 and 50,000 for Kutuzov's troops. Denniée's estimates, however, seem to exclude the losses (4–5,000 men) that the Grand Army suffered on 5 September, since it would be incredible to assume that the French lost less than 25,000 men at Borodino. Therefore, if one adds the casualties of 5 and 7 September – as Russian studies have done for Kutuzov's army – then the combined French losses sustained on 5–7 September would be in the vicinity of 34,000–35,000 men.

Details on French regimental losses are lacking but some data is available. Hourtoulle's study showed that the 17th Line lost twenty-five officers killed and forty-six wounded, while the 9th Line had eight officers and seventy-three men killed, thirty-one officers and 713 men wounded. The 30th Line, which had some 3,000 men in late August, tallied less than 300 after the battle. Montesquiou de Fezensac was

> struck by the exhaustion of the troops and their numerical weakness [...] The 4th Line was reduced to 900 men out of the 2,800 which had crossed the Rhine; thus four battalions now formed but two when mustered, and each company had a double complement of officers and non-commissioned officers. All of their equipment, and particularly their shows, were in a dilapidated state [...]

# The Battle of Borodino

Never had we suffered such heavy losses; never had the morale of the Army been so shaken.[535]

Among the cavalry units, the 4th Chasseurs had one officer killed and ten wounded, the 6th Lancers lost four officers killed and four wounded. Roth von Schreckenstein recorded the loss of thirty-nine officers and 287 men killed and twenty-nine officers and 323 men wounded in Thielemann's Saxon brigade, which also lost 610 horses. Preysing-Moos recorded in his diary that his Bavarian troops lost five officers and around 100 men. According to von Dittfurth, the Württemberg cavalry lost 34 killed, 274 wounded and 10 missing, and lost 323 of its 386 horses; the Württemberg infantry lost fifteen officers and 259 soldiers. The Westphalians fared no better and Junot's corps had some 3,000 killed, wounded and missing. Linsingen's regiment had about 700 men in the morning but lost ten officers and 341 men. Maurice Tascher's regiment, the 12th Chasseurs à Cheval, lost ten officers and eighty-seven soldiers, while Vossler of the 3rd Württemberg Jäger zu Pferde described how

of the 180 men the regiment had been able to muster that morning, half were either dead or wounded. The general commanding our division, General Waltier, and the brigadier of our brigade, as well as their seconds-in-command, had all been wounded and another senior divisional staff officer killed.

Casualties were high also among the carabiniers and as Schehl, of the 2nd Carabiniers, revealed, 'After the roll call on 8 September, we became aware that 360 troopers and seventeen officers were absent. My company lost all its officers; our sergeant-major led us in the battle.'

According to Brandt, the Polish losses amounted to about 2,000 men, while Marian Kukiel specified that one general, fifty-six officers and some 2,000 soldiers of the V Corps were killed or wounded in the battle.

More specific information is available on Compans' division, whose battle reports were later published. Thus, according to Charrière's report, the 57th Line lost over 1,230 men, including 236 missing. Martinien's study reveals that the regiment lost 14 officers killed and twenty-six wounded. General Guyardet reported that his 61st Line suffered one officer and twenty-nine men killed, twelve officers and 226 men wounded, and seventeen captured in the fighting of 5 September but discusses no casualties for Borodino; based on Martinien's data on officer casualties, the 61st Line probably lost about 400 men. Discussing the Battle of Shevardino, Longchamp, of the 111th Line, initially reported 157 killed and 600 wounded, including twenty officers. His report was revised on 30 September and showed four officers and eighty-two men killed, fifteen officers and 540 men wounded and thirty-three captured.[536] In the 2nd Division, Dedem referred to 1,500 men lost in the 33rd Line, including 404 killed (forty-eight of them officers). His estimates seems exaggerated since Martinien found only nine officers killed and nineteen wounded, which would indicate lower overall loss.

The data on Russian casualties is more available but, although it has been long studied, the debate still continues. The roll-calls of the 1st and 2nd

# Aftermath

Western Armies and reports by regimental, division and corps commanders remain one of the most important sources on this subject. However, they are not without blemishes, often contradicting each other or containing duplications and mistakes. So they must be considered with a critical eye.

The official roll-calls show that the 1st Western Army suffered the largest casualties (21,727 men) but the 2nd Western Army, with 16,845 killed and wounded, sustained a higher percentage of losses. Their combined casualties total 38,569 men, a figure that is often cited in Soviet studies. However, this number is misleading since it does not account for casualties among officers, Opolchenye and Cossack forces. Yet, another dossier, containing reports on the Russian casualties for the 1812–14 campaigns, includes a report on the actions of 5–7 September showing six generals and 166 officers killed, twenty-three generals and 438 officers wounded while up to 45,000 soldiers were dead and injured.[537]

Several attempts were made to correct these figures. Sergei Shvedov, who was among the first to challenge the official Soviet statistics back in the 1980s, has recently argued that the Russian losses were close to 50,000 men. Although some historians accepted his figures, others scholars questioned his methods and revealed considerable flaws in his research. Dmitri Tselorungo's research showed 39,060 casualties and about 1,000 captured, while Sergei Lvov's study produced 39,297 casualties, of which 21,756 were in the 1st Army and 17,541 – in the 2nd Army.[538] These findings, however, lack statistics on artillery, Cossack and Opolchenye losses. Taking them into account, the Russian casualties of 5–7 September will exceed 40,000 men and might be close to 45,000 men. The recently published *Otechestvennaya voina 1812 goda: Entsiklopediya*, written by leading Russian scholars, refers to between 45,000 and 50,000 losses.

As mentioned above, Russian regimental reports are often incomplete, since they list casualties of NCOs and rank-and-file to which those of officers and non-combatants should be added. Nevertheless, these documents reveal vast losses. The Combined Grenadier Division, which counted 4,059 men in its eleven battalions on the eve of the battle, sustained a staggering loss of 62 per cent, losing 526 killed, 1,224 wounded and 750 missing; it tallied only 1,559 men (95 out of 243 NCOs) or 38 per cent of its fighting force by 18 September. The VII Corps lost 5,978 NCOs and rank-and-file, including 1,346 killed, and the VIII Corps – 9,260 men. The II and III Corps lost about 3,718 and 3,799 men respectively, while the V Corps lacked 4,891 men. In the infantry, the 6th Jägers suffered the highest casualties with 910 killed, wounded and missing, followed by the Vilenskii Infantry Regiment (870), the Yeletskii Infantry Regiment (792), the Life Guard Izmailovskii (777) and the Life Guard Litovskii (693). The Life Guard Preobrazhenskii and Semeyonovskii Regiments, despite being held in reserve, still suffered substantial casualties from enemy artillery fire.

The cavalry fared no better, with 1,184 killed, wounded and missing in the II and III Cavalry Corps and over 320 men in the IV Cavalry Corps. The Astrakhanskii Cuirassiers lost 231 men, including fifty-six killed and

# The Battle of Borodino

*Casualty Figures for the Battle of Borodino*

| Author | Year | Russian | French | Total |
|---|---|---|---|---|
| 18th Bulletin | 1812 | 40–50,000 | 10,000 | 50–60,000 |
| Kutuzov's report | 1812 | 25,000 | 40,000 | 65,000 |
| Buturlin | 1837 | 50,000 | 60,000 | 110,000 |
| Mikhailovsky Danilevsky | 1839 | 55,000 | 50,000 | 105,000 |
| Thiers | 1856 | 60,000 | 30,000 | 90,000 |
| Bogdanovich | 1859 | 44,000 | 28,000+ | 73,000+ |
| George | 1899 | 40,000+ | 30,000+ | 70,000+ |
| Burton | 1914 | 44,000 | 28,000+ | 72,000+ |
| Kukiel | 1937 | 50,000 | 29,000 | 79,000 |
| Tarle | 1943 | 58,000 | 50,000+ | 108,000 |
| Beskrovny | 1951 | 42,438 | 58,578 | 101,016 |
| Garnich | 1958 | 38,500 | ~60,000 | ~98,500 |
| Tarle | 1962 | 42,000 | 58,500 | 100,500 |
| Chandler | 1966 | 44,000 | 30,000 | 74,000 |
| Thiry | 1969 | 50,000 | 28,000 | 78,000 |
| Holmes | 1971 | 42,000 | 40,000+ | 82,000 |
| Tranie | 1981 | 50,000 | 30,000 | 80,000 |
| Nicolson | 1985 | 44,000 | 35,000 | 79,000 |
| Cate | 1985 | 45,000 | 28,000+ | 73,000+ |
| Troitsky | 1988 | 45,600 | 30,000 | 75,600 |
| Nafziger | 1988 | 38.5–44,000 | 30,000 | 68.5–74,000 |
| Riehn | 1991 | 43,000 | 28,000 | 71,000 |
| Zamoisky | 2004 | 45,000 | 28,000 | 73,000 |
| Pigeard | 2004 | 46,000 | 28,000 | 74,000 |
| Encyclopedia of 1812 | 2004 | 45–50,000 | ~35,000 | 80–85,000 |

seventy-nine wounded; the Mariupolskii Hussars had 163 killed and thirty-five wounded, while the Pskovskii Dragoons, which distinguished themselves in charges around the Grand Redoubt, had 101 killed, fifty-one wounded and thirty-two missing. The Akhtyrskii Hussars lost 160 men, the Sibirskii Dragoons – 156 men, the Glukhovskii Cuirassiers – 150, the Novgorodskii Cuirassiers – 145, the Izumskii Hussars – 137 men, while the Sumskii Hussars and Yekaterinoslavskii Cuirassiers lost 117 men each.

The Russian artillery was also hard hit. The 1st Battery Company lost sixty-five men, the 5th Light Company – sixty-six, the 12th Light Company – forty-five, the 2nd Battery Company – thirty-two, the 17th Battery Company – thirty-three and the 33rd Light Company – thirty. The 5th Horse Artillery Company lost 110 men, including thirty-four killed, sixty-one wounded and fifteen missing, while 268 of its horses were dead or injured. The 6th Horse Company was also badly mauled, with fifty-eight men and eighty-three horses killed and wounded.[541] In the Guard Horse Artillery, commanders of both companies were killed and another 110 men were killed or injured. In the 2nd Artillery Brigade, the 11th Battery Company lost twenty killed and

212

*Casualties Among Russian Regular Troops*
(based on roll-calls of the 1st and 2nd Armies)[539]

| | Killed | | | Wounded | | | Missing | | |
|---|---|---|---|---|---|---|---|---|---|
| | NCOs | Privates | Non-Combatants | NCOs | Privates | Non-Combatants | NCOs | Privates | Non-Combatants |
| **1st Western Army** | | | | | | | | | |
| 2nd | 28 | 909 | 12 | 113 | 1,676 | 28 | 11 | 932 | 9 |
| 3rd | 22 | 358 | 11 | 117 | 1,687 | 36 | 17 | 977 | 12 |
| 4th | 28 | 765 | 6 | 98 | 1,999 | 21 | 6 | 871 | 5 |
| 5th | 88 | 1,227 | 13 | 217 | 2,527 | 76 | 33 | 707 | 3 |
| 6th | 45 | 949 | 9 | 100 | 1,325 | 19 | 30 | 1,131 | 8 |
| 1st Cavalry | 2 | 18 | – | 12 | 47 | 2 | – | 20 | – |
| 2nd & 3rd Cavalry | 21 | 322 | 85 | 49 | 499 | 2 | 3 | 203 | – |
| Artillery | 24 | 267 | 30 | 65 | 673 | 5 | 2 | 108 | 7 |
| Total | 258 | 4,815 | 166 | 771 | 10,433 | 189 | 102 | 4,949 | 44 |
| Total | | 5,239 | | | 11,393 | | | 5,095 | |
| **2nd Western Army** | | | | | | | | | |
| 7th | 46 | 1,300 | – | 184 | 2,608 | – | 22 | 1,818 | – |
| 8th | 133 | 2,262 | – | 285 | 3,941 | – | 74 | 2,565 | – |
| 2nd Cuirassier Division | 9 | 93 | – | 26 | 256 | – | 9 | 238 | – |
| 4th Cavalry | 4 | 55 | – | 14 | 176 | 5 | 4 | 64 | 3 |
| Artillery | 14 | 103 | 3 | 27 | 309 | 3 | 10 | 168 | 14 |
| Total | 206 | 3,813 | – | 536 | 7,290 | 8 | 119 | 4,853 | 17 |
| Total | | 4,019 | | | 7,834 | | | 4,989 | |

*Casualties Among Russian Regular Troops* (based on S. Lvov's 2003 study)[540]

| Corps | Killed | | | | Wounded | | | | Missing | | | | Total |
|---|---|---|---|---|---|---|---|---|---|---|---|---|---|
| | Officers | NCOs | Musicians | Privates | Officers | NCOs | Musicians | Privates | Officers | NCOs | Musicians | Privates | |
| **1st Western Army** | | | | | | | | | | | | | |
| 2nd Infantry | 17 | 25 | 9 | 784 | 88 | 75 | 24 | 1,257 | 2 | 7 | 7 | 720 | 3,015 |
| 3rd Infantry | 19 | 28 | 11 | 410 | 126 | 124 | 35 | 1,820 | 7 | 18 | 8 | 1,019 | 3,625 |
| 4th Infantry | 9 | 29 | 6 | 792 | 106 | 103 | 21 | 2,046 | 1 | 6 | 5 | 873 | 3,997 |
| 5th Infantry | 40 | 97 | 13 | 1,326 | 201 | 236 | 79 | 3,054 | 1 | 24 | 1 | 631 | 5,703 |
| 6th Infantry | 10 | 47 | 6 | 971 | 116 | 117 | 21 | 1,423 | 3 | 30 | 7 | 1,123 | 3,874 |
| 1st Cavalry | 0 | 2 | 0 | 19 | 6 | 15 | 2 | 57 | 0 | 0 | 1 | 35 | 137 |
| 2nd Cavalry | 1 | 13 | 2 | 105 | 34 | 23 | 1 | 304 | 3 | 1 | 0 | 100 | 587 |
| 3rd Cavalry | 7 | 17 | 4 | 271 | 43 | 38 | 1 | 325 | 1 | 2 | 0 | 109 | 818 |
| Total | 103 | 258 | 51 | 4,678 | 720 | 731 | 184 | 10,286 | 18 | 88 | 29 | 4,610 | 21,756 |
| **2nd Western Army** | | | | | | | | | | | | | |
| 7th Infantry | 33 | 55 | 14 | 1,467 | 130 | 172 | 27 | 2,524 | 8 | 23 | 8 | 1,815 | 6,276 |
| 8th Infantry | 42 | 124 | 13 | 2,007 | 279 | 272 | 30 | 3,501 | 6 | 99 | 12 | 3,088 | 9,473 |
| 4th Cavalry | 10 | 4 | 0 | 249 | 42 | 30 | 9 | 386 | 1 | 4 | 0 | 138 | 873 |
| 2nd Cuirassier Division | 10 | 14 | 1 | 135 | 47 | 35 | 5 | 370 | 6 | 11 | 1 | 284 | 919 |
| Total | 95 | 197 | 28 | 3,858 | 498 | 509 | 71 | 6,781 | 21 | 137 | 21 | 5,225 | 17,541 |
| Total in both armies | 198 | 455 | 79 | 8,536 | 1,218 | 1,240 | 255 | 17,067 | 39 | 225 | 50 | 9,935 | 39,297 |

# Aftermath

*Russian Regiments with the Heaviest Losses*
(1 = NCOs; 2 = Rank-and-File; 3 = Non-Combatants)

| Units | Killed 1 | Killed 2 | Killed 3 | Wounded 1 | Wounded 2 | Wounded 3 | Missing 1 | Missing 2 | Missing 3 | Total |
|---|---|---|---|---|---|---|---|---|---|---|
| 6th Jäger | 8 | 364 | x | 28 | 510 | x | x | x | x | 910 |
| Vilenskii IR | 23 | 372 | x | 19 | 301 | x | x | 155 | x | 870 |
| Yeletskii IR | 3 | 70 | x | 25 | 435 | 4 | x | 254 | 1 | 792 |
| L-G. Izmailovskii | 16 | 153 | 7 | 20 | 503 | 5 | 5 | 67 | 1 | 777 |
| L-G. Litovskii | 30 | 400 | 5 | 35 | 143 | 15 | 13 | 100 | x | 741 |
| L-G. Jäger | 3 | 43 | 1 | 54 | 473 | 16 | 5 | 96 | 2 | 693 |
| Simbirskii IR | 13 | 278 | x | 14 | 252 | x | 9 | 126 | x | 692 |
| Astrakhanskii GR | 8 | 167 | x | 16 | 422 | x | x | 61 | x | 674 |
| 5th Jäger | 3 | 53 | x | 21 | 438 | x | 3 | 141 | x | 659 |
| Moskovskii GR | 6 | 99 | x | 23 | 430 | x | 5 | 80 | x | 643 |
| Kievskii GR | 5 | 152 | x | 20 | 338 | x | 3 | 92 | x | 610 |
| Ufimskii IR | 10 | 208 | x | 10 | 160 | 3 | 12 | 179 | 6 | 588 |
| Tarnopolskii IR | x | 79 | x | 24 | 199 | x | 2 | 242 | x | 546 |
| Shirvanskii IR | 5 | 174 | 2 | 14 | 283 | 4 | x | 41 | x | 523 |
| Kaporskii IR | 6 | 110 | 1 | 12 | 250 | 1 | 2 | 118 | x | 500 |
| Volhynskii IR | 3 | 235 | 2 | 10 | 95 | 4 | 1 | 147 | 3 | 500 |
| Odesskii IR | 6 | 53 | x | 22 | 182 | x | 5 | 231 | x | 499 |

seventy-two wounded, the 20th Light Company saw seven men killed and twenty-four injured, while the 21st Light Company had eleven dead and thirty wounded. The batteries of the 3rd Reserve Brigade were not spared either; the 31st Battery Company of this brigade had twenty-six men killed, thirty-one wounded and 126 missing. The artillery roll-calls of the 2nd Western Army showed that fourteen NCOs and 103 privates were killed, twenty-seven NCOs and 309 privates wounded and ten NCOs and 168 privates were missing; the artillery also lost 143 horses.[542]

The Battle of Borodino is famous for the high casualty rates in officer corps. Caulaincourt noted that 'never had a battle cost so many generals and officers' and many French participants called the battle 'La Bataille des Généraux'. Information on the officer casualties is relatively thorough, largely due to A. Martinien's valuable study of French officers killed and wounded between 1805 and 1815. Still, neither Deniée nor Martinien provide total statistics as revealed in the works of Russian scholars researching the Grand Army. Thus Vasiliev asserted 1,792 officer losses, while Zemtsov found 480 killed and 1,448 wounded officers. The French casualty lists include the names of eighty-six aides-de-camp and over thirty staff officers. The battle also claimed thirty-seven colonels, of which nine were killed or mortally wounded. Out of some 316 chefs de battalion/d'escadron, 103 were wounded and another twenty-four killed. Among the majors, six (out of fifty-four) were killed and twenty-nine wounded.[543]

# The Battle of Borodino

Martinien's study, despite its shortcomings, remains an invaluable source for officer losses. It shows that the 30th Line, which stormed the Grand Redoubt, suffered twenty-one officers killed and thirty wounded, while the 17th Line lost twenty-six killed and twenty-eight wounded. The 106th Line, which rashly charged the Russian positions near Borodino, lost eighteen officers killed and thirty-two wounded. Among the units fighting at the flèches, the 57th Line lost fourteen officers killed and twenty-six wounded, while the 61st Line had six killed and thirteen wounded, the 48th – nine killed and twenty-two wounded, and the 72nd – fifteen killed and fourteen wounded. Light infantry fared no better with twenty-seven officers killed and wounded in the 13th Light and forty men (ten killed) lost in the 15th Light; the latter suffered twenty-two more casualties in the rearguard actions on 9–10 September. In the cavalry, the chasseur regiments sustained the highest losses, with twenty-one killed, ninety-one wounded, followed by the cuirassiers (seventy-nine men, including twelve killed) and hussars (forty-five men). Among the individual regiments, the 12th Chasseurs (seventeen men), 8th Cuirassiers (sixteen men), 25th Chasseurs (fifteen men), 7th Dragoons (fourteen men), and the 9th Chevau-léger lost more officers that others units.

During the battle, the Allied army lost eight generals, among them two generals of division (Caulaincourt and Montbrun) and six generals of brigade (Compère, Huard, Damas Lanabère, Marion and Plauzonne). Four more generals were mortally wounded and died over the next several weeks: Romeuf, Chief of Staff of the III Corps, died after the battle; Lepel, who was in charge of the Westphalian cuirassiers, ended his life at Mozhaisk on 21 September; he was followed by Tharreau, who commanded the 23rd Division and died on 26 September. The Württemberg Major General von Breuning, serving with the 14th Light Cavalry Brigade of the III Corps, passed away on 30 October. Among the wounded were thirty-nine generals, including Marshal Davout, Generals Grouchy, Nansouty, Latour-Maubourg, Friant, Rapp, Compans, Dessaix, and others. One general (Bonnamy) was captured by the Russians. In total, as Zemtsov noted, the officer losses (1,928 officers and forty-nine generals) on 5–7 September constitute 20 per cent of all officer losses (158 generals and 9,380 officers) the Grand Army sustained between June 1812 and February 1813.

The Russian Army also suffered heavy casualties in its officer corps. In total, 211 officers were killed and 1,184 wounded.[544] By the end of the battle, thirteen regiments were commanded by junior officers, including three led by lieutenants. In twenty-seven units the commanding officer was replaced once, in thirteen regiments – twice, and in six regiments – three times! Thus, in the Yekaterinoslavskii Cuirassier Regiment, Colonel Volkov was wounded and replaced by Lieutenant Colonel Uvarov III, who was soon replaced by Lieutenant Khomyakov II; after the latter was injured, the regiment was led by Lieutenant Chulkov III. Among eighty-nine Russian generals, five (Kantakuzen, Krasnov, Kutaisov, Palitsyn and Tuchkov IV) were killed and four received mortal wounds (among them Bagration and Tuchkov I). Twenty-three generals were wounded, including Lieutenant

# Aftermath

*Casualties in the Russian Officer Corps*
(based on D. Tselorungo)

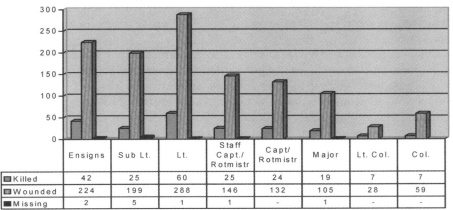

| | Ensigns | Sub Lt. | Lt. | Staff Capt./ Rotmistr | Capt/ Rotmistr | Major | Lt. Col. | Col. |
|---|---|---|---|---|---|---|---|---|
| ▪ Killed | 42 | 25 | 60 | 25 | 24 | 19 | 7 | 7 |
| ▪ Wounded | 224 | 199 | 288 | 146 | 132 | 105 | 28 | 59 |
| ▪ Missing | 2 | 5 | 1 | 1 | - | 1 | - | - |

Generals Golitsyn I, Gorchakov II, Konovnitsyn, and Osterman-Tolstoy, Major Generals Bakhmetyev I, Bakhmetyev II, Ivelich, Kretov, Karl von Mecklenburg, Neverovsky, Rossi, Vorontsov, Yermolov, and others. One general (Likhachev) was captured.

The combined casualties of the French and Russian armies at Borodino thus vary from 60,000 at their lowest to 110,000 at the highest, though the figure of 75–80,000 seems closer to reality. One must bear in mind, however, that this represents losses for the actions at Shevardino (5 September) *and* Borodino (7 September). Subtracting some 10,000 casualties for the action at Shevardino gives us about 64–65,000 losses sustained during the ten-hour battle on 7 September. The resulting 6,500 casualties per hour – or 108 men per minute – are truly staggering. Very few other *one-day* battles can approach such calamitous results. To fully understand the scale of Borodino's losses, it is illustrative that neither Rivoli (1797), Austerlitz (1805), Jena (1806), nor Eylau (1807), Friedland (1807), Salamanca (1812) or Bautzen (1813) can approach its murderous results. The *two-day* battles of Aspern–Essling (1809), Wagram (1809) and Dresden (1813) have an average of 22,000 to 40,000 victims per day. The massive *three-day* 'Battle of the Nations' at Leipzig in October 1813 was the largest Napoleonic battle, but its daily casualty rate averages 42,000–45,000. Waterloo (1815), with over 55,000 victims, is probably the second bloodiest *one-day* battle of the Napoleonic Era. Looking into other eras, the battles of antiquity should be discounted for the lack of precise numbers. One exception, however, can be made for the Battle of Cannae, where the Carthaginian Hannibal routed the Roman Army, with the combined loss of both sides exceeding 70,000 men. Other examples can be found only in modern era, since Medieval and Renaissance wars hardly produced carnage of comparable scale. Thus, the Third Battle of Nanking and the first day of the Somme (1916) certainly

# The Battle of Borodino

eclipsed Borodino in its deadly results. At the same time, the Battles of Stalingrad (165 days in 1942–43) and Verdun (297 days in 1916), the bloodiest battles in human history, claiming up to 2,000,000 and 720,000 casualties respectively, had average daily casualty rates below that of Borodino.

One last note is needed with respect to casualties. The loss of life did not stop with the end of the battle but rather continued for weeks as hundreds of wounded succumbed to their injuries, starvation or disease. Thus, both French and Russians participants noted that hundreds of Russian wounded died in the raging fires of Moscow in mid-September. Most studies discussing the casualties at Borodino tend to concentrate on army losses and overlook the fact that the battle had a tremendous effect on the local community, which remained devastated for many years. Entire villages were ravaged and, out of 239 homes and estates destroyed on the battlefield and its vicinity, only 104 were rebuilt by 1816. Furthermore, thousands of rotting corpses posed a major health hazard to the population. Stench of decomposing flesh smothered the area for weeks and, as some contemporaries acknowledged, diseases caused by so many unattended decaying bodies led to the death of many locals.

The work on gathering and burning cadavers was started by Junot's corps, which was left behind to carry out this grisly task. It is not clear how much work the weakened Westphalian troops did during their one-month stay on the battlefield, but we can assume that hundreds of bodies were disposed of. The Russian authorities became involved after the region was liberated in early November. The province was divided into four sectors ('distantsia') and some 10,000 peasants began searching ravines, roads and bushes for any human and animal corpses. As these works progressed, some 17,916 human bodies and over 8,200 horse cadavers were buried or burned by 4 January 1813, an additional 4,045 and 3,215 corpses by mid-January, and a further 6,859 and 9,147 corpses by late January. By early spring, some 52,048 human and over 41,700 horse corpses were removed from the entire Mozhaisk district. Human bodies, notwithstanding their allegiance and ethnic origin, were buried in deep pits (some containing up to 180 bodies) and large mounds with crosses were erected above them. Over time, the location of some of these mounds was forgotten but they were discovered in 1984, when the remains of over 450 men were found in three mounds near the Borodino Saviour Monastery. In August 2006, on the 194th anniversary of the battle, a religious service was held to consecrate large crosses in memory of the fallen.

Reminiscing on the sacrifice of soldiers of both armies, Eugène of Württemberg probably summed it up the best:

A friend of mine, whose ashes have long since been consigned to the earth, wrote the following about Borodino: 'To be honest, Kutuzov had no cause to have Emperor Alexander hold a *Te Deum* [to celebrate victory] and neither did Napoleon have reason to write a victorious report to his Empress. If we,

# Aftermath

warriors, could have forgotten the quarrels of the great men and shaken hands over the altar of justice next day, Posterity would have recognized all of us as brothers.'

## To Moscow and Back

Neither side was willing to concede defeat in this bloody battle. The French considered themselves victors since the Russians retreated from the battlefield. After the battle, Napoleon wrote to his wife Marie Louise, 'My dear, I write you from the battlefield of Borodino. Yesterday, I beat the Russians, their whole army [...] the battle was hot [...] and I had many killed and wounded.' The 18th Bulletin proudly proclaimed the French triumph on the field of Borodino and noted that 'the victory was never uncertain'. Yet the Russians had a different view.

As we have seen above, Kutuzov immediately drafted letters with the news of the Russian victory at Borodino. His report reached the Russian capital on the night of 10/11 September, when it was presented to Tsar Alexander and his close advisors. Alexander certainly saw through Kutuzov's claims of victory, since he ordered the report to be edited and excluded any reference to the Russian withdrawal. As Joseph de Maistre described, the following day, Kutuzov's courier, with the revised report in hand, 'triumphantly arrived' at St Petersburg, which was celebrating the Tsar's saint's day.[545] The imperial family was attending a mass at the Alexander of Neva Monastery and, after the liturgy, Kutuzov's report was announced to a joyous public. The edited version was then released for publication in the newspapers.[546]

News of the victory was rapturously celebrated throughout St Petersburg, where church bells pealed forth and trumpets blared. The American envoy to Russia, John Quincy Adams, wrote that 'St Petersburg was illuminated', while English traveller, Ker Porter, described that 'with the victory being publicly declared, the *Te Deum* was chanted, every voice united in the strain which gave glory to the God who had fought, and covered her people with immortal honours.'[547] And Mikhailovsky-Danilevsky noted that 'the Emperor's saint's day was never before celebrated with such rapture'.[548] The news spread to other towns and provinces and in the process became embellished. Thus Joseph de Maistre informed the Sardinian foreign minister that he had heard from an officer who fought at Borodino that 'by the end of the battle the French had completely run out of ammunition and were throwing stones'.

To commemorate the Russian victory, Tsar Alexander announced that Kutuzov was to be promoted to the rank of field marshal general and awarded a lump sum of 100,000 roubles, while his wife was named a state-dame of the court. Every participating soldier received 5 roubles. Officer corps was generously rewarded as well. Bagration was given a lump sum of 50,000 roubles (he died on 24 September 1812), Barclay de Tolly was awarded the Order of St George (2nd class), while Miloradovich and Dokhturov received the diamond signs of the Order of Alexander of Neva.

Osterman-Tolstoy and Rayevsky were also awarded the Order of Alexander of Neva but minus the diamond signs. Fourteen generals received the Order of St George (3rd class) and six more were given golden swords with diamonds. Eleven generals received the Order of St Anna (1st class), while seven major generals – Bakhmetyev, Dorokhov, Korf, Mecklenburg, Neverovsky, Stroganov and Vasilchikov – were promoted to lieutenant general.

The rest of the army was rewarded handsomely as well. Sixty-three officers received promotions. Two senior officers received the prestigious Order of St George (3rd class) while sixty-six (including twenty-seven colonels) earned the St George of the 4th class. Thirty-two officers received the Order of St Vladimir (3rd class), twenty-two – St Vladimir (4th class), and 554 – St Vladimir (4th class with ribbon). Seventeen officers were given the Order of St Anna (3rd class), twenty-seven – St Anna (2nd class with diamonds), while 159 officers received St Anna (2nd class), and 767 – St Anna (4th class). Over 340 officers were awarded with golden swords for courage, while six were commended with citations of the 'imperial goodwill'.

In Moscow, Governor Rostopchin, who had been publishing overly positive and patriotic proclamations for the past few weeks, issued more bulletins proclaiming that 'the accursed one [Napoleon] and his accomplices will perish through famine, fire and sword'. A *Te Deum* service was held at the Uspensky Cathedral and the air over the city was shaking from constant pealing of church bells. Yet, after receiving Kutuzov's new dispatches, Rostopchin found himself in a very awkward position. The Russian Commander informed Rostopchin that he had retreated behind Mozhaisk and desperately needed supplies and transports to evacuate the wounded to Moscow. As thousands of wounded troops and terrified peasants began arriving at the capital, rumours of a French victory rapidly spread and the mood of the populace dramatically changed.

The Russian Army, meantime, spent 8 September taking new positions behind Mozhaisk. The French remained idle until afternoon, when Murat's advance guard moved close to the town and fought minor skirmishes with the Russians. The Imperial Guard, Davout and Ney were following in Murat's wake, while Junot, as notes above, was ordered to remain on the battlefield. Prince Eugène, reinforced by the approaching 15th Division of General Pino, prepared to cross the Moscow river and proceed towards Ruza, while Poniatowski marched to Borisov. That evening Kutuzov reconnoitred the French positions and decided to continue his retreat. Murat's cavalry made several attacks on the Russian rearguard but failed to break through into Mozhaisk; Murat's chief of staff, Belliard, was wounded early in this combat. Late in the evening the French light infantry (four voltigeur companies from the 2nd Division) did manage to enter one of suburbs of Mozhaisk but the Russians were clinging on stubbornly. As Ségur noted, 'Murat fancied himself already in possession of it, and sent to inform the Emperor that he might sleep there.' As Napoleon and his entourage

# Aftermath

moved forward to Mozhaisk, they were warned that the town was still in the Russian possession. So the Emperor spent the night at Kukarino, about a mile from Mozhaisk.

The very fact the Mozhaisk was not seized that day revealed and Murat's advance was checked showed that the Russian Army was far from being routed. Furthermore, the successful advance guard action allowed Kutuzov to claim further feats of Russian arms. But his army still had to retreat ...

On 9 September, the Russian Army, in two columns, proceeded to Zhukovo and then Zemlino. Mozhaisk was occupied after a brief combat and, as Dedem informs us, French troops seized a large magazine with 'eau-de-vie' (i.e. vodka). Staff officers tried to confiscate the liquor from Dedem's soldiers, in order to distribute it among the Imperial Guard, but they were quickly overruled and it was given to regular units. Napoleon moved his headquarters to Mozhaisk later that day and remained for the next three days.

Murat's cavalry, meantime, continued to harass the Russian rearguard on 10–11 September and at one moment the Russian movement was jeopardized when Platov withdrew his rearguard too soon, allowing Murat to close on the main Russian Army.[549] Kutuzov, already dissatisfied with Platov's performance at Borodino, was furious at this latest slip-up and replaced him at once with Miloradovich.

Publicly, Kutuzov still considered fighting another battle. Many Russian historians claimed that he genuinely wanted to make a second battle before Moscow, but others argued convincingly that Kutuzov simply played to popular sentiments while rationally weighing his options. On 9 September, Kutuzov issued an order thanking his troops for their courage at Borodino and promising 'with the Lord's help we will inflict a crushing defeat on our enemy'.[550] Three days later, he reiterated, 'Every commander knows that the Russian Army must have another decisive battle under the walls of Moscow.' The search for a suitable battlefield finally produced a site near the Poklonnaya Gora, a few miles from the capital. The new battlefield proved to be too expansive for Kutuzov's weakened force, which still had not received necessary reinforcements. Senior officers voiced their objections to the position, which as Barclay de Tolly noted, presented a cobweb of ravines and gullies. According to Mikhailovsky-Danilevsky, 'If such a position were found several marches, even one march, from Moscow, it would have been abandoned at the very first glance but now, with Moscow itself in sight, generals deliberated and mulled over their decision, seeking at least some other means to give a battle.'[551] It was finally agreed to summon a council of war at the nearby village of Fili.

The council met in a small peasant hut on 13 September and was attended by the Commander-in-Chief and ten senior officers. In a heated debate, Barclay de Tolly, Rayevsky, Osterman-Tolstoy and Toll called for retreat, while Bennigsen, Konovnitsyn, Uvarov, Dokhturov, and Yermolov suggested fighting another battle. Kutuzov, shrewdly allowing everyone to express an opinion, in order to avoid being the first to advocate the abandonment of

# The Battle of Borodino

Moscow, had the last word: declaring his support for those proposing retreat, he stated that 'the loss of Moscow does not mean the loss of Russia'.

Over the next day and half the Russian Army passed through the capital, which was hastily being evacuated. 'The march of the Army, while being executed with admirable order considering the circumstances, resembled a funeral procession more than a military progress ...' noted Buturlin, adding that 'Officers and men wept with rage'. Meanwhile, Dokhturov voiced his indignation at Kutuzov's the decision 'to abandon one's cradle without a single shot and without a fight! I am in a fury ...' And many shared his views. Even more outspoken was Governor Rostopchin, who had spent the previous weeks convincing the people of Moscow that the Russians were winning the war: 'The blood is boiling in my veins,' he wrote to his wife, 'I think that I shall die of the pain.'

On 14 September Napoleon's troops entered Moscow. The previous day Miloradovich and Murat struck an impromptu armistice to allow the Russian rearguard to withdraw and, as Perovsky recalled, some were stunned to witness French troops allowing the Russians to march through their ranks.[552] But the majority in the French Army believed that, to all intents and purposes, the war was now over, and there was no reason to spill more blood. There was hardly any doubt that Tsar Alexander would have to make peace with Napoleon.

For the Russians, however, the war was far from finished. The French hardly occupied the capital when fires began throughout the city and continued to burn for the next three days, destroying two-thirds of the city. The fires were started on the orders of Rostopchin, who preferred to see the capital destroyed rather than in the hands of the triumphant enemy. 'It was the most grand, the most sublime and the most terrific sight the world ever beheld!' Napoleon reminisced in exile on St Helena. Yet the great fire had a tremendous impact on the French Army, which descended into chaos and disorder. Pion des Loches recalled that

> The army had dissolved completely; everywhere one could see drunken soldiers and officers loaded with booty and provisions seized from houses which had fallen prey to the flames. The streets were strewn with books, porcelain, furniture and clothing of every kind.

While the French remained in Moscow, the Russian Army manoeuvred from the Ryazan Road to the Kaluga Road, where Kutuzov established the Tarutino Camp. Through this manoeuvre, Kutuzov covered the southern provinces with abundant supplies and manufacturing enterprises. The Russians also threatened Napoleon's rear and lines of communication. At Tarutino, Kutuzov began intensive preparations for future operations and increased his army to 110,000–120,000 men, with additional militia forces to come. Kutuzov also encouraged guerrilla operations against the invaders and organized several regular cavalry detachments to harass French communications and supply lines. Napoleon made several peace proposals to Alexander, but they were all rejected.

# Aftermath

On 18 October, Marshal Murat's advance guard suffered a sudden defeat on the Chernishnya river, north of Tarutino. Hearing this news, Napoleon realized it was time to abandon the devastated Russian capital before he was surrounded, especially as the Russian winter, with its notorious frost and snow, was due. The retreat commenced on 19 October, when remnants of the Grand Army left Moscow, accompanied by thousands of non-combatants and an enormous train loaded with loot. The route from Moscow to Smolensk, via Gzhatsk, was devastated during the fighting of August–September, so Napoleon intended to move his forces via the south-western provinces, which were unharmed by the war and retained large supply stores.

The start seemed promising, as Napoleon successfully deceived Kutuzov as to his intentions, quietly moving his troops onto the Kaluga route. But heavy rains made the roads almost impassable and considerably delayed French progress on 21–22 October. During the night of the 23rd, Russian scouts finally realized that Napoleon was moving southward and Kutuzov immediately marched to Maloyaroslavets, the only point where he could strike the new Kaluga Road and block the French advance. In a battle on 23–24 October, the French captured the town but failed to break through the Russian lines. After a council of war on the evening of 25 October, Napoleon ordered the withdrawal to Smolensk, by the way of Borodino and Gzhatsk. The Battle of Maloyaroslavets had a crucial impact on the Russian campaign, as it prevented Napoleon from reaching the rich provinces in south-eastern Russia and forced him to return to the devastated route of his summer advance. The marching and fighting at Maloyaroslavets consumed seven crucial days and, a week after the battle, the snow began to fall.

In early November the Grand Army finally reached Smolensk, where huge supply depots had previously been established. But discipline broke down and looting became rampant. Napoleon hoped to rally his forces at Smolensk but Kutuzov's advance toward Krasnyi threatened to cut his route. On 3 November, Miloradovich and Platov attacked Davout near Vyazma and captured the town. Napoleon soon abandoned Smolensk and as the French withdrew, superior Russian forces attacked the French corps as they marched from Smolensk to Krasnyi. Each corps was temporarily cut off and Ney's corps even surrounded, but none of them was forced to lay down their arms and Ney made a heroic retreat across the Dnieper, earning the nickname 'the bravest of the brave'. Nevertheless, French losses were horrendous due to constant skirmishes, cold weather and lack of supplies. The poorly dressed French soldiers began to freeze and thousands of stragglers were killed or captured. The Russian Army also suffered severely in the harsh winter conditions.

As Napoleon retreated westwards, the Russians had a unique chance of trapping him on the Berezina river. Admiral Chichagov merged his forces with Tormasov's army and containing Schwarzenberg's corps in Volhynia, moved north to intercept Napoleon, taking Minsk on 16 November and Borisov on the 22nd. The main Russian Army under Kutuzov closely pursued

# The Battle of Borodino

Napoleon's forces from the east, while Wittgenstein's corps converged from the north-east and Chichagov's army from the south-west. But Napoleon demonstrated his dazzling military talents by diverting Russian attention to Uchlodi, while his forces crossed the river at Studienka. In desperate fighting, Napoleon extricated part of his army, but lost some 25,000 troops and up to 30,000 non-combatants. Although Chichagov was held responsible for the Berezina failure, Wittgenstein and Kutuzov also acted indecisively. Kutuzov's faltering actions at Krasnyi and Berezina served as a basis for the so-called 'golden bridge' or 'parallel march' thesis, which argued that Kutuzov had refrained from attacking the French in order to preserve his armies and let the winter and hunger do its business. On 5 December, Napoleon appointed Murat Commander-in-Chief of the Grand Army and left for Paris. Five days later, the Russian Army captured Vilna and halted its pursuit. By 25 December, the last remnants of the Grand Army recrossed the Nieman and quit Russian soil.

Thus the Russian campaign had disastrous consequences for Napoleon and his empire. His military might was shattered following the loss of up to half a million men in Russia. The loss of so many veterans and the influx of inexperienced recruits had a major impact on the quality of the French Army. Although there is hardly a doubt about the élan of the troops Napoleon led in 1813–14, they were never as good as the veterans of the earlier campaigns. The French cavalry was virtually wiped out and never fully recovered during the subsequent campaigns.

In the spring of 1813, the Battles of Lützen and Bautzen – remarkable victories in themselves – could have been of greater consequence had Napoleon had enough cavalry to mount an effective pursuit of the Allies. In the political dimension, Napoleon's reluctant allies, Austria and Prussia, exploited the French setback in Russia to break their alliances and joined their efforts against Napoleon. By 1815 French dominance of the Continent was over and a new political equilibrium established in Europe.

The Battle of Borodino is interesting for a number of reasons. Both armies demonstrated remarkable tenacity and gallantry. The Allied troops made repeated charges on fortified positions, while the Russians endured an artillery bombardment of unprecedented intensity. Napoleon used his cavalry in a surprising fashion. The battlefield itself was hardly suitable for cavalry actions and Napoleon's troopers were forced to endure heavy enemy fire for hours, before being finally thrown into direct assault on Rayevsky's Redoubt. The French artillery performed well, maintaining a devastating bombardment that decimated Kutuzov's forces. But most importantly, Napoleon himself was unrecognizable and his lethargy may have been the most decisive factor in the battle, as he rejected proposals that could have delivered victory.

The Russian troops fought with their usual resilience, fervent devotion and gallantry. Individual corps and regimental commanders gave outstanding performances and more Russian officers were killed and wounded at Borodino than any prior battle of this period. Yet Kutuzov's actions were

# Aftermath

less than satisfactory – although for years afterwards Russian historians sang his praises. Kutuzov's battle deployment was flawed, his tight formations presenting easy targets for Napoleon's gunners. Kutuzov's inactivity was akin to Napoleon's but it was balanced by the vigour of Barclay de Tolly and Bagration, who, in many respects, fought the battle independent of Kutuzov.

Borodino remains an example of how winning a major battle does not necessarily mean winning the campaign. The French gained a victory – albeit a narrow one – and triumphantly entered Moscow a week later, only to abandon it after a month. The Grand Army then suffered perhaps the most devastating retreat in history. In political terms, Napoleon's hopes of exploiting his success at Borodino (which, after all, had led to the capture of Moscow) proved futile, as the Russians continued to reject proposals for a negotiated peace. The battle, in fact, may be considered a key event in the downfall of the French First Empire, since Napoleon's failure to destroy the Russian Army and gain peace with Alexander led to ignominious retreat and the ultimate loss of his own, awesome, Grand Army. This, in turn, prompted the collapse of the Emperor's power base, facilitating a strong anti-French coalition in 1813. Meanwhile, the Russian Army carried the war from the walls of Moscow to the heart of Paris, where it triumphantly paraded on the Champs-Elysées in the spring of 1814.

The battle had a tremendous effect on the social and cultural landscape of the Russian empire. It was hardly ever acknowledged as a defeat, but rather lauded as a crucial moral victory, especially in view of the subsequent rout of Napoleon's forces. It helped mobilize the nation and provided a powerful morale boost. The subsequent defeat of an opponent previously deemed unstoppable left a permanent imprint on the Russian national psyche, and helped revive Messianic sentiments in the nation and its rulers. By 1815, Emperor Alexander would be enthralled by these mystical ideas, as revealed in his famous proposal for the creation of a 'Holy Alliance' to maintain conservative order and encourage monarchs to rule according to Christian principles. Under his successor, Nicholas I, Russia would be labelled the 'gendarme of Europe' for its role in protecting the existing status quo on the Continent. The origins of the Decembrist movement, which had a lasting effect on Russian upper society, can be traced to officers, who, following Borodino and the French defeat in Russia, had served in Western Europe and shared their experiences and impressions with other officers.

Finally, the Battle of Borodino influenced artistic and literary fields for the rest of the century and inspired such luminaries of Russian literature as Alexander Pushkin, Peter Vyazemsky, Vasili Zhukovsky, Mikhail Lermontov, Alexander Griboyedov and, above all, Leo Tolstoy, whose *War and Peace*, with its detailed discussion of the Battle of Borodino, remains one of the greatest literary accomplishments of the 19th century. The themes of 1812 were also woven into the musical masterpieces of Mikhail Glinka, Peter Tchaikovsky and Sergei Prokofiev.

# Appendices

---•◦•<(•)>•◦•---

## ORDER OF BATTLE
[Note: A more detailed order of battle is available at the www.napoleon-series.org.)

## THE RUSSIAN ARMY AT BORODINO
*COMMANDER-IN-CHIEF: General of Infantry Mikhail Golenishchev-Kutuzov*

*1ST WESTERN ARMY: General of Infantry Mikhail Barclay de Tolly*
**II INFANTRY CORPS: Lieutenant General Karl Gustav Baggovut**
*4TH DIVISION: Major General Eugène von Württemberg*
*1st Brigade: Major General Ignatii Rossi*
Tobolskii (Tobolsk) Infantry Regiment
Volynskii (Volhynia) Infantry Regiment

*2nd Brigade: Colonel Dmitri Pyshnitsky*
Kremenchugskii (Kremenchug) Infantry Regiment
Minskii (Minsk) Infantry Regiment

*3rd Brigade: Colonel Yegor Pillar*
34th Jäger Regiment
4th Jäger Regiment

*4th Artillery Brigade: Colonel Aleksey Voyeikov*
4th Battery Company (12 guns)
7th Light Company (12 guns)
8th Light Company (12 guns)

*17TH DIVISION: Lieutenant General Zakhar Olsufiev III*
*1st Brigade: Major General Peter Ivelich IV*
Ryazanskii (Ryazan) Infantry Regiment
Brestskii (Brest) Infantry Regiment

*2nd Brigade: Major General Yakov Vadkovsky*
Belozerskii (Belozersk) Infantry Regiment
Willmandstrandskii (Willmandstrand) Infantry Regiment

*3rd Brigade: Colonel Yakov Potemkin*
30th Jäger Regiment
48th Jäger Regiment

*17th Artillery Brigade: Colonel Ivan Ditterix II*
17th Battery Company (12 guns)
32nd Light Company (12 guns)
33rd Light Company (12 guns)

**III INFANTRY CORPS: Lieutenant General Nikolai Tuchkov I**
*1ST GRENADIER DIVISION: Major General Pavel Stroganov*
*1st Brigade: Colonel Peter Zheltukhin II*
Leib-Grenadier Regiment
Count Arakcheyev's Grenadier Regiment

*2nd Brigade: Major General Alexander Tsvilenev*
Pavlovskii (Pavlovsk) Grenadier Regiment
Yekaterinoslavskii (Yekaterinoslavl) Grenadier Regiment

*3rd Brigade: Major General Boris Foch I*
St Petersburgskii (St Petersburg) Grenadier Regiment
Tavricheskii (Taurida) Grenadier Regiment

*3rd DIVISION: Lieutenant General Peter Konovnitsyn*
*1st Brigade: Major General Alexander Tuchkov IV*
Muromskii (Murom) Infantry Regiment
Revelskii (Revel) Infantry Regiment
1st Combined Grenadier Battalion

*2nd Brigade: Colonel Demid Mesheryakov*
Chernigovskii (Chernigov) Infantry Regiment
Selenginskii (Selenginsk) Infantry Regiment
2nd Combined Grenadier Battalion

*3rd Brigade: Major General Ivan Shakhovsky*
20th Jäger Regiment
21st Jäger Regiment

*3rd Artillery Brigade*
Half Company of the 1st Battery Company (6 guns)
6th Light Company (12 guns)

**IV INFANTRY CORPS: Lieutenant General Alexander Osterman-Tolstoy**
*11th DIVISION: Major General Nikolai Bakhmetyev I*
*1st Brigade: Major General Pavel Choglokov*
Kexholmskii (Kexholm) Infantry Regiment
Pernovskii (Pernau) Infantry Regiment

*2nd Brigade: Major General Vasili Laptev*
Polotskii (Polotsk) Infantry Regiment
Yeletskii (Yeletsk) Infantry Regiment

*3rd Brigade: Colonel Adam Bistrom II*
1st Jäger Regiment
33rd Jäger Regiment

*11th Artillery Brigade: Lieutenant Colonel Alexander Maleyev I*
2nd Battery Company (12 guns)
3rd Light Company (12 guns)
Half Company of the 4th Light Company (6 guns)

**23RD DIVISION: *Major General Aleksey Bakhmetyev III***
*1st Brigade: Major General Prince Ivan Gurielov*
Yekaterinburgskii (Yekaterinburg) Infantry Regiment
Rylskii (Rylsk) Infantry Regiment

*2nd Brigade: Major General Fedor Aleksopol*
Koporskii (Koporsk) Infantry Regiment
18th Jäger Regiment

*23rd Artillery Brigade*
44th Light Company (12 guns)

*2nd Combined Grenadier Brigade: Colonel Sergei Ostrovsky of the Life Guard Preobrazhenskii Regiment*
1st Combined Grenadier Battalion
2nd Combined Grenadier Battalion

**V INFANTRY CORPS: Lieutenant General Nikolai Lavrov**
**GUARD INFANTRY DIVISION: *Lieutenant General Nikolai Lavrov***
*1st Brigade: Major General Baron Grigory Rosen I*
Life Guard Preobrazhenskii Regiment
Life Guard Semeyonovskii Regiment

*2nd Brigade: Colonel Matvei Khrapovitsky*
Life Guard Izmailovskii Regiment
Life Guard Litovskii Regiment

*3rd Brigade: Colonel Karl Bistrom I*
Life Guard Jäger Regiment
Life Guard Finlyandskii Regiment

*Life Guard Artillery Brigade: Colonel Alexander Eyler*
His Majesty Grand Duke Mikhail Pavlovich's 1st Battery Company (12 guns)
Count Arakcheyev's 2nd Battery Company (12 guns)
Major General Kaspersky's 1st Light Company (12 guns)
Captain Gogel's 2nd Light Company (12 guns)
Guard Equipazh's Artillery (2 guns assigned to the 1st Light Company)

*1st Combined Grenadier Brigade: Colonel Prince Grigory Kantakuzen*
1st Combined Grenadier Battalion of the 1st Division
2nd Combined Grenadier Battalion of the 1st Division
1st Combined Grenadier Battalion of the 4th Division
2nd Combined Grenadier Battalion of the 4th Division

# Appendices

**1ST CUIRASSIER DIVISION:** *Major General Nikolai Borozdin II*
*1st Brigade: Major General Ivan Shevich*
Chevalier Guard Regiment
Life Guard Horse Regiment

*2nd Brigade: Major General Nikolai Borozdin II*
His Imperial Majesty's Leib-Cuirassier Regiment
Her Imperial Majesty's Leib-Cuirassier Regiment
Astrakhanskii (Astrakhan) Cuirassier Regiment

*Life Guard Horse Artillery Brigade: Colonel Peter Kozen*
1st Horse Battery (8 guns)
2nd Horse Battery (8guns)


**VI INFANTRY CORPS: General of Infantry Dmitri Dokhturov**
**7TH DIVISION:** *Lieutenant General of Artillery Peter Kaptsevich*
*1st Brigade: Colonel Dmitri Lyapunov IV*
Moskovskii (Moscow) Infantry Regiment
Pskovskii (Pskov) Infantry Regiment

*2nd Brigade: Colonel Aleksey Aigustov*
Libavskii (Libau) Infantry Regiment
Sofiiskii (Sofia) Infantry Regiment

*3rd Brigade: Lieutenant Colonel Nikanor Kashirinov*
11th Jäger Regiment
36th Jäger Regiment

*7th Artillery Brigade: Lieutenant Colonel Danil Devel*
7th Position Battery (12 guns)
12th Light Battery (12 guns)
13th Light Battery (12 guns)


**24TH DIVISION:** *Major General Peter Likhachev I*
*1st Brigade: Major General Ivan Tsybulsky*
Ufimskii (Ufa) Infantry Regiment
Shirvanskii (Shirvan) Infantry Regiment

*2nd Brigade: Colonel Peter Denisyev*
Butyrskii (Butyrsk) Infantry Regiment
Tomskii (Tomsk) Infantry Regiment

*3rd Brigade: Colonel Nikolai Vuich*
19th Jäger Regiment
40th Jäger Regiment

*24th Artillery Brigade: Lieutenant Colonel Ivan Yefremov*
24th Battery Company (12 guns)
45th Light Battery (12 guns)
46th Light Battery (12 guns)

# The Battle of Borodino

**I RESERVE CAVALRY CORPS:** *Lieutenant General Fedor Uvarov*
*1st Brigade: Major General Anton Chalikov*
Life Guard Dragoon Regiment
Life Guard Uhlan Regiment

*2nd Brigade: Major General Vasili Orlov-Denisov*
Life Guard Hussar Regiment
Life Guard Cossack Regiment
Black Sea Guard Cossack Sotnya

*3rd Brigade: Major General Aleksey Vsevolozhsky I*
Yelisavetgradskii (Yelisavetgrad) Hussar Regiment
Nezhinskii (Nezhinsk) Dragoon Regiment

*Artillery*
2nd Horse Artillery Company of the 1st Reserve Artillery Brigade (12 guns)

**II RESERVE CAVALRY CORPS:** *Major General Fedor Korf*
*1st Brigade: Colonel Nikolai Davydov*
Moskovskii (Moscow) Dragoon Regiment
Pskovskii (Pskov) Dragoon Regiment

*2nd Brigade: Major General Semen Panchulidzev II*
Izumskii (Izumsk) Hussar Regiment
Polskii (Polish) Uhlan (Lancer) Regiment

*Artillery*
6th Horse Artillery Company of the 2nd Reserve Artillery Brigade (12 guns)

**III RESERVE CAVALRY CORPS:** *Major General Fedor Korf*
*1st Brigade: Major General Stepan Dyatkov*
Kurlandskii (Courland) Dragoon Regiment
Orenburgskii (Orenburg) Dragoon Regiment

*2nd Brigade: Colonel Baron Cyprian Creitz*
Irkutskii (Irkutsk) Dragoon Regiment
Sibirskii (Siberia) Dragoon Regiment

*3rd Brigade: Major General Ivan Dorokhov*
Mariupolskii (Mariupol) Hussar Regiment
Sumskii (Sumsk) Hussar Regiment

*Artillery*
7th Horse Artillery Company of the 3rd Reserve Artillery Brigade (12 guns)

**IRREGULAR FORCES:** *General of Cavalry Matvei Platov*
*Separate Units*
Ataman Don Cossack Regiment
1st Bug Cossack Regiment
1st Bashkir Cossack Regiment
1st Teptyarsk Cossack Regiment

*1st Brigade: Lieutenant Colonel Maxim Vlasov III*
Adrianov II's Don Cossack Regiment
Chernozubov VIII's Don Cossack Regiment
Vlasov III's Don Cossack Regiment
Perekop Horse Tatar Regiment

*2nd Brigade: Major General Nikolai Ilovaisky V*
Ilovaisky V's Don Cossack Regiment
Grekov XVIII's Don Cossack Regiment

*3rd Brigade: Major General Vasili Denisov VII*
Denisov VII's Don Cossack Regiment
Zhirov's Don Cossack Regiment

*5th Brigade: Major General Dmitri Kuteinikov II*
Kharitonov VII's Don Cossack Regiment
Simferopol Horse Tatar Regiment

*Artillery*
2nd Don Cossack Artillery (12 guns)


**RESERVE ARTILLERY**
*1st Artillery Brigade of the 1st Grenadier Division*
1st Light Company (12 guns)
2nd Light Company (12 guns)
*3rd Artillery Brigade of the 3rd Infantry Division*
5th Light Company (12 guns)
2nd Reserve Artillery Brigade
4th Horse Company (12 guns)
5th Horse Company (12 guns)
29th Battery Company (12 guns)
30th Battery Company (12 guns)
*3rd Reserve Artillery Brigade*
9th Horse Company (12 guns)
10th Horse Company (12 guns)
4th Pontoon Company

*4th Replacement Artillery Brigade*
22nd Horse Company (12 guns)


# 2ND WESTERN ARMY: *General of Infantry Peter Bagration*
**VII INFANTRY CORPS: Lieutenant General Nikolai Rayevsky**
*12TH DIVISION: Major General Illarion Vasilchikov I*
*1st Brigade: Lieutenant Colonel Andrei Bogdanovsky*
Narvskii (Narva) Infantry Regiment
Smolenskii (Smolensk) Infantry Regiment

*2nd Brigade: Colonel Karl Friedrich Pantzerbiter*
Novoingermanlandskii (New Ingermanland) Infantry Regiment
Aleksopolskii (Aleksopol) Infantry Regiment

# The Battle of Borodino

*3rd Brigade: Colonel Andrei Glebov*
6th Jäger Regiment
41st Jäger Regiment

*26TH DIVISION: Major General Ivan Paskevich*
*1st Brigade: Lieutenant Colonel Nikolai Kadyshev*
Nizhegorodskii (Nizhni Novgorod) Infantry Regiment
Orlovskii (Orel) Infantry Regiment

*2nd Brigade: Colonel Yeremei (Geronimo) Savoini*
Ladozhskii (Ladoga) Infantry Regiment
Poltavskii (Poltava) Infantry Regiment

*3rd Brigade: Colonel Fedor Gogel I*
5th Jäger Regiment
42nd Jäger Regiment

*26th Artillery Brigade: Lieutenant Colonel Gustav Shulman II*
26th Battery Company (12 guns)
47th Light Company (12 guns)

**VIII INFANTRY CORPS: Lieutenant General Mikhail Borozdin I**
*2ND GRENADIER DIVISION: Major General Karl von Mecklenburg-Schwerin*
*1st Brigade: Colonel Ivan Shatilov*
Kievskii (Kiev) Grenadier Regiment
Moskovskii (Moscow) Grenadier Regiment

*2nd Brigade: Colonel Ivan Buxhöwden*
Astrakhanskii (Astrakhan) Grenadier Regiment
Fanagoriiskii (Fanagoria) Grenadier Regiment

*3rd Brigade: Colonel Dmitri Levin*
Sibirskii (Siberia) Grenadier Regiment
Malorossiiskii (Little Russia) Grenadier Regiment

*2nd Artillery Brigade: Colonel Alexander Boguslavsky*
11th Battery Company (12 guns)
*Division* of the 21st Light Company (4 guns)

*27TH DIVISION: Major General Dmitri Neverovsky*
*1st Brigade: Colonel Maxim Stavitsky II*
Odesskii (Odessa) Infantry Regiment
Tarnopolskii (Tarnopol) Infantry Regiment

*2nd Brigade: Colonel Alexander Knyazhnin I*
Vilenskii (Vilna) Infantry Regiment
Simbirskii (Simbirsk) Infantry Regiment

*3rd Brigade: Colonel Alexei Voyeikov of the Life Guard Preobrazhenskii Regiment*
49th Jäger Regiment
50th Jäger Regiment

# Appendices

*Artillery*
32nd Battery Company (12 guns of the 3rd Reserve Artillery Brigade)

## 2ND COMBINED GRENADIER DIVISION: Major General Mikhail Vorontsov
*1st Brigade*
1st Combined Grenadier Battalion of the 7th Division.
2nd Combined Grenadier Battalion of the 7th Division.
1st Combined Grenadier Battalion of the 24th Division
2nd Combined Grenadier Battalion of the 24th Division

*2nd Brigade*
1st Combined Grenadier Battalion of the 2nd Grenadier Division
2nd Combined Grenadier Battalion of the 2nd Grenadier Division
1st Combined Grenadier Battalion of the 12th Division
2nd Combined Grenadier Battalion of the 12th Division
2nd Combined Grenadier Battalion of the 26th Division
1st Combined Grenadier Battalion of the 27th Division
2nd Combined Grenadier Battalion of the 27th Division

*Artillery*
1st Don Horse Company (12 guns)

## ARTILLERY ATTACHED TO THE VIII CORPS
*1st Brigade*
3rd Battery Company (12 guns)

*3rd Brigade*
Half Company of the 1st Battery Company (6 guns)
3rd Reserve Artillery Brigade
31st Battery Company (12 guns)

## CAVALRY OF THE 2ND WESTERN ARMY: Lieutenant General Dmitri Golitsyn V
### 2ND CUIRASSIER DIVISION: Major General Ilya Duka II
*1st Brigade: Major General Nikolai Kretov*
Yekaterinoslavskii (Yekaterinoslavl) Cuirassier Regiment
Voyennogo Ordena (Military Order) Cuirassier Regiment

*2nd Brigade: Colonel Mikhail Tolbuzin I*
Glukhovskii (Glukhov) Cuirassier Regiment
Malorossiskii (Little Russia) Cuirassier Regiment
Novgorodskii (Novgorod) Cuirassier Regiment

### IV RESERVE CAVALRY CORPS: Major General Karl Sievers I
*1st Brigade: Major General Ivan Panchulidzev I*
Kharkovskii (Kharkov) Dragoon Regiment
Chernigovskii (Chernigov) Dragoon Regiment

*2nd Brigade: Colonel Yegor Emmanuel*

# The Battle of Borodino

Kievskii (Kiev) Dragoon Regiment
Novorossiiskii (Novorossiisk) Dragoon Regiment

*3rd Brigade: Colonel Dmitri Vasilchikov II*
Akhtyrskskii (Akhtyrsk) Hussar Regiment
Litovskii (Lithuanian) Uhlan Regiment

*Artillery*
8th Horse Company (12 guns of the 3d Reserve Artillery Brigade)

*IRREGULAR TROOPS OF THE 2ND WESTERN ARMY: Major General
Akim Karpov II*
*Cossack Forces*
Bykhalov I's Don Cossack Regiment
Grekov XXI's Don Cossack Regiment
Ilovaisky X's Don Cossack Regiment
Ilovaisky XI's Don Cossack Regiment
Karpov II's Don Cossack Regiment
Komissarov I's Don Cossack Regiment
Melnikov IV's Don Cossack Regiment
Sysoyev III's Don Cossack Regiment

*ARTILLERY RESERVE OF THE 2ND WESTERN ARMY*
*12th Artillery Brigade (of the 12th Division)*
12th Battery Company (12 guns)
22nd Light Company (12 guns)
23rd Light Company (12 guns)

*2nd Artillery Brigade (of the 2nd Grenadier Division)*
20th Light Company (12 guns)
21st Light Company (8 guns)

*23rd Artillery Brigade (of the 23rd Division)*
23rd Battery Company (12 guns)

*26th Artillery Brigade (of the 26th Division)*
48th Light Company (12 guns)

*3rd Reserve Artillery Brigade*
4th Pontoon Company

*Engineer Troops*
Zotov's Pioneer Company of the 2nd Pioneer Regiment.

OPOLCHENYE FORCES
*MOSCOW OPOLCHENYE: Lieutenant General Irakly Morkov*
*1st Division*
1st Jäger Regiment (4 Battalions, armed with muskets)
4th Dismounted Cossack Regiment (armed with pikes)
6th Dismounted Cossack Regiment (armed with pikes)

*2nd Division*
7th Dismounted Cossack Regiment (armed with pikes)

# Appendices

*3rd Division*
2nd Jäger Regiment (armed with muskets)
3rd Jäger Regiment (armed with muskets)
1st Dismounted Cossack Regiment (armed with muskets)
3rd Dismounted Cossack Regiment (armed with pikes)

*Militia*
Troops of Vereya and Volokolamsk *uezds*

**SMOLENSK OPOLCHENYE: Lieutenant General Nikolai Lebedev**
Opolchenye of the Belsk, Vyazma, Gzhatsk, Dorogobuzh, Dukhovo, Yelna, Krasnyi, Roslavl, Smolensk, Sychev and Yukhnov *uezds*

# THE ALLIED ARMY AT BORODINO
## COMMANDER-IN-CHIEF: *Emperor Napoleon I*
## *IMPERIAL GUARD*
**Young Guard Infantry: Marshal Eduard Adolph Mortier**
*A brigade of Delaborde's Division: General of Brigade Pierre Berthezene*
4th Voltigeurs
4th Tirailleurs
5th Voltigeurs

*2ND GUARD DIVISION: General of Division François Roguet*
*1st Brigade: General of Brigade Jean Pierre Lanabere*
1st Guard Tirailleur Regiment
1st Guard Voltigeur Regiment

*2nd Brigade: General of Brigade Boyeldieu*
Fusilier Chasseur Regiment
Fusilier Grenadier Regiment

*Artillery: Colonel Villeneuve*
3rd Foot Artillery of the Young Guard (8 guns)
2nd Company of the Guard Artillery Train Battalion

*VISTULA LEGION: General of Division Michel Claparède*
1st Vistula Regiment
2nd Vistula Regiment
3rd Vistula Regiment
13th Company of the 8th Foot Artillery (6 guns)
Reserve Artillery: General of Brigade Henri Marie Noury
3rd Foot Artillery of the Old Guard (8 guns)
Detachment of the 1st Guard Artillery Train Battalion
5th and 7th Foot Batteries of the Prussian Artillery Brigade (without guns)

**OLD GUARD INFANTRY: Marshal François Joseph Lefebvre**
*3RD GUARD DIVISION: General of Division Philibert Curial*
*1st Brigade: General of Brigade Boyer*
1st Chasseur à Pied
2nd Chasseur à Pied

# The Battle of Borodino

Artillery:
1st Foot Artillery the Old Guard (8 guns)
2nd Foot Artillery of the Young Guard (8 guns)

*2nd Brigade: General of Brigade Claude Michel*
1st Grenadier à Pied
2nd Grenadier à Pied
3rd Grenadier à Pied
Artillery:
2nd Foot Artillery of the Old Guard (8 guns)
1st Foot Artillery of the Young Guard (8 guns)
4th Company of the 2nd Guard Artillery Train Battalion
Detachment of the 1st Guard Artillery Train Battalion
Detachments of the 4th and 7th Artillery Train Battalions

**GUARD CAVALRY: Marshal Jean Baptiste Bessières**
*GUARD CAVALRY DIVISION: General of Division Frederick Walther*
*1st Brigade: General of Division Charles Lefevbre-Desnouettes*
Guard Chasseur à Cheval Regiment
Mamluk Company

*2nd Brigade: General of Division Raymond Saint-Sulpice*
Empress Guard Dragoon Regiment

*3rd Brigade: General of Division Frederick Walther*
Grenadier à Cheval Regiment

*4th Brigade: General of Brigade Vincent Krasinski*
1st Chevau-léger Lancier de la Garde Regiment (Polish)

*5th Brigade: General of Brigade Edouard Colbert-Chabanais*
2nd Chevau-léger Lancier de la Garde Regiment (Dutch)

*6th Brigade: General of Division Antoine Durosnel*
Gendarmerie d'Élite

*Artillery*
1st Horse Artillery of the Old Guard (6 guns)
2nd Horse Artillery of the Old Guard (6 guns)
Detachment of the 2nd Guard Artillery Train Battalion
Detachment of the 7th Artillery Train Battalion.

**GUARD ARTILLERY RESERVE: *General of Division Jean Sorbier***
*Foot Artillery: Colonel Antoine Drouot*
4th Company of the Old Guard (8 guns)
5th Company of the Old Guard (8 guns)
6th Company of the Old Guard (9 guns)
Detachment of the 1st Guard Artillery Train Battalion
Detachment of the 2nd Guard Artillery Train Battalion

*Horse Artillery: General of Brigade Desvaux de St Maurice*
3rd Company of the Old Guard ( 6 guns)
4th Company of the Old Guard (6 guns)

# Appendices

*Guard Engineer Park: General of Brigade François Kirgener*
Sapper Company of the Old Guard
Detachment of Guard Marines
6th Company of the Guard Marines
7th Company of the Guard Marines


# I CORPS: *Marshal Louis Nicolas Davout*
## 1ST DIVISION: *General of Division Charles Morand*
*1st Brigade: General of Brigade d'Alton*
13th Light

*2nd Brigade: General of Brigade Pierre Gratien*
17th Line
3rd Brigade: General of Brigade Charles August Bonnamy
30th Line

*Artillery: Captain Beroville*
1st Company of the 7th Foot Artillery (8 guns)
7th Company of the 1st Horse Artillery (6 guns)
1st and 2nd companies of 1st Principal Train Battalion

*Auxiliary*
6th Company of the 3rd Sapper Battalion
1st Company of the 12th Battalion of Military Equipage.

## 2ND DIVISION: *General of Division Louis Friant*
1st Brigade: General of Brigade François Dufour
15th Light

*2nd Brigade: General of Brigade Antoine van Dedem de Gelder*
33rd Line

*3rd Brigade: Colonel Joseph Groisne*
48th Line
2nd and 3rd Battalions of the Joseph Napoleon (Spanish) Regiment

*Artillery: Chef de Bataillon Cabrie*
2nd Company of the 7th Foot Artillery (8 guns)
5th Company of the 3rd Horse Artillery (6 guns)
4th and 6th companies of the 9th Train (bis) Battalion.

*Auxiliary*
5th Company of the 5th Sapper Battalion
4th Company of the 12th Battalion of Military Equipage.

## 3RD DIVISION: *General of Division Etienne Maurice Gérard*
*1st Brigade: General of Brigade Leclerc des Essarts*
7th Light

*2nd Brigade: Colonel Henri-Aloyse-Ignace Baudinot*
12th Line

# The Battle of Borodino

*3rd Brigade: General of Brigade Etienne Maurice Gérard*
21st Line
127th Line (2 battalions and 2 light guns) and 1st Mecklenburg Battalion served as escort of parks of the I Corps and did not participate in battle.

*Artillery: Colonel Christophe Pelgrin*
3rd Company of the 7th Foot Artillery (8 guns)
4th Company of the 3rd Horse Artillery (6 guns)
7th and 4th companies of the 1st Principal Train Battalion
1st and 4th companies of the 1st Train Battalion

*Auxiliary*
9th Company of the 5th Sapper Battalion
1st and 3rd Companies of the 12th Battalion of Military Equipage.


**4TH DIVISION:** *General of Division Joseph Marie Dessaix*
*1st Brigade: General of Brigade Jean Friederichs*
85th Line

*2nd Brigade: General of Brigade François-Joseph Leguay*
108th Line
2nd Battalion of Hesse-Darmstadt 'Leib' Regiment [553]

*Artillery: Chef de Bataillon Thevenot*
9th Company of the 7th Foot Artillery (8 guns)
2nd Company of the 5th Horse Artillery (6 guns)
3rd and 6th companies of the 1st Train Battalion

*Auxiliary*
3rd Company of the 2nd Sapper Battalion
4th Company of the 12th Battalion of Military Equipage


**5TH DIVISION:** *General of Division Jean Dominique Compans*
*1st Brigade: General of Brigade Jean Duppelin*
25th Line

*2nd Brigade: General of Brigade François Antoine Teste*
57th Line

*3rd Brigade: General of Brigade Pierre Jules Guyardet*
61st Line

*4th Brigade: General of Brigade Louis Lonchamp*
111th Line

*Artillery: Chef de Bataillon Klie*
2nd Company of the 6th Horse Artillery (6 guns)
16th Company of the 7th Foot Artillery (8 guns)
2nd and 4th companies of the 9th Principal Train Battalion

*Auxiliary*
5th Company of the 3rd Sapper Battalion
3rd and 5th companies of the 12th Military Equipage Battalion

238

# Appendices

*Artillery Reserve*
3rd Company of the 1st Foot Artillery (8 guns)
17th Company of the 1st Foot Artillery (8 guns)
6th Company of the 7th Foot Artillery (8 guns)

*Artillery Park*
1st, 5th and 6th companies of the 1st Train Battalion
Engineer Park: Chef de Bataillon Proust
8th Company of the 5th Sapper Battalion
5 companies of the 9th Train
5 companies of the 12th Battalion of Military Equipage.

**LIGHT CAVALRY: *General of Brigade Alexandre Louis Girardin
d'Ermenonville – attached to the I Cavalry Corps***
*1st Light Cavalry Brigade: General of Brigade Girardin d'Ermenonville
(624 men)*
2nd Chasseurs
9th Polish Lancer Regiment

*2nd Light Cavalry Brigade: General of Brigade Etienne Bordessoulle
(454 men)*
1st Chasseurs
3rd Chasseurs

## III CORPS: Marshal Michel Ney
**10TH DIVISION: *General of Division François Ledru des Essarts***
*1st Brigade: General of Brigade Louis Thomas Gengoult*
24th Light
1st Portuguese Line

*2nd Brigade: General of Brigade Charles-Stanislas Marion*
46th Line

*3rd Brigade: General of Brigade Jean Baptiste Bruny*
72nd Line

*Artillery: Chef de Bataillon Ragmey*
12th Company of the 5th Foot Artillery (8 guns)
5th Company of the 6th Horse Artillery (6 guns)

*Auxiliary*
1st and 2nd companies of the 6th Principal Train Battalion
7th Company of the 3rd Sapper Battalion

**11TH DIVISION: *General of Division Jean Razout***
*1st Brigade: General of Brigade Claude-Antoine Compère*
2nd Portuguese Line

*2nd Brigade: General of Brigade Joseph Antoine Joubert*
18th Line
4th Line

# The Battle of Borodino

*3rd Brigade: General of Brigade François d'Henin*
93rd Line

*Artillery: Chef de Bataillon Bernard*
18th Company of the 5th Foot Artillery (8 guns)
6th Company of the 5th Horse Artillery (6 guns)

*Auxiliary*
1st and 3rd companies of the 6th Principal Train Battalion
9th Company of the 3rd Sapper Battalion

**25TH (WÜRTTEMBERG) DIVISION:** *General of Division Jean Gabriel Marchand*
Temporary Württemberg Infantry Regiment
1. Bataillon (Leichten Infanterie-Brigade)
1. Kompagnie (FußJäger König)
2. Kompagnie (FußJäger No. 2)
3. Kompagnie (1. Leichtes Infanterie-Bataillon)
4. Kompagnie (2. Leichtes Infanterie-Bataillon)
2. Bataillon (1. Infanterie-Brigade)
1. Kompagnie (1. Bataillon, Regiment No. 1)
2. Kompagnie (2. Bataillon, Regiment No. 1)
3. Kompagnie (1. Bataillon, Regiment No. 4)
4. Kompagnie (2. Bataillon, Regiment No. 4)
3. Bataillon (2. Infanterie-Brigade)
1. Kompagnie (1. Bataillon, Regiment No. 2)
2. Kompagnie (2. Bataillon, Regiment No. 2)
3. Kompagnie (1. Bataillon, Regiment No. 6)
4. Kompagnie (2. Bataillon, Regiment No. 6)
1st Württemberg Foot Artillery (6 guns)
2nd Württemberg Foot Artillery (6 guns)
1st Württemberg Horse Artillery (4 guns)

**LIGHT CAVALRY**
*9th Light Cavalry Brigade: General of Brigade Pierre Mourier*
11th (Dutch) Hussars
6th Chevau-léger Lanciers
4th Württemberg Chasseurs of the King

*14th Light Cavalry Brigade: General of Brigade Frederick Beurmann*
4th Chasseurs à Cheval
28th Chasseurs à Cheval
1st Württemberg Chevau-léger
2nd Württemberg Chevau-léger
2nd Württemberg Horse Artillery (6 guns)

**RESERVE ARTILLERY AND PARKS:** *Colonel Marie Claude Bernard Verrier*
*Artillery*
16th Company of the 1st Foot Artillery (8 guns)
Württemberg Reserve Battery (5 guns)

# Appendices

Württemberg Regimental Artillery (12 guns)
Artillery Park:
4th and 5th companies of the 6th Artillery Train Battalion

*Engineer Park*
3rd Company of the 1st Sapper Battalion
6th Company of Engineer Train
8th Company of the 1st Pontoon Battalion
5th Company of Artillery Artisans


## IV CORPS: *Prince Eugène de Beauharnais, Viceroy of Italy*
### 13TH DIVISION: *General of Division Alexis Joseph Delzons*
*1st Brigade: General of Brigade Huard de St Aubin*
8th Light
84th Line
1st Provisional Croat Regiment

*2nd Brigade: General of Brigade Louis Auguste Plauzonne*
92nd Line
106th Line

*Artillery: Chef de bataillion Demay*
9th Company of the 2nd Foot Artillery (8 guns)
2nd Company of the 4th Horse Artillery (6 guns)
2nd and 3rd companies of the 7th Train Battalion

*Auxiliary*
7th Company of the 1st Sapper Battalion

### 14TH DIVISION: *General of Division Jean Baptiste Broussier*
*1st Brigade: General of Brigade Bertrand de Sivray*
18th Light
53rd Line
1st and 4th Battalions of Joseph Napoleon (Spanish) Regiment

*2nd Brigade: General of Brigade Louis Alméras*
9th Line
35th Line

*Artillery: Chef de Bataillon Hermann*
7th Company of the 2nd Foot Artillery (8 guns)
3rd Company of the 4th Horse Artillery (6 guns)
1st and 6th companies of the 7th Train Battalion

*Auxiliary*
2nd Company of the 1st Sapper Battalion
Italian Royal Guard: General of Brigade Lechi
Infantry Brigade: General of Brigade Lechi
Royal Vélites
Guard Infantry Regiment
Guard Conscript Regiment

# The Battle of Borodino

*Cavalry Brigade: General of Brigade Joseph Triaire*
1st to 5th companies of the Gardes d'Honneur
Guard Dragoon Regiment
Queen's Dragoon Regiment
Artillery: Chef de Bataillon Clément
1st Italian Foot Artillery (6 guns)
2nd Italian Foot Artillery (6 guns)
1st Italian Horse Artillery (6 guns)
1st and 2nd companies of Italian Guard Artillery Train
2nd Company of Italian Guard Artisans

*Auxiliary*
1st Company of the 1st Italian Sapper Battalion
Italian Guard Marines

**CORPS CAVALRY:** *General of Division Philippe Antoine Ornano*
*12th Light Cavalry Brigade: General of Brigade Claude-Raymond Guyon*
9th Chasseurs à Cheval
19th Chasseurs à Cheval

*13th Light Cavalry Brigade: General of Brigade Giovanni Villata von Villatburg*
2nd Italian Chasseurs à Cheval
3rd Italian Chasseurs à Cheval

**BAVARIAN CAVALRY DIVISION:** *Major General Maximillian Joseph von Preysing-Moos*
*21st Light Cavalry Brigade: Major General von Seydewitz*
3rd Bavarian Chevau-léger Kron-prinz
6th Bavarian Chevau-léger Bubenhofen

*22nd Light Cavalry Brigade: Major General Maximillian Joseph von Preysing-Moos*
4th Bavarian Chevau-léger
5th Bavarian Chevau-léger

*Artillery Brigade*
1st Bavarian Horse Artillery (6 guns)

**RESERVE ARTILLERY**
5th Company of the 2nd Foot Artillery
12th Company of the 2nd Foot Artillery
2nd Company of 1st Italian Foot Artillery
7th Company of 1st Italian Foot Artillery

*Auxiliary*
5th Company and Detachment of 7th Train (bis) Battalion
5th and 6th companies and Detachment of the 9th Italian Train Battalion
1st Company and detachment of the 2nd and 6th companies of the 9th Battalion of Military Equipage.
1st Company of the 2nd Pontoon Battalion
1st and 3rd companies of the 1st Italian Battalion of Military Equipage.

# Appendices

**V CORPS:** *General of Division Prince Józef Poniatowski*
**16TH DIVISION:** *General of Division Isidor Krasinski*
*1st Brigade: General of Brigade Krasinski*
3rd Polish Line
15th Polish Line

*2nd Brigade: General of Brigade Franciszek Paszkowski*
16th Polish Line

*Artillery: Chef de Bataillon Sowinski*
3rd Polish Foot Artillery Company (6 guns)
12th Polish Foot Artillery Company (6 guns)
3rd Company of the Polish Artillery Train Battalion

*Auxiliary*
1st Company of the Polish Sapper Battalion
Detachment Polish Artillery Artisan Company

**18TH DIVISION:** *General of Division Charles Kniaziewicz*
*1st Brigade: General of Brigade Beganski*
2nd Polish Line
8th Polish Line

*2nd Brigade: General of Brigade Pototzki*
12th Polish Line

*Artillery: Chef de Bataillon Ushinski*
4th Polish Foot Artillery Company (6 guns)
5th Polish Foot Artillery Company (6 guns)
2nd Company of the Polish Artillery Train Battalion

*Auxiliary*
A Company of Polish Sapper Battalion

**CORPS CAVALRY:** *General of Division Kaminski*
*18th Light Cavalry Brigade: General of Brigade Joseph Niemojewski*
4th Polish Chasseurs à Cheval

*19th Light Cavalry Brigade: General of Brigade Tadeus Tyskiewicz*
1st Polish Chasseurs à Cheval
12th Polish Lancer Regiment

*20th Light Cavalry Brigade: General of Brigade Prince Antoine Sulkowski*
5th Polish Chasseurs à Cheval
13th Polish Hussars

**RESERVE ARTILLERY:** *Colonel Antoine Górski*
2nd Polish Horse Artillery Company (6 guns)
14th Polish Foot Artillery Company (6 guns)
Polish Regimental Artillery (3 guns)

*Auxiliary*
4th and 5th of the Polish Artillery Train Battalion
One Company of Polish Pontonniers
Two companies of Polish Sapper Battalion
4 companies of Polish Battalion of Military Equipage.


## VIII CORPS: *General of Division Andoche Junot*
### 23RD INFANTRY DIVISION: *General of Division Jean-Victor Tharreau*
*1st Brigade: General of Brigade François Auguste Damas*
3rd (Westphalian) Light Battalion
2nd (Westphalian) Line
6th (Westphalian) Line

*2nd Brigade: General of Brigade Karl Heinrich von Borstel*
2nd (Westphalian) Light Battalion
3rd (Westphalian) Line
7th (Westphalian) Line

*Artillery: Captain Frede*
1st Westphalian Foot (8 guns)
1st Westphalian Artillery Train Company


### 24TH INFANTRY DIVISION: *General of Division Adam Ludwig von Ochs*
*1st Brigade: General of Brigade Edouard Legras*
Westphalian Guard Grenadiers Battalion
Westphalian Guard Jäger Battalion
Westphalian Jäger-Carabinier Battalion
1st (Westphalian) Light Battalion

*Artillery: Captain Lamaitre*
2nd Westphalian Foot (8 guns)
Westphalian Guard Horse Artillery Battery (4 guns)
3rd Westphalian Train Company.


### CORPS CAVALRY: *General of Brigade Hans Georg von Hammerstein-Equord*
*24th Light Cavalry Brigade: General of Brigade von Hammerstein-Equord*
1st Westphalian Hussars
2nd Westphalian Hussars

*Guard Cavalry Brigade: General of Brigade Marc François Wolf*
Westphalian Chevau-léger Regiment of the Guard

*Artillery*
Westphalian Guard Horse Artillery Battery (2 guns).
Artillery Park: Chef de battailon Schulz
Detachment of Westphalian reserve artillery (no guns)
4th Westphalian Train Company
Westphalian sapper Company

# Appendices

Detachment of Westphalian Artillery Artisans
Detachment of Westphalian Military Equipage
Detachment of Westphalian gendarmerie.

## CAVALRY RESERVE: Marshal Joachim Murat, King of Naples
**1st RESERVE CAVALRY CORPS: General of Division Etienne-Marie-Antoine-Champion Nansouty**
### 1ST LIGHT CAVALRY DIVISION: General of Division Pierre Joseph Bruyères
*3rd Light Cavalry Brigade: General of Brigade Claude-Charles Jacquinot*
7th Hussar Regiment
9th Chevau-léger Regiment

*4th Light Cavalry Brigade: General of Brigade Hippolyte-Marie-Guillaume Pire*
16th Chasseurs à Cheval Regiment
8th Hussar Regiment

*15th Light Cavalry Brigade: General of Brigade Joseph Nienwieski*
6th Polish Lancer Regiment
8th Polish Lancer Regiment
2nd Combined Prussian Hussar Regiment
Brandenburg Hussar Regiment No. 3 (3rd & 4th Squadrons)
Pomeranian Hussar Regiment No. 5 (1st & 3rd Squadrons)

*Artillery*
7th Company of the 6th Horse Artillery (6 guns)

### 1ST CUIRASSIER DIVISION: General of Division Antoine Louis St Germaine
*1st Brigade: General of Brigade Adrien-François Bruno*
2nd Cuirassier Regiment

*2nd Brigade: General of Brigade Bertrand Bessières*
3rd Cuirassier Regiment

*3rd Brigade: General of Brigade Mathieu Quenot*
9th Cuirassier Regiment
1st Squadron of the1st Chevau-léger Regiment

*Artillery*
1st Company of the 5th Horse Artillery (6 guns)
3rd Company of the 5th Horse Artillery (6 guns)

### 5TH CUIRASSIER DIVISION: General of Division Valence de Timbrune de Thiembronne
*1st Brigade: General of Brigade Nicolas Reynaud*
6th Cuirassier Regiment

*2nd Brigade: General of Brigade Pierre-François-Marie-Auguste Dejean*
11th Cuirassier Regiment

*3rd Brigade: General of Brigade Armand-Charles-Louis de Lagrange le Lievre*
12th Cuirassier Regiment
1st Squadron of the 5th Chevau-léger Regiment

*Artillery*
4th Company of the 5th Horse Artillery (6 guns)
5th Company of the 5th Horse Artillery (6 guns)

**II RESERVE CAVALRY CORPS: General of Division Louis-Pierre Montbrun**
*2ND LIGHT CAVALRY DIVISION: General of Division Claude Pierre Pajol*
*7th Light Brigade: Colonel Desirat*
11th Chasseur à Cheval Regiment
12th Chasseur à Cheval Regiment

*8th Light Brigade: General of Brigade Andre Burthe*
5th Hussar Regiment
9th Hussar Regiment

*16th Light Brigade: General of Brigade Jacques-Gervais Subervie*
3rd Württemberg Jäger zu Pferd
1st Combined Prussian Lancer Regiment
Silesian Lancer Regiment No. 2 (3rd & 4th Squadrons)
Brandenburg Lancer Regiment No. 3 (3rd & 4th Squadrons)
10th Polish Hussar Regiment

*Artillery*
1st Company of the 4th Horse Artillery (6 guns)

*2ND CUIRASSIER DIVISION: General of Division Pierre Wathier (de Saint Alphonse)*
*1st Brigade: General of Brigade Louis-Chrétien Beaumont*
5th Cuirassier Regiment

*2nd Brigade: General of Brigade Jean Louis Richter*
8th Cuirassier Regiment

*3rd Brigade: General of Brigade Joseph-Philippe Dornes*
10th Cuirassier Regiment
1st Squadron of the 2nd Chevau-léger Regiment

*Artillery*
1st Company of the 2nd Horse Artillery (6 guns)
4th Company of 2nd Horse Artillery (6 guns)

*4TH CUIRASSIER DIVISION: General of Division Jean-Marie Antoine Defrance*
*1st Brigade: General of Brigade Louis-Claude Chouard*
1st Carabinier Regiment

# Appendices

*2nd Brigade: General of Brigade Pierre-Louis-François Paultre de Lamotte*
2nd Carabinier Regiment

*3rd Brigade: General of Brigade Joseph Bouvier des Eclaz*
1st Cuirassier Regiment
4th Squadron of the 4th Chevau-léger Regiment

*Artillery*
3rd Company of the 1st Horse Artillery (6 guns)
4th Company of the 1st Horse Artillery (6 guns)

**III RESERVE CAVALRY CORPS: General of Division Emmanuel Grouchy**
*3RD LIGHT CAVALRY DIVISION: General of Division Louis-Pierre-Aimé Chastel*
*11th Light Brigade: General of Brigade Pierre-Edme Gauthrin*
6th Hussar Regiment
8th Chasseur à Cheval Regiment

*10th Light Brigade: General of Brigade François-Joseph Gérard*
6th Chasseur à Cheval Regiment
25th Chasseur à Cheval Regiment

*17th Light Brigade: General of Brigade Jean Baptiste Dommanget*
1st Bavarian Chevau-léger Regiment
2nd Bavarian Chevau-léger Regiment
Saxon Prinz Albrecht Chevau-lèger Regiment

*Artillery*
6th Company of the 6th Horse Artillery (6 guns)

*6TH HEAVY CAVALRY DIVISION: General of Division Armand Lebrun La Houssaye*
*1st Brigade: General of Brigade Nicolas-Marin Thiry*
7th Dragoon Regiment
23rd Dragoon Regiment

*2nd Brigade: General of Brigade Denis-Etienne Seron*
28th Dragoon Regiment
30th Dragoon Regiment

*Artillery*
4th Company of the 6th Horse Artillery (6 guns)
5th Company of the 6th Horse Artillery (6 guns)

**IV RESERVE CAVALRY CORPS: General of Division Marie-Victor-Nicolas de Fay de Latour-Maubourg**
*4TH LIGHT CAVALRY DIVISION: General of Division Alexander Rozniecki*
*29th Light Brigade: General of Brigade Kazimierz Turno*
3rd Polish Lancer Regiment
15th Polish Lancer Regiment
16th Polish Lancer Regiment

*Artillery*
3rd Polish Horse Artillery (6 guns)
4th Polish Horse Artillery (6 guns)

## 7TH CUIRASSIER DIVISION: General of Division Jean-Thomas-Guillaume Lorge

*1st Brigade: Generalmajor Johann Adolf von Thielemann*
Zastrow Cuirassier Regiment
Saxon Gardes du Corps
14th Polish Cuirassier Regiment

*2nd Brigade: General of Brigade Helmut Auguste von Lepel*
1st Westphalian Cuirassier Regiment
2nd Westphalian Cuirassier Regiment

*Artillery*
2nd Westphalian Horse Battery (6 guns)
2nd Saxon Horse Battery von Hiller (6 guns)

# Glossary

━━━━◅(●)▻━━━━

| | |
|---|---|
| Abatis: | An obstacle or barricade of trees, often with bent or sharpened branches directed toward an enemy. |
| Auxiliary: | Non-combatant, support, troops. |
| Bataillon de Guerre: | Active battalion in a French regiment. |
| Brigade: | Military unit consisting of two or more regiments. |
| Brustwehr: | A defensive wall or elevation in a fortification. |
| Cantinière: | Female camp-follower selling food and drink to the troops. |
| Carabinier(s): | Mounted trooper armed with a carbine. |
| Chasseur(s) à Cheval: | In the French Army, a light cavalryman. |
| Chasseur(s) à Pied: | In the French Army, a light infantryman. |
| Chef d'Escadrons: | French military rank, in charge of two squadrons. |
| Chef de Bataillon: | French military rank, in charge of a battalion. |
| Chef(s): | In the Russian Army, a colonel-proprietor in charge of a regiment. |
| Chevau(x)-Léger: | In the French Army, light cavalry units, often Polish. |
| Company: | Tactical unit, part of a battalion. |
| Corps: | Self-contained military operational unit consisting of two or more infantry and cavalry divisions, with artillery and engineer forces. |
| Corps de Bataille: | At Borodino, *ad hoc* Russian military component that included two corps, e.g. *corps de bataille* of Gorchakov and of Miloradovich. |
| Cossack(s): | Irregular cavalry force in the Russian Army, famous for their harassing tactics. |
| Cuirassier(s): | Heavy cavalryman protected by an iron breastplate (cuirass). |
| Division: | Military unit consisting of two or more brigades. |
| Dragoon(s): | Heavy cavalryman armed with a short musket. |
| Ekipazh/Equipage: | Russian military unit established from the crews of the Imperial court's yacht and galleys in St Petersburg in 1810. |
| État Major: | General Staff of the French Army. |
| Fascine: | A long bundle of sticks bound together, used in building earthworks and in strengthening ramparts. |
| Flèche(s): | Small V-shaped military fortification. |
| Flügel Adjutant: | Special rank granted by the Russian Emperor to staff and junior officers of the imperial suite. |
| Fusilier(s): | Soldier armed with a light flintlock musket called a *fusil*. |
| Gendarmerie: | Military body charged with police duties. |
| General-proviantmaster: | In the Russian Army, an official in charge of supplies and forage. |
| Grand Equerry: | Master of the Horse, one of the Great Officers of the French court, in charge of the royal or imperial stables. |
| Grenadier(s) à Cheval: | Mounted grenadiers. |
| Grenadier(s) à Pied: | Foot grenadiers. |
| Grenadier(s): | Originally, a specialized assault soldier who would throw grenades and storm breaches; by early 19th century, élite troops drawn from veterans and noted for their size and discipline. |
| Horse Artillery: | Artillery drawn by horses, which allowed for higher manoeuvrability. |
| Howitzer: | Type of artillery piece with a relatively short barrel, used to propel large projectiles at medium velocities over a curved trajectory. |
| Hussar(s): | Light cavalryman, armed with sabre and dressed in an elaborate short cloak. |

249

# The Battle of Borodino

Imperial Guard:      Napoleon's élite military formation.

Jäger(s):      Light infantry, often employed to skirmish ahead of the main infantry lines, and harass and delay the enemy advance.

Leib:      In the Russian Army, a term indicating unit's special status, i.e. Leib-Grenadier or Leib-Cuirassier Regiments; used as "Leib-Gvardii" for élite Guard units.

Licorne:      In the Russian Army, a type of cannon that combined characteristics of howitzer and cannon.

Lieue:      French unit of measurement equal to an English league or 2.4 miles.

Lunette:      A wide-V shaped fortification with two projecting shoulders.

Musketeer(s):      Infantryman armed with a musket; in the Russian army, a generic term for infantry units until 1811.

Nagaika:      A short, thick whip with round cross-section used by Cossacks.

Old Guard:      Napoleon's élite unit, part of the Imperial Guard.

Opolchenye(s):      In the Russian Army, a militia force that was recruited in provinces.

Opisaniye:      Title of the official account of the Battle of Borodino written by Karl Toll

Palisade:      A fence of pales or stakes set firmly in the ground for enclosure or defence.

Peloton:      Tactical unit within a company or squadron.

Pioneer(s):      Combat engineers.

Pontoon:      Flat-bottomed boat or a float used to cross water obstacles.

Pontonnier(s):      Combat engineers used to construct crossings over the bodies of water.

Pud:      Russian measurement of weight, equal to 16.4 kg or 36.2 pounds.

Redan:      French term for a V-shaped fortification.

Redoubt:      Military fortification consisting of an enclosed defensive emplacement.

Rezervnii:      In the Russian Army, a reserve unit.

Rotmistr:      In the Russian cavalry, a rank of the 9th class (in the Guard cavalry – 7th class), equal to a captain in the infantry.

Roubles:      Russian currency.

Sapper(s):      Combat engineer(s).

Sazhen:      Russian measurement of length equal to 3m or 7 feet.

Shantsy:      Old Russian term for a fortification.

Sotnya:      A Cossack unit, literally meaning 'one hundred.'

Sous-Lieutenant:      French junior officer rank.

Sub Lieutenant:      Russian junior officer rank of the 13th class in regular infantry (in guard – 10th class; in artillery - 12th class), below a lieutenant.

Tartar(s):      Collective name applied to the Turkic speaking people within the Russian Empire.

Tirailleur(s):      Sharpshooters, light infantry trained to skirmish ahead of the main forces.

Toises:      French measurement of length equal to 1.94m or 2.13 yards.

Uezds:      Russian administrative unit.

Uhlan(s):      Light cavalrymen armed with lances and known for their double breasted jackets (*kurtka*) and a square topped Polish lancer cap (*czapka*).

Versta:      Russian measurement of length, equal to 1,066m or 3,500 feet.

Vzvod:      In the Russian Army, a tactical unit (platoon) within a company (which contained two *vzvods*) or a squadron (which contained four *vzvods*). Each *vzvod* was sub-divided into two half-vzvods (*poluvzvod*). In the Russian artillery, a *vzvod* contained two guns and six *vzvods* formed a battery.

Young Guard:      Napoleon's élite unit, part of the Imperial Guard.

Zapasnoi:      In the Russian Army, a replacement unit.

# Notes and Sources

1. L. Beskrovny, *Otechestvennaia voina 1812 g. i kontrnastuplenia Kutuzova*, (Moscow, 1951), 66.
2. N. Garnich, *1812 god*, (Moscow, 1956), 181.
3. V. Pugachev and V. Dines, *Istoriki, izbravshie put Galilea: statii, ocherki*, (Saratov, 1995), 137. Also see *Rodina* 6–7 (1992): 172.
4. N. Ryazanov, 'M.I. Kutuzov i ego pisma,' in *Kutuzov M.I.: pisma, zapiski*, (Moscow, 1989), 554; B.Abalikhin and V. Dunayevsky, *1812 god na perekrestkakh mnenii sovetskikh istorikov, 1917–1987*, (Moscow, 1990), 79, 112–113; O. Orlik, *Groza dvenadtsatogo goda ...*, (Moscow, 1987), 105.
5. Yu. Gulyaev and V. Soglayeva, *Feldmarshal Kutuzov: Ist.-biograficheskii ocherk*, (Moscow, 1995); V. Dunayevsky, *General-feldmarshal, svetleishii knyaz M.I. Golenishchev-Kutuzov v sotsiokulturnom kontekste*, (Moscow, 1997); I. Andrianova, *Spasitel otechestva: zhizneopisanie M.I. Golenishcheva-Kutuzova*, (Moscow, 1999); A. Shishov, *Neizvestnii Kutuzov: Novoye prochtenie biografii*, (Moscow, 2002).
6. Napoleon to Champagny, 5 April 1811, *Correspondance de Napoleon Ier*, XXII, No. 17571.
7. V. Pugachev, 'K voprosu o pervonachalnom plane voiny 1812 g.,' in *1812 god: sbornik statei*, (Moscow, 1962), 32–34.
8. Fabry, I, i.
9. Barclay de Tolly to Alexander, March 1812, *Otechestvennaya voina 1812 goda. Materialy Voenno-uchebnogo arkhiva Generalnogo Shtaba*, [hereafter cited as General Staff Archives], I, part II, 1–6.
10. Bagration to Alexander, *circa* March 1812, *General Bagration: Sbornik dokumentov i materialov* [hereafter cited as Correspondence of Bagration], ed. S. Golubov, (Moscow, 1945), 134–136.
11. V. Bezotosny, 'Analiticheskii proyekt voyennikh deistvii v 1812 g. P. A. Chuikevicha,' in *Rossiiskii arkhiv*, 7(1996): 43–49.
12. Instructions to General Adjutant Count Saint Priest, [n.d., June 1812]; Bagration to Alexander, No. 283, 18 June 1812; Bagration to Barclay de Tolly, No. 294 (secret), 18–22 June 1812, *General Staff Archives*, XIII, 49, 96–97, 414.
13. S. Shvedov, 'O plane otstupleniya russkoi armii vglub strany v 1812 g.,' in *Otechestvennaya voina 1812 g. Rossia i Evropa*, (Borodino, 1992), 35
14. Clausewitz, 24–25.
15. I. Radozhitsky, *Pokhodnie zapiski artilerista s 1812 po 1816 g*, (Moscow, 1835) I, 37.
16. *Russkaya starina*, 9(1885): 396–97. Zakrevsky to Vorontsov [n.d. July 1812] in *arkhiv knyazya Vorontsova*, (Moscow, 1891); vol. 37, 229. Rayevsky to Samoilov, 10 July 1812, *arkhiv Rayevskikh* (St Petersburg, 1908), I, 152–153; Odental to Bulgakov, 14 August 1812, *Russkaya starina*, 8(1912): 166.
17. Barclay de Tolly, *Description of Military Operations of the 1st Army*, Rossiiskii Gosudarstvenii Voenno-Istoricheskii arkhiv (Russian State Military Historical Archive, hereafter cited as RGVIA), f. VUA, op. 16, d. 3571, l. 10.
18. Zapiski Yakova Ivanovicha de Sanglena (1776–1831), *Russkaya starina*, 37/3 (1883): 546
19. Muravyeov, 89; Timiriazev, 'Stranitsy proshlogo,' *Russkii arkhiv*, 22/1 (1884): 156.
20. Radozhitsky, 37; Gribanov, 185; Yermolov, I, 155.
21. Bagration to Barclay de Tolly, 3 August 1812, No. 394, *General Staff Archives*, XIV, 199.
22. Bagration to Barclay de Tolly, 8 August 1812, No. 416, *General Staff Archives*, XIV, 250–251.
23. Yermolov, 157.
24. Zhirkevich, 648. Troitsky, 107; Voronovsky, 88.
25. Bagration to Yermolov, 10 August 1812, *Russkii Invalid,* 169 (August 1912): 5.
26. L.A. Simansky, 'Zhurnal,' in *Voenno-Istoricheskii sbornik* 1(1913): 158; Pushin, *Diary of 1812–1814,* Entry of 2 August.
27. Barclay de Tolly, *Description of Military Operations of the 1st Army*, RGVIA, f. VUA, op. 16, d. 3571, ll. 28–29.
28. Pushin, 45; Yermolov, I, 180; Grabbe, II, 66–67; Löwernstein, 234–35.
29. Vistitsky, 186; Zhirkevich, 653; Voronovsky, 155; Bagration to Barclay de Tolly, 28 August 1812, in Aglamov, 289; Barclay de Tolly, *Description of Military Operations of the 1st Army*, RGVIA, f. VUA, op. 16, d. 3571, l. 30.

30. *Neizvestnii Barclay*, 79. Also see Michael Glover, *A Very Slippery Fellow: The Life of Sir Robert Wilson, 1777–1849* (Oxford, 1978), 104.
31. Wilson (1860): 114–15; Dokhturov to his wife, *circa* August 1812, *Russkii arkhiv*, 1 (1874): 1101, 1118; Muravyev, 102; Vistitsky, 184.
32. Bagration to Rostopchin, July 1812, in Dubrovin, 72–73; Bagration to Chichagov, 15 August 1812, in A. Afanasiev, *1812–814: Sekretnaya perepiska General P.I. Bagrationa, iz sobrania Gosudarstvennogo Istoricheskogo Muzea [hereafter cited as Sekretnaya perepiska]*, (Moscow, 1992), 168; Yermolov to Bagration, 31-July-1 August 1812, *Sekretnaya perepiska*, 177–178 Bagration to Yermolov, [n.d] July 1812, Yermolov, I, 176.
33. Wilson (1860): 130.
34. M. Konshin, 'Iz Zapisok Konshina,' in *Istoricheskii Vestnik*, 8/17 (1884): 283; Uxkull, 74–75; Simansky, 159.
35. Radozhitsky, 128.
36. Grabbe, II, 57.
37. Zakrevsky to Vorontsov, 17–18 August 1812, in *arkhiv knyazya Vorontsova*, (Moscow, 1891), vol. 37, 229–230.
38. Radozhitsky, I, 125, 129.
39. Zhirkevich, 8(1874): 648; Muraviyev, 187.
40. P. Glebov, 'Slovo o Barklaye de Tolli,' *Sovremennik*, 1 (1858): 155.
41. Shuvalov to Alexander, 12 August 1812, in Dubrovin, 71–73.
42. Alexander Shishkov, *Zapiski, mnenia i perepiska*, (Berlin, 1870), I, 154; Zhilin (1988): 134–35.
43. Cathcart, 62.
44. Alexander to Bagration, 20 August 1812, *Correspondence of Bagration*, 239; *Correspondence of Kutuzov*, IV, 75; Odental' to Bulgakov, 28 August 1812, *Russkaya starina*, 8 (1912): 170.
45. Clausewitz, 139, 142.
46. Bogdanovich, II, 125; Voronovsky, 168.
47. Sherbinin, 20.
48. Bagration to Rostopchin, 3 September 1812, in Dubrovin, 109.
49. Kutuzov to Rostopchin, 31 August 1812, in *M.I. Kutuzov: sbornik dokumentov*, IV, 118–120.
50. Disposition for Advance to the village of Borodino, *M.I. Kutuzov: sbornik dokumentov*, IV, 121.
51. Levin Bennigsen, 'Zapiski grafa L.L. Bennigsen o kampanii 1812 goda,' in *Russkaya starina*, 139 (1909): 494; Barclay de Tolly, *Description of Military Operations of the 1st Army*, RGVIA, f. VUA, op. 16, d. 3571, l. 37; Vistitsky, 186; Kutuzov to Alexander, 4 August 1812, *M.I. Kutuzov: sbornik dokumentov*, IV, 129.
52. Clausewitz, 149–150
53. Norov, 189.
54. St Priest, 393.
55. Barclay de Tolly, *Description of Military Operations of the 1st Army*, RGVIA, f. VUA, op. 16, d. 3571, ll. 38–40.
56. Brandt, 215.
57. Girod de l'Ain, 252–253
58. Orders to Army, 31 August-2 September, in Bogdanovich, II, 531–532; Order to the 2nd Western Army, 4 September 1812, in *Borodino: dokumentalnaya khronika*, 74.
59. D. Davydov, 'Iz Dnevnika partizanskikh deistvii 1812 goda,' in *Borodino: Dokumenty, pisma, vospominaniya*, 348; Konovnitsyn to Bagration, 4 September 1812 in *Borodino: dokumenty, pisma, vospominaniya*, 73–74; Fleischmann, Ch, *Denkwütdigkeiten* (Berlin, 1892), 25.
60. Labaume, 127–128.
61. *Istoriya leib-gvardii Yegerskogo polka za sto let*, (St Petersburg, 1896), 84.
62. Labaume, 124; Adams, 184–185
63. Barclay de Tolly to Kutuzov, 8 October 1812, RGVIA, f. VUA, d.3652. l. 8.
64. Bogdanovich, II, 147; Rapport sur les affaires du 5 Septembre 1812, 6 September 1812, in Nicolas Ternaux-Compans, *Le general Compans (1769–1845), d'apres ses notes campagnes et sa correspondence de 1812 a 1813 par son petit-fils*, (Paris, 1912), 352.
65. Clausewitz, 166; Vistitsky, I, 186; Ofitsialnye izvestia iz armii ot 27 avgusta [Official New from the Army of 27 August], RGVIA, f. VUA, d.3652. l.48; *Description de la Bataille de Borodino livrée les 24 et 25 aout 1812*, RGVIA, fond VUA, delo 3562, l.6.
66. Mikhailovsky-Danilevsky, II, 211; Buturlin, I, 250.
67. Neyelov, 6–7, 16–17.
68. Garnich (1955), 189; Fedorova, O. and V. Ushakov, *Pole russkoi slavy*, (Moscow, 1979), 27–29; Abalikhin, B. ed, '*Bessmerten tot, Otechestvo kto spas:' Mikhail Illarionovich Kutuzov*, (Moscow, 1995), 98.
69. Norov, 190; Yermolov, 154.
70. Ofitsialnye izvestia iz armii ot 27 avgusta [Official New from the Army of 27 August], RGVIA, f. VUA, d.3652. l.48. Also see Zemtsov, V, 'Divizia Kompana v boiyu za Shevardinskii redut 5 Sentiabrya 1812 g.,' *Sergeant*, No.7 *(Moscow 2000), 3–8*.
71. Paskevich, 100.
72. J.J. Pelet, 'Moskovskaya bitva,' in *Borodino v vospominaniyakh sovremennikov* (St Petersburg, 2001), 322–323.
73. Gourgaud, 148; Denniée, 64–65; Vaudoncourt, 176; Lejeune, 203; Fain, 3; Thiry, 132; Kukiel, 172–173. Kolaczkowski, I, 117; Dumonceau, 131.

# Notes and Sources

74. Sievers to Kutuzov, 8 October 1812, No. 276, RGVIA, f. VUA, d. 3561, ll. 20–22b; Beskrovny, 52; Tarle, 29; Troitsky, 139; Oboleshev, 34. Zemtsov, without indicating his sources, referred to 18,000 men and 46 cannon, *Sergeant*, 7 (2000): 3–8; idem, *Bitva pri moskve reke* (Moscow, 1999), 34. Years later, Gorchakov himself estimated 11,000 men under his command at Shevardino. Gorchakov to Mikhailovsky-Danilevsky, 13 May 1837, RGVIA, f. VUA, d. 3465, ch. 2, l. 270.
75. Sievers to Kutuzov, 8 October 1812, No. 276, RGVIA, f. VUA, d. 3561, l. 20–21; Kolaczkowski, 117–118;
76. Griois, II, 29.
77. Ségur (1958): 54.
78. Löwenstern to Kutuzov, [?] September 1812, RGVIA. F. 103. op. 208a. sv. 0, d. 4, ch. 1, l.206; Saint Priest, Diary, 393; Bogdanovich, II, 148.
79. Rapport sur les différentes affaires ou le 57e regiment s'est trouvé pendant la campagne de 1812, in Ternaux-Compans, 344.
80. Kutuzov to Alexander, 8 September 1812, *General Staff Archives*, XVI, 108.
81. Sievers to Kutuzov, 8 October 1812, No. 276, RGVIA, f. VUA, d. 3561, l. 20–21.
82. Rapport sur les affaires du 5 septembre 1812, in Ternaux-Compans, 345, 352–353.
83. Sievers to Kutuzov, 8 October 1812, No. 276, RGVIA, f. VUA, d. 3561, l. 20–21.
84. A letter of Adjutant Lehucher of the 57th Line suggests that other battalions might have participated in this attack. Lahucher to Dournet, 16 September 1812, in Grunwald (1963): 121.
85. Ternaux-Compans, 353; Grunwald (1963): 121.
86. Journal de la division Friant in Chuquet, 61.
87. Gourgaud, 149.
88. Chambray, 44; Dumonceau, 131; Ternaux-Compans, 175; Thiers, XIV, 303; Bogdanovich, 149; Buturlin, 253.
89. Löwenstern to Kutuzov, [n.d, October 1812], in *Borodino: dokumenty, pisma,vospominaniya*, 182–183; Gorchakov, 197–98; Löwenstern, 248; Denniée, 65–66; Gourgaud, 201–206; Sievers to Kutuzov, 8 October 1812, No. 276, RGVIA, f. VUA, d. 3561, l. 21–22.
90. Kukiel, 28 (1929): 25.
91. Andreyev, 190–191.
92. Löwenstern to Kutuzov, [n.d.] September 1812, in *Borodino: dokumenty, pisma, vospominaniya*, 182.
93. Report of the 61st Line in Ternaux-Compans, 349.
94. Guillemard, 138.
95. Report of the 61st Line in Ternaux-Compans, 349; Vossen, 469; Berthezene, II, 44; Dutheille de Lamothe, 42; Boulart, 257; Fain, 4; Thiers, 303–306.
96, *Denkwurdigkeiten des Grafen v. Toll*, II, 27; Bogdanovich, 146, 537; Wilson (1860): 137.
97. Murat to Berthier, 9 September 1812 in Markham, *Imperial Glory*, 290.
98. A. Khatov, *Boi pri redute Shevardinskom 24-go avgusta 1812 g.* (St Petersburg, 1839), 30.
99. Sievers to Kutuzov, 8 October 1812, No. 276, RGVIA, f. VUA, d. 3561, l. 22; Panchulidzev to Golitsyn, 12 September 1812, RGVIA f. 846, op. 16, d. 3561. l.47; Yuzefovich to Panchulidzev, 22 September 1812, in *Borodino: dokumentalnaya khronika*, 218.
100. Ségur (1958): 55
101. Vossen, 468–469.
102. Boppe, *Les Espagnoles a la Grande Armée*, 146–147; Berthezene, II, 44.
103. Panchulidzev to Golitsyn, 12 September 1812, RGVIA f. 846, op. 16, d. 3561, l.47.
104. Kutuzov to Alexander; Kaisarov to Rostopchin, 6 September 1812, in *Borodino: dokumentalnaya khronika*, 102–103; Kutuzov to his wife, 6 September 1812, in *Borodino: dokumenty, pisma, vospominaniya*, 146; B. Kolubyakin, 'Voina 1812 g. Borodinskaya operatsiya i Borodinskoye srazheniye,' in *Trudy Imperatorskogo Russkogo voenno-istoricheskogo obshestva*, 6 (1912): 75.
105. For details see list of soldiers nominated to awards in *Borodino: dokumenty, pisma, vospominaniya*, 265–266.
106. See list of the officers and the rank-and-file, attached to Yuzefovich to Panchulidzev, 22 September 1812, in *Borodino: dokumentalnaya khronika*, 218–220.
107. Gorchakov to Bagration, 22 September 1812, in *Borodino: dokumentalnaya khronika*, 217.
108. Panchulidzev to Golitsyn, 12 September 1812, RGVIA f. 846, op. 16, d. 3561. l.47b.
109. Report of the 111th Line in Ternaux-Compans, 354–355.
110. Raswadowski of the 8th Polish Lancers referred to the 6th Polish Lancer while Wedel, who served in the 9th Chasseurs à Cheval describes the attack without specific details. Wedel, 80–82; Bielecki, *Dal nam przyklad Bonaparte* (Krakow, 1984), II, 97–98
111. Gorchakov to Mikhailovsky-Danilevsky, 13 May 1837, RGVIA, f. VUA, d. 3465, ch. 2, l. 270–271.
112. Kutuzov to Kutuzov, 6 September 1812, *Borodino: dokumenty, pisma, vospominaniya*, 87.
113. Saint Priest, 393.
114. Larrey, IV, 43; Griois, 30; Roos, 111.
115. Mayevsky, 370.
116. Mitarevsky, 173.
117. Bennigsen, 495–496.
118. Attestations du Docteur Ywan, in Ségur, VI, 15
119. Neverovsky, 379; Vorontsov; Ségur (1958): 56.
120. Rapport sur les affaires du 5 Septembre 1812; 111e Régiment de Ligne, état des pertes éprouv'ees par le susdit regiment a j'affaire du 5 Septembre 1812, in Ternaux-Compans, 352–356; Kukiel 28 (1929): 27; Castellane, I, 147.

# The Battle of Borodino

121. Report of the 61st Line in Ternaux-Compans, 349–351; Ségur (1958): 54; Labaume, 124; Lejeune, 204; François, 787; Ternaux-Compans, 356, 359; Martinien, 179, 250, 332, 580, 653; Girolamo Cappello *Gli Italiani in Russia nel 1812*, (Gitta di castello, 1912), 151; Guillemard, 138.

122. 'Rasskaz Georgiyevskogo Kavalera iz divizii Neverovskogo,' in *Chtenia imperatorskogo obschestva istorii drevnostei*, 1 (1872): 119.

123. Alexander to Kutuzov, 5 September 1812, in *Borodino: dokumentalnaya khronika*, 99.

124. Rosters of the 1st Western Army, 4–6 September 1812, in *Borodino: dokumentalnaya khronika*, 78, 92, 106. Several cavalry regiments were detached from the army and not included in the roll-call of 5–6 September.

125. *M.I. Kutuzov: sbornik dokumentov*, IV, 98.

126. Vasiliev and Eliseyev, 66.

127. Kutuzov to Alexander, 4 September 1812. in *Borodino: dokumentalnaya khronika*, 75.

128. Neverovsky to Gorchakov, 4 September 1812, in *Borodino: dokumentalnaya khronika*, 84.

129. Vasiliev and Eliseyev, 14–52; Larionov, 132

130. Kutuzov to Alexander, 31 August 1812, in *M.I. Kutuzov: sbornik dokumentov*, 98; Alexander to Kutuzov, 5 September 1812, in *Borodino: dokumentalnaya khronika*, 99.

131. Chambray, I, 274.

132. Laugier, 15–16.

133. Holzhausen, 27; Calosso, 51; Mikhailovsky-Danilevsky, III, 141.

134. Oleg Sokolov, 'Kapitan N: Portret frantsuzskogo ofitsera 1812 goda,' *Rodina*, 6/7(1992): 14–15; Jean-Paul Bertaud, 'Napoleon's Officers,' in *Past and Present* 112 (Aug., 1986): 104. *For further data on the French officer corps see Jacques Houdaille's studies 'Les officiers du Premier Empire (1803–1815),' Population* (French Edition), 4/5(1995): 1229–1235, and 'Les generaux francais,' *Population*, 4/5 (1994): 1169–1173.

135. For excellent discussion see Tselorungo, 154, 166, 189.

136. N. Dubrovin, 'Russkaya zhizn v nachale XIX v,' in *Russkaya starina*, 12 (1901): 494

137. Tselorungo, 78, 97.

138. 18th Bulletin, 10 September 1812, in Markham, *Imperial Glory*, 295; Caulaincourt, *Mémoires*, 424. The timing of the first reconnaissance is sometimes also given as 6:00 a.m (Thiers, Britten Austin, Denniée) or simply as 'the first light of day' (Ségur), 'at dawn' (Lejeune, Brandt) or 'early morning' (Pelet). Castellane refers to 1:00 A.M.

139. Pelet, 22; Kolaczkowski, 119–120.

140. Rapp, 199–200

141. Bausset, II, 77; Castellane, I, 148; Brandt, 217.

142. Fabvier is often referred to as 'colonel' but, in September 1812, he was a captain of the Guard. Quintin, 322.

143. Rory Muir, *Salamanca 1812* (New Haven, 2001), 208.

144. Gourgaud, 127–128.

145. Rapp, 200.

146. Muravyev, 375.

147. Denniée, 69

148. Holzhausen, 82–83.

149. Suckow, 178; Pajol, 41; Vossler, 59; Boulart, 252;

150. Kutuzov to E. Kutuzova, 6 September 1812, in *Borodino: dokumenty, pisma, vospominaniya*, 87.

151. Gourgaud, 130.

152. Ordre pour la bataille, 6 September 1812, *Correspondance de Napoléon Ier*, No.19181, XXIV, 239; Albert Du Casse, *Mémoires et correspondance politique et militaire du prince Eugène*, (Paris, 1859), VIII, 2–3; Denniée, 67.

153. Ségur, IV, 362; Davout, *Mémoires et souvenirs*, II, 95; Gallaher, 246; Thiers, VIII, 130.

154. Bogdanovich, II, 166.

155. Duffy, 85.

156. For an interesting note see Chandler, 798.

157. Ordre, 7 September 1812, *Correspondance de Napoléon 1er*, No. 19181. For interesting discussion, see Kukiel, 28 (1929): 28.

158. Zemtsov, 61.

159. Denniée, 81; Fain, II, 47; Castellane, 150–151; Roguet, IV, 482. Cate incorrectly calculated 140,000 and 120,000 cartridges expended by the French and Russian infantry, which only gives 1,5–2 expended cartridges per soldier. Denniée and Roguet referred to '1,400,000 cartouches.' *The War of the Two Emperors*, 235.

160. Planat de la Faye, 81.

161. Pion des Loches, 288–289.

162. Barclay de Tolly to Kutuzov, 8 October 1812, RGVIA, f. VUA, d. 3561, l. 8–9; Bagration to Alexander I, 8 September 1812, No. 488, in *Borodino: dokumenty, pisma, vospominaniya*, 109.

163. Dedem, 236.

164. Kaisarov to Rostopchin, 7 September 1812, in *Borodino: dokumenty, pisma, vospominaniya*, 92–93.

165. Ségur (1958): 57.

166. Bourgogne, 7.

167. Fezensac, 30.

168. Griois, II, 33.

169. Girod de l'Ain, 255.

170. Vionnet de Maringoné, 12

171. Boulart, 252; Combe, 79; Holzhausen, 97; Fezensac, 30; Dedem, 235–236.

# Notes and Sources

172. Ségur (1958): 62.
173. Brandt, 218.
174. Dumonceau, II, 133.
175. Biot, 31–32
176. Rotenhan, 25–27.
177. Disposition of the 1st and 2nd armies, 5 September 1812, *Feldmarshal Kutuzov: sbornik dokumentov i materialov* (Moscow, 1947) 159.
178. Garnich, 141.
179. Kutuzov to Alexander, 6 September 1812, in *Borodino: dokumentalnaya khronika*, 102.
180. 'Rasskaz o Borodinskom srazhenii otdelnnogo Unter-Ofitsera Tikhonova,' in *Chtenia imperatorskogo obshchestva istorii drevnostei*, 1 (1872), 119.
181. Barclay de Tolly, *Izobrazheniye*, RGVIA, f. VUA, op. 16. d. 3571, l. 42–43
182. Journal of Military Operations of the 1st and 2nd Western Armies, RGVIA, f. VUA, op. 16, d. 3485, l.43b; Barclay de Tolly to Kutuzov, 8 October 1812, RGVIA, f. VUA, op. 16, d. 3561, l. 8; Sherbinin, 395.
183. *Borodino: dokumenty, pisma, vospominaniya*, 112, 135, 138.
184. Sherbinin, 397; Bolgovsky, 339–340.
185. Dmitri Buturlin, 'Kutuzov v 1812 g.,' in *Russkaya starina*, 10 (1894): 207; St Priest, 393; Eugène of Württemberg, 1 (1848): 52, 73, 83.
186. Gerua, 30–32.
187. N. Pavlenko, 'Nekotorye voprosy Borodinskogo srazheniya,' in *Voenno-istoricheskii zhurnal*, 5 (1941): 34–35.
188. Garnich (1955): 203, 223–224
189. Popov (1998): 122–143
190. Aglamov, 51.
191. Major General P.N. Ivashov's Daily Journal, *Voenno-istoricheskii zhurnal*, 4 (1939): 128.
192. Kutuzov's Order on Supervising Engineer Units and Establishment of Communications between the Armies, 3 September 1812; Bagration's Order to the 2nd Western Army, 3–4 September 1812, in *Borodino: dokumenty, pisma, vospominaniya*, 62–63.
193. Bagration's Orders to the 2nd Western Army, 4 September 1812, in *Borodino: dokumenty, pisma, vospominaniya*, 70–72.
194. For detailed discussion see B. Kolyubakin, *Borodinskoye srazheniye i podgotovka polya srazhenya v inzhenernom itnoshenii*, Moscow, 1999.
195. 'Rasskaz o Borodinskom srazhenii otdelnnogo Unter-Ofitsera Tikhonova,' in *Chtenia imperatorskogo obshchestva istorii drevnostei*, 1 (1872), 119–20.
196. Liprandi (1867), 18–21.
197. Bogdanov, 338.
198. Bogdanovich, II, 171.
199. Yermolov's Order to the 1st Western Army; Bagration's Order to the 2nd Western Army, 6 September 1812, in *Borodino: dokumenty, pisma, vospominaniya*, 84, 91–92.
200. Disposition of the 1st and 2nd Armies, 5 September 1812, in *Borodino: dokumentalnaya khronika*, 93.
201. Yermolov's Order to the 1st Western Army, 6 September 1812, in *Borodino: dokumentalnaya khronika*, 108.
202. Sukhanin, 281.
203. Skobelev, 188; Radozhitsky, 140; Dushkevich, 114.
204. Mayevsky, 370; Ivchenko, 35.
205. Radozhitsky, 142; Muravyev, 375.
206. Vionnet de Maringoné, 12–13.
207. Glinka, *Pisma russkogo ofitsera*.
208. Mitarevsky, 51–56.
209. *Wider Napoleon! Ein deutsches Reiterleben, 1806–1815. Herausgegeben von Friedrich M. Kircheisen*, (Stuttgart, 1911), II, 132.
210. Glinka, *Ocherki Borodinskogo srazheniya*.
211. Bogdanovich, II, 199.
212. Mitarevsky, 55–56.
213. Ségur (1958): 62–63; Rapp, 200–202; Fain, II, 18–19.
214. Seruzier, 198.
215. Correspondance de Napoleon 1er, XXIV, 207.
216. Guillemard, 139; Chambray, 298; Laugier, 80; Fezensac, 31.
217. Bogdanov, 338.
218. Bogdanovich, II, 177.
219. Rodozhnitsky, 386; Duffy, 95; I.S. Tikhonov, 'Ob ustanovlenii neizvestnogo avtora vospominanii 'Istoricheskie svedenia o Borodinskom srazhenii," in *Otechestvennaia voina 1812 goda. Rossia i Evropa*, (Borodino, 1992), 16–20.
220. Barclay de Tolly to Kutuzov, 26 September 1812, RGVIA, f. VUA, d. 3561, op. 16, l. 8. Kutuzov's report also noted that the French made first attacks around 4:00 A.M. Kutuzov to Alexander, [n.d.] RGVIA, f. VUA, op. 16, d. 3561. l.52b. For a French printed version see, *Description de la Bataille de Borodino livrée les 24 et 26 aout 1812*, (St Petersburg, 1839), RGVIA, f. VUA, op. 16. d. 3562. Kutuzov to Alexander, 8 September 1812, in *Borodino: dokumentalnaya khronika*, 165.

221. Bistrom to Lavrov, 12 September 1812, N. 656, in *Istoriya leib-gvardii Yegerskogo polka za sto let*, (St Petersburg, 1896), 47.
222. Ofitsialnye izvestia iz armii ot 27 Avgusta in *Borodino: dokumenty, pisma, vospominaniya*, 112.
223. Eugène to Berthier, 10 September 1812, in Markham, *Imperial Glory*, 293.
224. Windmann, 106–107.
225. Eugène to Berthier, 10 September 1812, in Markham, *Imperial Glory*, 293.
226. Bistrom to Lavrov, 12 September 1812, N. 656, in *Istoriya leib-gvardii Yegerskogo polka*, 47.
227. Löwenstern, 12(1900): 573.
228. Grabbe, 406.
229. Bistrom to Lavrov, 12 September 1812, N. 656, in *Istoriya leib-gvardii Yegerskogo polka*, 47.
230. Durnovo, 107.
231. Bistrom to Lavrov, 12 September 1812, N. 656, in *Istoriya leib-gvardii Yegerskogo polka*, 47. According to N. Muravyev, a Russian guard Jäger brought one of the French captives, holding his sword in hand. The French officer told Kutuzov that the Jäger did not mistreat him and Kutuzov rewarded him with the medal of the Military Order, also known as the soldiers' St George order.
232. Bistrom to Lavrov, 12 September 1812, N. 656, in *Istoriya leib-gvardii Yegerskogo polka*, 47; Shepotiev, *Pamyatka gvardeiskogo ekipazha* (St Petersburg, 1910), 18.
233. Liprandi, 28–29.
234. Durnovo, 107.
235. Bistrom to Lavrov, 12 September 1812, N. 656, in *Istoriya leib-gvardii Yegerskogo polka*, 48.
236. Lowernstern, 574.
237. Eugène to Berthier, 10 September 1812, in Markham, *Imperial Glory*, 293.
238. Petrov, 182.
239. Grabbe, 75.
240. Grabbe 75; Divov, 1336.
241. Merlin to Yermolov, 22 September 1812, No. 618, *General Staff Archive*, XVIII, 50–51.
242. Spisok generalitetu, shtab-i ober-ofitseram, osobenno otlichivshimsia v dele 26-go chisla avgusta pri selenii Borodine, koim isprashivaetsia voznagrazhdenie, 26 September 1812, in *Borodino: dokumenty, pisma, vospominaniya*, 277–280.
243. Adam, 189.
244. Saint-Hilaire, II, 20; Eugène, *Correspondance*, VIII, 5. The unit had listed 66 officers and 1,904 men in late AuguSt Hourtoulle, 88.
245. Eugène to Berthier, 10 September 1812, in Markham, *Imperial Glory*, 294. Also see Laugier, 56; Labaume, 128; Adam, 189.
246. Skobelev, 217.
247. Petrov, 182–183; Karpenko, 340.
248. Bistrom to Lavrov, 12 September 1812, N. 656, in *Istoriya leib-gvardii Yegerskogo polka*, 48.
249. List of Officers Receiving Awards for Borodino, in *Istoriya leib-gvardii Yegerskogo polka*, annex II, 49–50.
250. Bogdanovich, II, 168.
251. Ney to Berthier, 9 September 1812, in Markham, *Imperial Glory*, 292.
252. Murat to Berthier, 9 September 1812, in Markham, *Imperial Glory*, 290.
253. Ségur, I, 390.
254. Dumonceau, II, 135–136.
255. Ternaux-Compans, 184–185, 346, 357–359; Dutheillet de Lamothe, 42; Thiry, 137, Girod de l'Ain, 79; Teste, 667; 'Journal de la division Friant' in Chuquet, 50; Pelet, 72, 100–101; Friant, 233.
256. Shakhovsky to Konovnitsyn, 19 September 1812, in *Borodino: dokumentalnaya khronika*, 187–188.
257. Ternaux-Compans, 184–187; Teste, 669; Pelet, 74.
258. Löwenstern to Kutuzov, [n.d, October 1812], in *Borodino: dokumenty, pisma, vospominaniya* , 184.
259. Rapport sur les différentes affaires ou le 57e regiment s'est trouvé pendant la campagne de 1812; 111e regiment d'infanterie de ligne: rapport sur la journée du 7 septembre 1812, Ternaux-Compans, 346, 359. Teste, 669.
260. Muravyev, 377; 'Capitulation of Paris in 1814: Razskaz M.F. Orlova,' *Russkaya starina*, 20 (1877): 647; Tarle, 192; Davidov, 527
261. Dutheillet de Lamoth, 42–43.
262. Rapport sur les différentes affaires ou le 57e regiment s'est trouvé pendant la campagne de 1812; Rapport du 61e de la bataille du 7 septembre 1812, 111e regiment d'infanterie de ligne: rapport sur la journée du 7 septembre 1812, in Ternaux-Compans, 346, 357, 359.
263. Ternaux-Compans, 148; Girod de l'Ain, 81; Dessaix et Folliet, 248–249.
264. According to Fain, Dupelain, commander of the 1st Brigade of the 5th Division, initially took over the division command. However, Compans' letter reveals that he was also wounded during the battle of Shevardino on the 5th. Fain, II, 25; Ternaux-Compans, 186.
265. Ternaux-Compans, 186; Teste, 670; Dutheillet de Lamothe, 44.
266. Vorontsov, 342; Neverovsky to Kutuzov, 24 September 1812, RGVIA, f. VUA, op. 16, d. 3561, l. 45–45b.
267. Blocqueville, 168–170; Gourgaud, 218; Vigier, 96.
268. Murat to Berthier, 9 September 1812, in Markham, *Imperial Glory*, 290.
269. Le Roy, 157.
270. Ney to Berthier, 9 September 1812, in Markham, *Imperial Glory*, 292; Ségur (1958): 66; Bertin, 70; Davout, II, 97; Joly, 87–88; Thiers, VIII, 137; Vigier, 96–98; Lejeune, II, 175–79; Rossetti, 117; Buturlin, I, 334–35; Chambray, 304–305; Sainte-Hillaire, II, 16–17.

# Notes and Sources

271. Ségur (1958): 66. Also see Davout, II, 97; Vigier, 96–98; Lejeune, II, 180–81; Rossetti, 117; Castellance, 149; Ternaux-Compans, 186; Fain, 25; Pelet, 74.
272. Rayevsky, 380; Buturlin, I, 267; Sievers to Kutuzov, 8 October 1812, No. 278, RGVIA, f. VUA, d. 3561, l. 23.
273. Mayevsky, 371.
274. Vistitsky, 187.
275. Bennigsen, 139 (1909): 497
276. Lavrov to Dokhturov, 15 September 1812, RGVIA, f. VUA, d. 3561, ll.30–31.
277. Lavrov to Dokhturov, 15 September 1812, RGVIA, f. VUA, d. 3561, ll.30–31.
278. Kutuzov to Lavrov, 13 September 1812, RGVIA, f. VUA, d. 3561, l. 34.
279. Ivchenko, 47.
280. Ney to Berthier, 9 September 1812, in Markham, *Imperial Glory*, 292.
281. Bogdanovich, II, 183.
282. Ney to Berthier, 9 September 1812, in Markham, *Imperial Glory*, 292.
283. Durova, 143.
284. Dessaix, 251; Girod de l'Ain, 83; Vossen, 470–471.
285. Bagration to Alexander, 8 September 1812, No. 488, *Borodino: dokumenty, pisma, vospominaniya*, 100.
286. Vorontsov, 342.
287. Neverovsky, 379; Neverovsky to Kutuzov, 24 September 1812, RGVIA, f. VUA, op. 16, d. 3561, l. 45–45b.
288. Andreyev, 10 (1879): 191–93
289. Vorontsov, 343.
290. Sievers to Kutuzov, 8 October 1812, No. 278, RGVIA, f. VUA, d. 3561, l. 23–23b
291. Sievers to Kutuzov, 8 October 1812, No. 278, RGVIA, f. VUA, d. 3561, ll.23–23b
292. Bogdanovich, II, 184.
293. Guyardet's Rapport de la bataille du 7 septembre 1812, in Ternaux-Compans, 357–358.
294. Girod de l'Ain, 84; Dessaix, 252–254
295. Rapport sur les différentes affaires ou le 57e regiment s'est trouvé pendant la campagne de 1812, in Ternaux-Compans, 346–347.
296. Pieces officielles et bulletins de la Grand Armee, Anne 1812, (Extrait du Journal official), 325–327.
297. Suckow, 183–184.
298. Murat to Berthier, 9 September 1812, in Markham, *Imperial Glory*, 290.
299. Feodor Glinka, *Pisma Russkogo ofitsera*, (Moscow, 1985), 88.
300. Murat to Berthier, 9 September 1812, in Markham, *Imperial Glory*, 290.
301. Holzhausen, 88, 90–91; Suckow, 184–185; Burkersroda, 10; Maceroni, 483–84; Rossetti, 119–20; Lucas-Dubreton, 193–94; Zhilin, 155; Troitsky, 149; Popov (1994): 43–44.
302. Holzhausen, 91.
303. Aleksey Vasiliev, 'O vremeni padenia Bagrationovskikh fleshei,' *Rodina*, 6/7 (1992): 62–67.
304. Ofitsialnye izvestia iz armii ot 27 avgusta, RGVIA, f. VUA, d.3652, l. 48; *Opisaniye srazheniya pri sele Borodine, in Borodino: dokumenty, pisma, vospominaniya*, 323–324.
305. Glinka, *The Battle of Borodino*, II, 13–17.
306. 'Rasskaz o Borodinskom srazhenii otdelnnogo Unter-Ofitsera Tikhonova,' in *Chtenia imperatorskogo obschestva istorii drevnostei*, 1 (1872), 119–20.
307. Ségur (1958): 68.
308. Mikhailovsky-Danilevsky, II, 241.
309. Butenev, 41. Bagration was lightly wounded several times in 1799 and 1807.
310. Quotes from Tarle, 193.
311. Muravyev (1986), 111; Glinka, *Battle of Borodino*, 17–20; Löwernstein, 260; Norov, 196.
312. Konovnitsyn to Kutuzov, 1 October 1812, RGVIA, f. VUA, d. 3561, ll. 27–29b.
313. Sherbinin, 20.
314. Mikhailovsky-Danilevsky, II, 241.
315. Suckow, 183; Holzhausen, 89; Planat de la Fay, 83.
316. Rayevsky, 381.
317. Rayevsky, 380; Paskevich, 102–103.
318. Rayevsky, 380–381.
319. Rayevsky to Dokhturov, 23 September 1812, No. 280, General Staff Archives, XVIII, 59.
320. Zemtsov, 113; Larionov, 124–125.
321. Mikhailovsky-Danilevsky (1839), II, 242–243.
322. Creitz, 359.
323. Larionov, 126.
324. Bogdanovich, II, 195.
325. Tarle (1992), 140; Troitsky, 168; Larionov, 125.
326. Paskevich, 102.
327. Mayevsky, 371.
328. Some authors refer to the 2nd Baden Infantry Regiment participating in the attack but it does seem to be true since the Badenese regiment was assigned to the Imperial Guard that day. Bogdanovich, II, 195; Nafziger, 238; Gerua, 49.
329. Chambray, 68; Vaudoncourt, 183; François, 791.
330. Mitarevsky, 62.

# The Battle of Borodino

331. Some authors claim that Rayevsky's decision to sent back caissons with ammunition deprived his guns of sufficient ammunition and allowed the French to seize the redoubt. However, memoirs of participants indicate that the Russian guns maintained fire until the very last moment.
332. Rayevsky, 381. Also see Rayevsky to Dokhturov, 23 September 1812, No. 280, General Staff Archives, XVIII, 59–60.
333. Popov (1997): 20; Thiry, 147; Larrey, 45; Chuquet, 369.
334. Bulletins, 132.
335. Divov, 1337–1338; *Rossii dvinulis siny*, 406–407; Davydov (1962): 528–529.
336. Barclay de Tolly, *Izobrazhenie voyennykh deistvii 1-oi armii v 1812 g,*, RGVIA, f. VUA, op. 16, d. 3571, ll. 23–23b.
337. Paskevich, 103; *Description de la Bataille de Borodino livrée les 24 et 25 aout 1812*, RGVIA, fond VUA, delo 3562, l. 28–29; Kutuzov to Alexander, [n.d.] RGVIA, fond VUA, delo 3561, l.55–56; Barclay de Tolly to Kutuzov, 8 October 1812, RGVIA, fond VUA, delo 3561, 10–10b.
338. Pierre Bertrand, *Historique abrégé du 30e Régiment d'infanterie*, (Paris, 1887), 58–59; Nikitin, 144; Wolzogen, 141; Eugène, *Correspondance*, VIII, 6.
339. Rayevsky to Dokhturov, 23 September 1812, No. 280, *General Staff Archives*, XVIII, 59–60.
340. Yermolov (2005), 161.
341. Yermolov to Barclay de Tolly, 2 October 1812, RGVIA, f. VUA, d. 3561, ll. 49–50; Barclay de Tolly to Kutuzov, 8 October 1812, RGVIA, f. VUA, d. 3561, ll. 8–13.
342. Creitz, 359.
343. Eugène to Berthier, 10 September 1812, in Markham, *Imperial Glory*, 294.
344. Paskevich, 103.
345. Baggovut to Barclay de Tolly, [n.d.] September 1812, RGVIA, f. VUA, op. 16, d. 3561, ll. 42b-43.
346. Bogdanovich, II, 201.
347. Helldorf's account in Duffy, 110.
348. Bogdanovich, II, 202.
349. Nafziger, 240; Duffy, 110; Bleibtreu, 250–251, 256; Ditfurth, 94–95; Kukiel (1919), 60
350. Murat to Berthier, 9 September 1812, in Markham, *Imperial Glory*, 290.
351. Spisok nizhnim chinam razznikh artilleriiskikh brigad … in *Borodino: dokumenty, pisma, vospominaniya*, 298–299
352. Rayevsky to Dokhturov, 23 September 1812, No. 280 in Mikhailovsky-Danilevsky, II, 244.
353. Kutuzov's Order to the Army, 9 September 1812, No.11. RGVIA, f. VUA, d. 3524, l. 8; Kutuzov to Alexander [n.d. September 1812], RGVIA, f. VUA, d. 3561, l.56. Meshetich and Radozhitsky claim the soldier 'dragged' the French general to Kutuzov and was also awarded the St George cross but they might be confusing him with another Jäger who, according to Muravyev, captured a staff officer at the village of Borodino and brought him to Kutuzov. Meshetich, 48; Radozhitsky, I, 144–145; Muravyev, *Russkii arkhiv* (1885): 255.
354. Radozhitsky, I, 144–145.
355. Clausewitz, 159.
356. For details on Bonammy's captivity see Leysser's letters in Meerheim, 297. Yermolov later sent Bonammy to his family estate in Orel and asked his father to take particular care of him.
357. Bogdanovich, II, 199–200; Nikitin, 149; Yermolov (2005), 161; Mikhailovsky-Danilevsky, Imperator Aleksandr I i ego spodvizhniki, vol I (no pagination); Meshetich, 48.
358. Divov, 1337–1338.
359. Durnovo, 90–91.
360. Mikhailovsky-Danilevsky, Imperator Aleksandr I i ego spodvizhniki, *vol. I (no pagination)*.
361. Ratch, G, 'Publichniye lektsii, chitanniye gospodam ofitseram gvardeiskoi artillerii,' in *Artilleriiskii zhurnal*, 11(1861): 843.
362. Winzegorode to Alexander, 25 September 1812, *Otechestvennaya voina v pismakh sovremennikov* (St Petersburg, 1882), 136–137.
363. Golitsyn, 343.
364. Mikhailovsky-Danilevsky, II, 245–246.
365. Bolgovsky, 340.
366. Bogdanovich, II, 199
367. A. Larionov, 'Ispolzovaniye artillerii v Borodinskom srazhenii,' in *1812 god: sbornik statei* (Moscow, 1962), 130–131.
368. Barclay de Tolly, *Izobrazhenie*, RGVIA, f. VUA, op. 16, d. 3571, ll. 23b-24.
369. Chlapowski, 119.
370. Stroganov to Konovnitsyn, 18 September 1812, in *Borodino: dokumenty, pisma, vospominaniya*, 151.
371. Poniatowski to Berthier, 7 September 1812, in Markham, *Imperial Glory*, 288.
372. *Description de la Bataille de Borodino*, RGVIA, f. 846, op. 16, d.3562, l. 21; Kukiel (1929), 79; Mikhailovsky-Danilevsky (1839), 239.
373. Konovnitsyn to Kutuzov, 1 October 1812, RGVIA, f. VUA, d. 3561, ll. 27b; Stroganov to Konovnitsyn, 18 September 1812, in *Borodino: dokumenty, pisma, vospominaniya*, 151.
374. Poniatowski to Berthier, 7 September 1812, in Markham, *Imperial Glory*, 288.
375. Smith incorrectly refers to 'Prince Shakhovsk's 4th Jäger Regiment,' probably wrong translation of Bogdanovich's line 'Prince Shakhovsky's four Jäger regiments.' Smith, 107; Bogdanovich, II, 193.
376. Poniatowski to Berthier, 7 September 1812, in Markham, *Imperial Glory*, 288.
377. Soltyk, 228, Gourgaud, 238; Fain, II, 29.

# Notes and Sources

378. Stroganov to Konovnitsyn, 18 September 1812, in *Borodino: dokumenty, pisma, vospominaniya*, 152; *Spisok ob otlichivshikhsia v srazhenii 26 avgusta 1-i grenaderskoi divizii generalitet, shtab i ober-ofitserakh*, [n.d.] September 1812, in *Borodino: dokumentalnaya khronika*, 186–187.
379. Baggovut to Barclay de Tolly, [n.d.] September 1812, RGVIA, f. VUA, op. 16, d. 3561, l. 43; Bogdanovich, 202. D. Smith cited abridged version of Baggovut's report but translation contains several errors, including misnaming the 39th Company as 33rd, *Borodino*, 104.
380. Paskevich, 103.
381. Kukiel (1929): 34; Jomini, IV, 127.
382. Baggovut to Barclay de Tolly, [n.d.] September 1812, RGVIA, f. VUA, op. 16, d. 3561, l.43–43b.
383. Kolaczkowski, I, 120.
384. Baggovut to Barclay de Tolly, [n.d.] September 1812, RGVIA, f. VUA, op. 16, d. 3561, l.43–43b; Stroganov to Konovnitsyn, 18 September 1812, in *Borodino: dokumenty, pisma, vospominaniya*, 152; Bogdanovich, 203; Mikhailovsky-Danilevsky (1839):239–240; Soltyk, 232–233.
385. Dembinski's *Mémoires*, in Kukiel (1929): 85.
386. Poniatowski to Berthier, 7 September 1812, in Markham, *Imperial Glory*, 288.
387. Brandt, 220.
388. Wiedemann, 106–107; Flotow, 194; Preysing, 13. French sources, among them Vaudoncourt and Laugier, misspell the name of Zakharino and often mislead author to refer to Lacharisi, which then found its way into some modern accounts of the battle (Austin Britten, 293).
389. Platov to Kutuzov [n.d. September 1812] RGVIA, f. VUA, d. 3465/2, l. 113.
390. Clausewitz, 158.
391. Bennigsen, 139 (1909): 497–498.
392. Lowernstern, 366–367.
393. Mikhailovsky-Danilevsky, 255.
394. Bennigsen, 139 (1909): 498; Wolzogen, 145; *General kvartimeister K.F. Toll v otechestvennuyu voinu* (St Petersburg, 1912), 214–215.
395. Liprandi (1861): 40–49. Liprandi's claim that Platov was not given command is a bit misleading. The Cossack ataman's report indicated that, as a senior officer, he did enjoy some authority, and some participants noted in their memoirs that Platov initially held the command and later transferred it to Uvarov. Muravyev, 249–250.
396. Beskrovny (1951): 63; Tarle (1962): 47–49; Garnich, 167; Beskrovny (1968): 37.
397. Kutuzov to Alexander, 4 December 1812, *M.I. Kutuzov: sbornik dokumentov*, IV, 219.
398. The strength of the I Cavalry Corps is based on the 6 September returns of the 1st Western Army, *Borodino: dokumenty, pisma, vospominaniya*, 90. Bogdanovich referred to 28 squadrons and 12 horse guns in the I Cavalry Corps. Bogdanovich, II, 206. Nafziger estimates the Russian cavalry at 8,000 men (Uvarov) and 5,000 Cossacks (Platov), Smith and Duffy cited 5,500 Cossacks and 2,500 men of the I Cavalry Corps. These authors, however, cite the strength of the entire Cossack force under Platov's command when only part of it was committed to the raid. Nafziger, 244; Smith, 112; Duffy, 119.
399. Löwenstern, 367.
400. Hailbronner, 106.
401. Platov to Kutuzov [n.d. September 1812] RGVIA, f. VUA, d. 3465/2, l. 113.
402. Eugène, *Correspondance*, VIII, 7–8; Laugier, 81; Anthouard, 341.
403. Clausewitz, 162–163.
404. Flotow, 195; Wiedemann, 107; Preysing, 13; Boppe, P, *La Croatie militaire*, 126; Chambray, 70; Vaudoncourt, 184.
405. Mitarevsky, 67.
406. Glinka, 359.
407. Eugène to Berthier, 10 September 1812, in Markham, *Imperial Glory*, 294.
408. Griois, 35; Anthouard, 341; Combe, 83; Cerrini, 434. Laugier, 83; Capello, 160–161; Langlois, 5; Saint-Hilaire, II, 21; Pinelli, 225
409. Laugier, 83–84.
410. Clausewitz, 163.
411. Uvarov to Barclay de Tolly, 15 September 1812, RGVIA, f. VUA, d. 3561, l. 1–2; Mikhailovsky-Danilevsky, 255; Bogdanovich, II, 207.
412. Bogdanovich, II, 207.
413. P. Bobrovsky, *Istoriya leib-gvardii Ulanskogo Polka* (St Petersburg, 1903), I, 153.
414. Heilmann, 195; Bobrovsky, 153; Preysing, 13–14.
415. Roth von Schreckenstein, 41–42.
416. Clausewitz, 161–162, 164.
417. Clausewitz, 164.
418. Toll, 217.
419. Clausewitz, 163.
420. Platov to Kutuzov [n.d. September 1812], RGVIA, f. VUA, d. 3465/2, l. 113.
421. Flotow, 195.
422. Wiedemann, 107.
423. Clausewitz, 165.
424. Liprandi (1861): 60.
425. Mikhailovsky-Danilevsky, II, 258; Tarle (1962), 48–49; Garnich, 167; Beskrovny (1968): 37.
426. Bieber, 105.

427. Wiedemann, 107–108.
428. Laugier, 84.
429. Dautancourt, 124–125.
430. Platov to Kutuzov [n.d. September 1812] RGVIA, f. VUA, d. 3465/2, l. 113.
431. Liprandi (1861): 61.
432. Report on Casualties of the 1st Western Army, in *Borodino: dokumenty, pisma, vospominaniya*, 197.
433. Clausewitz, 161–162, 164.
434. Golitsyn, 343.
435. Kutuzov to Alexander, 4 December 1812, *M.I. Kutuzov: sbornik dokumentov*, IV, 219.
436. *Borodino: dokumenty, pisma, vospominaniya*, 340–343; Kharkevich, 30–31.
437. Brandt, 219.
438. Dedem, 236.
439. Holzhauzen, 92–93.
440. Borozdin to Barclay de Tolly, 19 September 1812, RGVIA, f. VUA, d. 3561, ll. 14–19b.
441. Konovnitsyn, 358; Kutuzov to Lavrov, 13 September 1812, RGVIA, f. VUA, d. 3561, l. 34–35; Udom to Lavrov, 12 September 1812, in *Borodino: dokumenty, pisma, vospominaniya*, 147.
442. Chuquet, 50, 127–128, 345–346; Lejeune, II, 181; Schreckenstein, 53; Pelet, 80; Chambray, 63.
443. Chuquet, 50, 345–346; Dedem, 238; Friant, 234–235
444. Udom to Lavrov, 12 September 1812, in *Borodino: dokumenty, pisma, vospominaniya*, 147.
445. Dedem, 238–239; Friant, 234–235; Chuquet, 51; Rivolet, 252; Lubenkov, 49–50; St Priest, 168–170.
446. Bausset, II, 81–82
447. Dumas, *Souvenirs*, III, 440
448. Malachowski, 106; Griois, 36; Combe, 81; Pawly, 18.
449. Brandt, 219.
450. Pajol, 43.
451. Thirion, 185–187.
452. Biot, 35–37.
453. Roth von Schreckenstein, 85–86.
454. Barclay de Tolly, 'Izobrazhenye . . .' RGVIA, f. VUA, d. 3571, l. 48; Paskevich, 103; Rayevsky to Dokhturov, 23 September 1812, No. 280, General Staff Archives, XVIII, 59–60; Mikhailovsky-Danilevsky, II, 260.
455. Muravyev-Apostol 2(1886): 226. A slightly different version is in Muravyev, 'Zapiski,' *Russkii arkhiv*, 10(1885), 261.
456. *General Staff Archives*, XVI, 117; 139; Skugarevsky, 56–57, 71–72.
457. Larionov, 129.
458. Vasiliev, 'Frantsuzskie karabinery . . .' 8; Popov, 'Mezh dvukh 'vulkanov',' 44, 49; Roth von Schreckenstein, 84–85; Meerheim, 94, 96, Minckwitz, 10; Ditfurth, 95; Dumonceau, 139–140; Chlapowski, 268.
459. Eugène to Berthier, 10 September 1812, in Markham, *Imperial Glory*, 294.
460. Grunwald, 150; Griois, 36–37; Holzhausen, 98; Heckens, 128.
461. Pajol, 44; Biot, 36.
462. Korf to Barclay de Tolly, 21 September 1812, RGVIA, f. VUA, d. 3561, ll. 3b-4.
463. Creitz, 360.
464. Schubert, 235–236; Wolzogen, 142–143.
465. Ségur, IV, 391–392; Saint-Hilaire, 22.
466. Griois, II, 37; Murat to Berthier, 9 September 1812, in Markha, *Imperial Glory*, 291; Caulaincourt, I, 425–426; Derrécagaix, 503; Bausset, II, 79; Ségur, IV, 392; Coignet, 318–319; Vaudoncourt, 185; Roth von Schreckenstein, 93; Saint-Hilaire, 22–23.
467. Holzhausen, 98; Bertin, 73; Labaume, 144; Radozhitsky, I, 142.
468. Murat to Berthier, 9 September 1812, in Markham, *Imperial Glory*, 291; Griois, II, 38.
469. Griois, II, 38.
470. Brandt, 221–222; Caulaincourt, II, 429–430; Castellane, I, 150; Coignet, 319; Ségur, IV, 392.
471. Grunwald, 150.
472. Roth von Schreckenstein, 97–98; Minckwitz, 12–13.
473. Eugène to Berthier, 10 September 1812, in Markham, *Imperial Glory*, 291; Vaudoncourt, 185.
474. Labaume, 146; Laugier, 85.
475. Petrov, 184.
476. Karpenko, 340–341.
477. Meshetich, 47.
478. Mikhailovsky-Danilevsky, II, 261; Vyazemsky,84.
479. Barclay de Tolly, 'Izobrazhenye . . .' RGVIA, f. VUA, d. 3571, l. 49–50.
480. Roth von Schreckenstein, 94–96; Dutfurth, 109.
481. Kutuzov to Alexander, [n.d.] September 1812, RGVIA, f. VUA, d. 3561, ll. 56b-57; 'Opisaniye srazheniya pri sele Borodine,' *General Staff Archives*, XVI, 117.
482. Bogdanovich, II, 212.
483. Barclay de Tolly to Kutuzov, 8 October 1812, RGVIA, f. VUA, d. 3561, ll. 11–11b.
484. Barclay de Tolly to Kutuzov, 8 October 1812, RGVIA, f. VUA, d. 3561, ll. 11b-12.
485. Pawly, 18.
486. Vasiliev, 'Frantsuzkie karabinery,' 8–10; Holzhausen, 102.
487. Barclay de Tolly, 'Izobrazhenye . . .' RGVIA, f. VUA, d. 3571, l. 50–51.
488. Löwenstern, I, 262–265.

489. Barclay de Tolly, 'Izobrazhenye ...' RGVIA, f. VUA, d. 3571, l. 51.
490. Grunwald, 150–151.
491. Eugène to Berthier, 10 September 1812, in Markham, *Imperial Glory*, 291.
492. Griois, 38–39
493. Bogdanovich, II, 214.
494. Borozdin to Barclay de Tolly, 19 September 1812, No. 8, *General Staff Archives*, XVIII, 28–29.
495. Korf to Barclay de Tolly, 21 September 1812, RGVIA, f. VUA, d. 3561, ll. 4–5.
496. Korf to Barclay de Tolly, 21 September 1812, RGVIA, f. VUA, d. 3561, ll. 4–5; Kutuzov to Alexander, [n.d.] September 1812, RGVIA, f. VUA, d. 3561, ll. 56b-57.
497. Cited in Larionov, 129.
498. Mikhailovsky-Danilevsky, II, 260.
499. Radozhitsky, I, 152–154.
500. Meshetich, 49.
501. Mikhailovsky-Danilevsky, *Imperator Aleksandr I i ego spodvizhniki*, vol. 1.
502. Ségur, IV, 395–396.
503. Ségur, IV, 396.
504. Brandt, 221–222; Ségur, IV, 393–394.
505. Brandt, 222; Labaume, 152; Paskevich, 104.
506. Sievers to Kutuzov, [n.d.] September 1812, in Bogdanovich, II, 575–576.
507. Baggovut to Barclay de Tolly, [n.d] September 1812, in *Borodino: dokumenty, pisma, vospominaniya*, 184–185.
508. Sievers to Kutuzov, [n.d.] September 1812, Bogdanovich, II, 574–576.
509. Report cited in Larionov, 128.
510. Sievers to Kutuzov, [n.d.] September 1812, in Bogdanovich, II, 577
511. Baggovut to Barclay de Tolly, [n.d] September 1812, in *Borodino: dokumenty, pisma, vospominaniya, 186*.
512. Mikhailovsky-Danilevsky, II, 265.
513. Bogdanovich, II, 217–218.
514. Wolzogen, 145–146.
515. Rayevsky, 382; Kutuzov to Barclay de Tolly and Dokhturov, 7 September 1812, in *Borodino: dokumenty, pisma, vospominaniya, 96–97*.
516. Löwenstern, 368–369.
517. Timiryazev, *Russkii arkhiv*, 22/1 (1884): 167.
518. *Izobrazhenie voyennykh deistvii 1-oi armii v 1812 g*, RGVIA, f. VUA, op. 16, d. 3571, ll. 27–28.
519. Petrov, 1806–1807. Meshetich also wrote that 'the enemy retreated ... 7 versts from the battlefield.' Meshetich, 49.
520. Bennigsen, 'Memoirs,' *Russkaya starina*, 139 (1909): 499; Mikhailovsky-Danilevsky, II, 283; Sherbinin, 399.
521. Kutuzov to Rostopchin, 7 September 1812, in *Borodino: dokumenty, pisma, vospominaniya*, 97.
522. Kutuzov to Alexander, 8 September 1812; 'Ofitsialnye izevstiya,' [n.d.] September 1812, *Borodino: dokumenty, pisma, vospominaniya*, 101–102, 112; Kutuzov to Ekaterina Kutuzova, 9 September 1812, *M.I. Kutuzov: Sbornik dokumentov*, IV, 181.
523. *Bumagi Shukina*, 8 (1904): 109–110.
524. Petrov, 185–186.
525. Ségur, IV, 398.
526. Fantin des Odoards, 318–319
527. Caulaincourt, 103–104; Bausset, II, 87; Ségur, IV, 401–403; VI, 11
528. Dedem, 240; Kurz, 90; Brandt, 223–224; Boulart, 255; Labaume, 153–154; Dumonceau, II, 142–143; Griois, 41–42.
529. Bertin, 87–88.
530. Ségur, IV, 404.
531. Bellot de Kergorre, 59–64.
532. Kutuzov to Alexander I, 9 September 1812, No. 105, in *M.I. Kutuzov: sbornik dokumentov*, IV, 175–176.
533; Smith, 132.
534. Napoleon to Francis, 9 September 1812, *Correspondance de Napoleon Ier*, No.19183, XXIV, 241; The 18th Bulletin, 10 September 1812, in Markham, *Imperial Glory*, 297; Kutuzov to Alexander, 10 September 1812, in *Borodino: dokumenty, pisma, vospominaniya*, 117; Kutuzov to Alexander I, [n.d.] September 1812, RGVIA, f. VUA, d. 3561, l. 58.
535. Montesquiou de Fezensac, *Journal*, 51.
536. Report of Voltigeurs Réunis, 6 September 1812; Report of the 61st Line, 6 September 1812; Report of the 111th Line, 6 September 1812; Report of the 111th Line, 30 September 1812; Report of the 111th Line, 1 October 1812, Ternaux-Compans, 353, 355–356, 359.
537. 'Iz spiskov ubitykh, ranenykh I nagrazhdennikh voinsikh chinov v voinu 1812–1814 gg,' in *M.I. Kutuzov: Sbornik dokumentov*, IV, 208–209.
538. Tselorungo (2003), 33–38; Lvov (2003), 52–66.
539. 'Vedomost nizhnim voinskim chinam byvshei 2-I Zapadnoi armii ...' [n.d.] September 1812; 'Vedomost 8-go korpusa ...' 18 September 1812; 'Vedomost [...] artilleriiskhikh nizhnikh chinov ...' [n.d.] September 1812; 'Vedomost o poteryakh 1-i Zapadnoi Armii ...' [n.d.] September 1812; 'Vedomost [...] artillerrii 1-i Zapadnoi Armii,' 26 Septemebr 1812, in *Borodino: dokumenty, pisma, vospominaniya*, 189–212.
540. Lvov (2003): 52–66.

# The Battle of Borodino

541. 'Vedomost ob ubitykh, ranenykh, bez vestu propavshikh i o protchem artillerii 1-i Zapadnoi armii,' 26 September 1812, in *Borodino: dokumenty, pisma, vospominaniya*, 202–212.
542. 'Vedomost nizhnim chinam byvshei 2-i Zapadnoi armii . . .' [n.d.] September 1812, in *Borodino: dokumenty, pisma, vospominaniya*, 191–192.
543. Quintin, 27; Aleksey Vasiliev, 'Poteri frantsuzskoi armii pri Borodino,' *Rodina*, 6/7(1992): 68–71.
544. Tselorungo, 194.
545. Joseph Marie de Maistre, *Correspondence diplomatique*, 177
546. Bogdanovich, II, 230.
547. Writings of John Quincy Adams, IV, 395; Ker Porter, 101
548. Mikhailovsky-Danilevsky (1839), II, 289–290.
549. Panchulidzev, *Istoriya Kavalergardov*, III, 219; Bogdanovich, II, 239.
550. Order to the Armies, No. 12, 9 September 1812, *General Staff Archives*, XVI, 139–140
551. Mikhailovsky-Danilevsky (1839), II, 321.
552. Vasili Perovsky, 'Iz zapisok Grafa Vasilia Aleksandrovicha Perovskogo,' in *Russkii arkhiv* (1865): 1033.
553. Served as escort of parks of the I Corps and did not participate in battle.

# Select Bibliography

A complete bibliography is available at www.napoleon-series.org. Entries are organized based on the language of publication. Thus, memoirs by French participants that were consulted in their Russian editions are included in the Russian section. Dozens of Napoleonic titles are available through the Gallica project of *La Bibliothèque Nationale de France* (http://gallica.bnf.fr) and the *Google Book Project* (http://books.google.com).

Abbreviations
Beskrovny 1962 – Beskrovny, Liubomir and G. Mesheryakov, eds, *Borodino: dokumenty, pisma, vospominaniya*, Moscow, 1962.
Kharkevich, 1900–Kharkevich V, *1812 god v dnevnikakh, zapiskakh i vospominaniyakh sovremennikov* Vilna, 1900

## RUSSIAN SOURCES
### Archival
Rossiiskii Gosudarstvennii Voenno-Istoricheskii arkhiv (RGVIA)
[Russian State Military Historical Archive]
Cartons (*delo*) 3465, 3467, 3561, 3562, 3563, 3571, 3572, 3638, 3651, 3655 and 3690.

### Primary
Afanasiyev, V, *Podlinnye dokumenti o Borodinskom srazhenii*, Moscow, 1912.
Andreyev, N, 'Iz vospominanii,' *Russkii arkhiv*, 1879, N10.
Barclay de Tolly, Mikhail, *'Opravdanie v deistviyakh ego vo vremia Otechestvennoi voini s frantsuzami v 1812 godu,'* in *Zhurnal Imperatorskogo Russkogo voenno-istoricheskogo obshestva*, St Petersburg, 1911.
Bennigsen, Levin, 'Zapiski o kampanii 1812 g.,' *Russkaya starina*, Nos. 138–139 (1909).
Beskrovny, Liubomir, ed, *M.I. Kutuzov: Sbornik Dokumentov*, Moscow: Voenizdat, 1954.
Bieber, E, 'Zapiski mayora Z.F. Biebera,' in Popov, 1995 (b): 105.
Bogdanov, Dementii, 'Iz vospominanii D. Bogdanova,' in Beskrovny, 1962: 336–339.
Bolgovsky, D, 'Iz vospominanii D.N. Bolgovskogo,' in Kharkevich, 1900: 226–243.
*Bumagi, otnosiashiesia do Otechestvennoi voini 1812 g.*, sobrannye i izdannye P.I. Shukinim. Moscow, 1904.
Divov, N, 'Vospominaniya.' *Russkii arkhiv*: 1333–1340.
Dreyling, Johann Reinhold von, 'Vospominaniya ...' in *1812 god: Vospominaniya voinov russkoi armii*, Moscow, 1991, 356–400.
Dubrovin, Nikolai, *Otechestvennaya voina v pismakh sovremennikov, (1812–1815)* , St Petersburg, 1882.
Durnovo, Nikolai, 'Dnevnik 1812 g' in *1812 god: voyennie dnevniki*, Moscow, 1985.
Dushenkevich, Dmitri, 'Iz moikh vospominanii' in *1812 god v vospominaniyakh sovremennikov*, Moscow, 1985, 105–136.
Eugène of Wurttemberg, 'Vospominania' in *Voennyi zhurnal*, 4 (1847); 1 (1848).
Eyler, A, 'Iz zapisok A. Kh. Eyler,' in *Russkii arkhiv*, 2(1880): 359–360.
*Feldmarshal Kutuzov: sbornik dokumentov i materialov*, Moscow, 1947.
Glinka, Fedor, *Ocherki Borodinskogo srazhenia (vospominaniya o 1812 gode)*, Moscow, 1839.
Glinka, Fedor, *Pisma Russkogo ofitsera*, Moscow, 1985.
Golitsyn, A, 'Iz vospominanii A.B. Golitsyna,' in Beskrovny, 1962: 343–344.
Golitsyn, Nikolai, *Ofitserskiye zapiski ili vospominaniya o pokhodakh 1812, 1813, 1814 godov*, Moscow, 1838.
Golitsyn, Nikolai, *Perenesenie tela kniazya Bagrationa na Borodinskoye pole*, Moscow, 1839.
Gorchakov, Andrey, 'Iz vospominanii knyazya Gorchakova,' in Kharkevich, 1900: 196–198.
Grabbe, Paul, *Iz Pamiatnikh Zapisok* Moscow, 1873.
Heilbronner, K, 'Zapiski o perezhitom leitenanta K. Heilbronnera,' in Popov, 1995(b): 105–106.
Kallash V, *Dvenadtsatii god v vospominaniyakh i perepiske sovremennikov*, Moscow, 1912.
Karpenko, Moses, 'Pismo starogo voina' in *1812 god: vospominaniya voinov russkoi armii*, Moscow, 1991, 340–341.

# The Battle of Borodino

Konovnitsyn, Peter, 'Iz vospominanii' in Kharkevich, 1900: 121–134.
Creitz K, 'Iz zapisok' in Beskrovny, 1962: 359–360
Liprandi, Ivan, *Borodinskoye srazheniye, zaklucheniya s nekotorymi primiechaniyami na istoriyu etoi voiny*, St Petersburg, 1861.
Liprandi, Ivan, *Materialy dlya Otechestvennoi voiny 1812 goda*, St Petersburg, 1867.
Liprandi, Ivan, 'Zamechaniya I.P. Liprandi na 'Opisaniye Otechestvennoi voiny 1812 goda' Mikhailovskago Danilevskago,' in Kharkevich, 1900: 1–36.
Lubenkov, N, *Rasskaz artillerista o dele Borodinskom*, St Petersburg, 1837.
Löwenstern, Waldemar Hermann, 'Iz zapisok ...' *Russkaya starina*, 12 (1900): 572–582.
Mayevsky, Sergey, 'Moi vek ili istoria generala S.I. Mayevskogo.' *Russkaya starina*, 8(1873): 136–141. Excerpts in Beskrovny, 1962: 370–373.
Meshetich, Gavriil, 'Istoricheskie zapiski ...' in *1812 god: Vospominaniya voinov russkoi armii*, Moscow, 1991, 24–103.
Mikhailovsky-Danilevsky, Alexander, 'Zapiski. 1812 god,' in *Istoricheskii Vestnik*, 10(1890).
Mitarevsky, N, 'Iz zapisok ...' in *Borodino v vospominaniyakh sovremennikov*, St Petersburg, 2001, 171–188.
Muravyev, A, 'Iz avtobiograficheskikh zapisok ...' in Beskrovny, 1962: 373–379.
Muravyev, N, 'Zapiski' in *Russkii arkhiv*, 10 (1885).
Muravyev-Apostol, M.I. , 'Zapiski,' *Russkii arkhiv* 2 (1886).
Neverovsky, Dmitri, 'Iz zapisok ...' in Beskrovny, 1962: 379–380.
Nikitin, Aleksey, 'Vospominaniya ...' in *1812 god v dnevnikakh, zapiskakh i vospominaniyakh sovremennikov* Vilna, 1903, 139–150.
Nikolai Mikhailovich, Grand Duke, *Perepiska imperatora Aleksandra s sestroi velikoi kniazhnoi Ekaterinoi Pavlovnoi*, St Petersburg, 1910.
Norov, Avraam, 'Iz vospominanii ...' in *Borodino v vospominaniyakh sovremennikov*, St Petersburg, 2001, 188–204.
Orlov-Denisov, Vasili, 'Iz vospominanii ...' in Kharkevich, 1900: 213–225.
*Otechestvennaia voina 1812 g.: Materiali Voenno-Uchebnogo arkhiva Glavnogo Shtaba*, St Petersburg, 1900–1904, vols. I, XV–XVIII
Paskevich, Ivan, 'Zapiski Paskevicha' in Kharkevich, 1900: 82–112.
Pelet, Jean-Jacques, 'Borodinskoe srazheniye' in *Chteniya v imperatorskom obschestve istorii i drevnostei rossiiskikh*, 1 (1872).
Petrov, Mikhail, 'Rasskazy ...' in *1812 god: Vospominaniya voinov russkoi armii*, Moscow, 1991, 104–355.
Pushin, Pavel, 'Dnevnik ...' Leningrad, 1987. Also excerpts in Aglaimov, S, *Historical Materials of the Semyenovskii Lifeguard Regiment*, Poltava, 1912.
'Rasskaz Georgievskogo Kavalera iz divizii Neverovskogo,' in *Chtenia imperatorskogo obschestva istorii drevnostei*, 1 (1872), 119.
'Rasskaz o Borodinskom srazhenii otdelennogo Unter-Ofitsera Tikhonova' in *Chtenia imperatorskogo obschestva istorii drevnostei*, 1 (1872), 119–20.
Rayevsky, Nikolai, 'Iz zapisok ...' in Beskrovny, 1962: 380–382.
Rodozhitsky, Ilya, *Pokhodnye zapiski artillerista s 1812 po 1816 god*, Moscow, 1835.
Romanov, Mikhail, 'Zapiski otstavnogo podpolkovnika ...' in *1812 god: Vospominaniya voinov russkoi armii* Moscow, 1991, 403–409.
Roos, Heinrich von, *S Napoleonom v Rossiu. Zapiski vracha Velikoi armii*, Moscow, 1912.
Saint Priest, Emmanuel, 'Bumagi grafa Sen Priesta,' in Kharkevich, 1900: 134–180.
Sherbinin, A, 'Zapiski ...' in Kharkevich, 1900: 14–23.
Skobelev, I, 'Soldatskaya perepiska 1812 goda' in *1812 god v vospominaniyakh i rasskazakh sovremennikov*, Moscow, 2001.
Sukhanin, N, 'Iz zhurnala uchastnika voiny 1812 goda.' *Russkaya starina*, February 1912.
Toll, Karl, *Opisaniye bitvy pri s. Borodine*, St Petersburg, 1839.
Wiedemann, Karl, 'Bavarskaya shevolezherskaya divizia generala grafa Preysinga v voine protiv Rossii v 1812 godu' in Popov, 1995(b): 106–108.
Valkovich, A. and A. Kapitonov. eds, *Borodino: dokumentalnaya khronika*, Moscow, 2004.
Vistitsky, Mikhail, 'Iz zapisok ...' in Kharkevich, 1900: 181–195.
Vorontsov, Mikhail, 'Iz vospominanii ...' in Kharkevich, 1900: 199–204; and in Beskrovny, 1962: 342–43.
Vossen, Wilhelm Anton, 'Dnevnik poruchika Fossena.' *Russkii arkhiv* 11(1903): 468–471.
Voyensky, K, *Otechestvennaya voina 1812 goda v zapiskakh sovremennikov*, St Petersburg, 1911.
Vyazemsky, Peter. 'Iz vospominanii ...' in *Borodino v vospominaniyakh sovremennikov*, St Petersburg, 2001, 82–87.
Yermolov, Alexei, *Zapiski A.P. Yermolova*, Moscow, 1991.
Zhirkevich, Ivan, 'Zapiski,' *Russkaya starina*, 8 (1874).

## Secondary
Antelava, Irakli, *Gruzini v Otechestvenoi voine 1812 goda*, Tbilisi, 1983.
Beskrovny, Liubomir, *Russkaya armiya i flot v XIX veke*, Moscow, 1973.
Beskrovny, Liubomir, *Borodinskoye srazheniye*, Moscow, 1971.
Beskrovny, Liubomir, *Otechestvennaia voina 1812 goda*, Moscow, 1968.
Beskrovny, Liubomir, *Tysiacha vosemsot dvenadtsatyi god: k stopiatidesiatiletiiu Otechestvennoi voiny*, Moscow, 1962(a).

# Select Bibliography

Bezotosny, V ed, *Otechestvennaia voina 1812 goda: Entsiklopedia*, Moscow, 2004.
Bezotosny, V, *Donskoi generalitet i Ataman Platov v 1812 godu: Maloizvestnye i neizvestnye fakty na fone znamenitykh sobytii*, Moscow, 1999.
Bezotosny, V, 'Analiticheskii proyekt voyennikh deistvii v 1812 g. P. A. Chuikevicha.' *Rossiiskii arkhiv*, 7(1996): 43–49.
Bogdanovich, Modest, *Istoria Otechestvennoi voiny 1812 g. po dostovernym istochnikam*, St Petersburg 1859.
Buturlin, Dmitri, *Istoriya nashestviya Imperatora Napoleona na Rossiyu v 1812 godu*, St Petersburg, 1837.
Buturlin, Dmitri, 'Kutuzov v 1812 g.' *Russkaya starina*, 10 (1894).
Djevegelov A., Makhnevich N., eds, *Otechestvennaia voina i Russkoye obshestvo*, 7 vols. Moscow, 1911–1912.
Garin F, *Izgnaniye Napoleona*, Moscow, 1988.
Garnich, N, *1812*, Moscow, 1956.
Garnich, N, 'Borodinskoye srazheniye' in *Polkovodets Kutuzov: sbornik statei*, Moscow, 1955.
Garnich, N, *Borodinskoye srazhenie*, Moscow, 1949.
Gerua, A, *Borodino (po novym dannym)*, St Petersburg, 1912.
Grunberg, P, 'Deistvitelno li 'perevodil strelki' general-kvartimeister Karl Tol'?' in *Epokha Napoleonovskikh voin: liudi, sobitiya, idei*, Moscow, 2004.
Grunberg, P, 'O chislenotsi velikoi armii v srazhenii pri Borodine,' in *Epokha Napoleonovskikh voin: liudi, sobitiya, idei*, Moscow, 2002.
Ivchenko, Lydia, *Borodino: Legenda i deistvitelnost*, Moscow, 2002.
Ivchenko, Lydia, 'Raport M.I. Golenisheva-Kutuzova o borodinskom srazhenii. Podlinnik ili apokrif,' in *Epokha Napoleonovskikh voin: liudi, sobitiya, idei*, Moscow, 2002.
Ivchenko, Lydia, 'Plany russkogo komandovaniya v Borodinskom srazhenii i ikh realizatsiya,' in *Borodinskoye srazheniye*, Mozhaisk, 2001.
Ivchenko, Lydia, 'Boi za Semeyonovskie vysoty,' in *Otechestvennaiya voina 1812 g: Istochniki, Pamyatniki, Problemy*, Borodino, 2001.
Ivchenko, Lydia, 'Sravnitelnii analiz pervikh ofitsialnikh izvestii o Borodinskom srazhenii,' in *Epokha Napoleonovskikh voin: liudi, sobitiya, idei*, Moscow, 2001.
Ivchenko, Lydia, 'Boevye deistviya russkikh voisk u der. Semeyonovskoe,' in *Otechestvennaiya voina 1812 g: Istochniki, Pamyatniki, Problemy*, Borodino, 1994.
Ivchenko, Lydia, 'K. F. Toll i istoriografiya Borodinskogo srazheniya,' in *Otechestvennaiya voina 1812 g: Istochniki, Pamyatniki, Problemy*, Borodino, 1993.
Kharkevich, V, *Barklai de Tolly v Otechestvennuyu voinu posle soedineniya armii pod Smolenskom*, St Petersburg, 1904.
Kharkevich, V, *Voina 1812 goda. Ot Nemana do Smolenska*, Vilna, 1901.
Kochetkov, A, 'O nekotorykh oshibkakh v osveshenii Borodinskogo srazheniya.' in *Voenno-Istoricheskii Zhurnal*, 1963, No. 12.
Kochetkov, A, *Barclay de Tolly*, Moscow, 1970.
Kolyubyakin, B, *1812 g. Borodinskoye srazhenie*, St Petersburg, 1912.
Kolyubyakin, B and A. Nefedovich, *Borodinskoye srazheniye i podgotovka polya srazhenya v inzhenernom otnoshenii*, Moscow, 1999.
Kozlovsky, I, 'Gvardeiskii ekipazh v Borodinskom srazhenii i pri izgnanii protivnika iz Rossii i okkupirovannikh stran Evropy,' in *Epokha Napoleonovskikh voin: liudi, sobitiya, idei*, Moscow, 1999.
Levchenko, V, *Geroi 1812 goda*, Moscow, 1987.
Levitsky, N, *Voina 1812 goda*, Moscow, 1938.
Lvov, Sergey, 'Borba s formalizmom ili chto delal Wittgenstein v Mozyre: K diskusii o chislenosti i poteryakh Rossiiskoi armii pri Borodino' in *Epokha Napoleonovskikh voin: liudi, sobitiya, idei*, Moscow, 2005.
Lvov, Sergey, 'Poteri 6-go pekhotnogo korpusa pri Borodino' in *Epokha Napoleonovskikh voin: liudi, sobitiya, idei*, Moscow, 2004.
Lvov, Sergey, 'O poteryakh Rossiiskoi armii v srazhenii pri Borodino 24–26 avgusta 1812 goda' in *Epokha Napoleonovskikh voin: liudi, sobitiya, idei*, Moscow, 2003.
Mikhailovsky-Danilevsky, Alexander, *Opisaniye Otechestvennoi voiny v 1812 godu*, St Petersburg, 1839.
Mikhailovsky-Danilevsky, Alexander, *Imperator Aleksandr I i ego spodvizhniki v 1812, 1813, 1814, 1815 godakh: Voennaia galereia Zimnego Dvortsa*, 6 vols. St Petersburg, 1845–1850.
Monakhov, A, 'M.B. Barclay de Tolly i plani nastupatelnoi voini v 1811–1812 gou,' in *Epokha Napoleonovskikh voin: liudi, sobitiya, idei*, Moscow, 2001.
Neyelov, N, *Opyt opisaniya Borodinskogo srazheniya*, Moscow, 1839.
Podmazo, Alexander, *Shefy i komandiry regulyarnykh polkov Russkoi armii v 1796–1815*, Moscow, 1997.
Polikarpov, N, *K istorii Otechestvennoi Voini 1812 g.: po pervositochnikam*, Moscow, 1911.
Popov, Andrey, 'Wurtemberzhtsy v Borodinskom srazhenii' in *Voin*, 2000, No. 4.
Popov, Andrey, 'Zasadnyi otryad' N.A. Tuchkova (somneniya v ochevidnom ili apologia Bennigsena),' in *Otechestvennaya voina 1812 goda: istochniki, pamyatniki, problemy*, Borodino, 1998
Popov, Andrey, 'Boyevye deistviya v tsentre Borodinskogo polya,' in *Otechestvennaya voina 1812 g.: Istochniki, Pamyatniki, Problemy*, Borodino, 1997.
Popov, Andrey, 'Mezh dvukh 'vulkanov:' Boyevye deistviya v tsentre Borodinskogo polya*, Kharkov, 1997.
Popov, Andrey, 'Deistviya Westphaltsev v Borodinskom srazhenii' in *Otechestvennaya voina 1812 g.: Istochniki, Pamyatniki, Problemy*, Borodino, 1995(a).
Popov, Andrey, *Borodinskoe srazhenie (boyevye deistviya na severnom flange)*, Samara, 1995(b).
Popov, Andrey, 'Nemetskie voiska v boyu za Bagrationovy fleshi' in *Problemy istorii i istoriografii zarubezhnogo mira*, Samara, 1994.

# The Battle of Borodino

Shvedov, S, 'Chislenost i poteri russkoi armii pri Borodino' in *Epokha Napoleonovskikh voin: liudi, sobitiya, idei*, Moscow, 2004.

Shvedov, S, 'Chislenost i poteri russkoi armii v Borodinskom srazhenii,' in *Otechestvennaya voina 1812 goda: Istochniki. Pamyatniki. Problemy*, Borodino, 1994.

Shvedov, S, 'O plane otstupleniya russkoi armii vglub strany v 1812 g' in *Otechestvennaya voina 1812 g. Rossia i Evropa*, Borodino, 1992.

Shvedov, S, 'Komplektovaniye, chislenost' i poteri russkoi armii v 1812 g.,' in *Istoriya SSSR*, 1987, No. 4.

Skugarevsky, A, *Borodino*, St Petersburg, 1912.

Smirnov, A, 'Kakim byl Shevardinskii redut?' in *Epokha Napoleonovskikh voin: liudi, sobitiya, idei*, Moscow, 2004.

Smirnov, A, 'Shevardinskii redut glazami vzyavshikh ego,' in *Epokha Napoleonovskikh voin: liudi, sobitiya, idei*, Moscow, 2003.

Tarle, Eugène, *Borodino*, Moscow, 1962.

Tarle, Eugène, *Nashestvie Napoleona na Rossiyu 1812*, Moscow, 1992 (reprint).

Tartarovsky, A, *Nerazgadannyi Barklai: legendy i byl' 1812 goda*, Moscow, 1996.

Tartarovsky, A, *1812 god i russkaia memuaristika*, Moscow, 1980.

Troitsky, Nikolai, *Otechestvennaya voina 1812 goda: istoriya temy*, Saratov, 1991.

Troitsky, Nikolai, *1812: Velikii god Rossii*, Moscow, 1988

Tselorungo, Dmitri, 'Nekotorye svedeniya, otnosyashiesya k publikatsii F.V. Rostopchinym 'Podrobnogo spiska vsekh korpusov, sostavlyaushikh frantsuzskuyu armiyu …' in *Otechestvennaya voina 1812 goda: Istochniki. Pamyatniki. Problemy*, (Moscow, 2006), 43–46.

Tselorungo, Dmitri, 'Boyevoi opyt unter-ofitserov Russkoi armii – uchastnikov Borodinskogo srazheniya.' *Otechestvennaya voina 1812 goda: Istochniki. Pamyatniki. Problemy*, (Moscow, 2005), 21–27.

Tselorungo, Dmitri, 'Ofitsery russkoi armii nemetskogo proiskhozhdeniya –uchastniki Borodinskogo srazheniya,' in *Otechestvennaya voina 1812 goda: Istochniki. Pamyatniki. Problemy*, (Moscow, 2004), 394–401.

Tselorungo, Dmitri, 'K voprosu o poteryakh Russkoi armii v Borodinskoi srazhenii,' in *Borodino i Napoleonovskie voiny*, (Moscow, 2003), 33–38.

Tselorungo, Dmitri, *Ofitsery russkoi armii–uchastniki Borodinskogo srazheniya: istoriko-sotsiologicheskoe issledovanie*, Moscow, 2002.

Tselorungo, Dmitri, 'Russkiye ofitsery v Borodinskom srazhenii,' in *Otechestvennaya voina 1812 goda: Istochniki. Pamyatniki. Problemy*, (Moscow, 2000), 268–284.

Vasiliev, Alexei, 'Komentarii k raportu o srazhenii pri Mozhaiske.' *Orel*, 1991, Nos. 15, 17.

Vasiliev, Alexei, 'Lukavaya tsifra avanturista. Poteri podlinnye i pridumannye,' *Rodina*, 1992, Nos. 6–7, 68–71.

Vasiliev, Alexei, 'Frantsuzskie karabinery pri Borodino.' *Tseikhgauz*, No. 2, 6–10.

Vasiliev, Alexei, 'Kavaleria Napoleona v Borodinskom srazhenii. Boevoye raspisanie na 5–7 sentyabrya 1812 g.' *Tseikhgauz*, No. 4 (1995): 13–15; No. 5 (1996): 13–15; No.6 (1997): 25–27.

Vasiliev, Alexei, 'Ispanskii polk 'Józef-Napoleon' v Russkoi kampanii.' *Tseikhgauz*, No. 6 (1997): 20–23.

Vasiliev, Alexei and Lydia Ivchenko, 'Devyat na dvenadtsat ili povest o tom kak nekton perevel chasovuyu strelku.' *Rodina*, 6–7(1992): 62–67.

Vasiliev, Alexei, and Yeliseyev, A, *Russkie soyedinennye armii pri Borodine 24–26 avg. 1812 g. Sostav voisk i ikh chislenost*, Moscow, 1997.

Vasiliev, Alexei, and Popov, A, *Voina 1812 g. Khronika sobytii. Grande Armée. Sostav armii pri Borodino*, Moscow, 2002.

Witmer, A, 'Borodino v ocherkakh nashikh sovremennikov,' in *Voenno-istoricheskii sbornik*, 1913, No.1

Witmer, A, 'Borodinskii boi' in *Voenno-istoricheskii sbornik* 1912, No. 3

Yepanchin, Yuri, 'Rol sedmogo korpusa N.N. Rayevskogo v Borodinskoi bitve.' *Voprosy Istorii*, 8 (1996): 144–146.

Zemtsov, Vladimir, ''Frantsuzskoe' Borodino (Frantsuzskaia istoriografiya Borodinskogo srazheniya,' in *Otechestvennaia Istoria*, 6 (2002): 38–51.

Zemtsov, Vladimir, *Bitva pri Moskve-reke: armiya Napoleona v Borodinskom srazhenii*, Moscow, 2001.

Zemtsov, Vladimir, 'Napoleon v Borodinskom srazhenii (opyt mikroistoricheskogo issledovanya),' in *Otechestvennaya voina 1812 g.: Istochniki, Pamyatniki, Problemy*, Borodino, 2000, 56–85.

Zemtsov, Vladimir, 'Divizia Kompana v boyu za Shevardinskii redut 5 Sentiabria 1812 g,' in *Sergeant*, 7 (2000): 3–8.

Zemtsov, Vladimir, *Bitva pri Moskve-reke*, Moscow, 1999

Zemtsov, Vladimir, 'Frantsuzskaya armiya 6 Sent. 1812 g.,' in *Otechestvennaya voina 1812 g.: Istochniki, Pamyatniki, Problemy*, Borodino, 1998,

Zhilin, Pavel, *Borodinskoe srazhenie*, Moscow, 1952.

Zhilin, Pavel, *M.I. Kutuzov*, Moscow, Nauka, 1987.

Zhilin, Pavel, *Gibel' Napoleonovskoi armii v Rossii*, Moscow, Nauka, 1974

Zhilin, Pavel, *Otechestvennaya voina 1812 goda*, Moscow, Voenizdat, 1988

## FRENCH SOURCES
### Primary

Anthouard de Vraincourt, Charls Nicholas, 'Notes et documents …' in *Carnet de la Sabretache*, Serie 2, 1906, No. 162.

Aubry Th.-J, *Souvenirs du 12-ème de chasseurs*, Paris, 1889

# Select Bibliography

Bausset, Louis-François-Joseph, *Mémoires anecdotiques sur l'intérieur du palais et sur quelques évènemens de l'Empire depuis 1805 jusqu'au 1er mai 1814 pour servir à l'histoire de Napoléon*, Paris, 1827.

Bellot de Kergorre, Alexandre. *Un commissaire des guerres pendant le premier empire. Journal de Bellot de Kergorre*, Paris, 1899.

Berthezene, Pierre, *Souvenirs militaries de la République et de l'Empire*, Paris, 1855.

Bertin, Georges, *La Campaign de 1812: d'après des témoins oculaires*, Paris, 1895.

Bertrand, Vincent, *Mémoires du capitaine Bertrand*, Augers, 1909.

Biot, Jouber François, *Souvenirs anecdotique et militaires du colonel Biot, aide-de-camp du general Pajol*, Paris, 1901.

Bonnet, Guillaume, 'Journal du captaine Bonnet du 18-e de ligne (campagne de 1812),' in *Carnet de la Sabretache*, 1912, 641–672.

Boulart, Jean François. *Mémoires militaires du général baron Boulart sur les guerres de la république et de l'empire*, Paris, 1892.

Bréaut des Marlots. Jean, *Letter d'un capitaine de cuirassiers sur la campagne de Russie*, Poitiers, 1885.

Bro, Louis. *Mémoires du général Bro (1796–1844)*, Paris, 1914.

Calosso, Colonel, *Mémoires d'un vieux soldat*, Turin, 1857.

Castellane, Victor, *Journal du maréchal de Castellane, 1804–1862, Paris, 1895*.

Chambray, Georges de, *Histoire de l'expedition de Russie*, Paris, 1838.

Chapowski, Dezydery. *Mémoires sur les guerres de Napoléon, 1806–1813*, Paris, 1908.

Chuquet, Arthur. *1812: La guerre de Russie. Notes et documents*, Paris: Fontemoing, 1912.

Coignet, Jean-Roch. *Les cahiers du capitaine Coignet (1799–1815)*, Paris, 1883.

Davout, Louis Nicholas, *Correspondance du Marechal Davout, Prince d'Eckmuhl, ses commandements, son ministére, 1801–1815*, Paris, 1885.

Davout, Louis Nicholas, *Mémoires et souvenirs*, Paris, 1898.

Dedem de Gelder, Antoine, *Mémoires du General Dedem de Gelder, 1774–1825*, Paris, 1900.

Dellard, Jean Pierre. *Mémoires militaires sur les guerres de la République et l'empire*, Paris, 1892.

Denniée, Pierre Paul, *Itinéraire de l'empereur Napoléon pendant la campaigne de 1812*, Paris, 1842.

Du Casse, Albert, ed, *Mémoires et correspondance politique et militaire du prince Eugène*, Paris, 1859.

Dumas, Mathieu, *Souvenirs* Paris, 1839.

Dumonceau, François. *Mémoires*, Bruxelles, 1958–1963.

Dupuy, Victor, *Souvenirs*, Paris, 1892.

Durdent, R, *Campagne de Moscou en 1812*, Paris, 1814.

Dutheillet de Lamoth, A, *Mémoires* Bruxelles, 1899.

Faber du Faur, G. de, *La Campagne de Russie (1812) d'après le journal illustré d'un témoin oculaire*, Paris, 1895.

Fain A.J.F, *Manuscript de 1812*, Paris, 1827.

Fantin des Odoards, Louis Florimond. *Journal*, Paris, 1895.

Fezensac de Montesquiou, Raymond, *Souveniers Militaires de 1804 a 1814*, Paris, 1863.

Flotow, Lieutenant, 'Journal' in Gabriel Fabry, *Campagne de Russie* (Paris, 1903), vol. 3.

François, C., *Journal du capitaine François*, Paris, 1904.

Gardier, Louis, *Journal de la campagne de Russie (1812)*, Paris, 1999.

Girod de l'Ain, Felix Jean Marie, *Dix Ans de mes Souvenirs militaires, de 1805 a 1815*, Paris, 1873.

Gourgaud, Gaspard, *Napoléon et la grande armée en Russie*, Paris, 1825.

Griois, Charles Pierre Lubin, *Mémoires*, Paris, 1909.

Grouchy, Emmanuel, *Mémoires* Paris, 1873–1879.

Henckens, J.L, *Mémoires*, La Haye, 1910.

Jomini, Antoine-Henri, *Vie Politique et Militaire de Napoleon, racontée par lui meme*, Paris, 1827.

Labaume, Eugène, *Relation circonstancée de la Campagne de Russie en 1812*, Paris, 1815.

Lagneau, Louis Vincent. *Journal d'un chirurgien de la Grande Armée, 1803–1815*, Paris, 1913.

Larrey, Dominique Jean, *Mémoires de Chirurgie militaire, et campagnes du Baron D-J Larrey*, Paris, 1817.

Laugier, Cesare de, *Épopées centenaires, la grande armée*, Paris, 1910.

Le Roy, Claude François Madeleine. *Souvenirs*, Dijon, 1914.

Napoleon I, Emperor of the French, *Correspondance de Napoleon Ier*, Paris, 1858–1869.

Pelleport, Pierre, *Souvenirs militaries et intimes*, Paris, 1857.

Pion des Loches, Antoine. *Mes campagnes (1792–1815)*, Paris, 1889.

Planat de la Faye, Nicolas Louis, *Vie de Planat de la Faye, aide de camp des generaux Lariboisiere et Drouot, officier d'ordonnance de Napoleon I*, Paris, 1895.

Rapp, Jean, *Mémoires*, Paris, 1823.

Roguet, François, *Meimoires militaires*, Paris, 1865.

Rossetti, general, *Journal d'un compagnon de Murat*, Paris, 1998.

Saint-Hilaire, Emile Marco, *Histoire de la campagne de Russie*, Paris, 1846.

Ségur, Philippe Paul, *Histoire et meimoires*, Paris, 1873–1877.

Ségur, Philippe Paul, *Histoire de Napoléon et de la grande-armée pendant l'année 1812*, Paris, 1825.

Seruzier, Theodore Jean Joseph. *Mémoires* Paris, 1823.

Soltyk, Roman, *Napoleìon en 1812: Meimoires historiques et militaires sur la campagne de Russie*, Paris, 1836.

Suckow, Karl Friedrich Emil von. *Fragments de ma vie*, Paris, 1901.

Teste, F.A., 'Souvenirs,' in *Carnet de la Sabretache*, 1911, No. 223, 666–742.

Thirion de Metz, Auguste, *Souvenirs militaires. 1807–1818*, Paris, 1892.

Vaudoncourt, Frédéric François Guillaume, *Mémoires pour servir a l'histoire de la guerre entre la France et la Russie en 1812*, Paris, 1817.

Vionnet de Maringoné, Louis Joseph. *Souvenirs*, Paris, 1913.

# The Battle of Borodino

## Secondary

Baye, Joseph, *Borodino*, Paris, 1904.

Blocqueville, Louise Adélaïde d'Eckmühl. *Le maréchal Davout, prince d'Eckmühl; correspondance inédite, 1790–1815. Pologne–Russie–Hambourg*, Paris, 1887.

Boppe, Paul Louis Hippolyte, *La Croatie militaire. Les regiments Croates a la Grande Armee*, Paris, 1900.

Boppe, Paul Louis Hippolyte, *Les Espagnoles a la Grande Armee*, Paris, 1899.

Derrécagaix, Victor Bernard, *Les Etats-Majors de Napoléon: le Lieutenant-Général Comte Belliard, Chef d'Etat-Major de Murat*, Paris, 1908.

Dessaix, Joseph, and Andre Folliet, *Étude historique sur la Révolution et l'Empire en Savoie: le général Dessaix, sa vie politique & militaire*, Paris, 1879.

Fabry, Gabriel Joseph, *Campaign de Russie*, Paris, 1900.

Friant J.-F, *La vie militaire du lieutenant-general comte Friant*, Paris, 1857.

Girod de l'Ain, Maurice, *Grande artilleurs: Drouot, Senarmont, Eblé*, Paris, 1895.

Grunwald, Constantine, *La Campagne de Russie, 1812*, Paris, 1963.

Hourtoulle, François-Guy, *La Moskowa-Borodino: La Bataille des Redoutes*, Paris, 2001.

La Seigneur, B.-J., and E. Lacombe, 'La valeur du comandement: l'exemple de la Moskowa,' in *Revue historique des armees*, 181(1990): 64–72.

Martinien, Aristide, *Tableaux par corps et par batailles des officiers tués et blessés pendant les guerres de l'Empire (1805–1815)*, Paris, 1899.

Martinien, Aristide, *Liste des officiers généraux tues ou blessés sous le Premier Empire de 1805 à 1815*, Paris, 1895.

Pajol, Charles Pierre, *Pajol, général en chef*, Paris, 1874.

Rivollet, Georges. *Général de bataille Charles Antoine Louis Morand, comte d'Empire, (1771–1835). Généraux Friant et Gudin du 3e Corps de la Grande Armée*, Paris, 1963.

Ternaux-Compans, Nicolas, *Le general Compans (1769–1845), d'apres ses notes campagnes et sa correspondence de 1812 a 1813 par son petit-fils*, Paris, 1912.

Thiers, Adolphe, *Histoire du Consulat et de l'Empire*, Paris, 1845.

Thiry, Jean, *La Campagne de Russie*, Paris, 1969.

Tranié, Jean and C. Carmigniani, *La campagne de Russie: Napoléon, 1812*, Paris, 1981.

Vallette, Rene, *Le centenaire de 1812: un héros vendéen de la Moskowa, le Général Bonnamy de Bellefontaine*, Extract from *Revue de Bas-Poitou*, Paris, 1912.

## ENGLISH SOURCES

### Primary

Brandt, Henrich von, *In the Legions of Napoleon: The Memoirs of a Polish Officer in Spain and Russia, 1808–1813*, London, 1999.

Brett-James, Antony, ed, *1812: Eyewitness Accounts of Napoleon's Defeat in Russia*, New York, 1966.

Bourgogne, Adrien Jean Baptiste François, *The Memoirs of Sergeant Bourgogne, 1812–1813*, New York, 1979.

Cathcart, George, *Commentaries on the War in Russia and Germany in 1812 and 1813*, London, 1850

Caulaincourt, Armand Augustin Louis, *With Napoleon in Russia: Memoirs of the General de Caulaincourt, Duke of Vicenza*, New York, 1935.

Chuquet, Arthur, *Human Voices from the Russian campaign of 1812*, Cambridge, 1994.

Clausewitz, Carl, *The Campaign of 1812 in Russia*, London, 1970 (reprint of the 1843 ed.).

Guillemard, Robert, *Adventures of a French Serjeant during His Campaigns in Italy, Spain, Germany, Russia, etc. from 1805 to 1823*, London, 1826.

Lejeune, Louis François, *Memoirs of Baron Lejeune, aide-de-camp to Marshals Berthier, Davout and Oudinot*, London, 1897.

Markham, J. David, ed, *Imperial Glory: The Bulletins of Napoleon's Grande Armée, 1805–1814*, London, 2003.

Porter, Sir Robert Ker, *A Narrative of the Campaign in Russia During the Year 1812*, London, 1813.

Ségur, Philippe-Paul, *Napoleon's Russian Campaign*, Boston, 1958.

Wilson, Sir Robert, *Narrative of the events during the invasion of Russia by Napoleon Bonaparte and the retreat of the French army*, London, 1860.

Wilson, Sir Robert, *Private Diary of Travels, Personal Services and Public Events During Mission and Employment in 1812, 1813 and 1814 Campaigns*, ed. By H. Randolph. London, 1861.

Yermolov, Alexei, *The Czar's General: The Memoirs of a Russian General in the Napoleonic Wars*, trans. by A. Mikaberidze, Welwyn Garden City, 2005.

### Secondary

Austin, Paul Britten, *1812: Napoleon Invasion of Russia* (combined edition). London, 2000.

Belloc, Hillaire, *Napoleon's Campaign of 1812 and the Retreat from Moscow*, New York, 1926.

Brnardic, Vladimir, *Napoleon's Balkan Troops*, Oxford, 2004.

Burton, Reginald, *Napoleon's Invasion of Russia*, London, 1914.

Cate, Curtis, *The War of the Two Emperors. The Duel between Napoleon and Alexander: Russia 1812*, New York, 1985.

Chandler, David, *The Campaigns of Napoleon*, London, 1967.

Duffy, Christopher, *Borodino and the War of 1812*, London, 1972.

Foord, Edward. *Napoleon's Russian Campaign of 1812*, London, 1914.

Holmes, E.R, *Borodino, 1812*, London, 1971.

# Select Bibliography

MacKay, Charles, *The Tempest: The Life and Career of Jean-Andoche Junot, 1771–1813*, Ph.D. dissertation, Florida State University. 1995.
Mikaberidze, Alexander, *The Russian officer corps in the Revolutionary and Napoleonic Wars : 1795–1815*, New York, 2005.
Palmer, Alan, *Napoleon in Russia*, London, 1967.
Pawly, Ronald, *Napoleon's Carabiniers*, Oxford, 2005.
Nafziger, George, *Napoleon's Invasion of Russia*, Novato CA, 1988.
Riehn, Richard, *1812. Napoleon's Russian Campaign*, New York, 1991.
Smith, Digby, *Borodino*, Moreton-in-Marsh, 1998.
Smith, Digby, *Napoleon against Russia: a new history of 1812*, Barnsley, 2004.
Zamoyski, Adam, *Moscow 1812: Napoleon's Fatal March*, New York, 2004.
Zemtsov, Vladimir, 'The Battle of Borodino: The Fall of the *Grand Redoute*,' *Journal of Slavic Military Studies*, 13/1 (2000): 90–112.
Zhmodikov, Alexander and Yuri Zhmodikov, *Tactics of the Russian Army in the Napoleonic Wars*, West Chester, 2003.

## GERMAN SOURCES
Adams, Albrecht, *Aus dem Leben eines Schlachtenmalers*, Stuttgart, 1886.
Bernhardi, Theodor von, *Denkwurdigkeiten aus dem Leben des Kaiserl russ. Generals von der Infantrie Carl Friedrich Grafen von Toll*, Leipzig, 1856–1858.
Bödicker, L, 'Die militarische Lauftbahn,' in *Beiheft zum Militär-Wochenblatt*, 1880, Hft. 1.
Borcke, Johann von, *Kriegerleben des Johann von Borcke, 1806–1815*, Berlin, 1888.
Burkersroda, A.H. von, *Die Sachsen in Russland*, Naumburg, 1846
Cerrini de Monte Varchi, Clemens Franz Xavier von, *Die Feldzuge der Sachen in den Jahren 1812 und 1813*, Dresden, 1821.
Ditfurth, M, *Die Schlacht bei Borodino*, Marburg, 1887.
Fleischmann, Ch, *Denkwürdigkeiten*, Berlin, 1892.
Eugène, Duke of Württemberg, *Memoiren des Herzogs Eugen von Wurttemberg*, Frankfurt, 1862.
Heilmann, 'Die Bayerische Cavallerie Division Preysing im Feldzuge von 1812,' *Jahrbücher für die Deutsche Armee und Marine*, Vol. 17, 1875.
Hoffmann, von, *Die Schlacht von Borodino*, Koblenz, 1846.
Hohenhausen, Leopold, *Biographie des Generals von Ochs*, Cassel, 1827.
Holzhausen, Paul, *Die Deutschen in Russland, 1812*, Berlin, 1912.
Krauss, Th, *Geschichte der bayerischen Heeresabtheilung im Feldzuge gegen Russland 1812.* Augsburg, 1857.
Kurz, Hauptmann von, *Der Feldzug von 1812. Denkwürdigkeiten eines württembergischen Offiziers*, Leipzig, 1912.
Linsingen, 'Auszug aus dem Tagebuch . . ,' in *Beihefte zum Militär-Wochenblatt*, 1894, Hft. 7
Löwenstern, Eduard von, *Mit Graf Pahlens Reiterei gegen Napoleon Denkwurdigkeiten des russischen generals Eduard von Löwenstern (1790—1827)*, Berlin, 1910.
Martens, Carl von, *Denkwurdigkeiten aus dem Leben aines alten Offiziers. Ein Beitrag zur Geschichte der letzten vierzig Jahre*, Dresden, 1848.
Meerheim, Franz Ludwig, *Erlebnisse eines Veteranen der grossen Armee wahrend des Feldzuges in Russland, 1812*, Dresden, 1860.
Minckwitz, August von, *Die Brigade Thielemann in dem Feldzuge von 1812 in Russland*, Dresden, 1879.
Preysing-Moos M, *Tagebuch*, Munich, 1912.
Rotenhan, Hermann Jul von *Denkwurdigkeiten eines wurttembergischen Offiziers aus dem Feldzuge im Jahre 1812, Munich, 1900*.
Roth von Schreckenstein, Ludwig, *Die Kavallerie in der Schlacht an der Moskwa*, Münster, 1858.
Rüppell, Eduard, *Kriegsgefangene im Herzen Russlands, 1812–1814*, Berlin, 1912.
Schubert, Friedrich, *Unter dem Doppeladler: Erinnerungen eines Deutschen im russischen Offizierdienst (1789–1814)*, Stuttgart, 1962.
Völderndorf und Waradein, Eduard, Frieherr von, *Kriegsgeschichte von Bayern unter König Maximilian Joseph I*, München, 1826.
Völderndorf und Waradein, Eduard, Frieherr von, *Betrachtung über das Werk des Herrn Grafen Ph. von Ségur, betittelt Geschichte Napoleons und der grossen Armee im Jahre 1812: nach dem Französischen*, Nördlingen, 1827.
Wagner, F.L, 'Tagebuch' in *Jahrbücher fur die deutsche Armee und Marine*, 1899. Bd. 111.
Wedel, Carl Anton Wilhelm von, *Geschichte eines Offiziers im Kriege gegen Russland, 1812, in russischer Gefangeschaft 1813 bis 1814, im Feldzuge gegen Napoleon 1815. Lebenserinnerungen*, Berlin, 1897.
Wolzogen und Neuhaus, Ludwig, *Memoiren des Königlich Preussischen Generals der Infanterie Ludwig Freiherrn von Wolzogen*, Leipzig, 1851.

## POLISH SOURCES
Droìzdz, Piotr, *Borodino 1812*, Warsaw, 2003.
Koaczkowski, Klemens, *Wspomnienia*, Krakow, 1898–1901.
Kukiel, Mariel, *Jazda polska nad Moskwa*, Poznan, 1919.
Kukiel, Mariel, *Wojna 1812 roku*, Krakow, 1937. vol. 2.
Kukiel, Mariel, 'Les Polonais a la Moskova,' *Revue des etudes napoléoniennes*, 28 (1929): 10–32.
Malachowski, Stanislaw. *Pamietniki*, Poznan, 1885.
Weyssenhoff, Jan, *Pamietnik*, Warsaw, 1904

# Index

# Index

# Index

# Index